AN INTERNATIONAL HISTORY OF THE VIETNAM WAR

Volume II
The Struggle for South-East Asia, 1961–65

By the same author

VIET-NAM AND THE WEST
EARLY SOUTH-EAST ASIA (*editor with William Watson*)
LAND AND POLITICS IN THE ENGLAND OF HENRY
VIII
AN INTERNATIONAL HISTORY OF THE VIETNAM
WAR Volume I: Revolution versus Containment, 1955–61

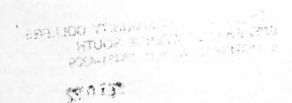

AN INTERNATIONAL HISTORY OF THE VIETNAM WAR

Volume II
The Struggle for South-East Asia, 1961–65

R. B. SMITH

St. Martin's Press   New York

© R. B. Smith 1985

All rights reserved. For information, write:
Scholarly & Reference Division,
St. Martin's Press, Inc., 175 Fifth Avenue, New York, NY 10010

Printed in Hong Kong

First published in the United States of America in 1985
Paperback reprint 1987

ISBN 0–312–42206–7

Library of Congress Cataloging in Publication Data
(Revised for v. 2)
Smith R. B. (Ralph Bernard), 1939–
An international history of the Vietnam War.
Includes bibliographies and indexes.
Contents: v. 1. Revolution versus containment,
1955–61—[v. 2] The Kennedy strategy.
1. Vietnamese Conflict, 1961–1975. 2. Vietnam–
History–1945–1975.   I. Title.
DS557.7.S64 1983 959.704′3 83–3248
ISBN 0–312–00551–2

Contents

PART IV 1964

PART V 1964–5

List of Tables

List of Maps

Acknowledgements

My debts of gratitude are essentially the same for this volume as for Volume I. The practical assistance and moral support given by Judith Stowe has been invaluable as ever. I am also grateful to Bryen McManus for helpful comments on the final draft. My debt to the translators of FBIS and BBC monitoring services will also be as evident as before. During all-too-brief visits to the John F. Kennedy and Lyndon Baines Johnson Libraries, I was grateful for the assistance readily offered by members of their staffs; in particular I must mention the help given me by David Humphrey at Austin.

As in the case of Volume I, I have for the most part avoided any systematic use of oral evidence. I owe it to the reader, however, as well as to those concerned, to mention that my whole approach to this period was given clearer shape as a result of meetings, during a visit to the United States in the spring of 1978, with Roger Hilsman, with William Bundy and with McGeorge Bundy. I have refrained from seeking their endorsement of any of the conclusions I have reached on the basis of documentary research, but I am most grateful to them for sparing me valuable time on that occasion. I was also grateful for the opportunity to meet Walt W. Rostow on two occasions in 1982-3.

I also owe thanks to Lillian Chia and to Ho Chui-mei for typing, and frequently retyping, successive versions of the final draft of the book; and for showing more patience than I deserve.

May 1984   R.B.S.

List of Abbreviations

For additional abbreviations, used in note references, see Bibliography.

United States and anti-Communist side

ARVN	Army of the Republic of Vietnam
CIA	Central Intelligence Agency
CINCPAC	Commander-in-Chief Pacific Forces (Honolulu)
JCS	Joint Chiefs of Staff
MAAG	Military Assistance Advisory Group
MACTHAI	Military Assistance Command, Thailand
MACV	Military Assistance Command, Vietnam
NATO	North Atlantic Treaty Organisation
NSAM	National Security Action Memorandum
NSC	National Security Council
RVN	Republic of Vietnam
SEATO	South-East Asia Treaty Organisation (Manila Pact)

Communist side (including North Vietnam)

CCP	Chinese Communist Party
CMEA	Council of Mutual Economic Assistance (Comecon)
COSVN	Central Office, South Vietnam (of VNWP)
CPSU	Communist Party of the Soviet Union
DRVN	Democratic Republic of Vietnam
KGB	Committee on State Security (*Komitet Gosudarstvennoi Bezopasnosti*)
NLFSVN	National Liberation Front of South Vietnam
PAVN	People's Army of Vietnam (North Vietnamese)
PKI	Indonesian Communist Party (*Partai Komunis Indonesia*)
PLA	People's Liberation Army (Chinese)
PLAFSVN	People's Liberation Armed Forces of South Vietnam
TASS	Soviet Telegraph Agency (*Telegrafinoye Agentsvo Sovietskoyo Soyuza*)
VNWP	Vietnam Workers' Party

A Note on Chinese and Vietnamese Names

Chinese names are given in the 'standard' Chinese form of Romanisation (*pin-yin*), which has been generally adopted by Western news media since January 1979. Vietnamese now has a Romanised script (*quoc-ngu*) which became 'standard' long before 1945 and requires no transliteration; diacritical marks, however, have been omitted. In the use of 'surnames' the Chinese usage is invariably to take the first (family) name, as in 'Chairman Mao', 'Premier Zhou'. The Vietnamese normally use the last (personal) name, as in 'President Diem', or 'Premier Dong', but in very special cases they may use the first (family) name, as in 'President Ho'.

Vietnamese terminology is used for the three regions of Vietnam, as follows:

North (Tongking):	Bac-Bo
Centre (Annam):	Trung-Bo
South (Cochinchina):	Nam-Bo.

Before 1954, non-Communist usage referred to the same divisions as Bac-Ky, Trung-Ky and Nam-Ky.

1 Introduction

I

Volume I of the present work took as its central theme the gradual breakdown of the 1954 Geneva settlement in Indochina and the almost imperceptible return to revolutionary armed struggle in South Vietnam which occurred during the years 1957–61. In terms of United States policy, it traced the consequences for Indochina of a strategy based on the principles of 'containment' and 'massive retaliation', which followed on from the establishment of NATO in 1949 and the United Nations intervention in Korea in 1950. Essential to that strategy was the notion of a powerful and rich American government providing economic aid and defence support to Asian countries belonging to the 'free world'. From the Communist point of view, the same period saw the beginning of what would eventually become the most ambitious – as well as the most traumatic – of 'wars of national liberation' across Asia and Africa. In both the American and the Marxist–Leninist context, South Vietnam – an agrarian country of fewer than 15 million people – thus acquired an international significance out of all proportion to its size.

When John F. Kennedy entered the White House in January 1961, his initial response to the situation in Indochina was somewhat cautious. By the end of his first year in office, however, he had succeeded in formulating a strategy of his own for both South Vietnam and Laos. What might be called the 'Kennedy Strategy' – as opposed to the 'Dulles Strategy' of the 1950s – is one of the principal starting points of the present volume. Later chapters of the book will explore the stages by which Kennedy's policies eventually disintegrated, in the face of a rapidly changing

situation during the years 1963–4; with the result that, following
Kennedy's tragic death in November 1963, Lyndon Johnson
inherited even greater problems than those which had confronted
his predecessor three years before. Johnson's own response to the
developing crisis was even more hesitant than Kennedy's had
been, and it was not until the end of the period covered by the
present volume (early 1965) that he began to commit himself to
what would become a distinctive 'Johnson Strategy'.

At a time when the war in Vietnam was being fought by more
than half a million American troops, it was easy to see the decisions
of 1961–3 as no more than the prelude to that larger war. But the
historian, whilst he must not become an apologist for any one
individual or group, has an obligation to examine each period in its
own terms. There is need for a serious reassessment of Kennedy's
decisions on Indochina in relation to his own long-term objectives
– and to his awareness, as a young and ambitious president, of the
importance of what was coming to be called the 'Third World'.
Seen in its own terms, and not as a prelude to escalation,
Kennedy's strategy of 'counterinsurgency' in South Vietnam was
not necessarily at variance with the supposedly more 'moderate'
aspects of his strategy elsewhere in Asia. Nor should it be assumed
that he would have given in to Communist demands in South
Vietnam had he continued in charge of United States policy in
1964.

In exploring the larger context of the Kennedy and early
Johnson decisions, the present volume seeks to apply the same
principles which governed the approach of Volume I. It looks at
both sides of the conflict simultaneously; and it places events in
Indochina into the wider international picture – both of Asian
relations and of conflict among the global powers – on the basis of a
historical rather than a thematic or conceptual approach. The
most important conclusion to emerge is that the war to which the
United States became committed in the early months of 1965 was
not the outcome merely of a self-imposed, purely bilateral
obligation to defend South Vietnam; nor can it be explained in
terms of a single theme in United States foreign policy – 'anti-
Communism'. At the beginning of the Kennedy period, South
Vietnam was one among many areas of tension in Asia and Africa.
The question for the historian is how it became – a mere four years
later – a strategic focal point which had to be protected: by the use
of tactical air power, and if necessary by the deployment of United

States combat troops. That is not a question we can hope to answer by studying events in Washington and in Vietnam alone. The war was the product of a global pattern of conflict which must be analysed in global terms.

In attempting to come to terms with the sequence of debates and decisions on the Communist side, we must recognise that the problems for the Western historian studying the early 1960s are even greater than for the preceding period, making it more difficult than ever to come to firm conclusions. With the 'benefit of hindsight' which is now possible the historian has an opportunity to re-examine the connection between events on the ground and the course of Soviet–Chinese–Vietnamese relations between 1961 and 1965. Nevertheless, he will be wise to admit that at certain critical moments during the evolution of the conflict in South Vietnam, it is difficult if not impossible to assemble the available fragments of hard information into a coherent story. Certainly American scholars – in published writing at least – failed to produce an effective analysis of the politics and strategy of the Vietnam Workers' Party while the war was still going on. That failure may help to explain why so many outside observers were taken aback by the intensity of the Sino-Vietnamese conflict which broke out in 1978, leading to actual hostilities the following year.

Primary sources on the Communist side are essentially the same for the 1960s as for the 1950s: the most important being, for our purposes, the output of the North Vietnamese, Chinese and Soviet media – including broadcasts monitored (and in part translated) by the FBIS and the BBC. These can, however, be supplemented to a limited extent by reference to two other kinds of information. While the war was still going on, a large number of Vietnamese Communist documents were captured by American and South Vietnamese military and security forces. For the most part they were low-level reports and directives; but sometimes they included also communications from a higher level, providing insight into decisions too secret to be mentioned in the public media.

Secondly, in the period since 1975 both the Vietnamese and Chinese governments have been more ready to publish details about past events which they were unwilling to reveal at the time. Vietnamese Communism has not experienced any internal upheaval comparable with China's 'cultural revolution', which might have led to the dramatic revelation of internal political secrets. Consequently we have no Party sources which approach the candour of Mao Zedong's 'unrehearsed' speeches, circulated by various groups of Red Guards. The Vietnamese have however published a number of memoirs and other accounts of the war, notably an official history of military decisions (in 1980) and a much more controversial analysis of the last stage of the war by one of the leading Communist generals in the South. None of these recent writings makes any secret of the fact that the whole campaign of the NLFSVN and PLAFSVN was directed from the beginning by the Politburo and Central Committee of the Vietnam Workers' Party in Hanoi. Unfortunately they do not tell us much about North Vietnam's own dependence on Soviet, as well as Chinese, aid at various stages of the conflict. But the 'White Book' of October 1979, dealing with the history of Sino-Vietnamese relations since the early 1950s, made a number of accusations which led the Chinese to produce revelations of their own concerning the extent to which they had aided both the Viet-Minh war effort and the anti-American struggle.[1]

It is most unlikely that decisions in Hanoi were based on specific directives from either Moscow or Peking. Nevertheless the documentary record of the statements and decisions of a number of different Communist Parties – including the CPSU, the CCP and the VNWP – suggests that their respective debates about tactics and strategy at a given time were often closely interrelated. In some cases the decisions of one Party may well have been predicated on those of another; and the Vietnamese were probably especially sensitive to Soviet and Chinese attitudes both to the struggle in South Vietnam and also to the provision of material aid for 'socialist construction' in the North. Only access to the internal archives of all three Parties and governments would allow us to know precisely how such debates were conducted, and how far decisions were truly international in character.

The Moscow meeting of Communist Parties in November 1960 proved to be the last point at which it was possible to produce an agreed definition of the Marxist–Leninist 'international line'. By 1963, when a similar conference ought to have been convened, the world at large was becoming aware that the Soviet and Chinese communist Parties took radically different positions on the issues of the 'nature of imperialism' and the 'question of war and peace'.

Instead of a meeting there began a long and bitter series of polemical exchanges. Equally important from our present point of view is the accumulation of evidence for important divisions *within* both the CPSU and the CCP – which again are more difficult to study than those of the late 1950s.[2] It is impossible in the present volume to attempt a thoroughgoing re-interpretation of events in the international movement as a whole during this critical period. But neither can the subject be ignored, since it is quite obvious from their own statements that Vietnamese Communist leaders paid close attention to what was happening amongst their fraternal allies.

It was logical for the North Vietnamese to behave with caution in the face of the growing complexity of international Communist relations. Anxious to retain the support of both Moscow and Peking for their own struggle against the United States and the regime in Saigon, they had more interest in preserving the unity of the communist world than in contributing to further 'splits'; and on a number of occasions the CPSU was able to exploit Hanoi's caution and to dissuade the VNWP from joining the Chinese in open revolt against its own line. The obvious importance of the Sino-Soviet dispute for North Vietnam led some Western commentators to study its own internal politics entirely in terms of a conflict between 'pro-Moscow' and 'pro-Peking' factions – even though they had difficulty in identifying the individual members of the two groups. The reality was clearly far more complicated than that.

Relating the various sources to one another, however, it is possible to define at least the main outlines of Vietnamese Communist decision-making and even to identify some of the issues which appear to have caused differences of opinion amongst them at especially critical moments. It is also possible to trace some – probably by no means all – of the occasions when one or more of the Vietnamese leaders visited the Soviet and Chinese capitals; and when high-level Soviet and Chinese delegations were received in Hanoi. Although we can do no more than guess what may have been said at such meetings, they were probably at least as important for decision-making as the frequent visits of top American officials to Saigon during these years.

In the absence of firm knowledge we are likely to be reduced to speculation. But from the point of view of understanding North Vietnam the international dimension is too important to be left out of account merely because it is inadequately documented. The 'international' character of a great deal of Marxist–Leninist writing in this period moreover, seems to belie the tendency of Western scholars to study individual Communist countries (or Parties) as separate entities. Each historical perspective has its own source material, and to some extent its own 'methodology'; but that is not a reason for treating each perspective as a hermetically sealed compartment of scholarship. In the words of Mao Zedong, 'ever since the monster of imperialism came into being, the affairs of the world have become so closely interwoven that it is impossible to separate them'.[3] The way the Chinese and Vietnamese Communists viewed Western 'imperialism' certainly deserves to be taken seriously in a study of an international conflict in which they were leading protagonists.

II

By comparison with the relative poverty of research on the Communist side, the historian of United States policy in the early 1960s faces an embarrassment of riches. In addition to finding a substantial body of 'primary' source materials, he has also to come to terms with a larger output of secondary writing – and consequently with the existence of a number of established interpretations of key events which will tend to influence the initial direction of his own enquiries.

Vietnam was already sufficiently important in world affairs by the mid-1960s to merit a growing number of books by authors with first-hand experience of what was going on there. Some were by journalists, trying to elucidate for the benefit of a Western public the problems and politics of a 'small' Asian country about which very little was known.[4] Already there was a tendency for some journalists – not all – to emerge from a period in Saigon as critics of both United States policy and the government of South Vietnam. Even so, the books published at that time evidence a measure of respect for Vietnam as a country worthy of attention in its own right. (The heyday of the war correspondent who saw only the war would come later.) In addition, a few books were published by people who had worked in Vietnam in one or another official capacity, and who were able to write with greater authority than journalists about the nature of counterinsurgency or about the activities of the 'Viet Cong'.[5]

Also important for the Kennedy period are a number of books based on first-hand knowledge of the higher levels of decision-making in Washington – where Vietnam was, of course, only one among many problems with which the Administration had to cope; and until at least mid-1963, by no means the most important. Neither John F. Kennedy nor his brother Robert lived to write memoirs of the period. Instead we must turn to their biographers, including some who served in government at the time and had at least some 'inside' knowledge. For Asian affairs, an especially useful example is the analysis of Kennedy's foreign policy by Roger Hilsman, who knew a good deal about Vietnam in his capacity first as Director of the State Department Intelligence Bureau and later as Assistant Secretary of State for Far Eastern Affairs.[6] In relation to areas other than Vietnam, one important 'success story' which generated a certain amount of writing of this kind was the Cuba Missiles Crisis of October 1962; and the resulting insights into decision-making at the highest level are of considerable value in approaching the documentary record on Laos and Vietnam.[7] On the other hand, those top officials who served under both Kennedy and Johnson, and who became intimately involved in Vietnam policy during the years when the war was the principal United States concern in Asia, have been remarkably reluctant to publish detailed memoirs. Lyndon Johnson himself wrote an account of his presidency, including several chapters on Vietnam; but we have nothing from Secretary of State Rusk, or from Secretary of Defense McNamara, or from National Security Adviser McGeorge Bundy.[8]

The experience of the Vietnam War itself was largely responsible for a significant transformation of American attitudes towards politics and international affairs during the years after 1968. The change can be attributed very largely to two specific events. First came the revelation that high officials of the Johnson Administration had told less than the whole truth about the Gulf of Tonkin incidents when they appeared before Congressional Committees to justify the South-East Asia Resolution in August 1964. Senator William Fulbright, already a critic of the war by 1966, was responsible for fresh Hearings before the Senate Foreign Relations committee in February 1968 which directly challenged the official version of the incidents – and cast doubt on whether the alleged 'second attack' on the USS *Maddox* had occurred at all. During the next three years, at least four books were devoted specifically to unravelling the 'truth' about the Gulf of Tonkin affair.[9] The effect was to make members of the public and political scientists alike call into question the credibility of a government system whose inner workings they had previously taken for granted. The second turning-point came in June 1971 with the publication, by the *New York Times*, of large sections of an internal Defense Department 'history' of United States decisions on Vietnam since the late 1940s. Compiled in 1967–8 but never intended for publication, the *Pentagon Papers* drew together a series of secret documents which provided a far more authentic 'inside story' of the way key decisions had been reached than one could hope to obtain from even the most honest of political memoirs or the most painstaking of presidential biographers. The impact was dramatic, and the original 'short' version was soon followed by two more substantial editions.[10]

The *Pentagon Papers* also went a long way towards shaping subsequent interpretations of the origins of the war. In that regard an influential role was played by the overall director of the Defense Department project, L. H. Gelb, who later published his own ideas in a separate book.[11] However, the release of so many documents tended to render out of date much of the work of more radical critics of the war by making it possible to replace unsubstantiated – even if correct – inferences and suspicions with records of actual decision-making.

In the wake of these developments – to be followed only a few years later by 'Watergate' – the 1970s became a veritable 'age of revelations' in American public life. The passage of a Freedom of Information Act, combined with a more liberal presidential order for the automatic declassification of many types of government record, led to the opening for research purposes of a large body of archival material. The 1960s archives of the State and Defense Departments and of other government agencies are unlikely to be transferred to the US National Archives for at least another decade. But the White House National Security Files are normally deposited in presidential libraries, where it is possible for some records to be made available for research as soon as they have been declassified. As a result, a growing body of material relating to Vietnam – and to United States relations with South-East Asia in general – can now be consulted at the John F. Kennedy Library in

Boston and at the Lyndon Baines Johnson Library at Austin (Texas).[12] Already it is impossible to do justice in a single volume to all aspects of the available sources on Vietnam alone. Some of this material duplicates what was included in the *Pentagon Papers*. But the compilers of the latter did not have direct access to White House files or to the records of the National Security Council. In certain cases we can now follow in detail the course of important decisions from the deliberations of low-level interagency groups all the way up to the Oval Office.

Also by the mid-1970s, following the withdrawal of United States combat forces from Vietnam and the final collapse of Saigon two years later, work began on what is likely to be the lengthy task of writing the official military history of the Vietnam War – or at least, of the United States 'involvement' in Vietnam. It must be noted that, despite their name, the *Pentagon Papers* are in no sense a military record. From time to time they tell us about recommendations made by the Joint Chiefs of Staff to the Secretary of Defense. But the compilers would appear to have had little or no access to the strictly military archives of the Pentagon itself – including those of the all important Special Assistant for Counterinsurgency and Special Activities (SACSA) who was responsible for much of the Vietnam programme between 1961 and 1964. Nor was it part of their assigned task to attempt a history of the actual fighting in Vietnam. For the time being the only historians likely to be allowed access to the whole range of military and intelligence archives are those appointed to write the official history of the activities in Vietnam of each individual armed service.

Several volumes have already been produced by the US Air Force and the US Marine Corps. But the main series of volumes will be that recording the role of the US Army, to be compiled by the Center for Military History. The volume covering the period with which we are concerned in the present study (1961–5) has not yet appeared. However, starting in 1973 a number of essays on specific aspects of the war were published in the Department of the Army's 'Vietnam Studies' series.[13] Some aspects of the military history of the war are also covered in memoirs and other studies by military officers who served in Vietnam. Not being official records, these sometimes contain outspoken criticism of the civilian decision-makers whose policies the military commanders had to obey while the war was going on.[14] But it will be a long time before scholars who are completely independent of the United States

government and armed forces are allowed unrestricted access to all
the relevant materials, and are able to weigh the various opinions
against one another.

Perhaps the most frustrating of all among the limitations
imposed on the independent historian is his lack of access to
intelligence archives. The highly processed 'intelligence estimates'
which figure prominently in the *Pentagon Papers* – and sometimes
also amongst records declassified more recently – are no substitute
for access to the 'raw' data on which they were ultimately based:
especially that derived from the latest methods of communications
and electronic intelligence gathering.[15] The denial of access is both
inevitable and understandable. But that does not alter the fact that
in any situation of international conflict intelligence is often the
most consequential factor of all. The absence of that dimension
makes it impossible to assess with any degree of confidence the
extent to which the Americans and their South Vietnamese allies
truly understood the strategy and tactics of their 'enemy' –
whether in the Vietnamese jungles or in the Kremlin and Peking.
The suspicion that the Communist side finally won because they
had better intelligence than the Americans – or could assess that
intelligence more effectively – must remain for the time being no
more than a suspicion.

A further limitation of the *Pentagon Papers* is that they were not
much concerned with the diplomacy surrounding the commitment
to Vietnam. Four volumes which were withheld from the public
until 1975 dealt with secret efforts to negotiate directly with North
Vietnam after mid-1964.[16] But the compilers were not asked to
examine United States diplomacy in relation even to the other
countries of Indochina. We cannot hope to see the war in proper
international perspective, however, without looking at the wider
diplomatic context. United States relations with Indonesia are
admirably covered by the memoirs of the American ambassador to
Jakarta from 1958 to 1965, which can now be supplemented by
reference to a series of declassified cables.[17] Diplomatic cables,
indeed, are one of the more important types of record to be released
during the period since about 1975, mainly as a result of
declassification procedures at the presidential libraries. For the
present volume it has been particularly useful to have access to
such cables between Washington, Bangkok, Vientiane and Phnom
Penh during the early months of the Johnson Administration. The
diplomacy of successive crises in Laos can be documented from

published sources, partly as a result of Britain's fulfilment of its responsibility as Co-chairman (with the Soviet Union) of the Geneva Conferences of 1954 and 1962.[18] It is also possible to refer to a number of British and Australian academic studies for information about the Indonesian 'confrontation' of Malaysia, which was the dominant theme in maritime South-East Asia during the latter part of our period (1963–5).

What is less easily studied is United States diplomacy in relation to the Soviet Union and China – beyond, that is, the public record of meetings and statements reported in the newspapers of the time. Thus attempts to place decision-making on Vietnam into the wider context of relations with Hanoi's principal allies cannot be pursued with great confidence. But that aspect of the subject cannot be left out of account entirely. Any efforts that either Kennedy or Johnson may have made towards achieving a reduction of tension through diplomatic means would sooner or later have to involve the major Communist powers as well as North Vietnam. The full story of 'East–West' relations during the Kennedy and early Johnson period will not be known for many years to come. From our present point of view it is particularly unfortunate that we have no 'inside' information concerning the meetings between American and Chinese ambassadors which took place periodically in Warsaw throughout these years.[19]

Yet another area where the source materials are less than adequate for a full understanding of what was going on during this period is that of the internal politics and decision-making of the countries of South-East Asia, including South Vietnam. No access to the archives of Asian governments is possible for a period as recent as the 1960s; and relatively few memoirs have been written, either in English or in Asian languages.[20] Our principal source must remain the news stories which appeared in the Western and South-East Asian press at the time, together with monitoring of Asian news agency transmissions and other broadcasts. Whilst the latter may often provide more detailed information than the Western press, it has to be admitted that there are important aspects of the internal politics of South Vietnam, Cambodia, Laos and Thailand about which outsiders must remain woefully ignorant. Nor do we have more than an outline knowledge of diplomacy between the various countries of South-East Asia, which played an increasingly important role in the period from late 1963 onwards. We must wait for Asian historians themselves to provide, in the fulness of time, a clearer picture of the way the conflict in South Vietnam was viewed in the other countries of the region.

In the early 1960s the countries of Asia were ceasing to be impotent spectators in a world dominated by the 'East–West' confrontation. Relations among Asian governments, in particular, were coming to matter more and more: with China, Japan and India each seeking to develop its own distinctive role in international affairs. Antagonism between China and India reached the point of open war between them in the autumn of 1962. Relations between China and Japan were more complex, but were of even greater importance for events in South-East Asia. Japanese economic interest in the latter region, which had taken a leap forward with the conclusion of reparations agreements in the 1950s, continued to expand. Direct economic relations between Japan and China, on the other hand, had been severely hampered by the crisis of 1958. They became active again in the years 1962–3, only to be interrupted by a worsening of Sino-Japanese relations towards the end of 1964. By then Peking was vigorously pursuing its own ambitions in South-East Asia. A much fuller analysis of international relations between the major countries of Asia in this period will eventually be necessary; here we can do no more than take account of the importance of that dimension in looking at the situation in Indochina.

Limitations of access to primary source materials have undoubtedly had an effect on the pattern of emphasis to be found in scholarly studies of United States policy in Vietnam. There is a natural tendency for researchers to concentrate on themes for which detailed sources are available, and to ignore others – often equally important – which cannot be documented so easily. But it was inevitable that a great deal of research should be directed towards explaining how the United States became 'involved' in Vietnam at all – often with the innuendo that such involvement was politically or morally wrong, regardless of the outcome.

The question of 'origins' was already implicit in the terms of reference given to the compilers of the *Pentagon Papers* in June 1967, and it dominated the interpretation which emerged. Dr Gelb's answer to the question – which has become so influential that one might almost speak of a 'Gelb Thesis' – was that everything the

Americans did in Vietnam down to 1968 followed logically and remorselessly from President Truman's commitment to assist the French against the Viet-Minh in 1950. He also argued that the basis of the commitment – which no subsequent Administration was able to escape – was an essentially ideological belief that the United States must oppose 'Communism' throughout the world.[21] If one is seeking a single, all-embracing 'explanation' for the whole Vietnam War from beginning to end, and if that explanation has to be derived solely from an analysis of United States attitudes, policies and decisions, then the 'Gelb Thesis' seems at first sight to have much to recommend it. On more careful examination, however, it can be seen to suffer from precisely the limitations of the documentary study which inspired it.

By paying attention only to the documents of the American side, the *Pentagon Papers* were unable to relate each succeeding decision to moves being made – or contemplated – by the Communist side at the same stage of the conflict. Likewise the fact that the project was confined to the study of bilateral relations between the United States and Vietnam meant that any consideration of the wider context of relations with China and the Soviet Union, or of the struggle for South-East Asia, was automatically excluded from the enquiry. United States global strategy cannot be disposed of merely by quoting the memoranda of the JCS which adduced the 'domino theory' as a reason for persisting in Vietnam. Nor can the significance of decisions geared to that broader strategy, and to Washington's perceptions of the world situation at a given time, be fully understood in terms of the sequence of events in Vietnam alone. It is even less reasonable to interpret the whole sequence of Vietnam decisions over a period of 18 years (from 1950 to 1968) in terms of the single concept of 'anti-Communism'. That notion may have figured prominently in the rhetoric both of presidential speeches and of Pentagon memoranda. But actual presidential decisions are unlikely to have been so completely divorced from the political realities of a world in which one of the first duties of a president was to preserve United States global power. At certain critical moments during the Kennedy and Johnson periods, the challenge to that power was very real indeed; so, too, were the consequences of the eventual American failure in Vietnam. Both presidents were aware that their power to help shape the future of South-East Asia was being challenged – by Peking and to some extent also by Moscow – and that their influence in the region might decline altogether if they were obliged to retreat in the face of a Communist-led 'liberation struggle' in Vietnam. It was concern about the future of the region as a whole which finally led them to conclude that the United States must reinforce its established aid policies by making a more direct military commitment to defend the status quo in Indochina.

There were, in practice, two quite different versions of the 'domino theory' present in American thinking during the early and mid-1960s. Military men, particularly the JCS, still thought mainly in terms of the strategy of 'containment' and its implications not only for South-East Asia but for the global chain of military alliances and 'defense support' countries, stretching across Asia from Turkey and Iran in the west to Taiwan and South Korea in the east. South Vietnam was seen as the weakest link in that chain. If the United States were to abandon its commitment to the Saigon regime, once made, the effects might be felt throughout the system, making other American allies in Asia wonder whether they too might one day be abandoned in adversity.

Civilian officials on the other hand, especially in the State Department, were more immediately concerned about the political future of South-East Asia – and the need to defeat any attempt by the Communist powers to draw individual countries away from existing political and economic relations with the West. In that context, the most important country of the region was not South Vietnam but Indonesia, whose participation was essential to the success of any long-term plan for greater regional co-operation. Whilst good relations between Washington and Jakarta depended on the successful conduct of diplomacy and aid programmes, it was generally believed that the outcome of the political conflict inside Indonesia would be directly affected by what happened in South Vietnam. An American defeat there would be interpreted throughout the region as evidence of a lack of commitment to South-East Asia as a whole. Fears that that might happen were a more cogent reason for persisting in Vietnam than the vague notion that withdrawal from Indochina would *eventually* be followed by revolutionary armed struggles elsewhere. By 1963 the original formulation of the 'domino theory' had given place to more pressing anxieties about the *immediate* political consequences of failure in Vietnam. For that reason we must pay special attention to events in maritime South-East Asia at moments when the Americans were reaching key decisions about Vietnam.

Gelb's interpretation of United States policy in Vietnam is not the only one that can be drawn even from the documents contained in the *Pentagon Papers* themselves. An important influence on the present study has been a series of memoranda contributed to the Vietnam debate during 1964 by William Bundy, Hilsman's successor as Assistant Secretary of State for Far Eastern Affairs.[22] Bundy's developing perception of the problem in Vietnam can be seen as transitional, in many respects, between the type of thinking that had characterised Kennedy's approach to the Cuba Missiles Crisis and the strategy Johnson eventually adopted in Vietnam. Those earlier crises, moreover, are not entirely irrelevant to the study of Johnson's handling of Vietnam during 1964. (For that reason rather more attention will be devoted to the Cuba Missiles Crisis itself than might be expected in a book about South-East Asia.) One of the most important questions to be asked is *why* it proved impossible, in the end, to resolve the problems of Indochina with the same degree of success as Kennedy had achieved elsewhere in 1961 and 1962. Was the situation itself very different from those earlier crises? Or did the main reason lie in a difference of approach between the two presidents?

At one point it became fashionable amongst critics of President Johnson to argue that 'if Kennedy had lived' things would have been very different – in short, that he would have found a 'way out' of the Vietnam commitment rather than send whole divisions of American troops into combat there.[23] For his part Johnson was at pains to insist that his own decisions were no more than a continuation of those taken by earlier presidents; and that in the face of a comparable threat to United States interests Kennedy himself would have done much the same thing. The controversy, expressed in those simple terms, can never be resolved. Nevertheless it may be worth asking whether there were not fundamental differences between the actual Kennedy and Johnson strategies.

There can be little doubt that the situation Johnson faced by the middle of 1964 was far more critical than that which had existed in Vietnam only one year earlier; we shall see, in fact, that a marked change occurred in the weeks just before and after President Kennedy's death. But would Kennedy have responded to that deteriorating situation in precisely the same cautious way as his successor in the White House? A study of the Kennedy period as a whole, including his handling of the Berlin Crisis, of the Laos Crisis of 1961–2, and above all of the Cuba Missiles Crisis, suggests that he *might* have tried to find some way of dramatising a 'Vietnam Crisis' – which would have meant risking another global confrontation in the hope of averting a larger war.

The question whether it might actually have been possible at some stage between 1961 and 1965 to negotiate a compromise solution to the Vietnam conflict, which would have permitted the withdrawal of United States support troops and advisers, is an extremely difficult one to answer on the basis of the diplomatic records so far available. On one level 'East–West' negotiations began to yield positive results during 1963: in July of that year, the United States, Britain and the Soviet Union reached agreement on the partial banning of nuclear weapons tests. But by early 1964 it was becoming clear that 'great power' negotiations were unlikely to provide a simple solution in Indochina, which in any case must involve China as well as the Soviet Union. The 'domino theory' had been formulated at a time when it was assumed in Washington that, for all practical purposes, the two principal Communist powers could be expected to act in essential harmony with one another – and that the 'threat' to South-East Asia came from both of them. Likewise any international guarantees relating to the area must also involve them both. The last occasion on which it proved possible to base an international agreement on Indochina on the attendance of both the Russians and the Chinese at the same conference was the signature of the Geneva Declaration and Protocol on Laos in July 1962. Barely a year later the 'Sino-Soviet dispute' was a recognised feature of the international political spectrum, with Peking bitterly denouncing Moscow for its willingness to sign the test-ban treaty. Whilst the Russians continued to speak of 'peaceful coexistence', the Chinese asserted that 'the nature of imperialism cannot change' and that new wars were inevitable despite the invention of nuclear weapons.

The uncompromising tone of Chinese polemical outbursts against both 'imperialism' and 'revisionism' in the years 1963–4 was seen by many Americans as evidence that the Chinese revolution was still in a militant phase; whereas the Soviet revolution, after 45 years, seemed to have lost its internationalist fervour. The American scholar, Crane Brinton, had compared the course of a revolution with that of a bodily fever: a metaphor which, applied initially to the French Revolution of 1789, led to the supposition that the Marxist–Leninist revolutions of the 20th century would in time also reach the point where the fever had passed and there would be a return to 'moderation'. The Soviet Union seemed to have reached that stage; China clearly had not. It was therefore logical to identify a militant North Vietnam with the Chinese rather than with the Russians, and to imagine that any influence exerted by Moscow on Hanoi would be in the direction of 'moderation'.

It was natural for the West to find Khrushchev's formulation of international relations more attractive than Mao's – especially at a time when the 'parity' between the two superpowers was more theoretical than actual. For their part the Russians may actually have gone out of their way to encourage the view of themselves as 'moderate' and the Chinese as more 'militant'. But neither the actual pattern of global rivalry nor the theoretical framework of Marxism–Leninism could be disposed of completely merely by applying Brinton's metaphor. A revolution in South Vietnam was a development which Moscow could not afford to ignore indefinitely. What mattered most in the end was the rivalry of two major powers for leadership of the world revolution – and more immediately, for political influence throughout Asia and Africa. Perhaps the most serious failing of both the Kennedy and the Johnson Administrations was their assumption that China was the principal 'enemy' in Asia, whilst the Soviet Union was potentially a 'friend'.

In view of the direction taken by Vietnam diplomacy ten years later, when Henry Kissinger was negotiating with Le Duc Tho in between visits to Moscow and Peking, it is perhaps necessary to add that in the early 1960s neither Kennedy nor Johnson allowed the notion of 'linkage' to enter into their thinking about South-East Asia. The United States still took its own global power for granted, and there was no question of allowing South Vietnam or Laos to become a bargaining chip which might be surrendered in return for concessions by the Communist powers in some other sphere. There might be some possibility of an understanding to 'live and let live', under which American restraint towards Cuba might be matched by Communist restraint in Vietnam. But there was no room for a direct relationship between the question of Vietnam and that of arms control. The fundamental principle of Western strategy was still the maintenance of the international *status quo* on the basis of agreements reached during the decade after 1945. The ability of the West to defeat any Communist attempt to change the global balance by force of arms was itself a precondition for the pursuit of *détente* in other spheres. In Vietnam it seemed as if that ability was being put to the test.

One final point must be made, by way of introduction to the chapters which follow. The distance in time between the early 1960s and the mid-1980s is substantial, in the sense that the events and assumptions of the earlier period are already sufficiently remote to require an effort of historical imagination in order to reconstruct them.

At the same time it has to be admitted that the historical perspective invariably cuts across the realities of individual experience. It is in the nature of the historian's craft that he can never, in the end, recreate the past as it actually happened. Many of the participants in the events of the 1960s are still alive and will have their own memories and perceptions of the period. To those who were involved, and who remember things differently, I can only apologise. In any age, the contemporary historian probably cannot improve on the sentiments with which Machiavelli introduced his *Florentine History*:

I have done my best, without violating the truth, to satisfy everybody; and perhaps I have not satisfied anyone. If this be the case, I shall not marvel, for I consider it impossible for anyone to write the history of his own time without offending many. Nevertheless, I shall go my way cheerfully, hoping that as I am honoured and sustained by the beneficence of your Holiness, so I shall be aided and defended by the armed legions of your most sacred judgement.

Part I
1961−2

2 December 1961:
Counterinsurgency

Your letter underlines what our own information has convincingly shown: that the campaign of force and terror now being waged against your people and your government is supported and directed from outside by the authorities at Hanoi. They have thus violated the provisions of the Geneva Accords designed to ensure peace in Vietnam, to which they bound themselves in 1954. At that time the United States, although not a party to the Accords, declared that it 'would view any renewal of aggression in violation of the agreements with grave concern and as seriously threatening international peace and security'. We continue to maintain that view. In accordance with that declaration and in response to your request, we are prepared to help the Republic of Vietnam to protect its people and to preserve its independence....

President Kennedy to Ngo Dinh Diem,
14 December 1961

Speaking on 12 October this year in North Carolina, President Kennedy was forced to admit that times have changed, that the USA is passing through an unusual period. Angola and Algeria, Brazil and Bizerta, Syria and South Vietnam, Korea and Kuwait, the Dominican Republic, Berlin, and the United Nations itself – all these are problems about which we could not even dream twenty years ago; and all this in conditions where two powers standing face to face are capable of destroying each other. We agree with President Kennedy. Much has changed in twenty years, a different epoch has arrived. If one adds to this the other burning problems – such as the Congo, the Republic of South Africa, Iran, West Irian, Cuba, the Palestinian question, the lynching of negroes, the chronic unemployment and the deficit of over $3 billion to be observed in the USA – then the prospects for the American imperialists are certainly not cheerful.

Marshal Malinovsky, speaking at
CPSU 22nd Congress, October 1961

I

Although it contained none of the drama of Pearl Harbor almost exactly twenty years before, mid-December 1961 can now be recognised as a turning-point of some significance in the evolution of United States foreign policy. No single area of the world commanded the President's overriding attention, and in that sense no major 'crisis' was about to erupt. But Kennedy and his advisers were increasingly aware of a persistent challenge to the global power which Americans had taken for granted since 1945: a challenge which required small but determined responses at a number of points across the world, rather than one vast and finite trial of strength.

The tension which had prevailed in Europe during the Berlin Crisis of the previous summer and autumn seemed to have eased, in that Khrushchev would not now carry out his threat to sign a separate peace treaty with East Germany at the end of the year; and the annual meeting of the NATO Council which completed its deliberations on 15 December was a relatively routine occasion. Tough statements on the German issue would continue to emanate from the Soviet media from time to time, but the need to defend West Berlin was no longer the most central of Washington's many concerns. In Asia, Africa and Latin America, however, Washington had fewer grounds for complacency. The sense of a changing pattern of world affairs was stronger now than at any time since 1945, and Kennedy was becoming increasingly aware of the challenge implicit in Khrushchev's use of the phrase 'peaceful competition'. But he still hoped that change would lead to an expansion rather than a contraction of United States power in the world.

Two events during December 1961 seemed to indicate a new militancy in the determination of nationalist governments in Asia to resolve by force some of the issues left over from the constitutional transfers of power of the period after 1945. On 17 December Indian forces entered the Portuguese colony of Goa and within two days completed its annexation. The move did not directly affect any American interests, but it seemed to imply an Indian bid for leadership of a non-aligned movement which might become increasingly anti-American as time went on. Moreover, it took place only two days after the arrival in New Delhi of the Soviet head-of-state, Leonid Brezhnev. Further East, in Indonesia, Sukarno was being pressed by left-wing elements to step up his campaign to force the Dutch out of western New Guinea (West Irian). On 19 December he issued his *Trikora* command ordering the liberation of that territory. Again Soviet encouragement was implicit, in the gift of torpedo boats made to the Indonesian Navy when Admiral Gorshkov had visited Jakarta and Surabaya the previous October. During his first year in office Kennedy had gone out of his way to indicate a desire for friendly relations with both Sukarno and Nehru. But he knew that neither of them was willing to take American influence in the Third World for granted – and that on some occasions they might find Moscow a more natural ally than Washington.

Another manifestation of the new mood in Asia and Africa was the convening in Belgrade of the first summit conference of non-aligned leaders in September 1961: a meeting which condemned both superpowers for their recent decision to resume the testing of nuclear weapons. Again, Kennedy appreciated that in the long run the West might have more to gain than the Russians from the emergence of a genuinely non-aligned Afro-Asian movement. It would become a serious threat to the United States only if the Communist powers succeeded in transforming it into an 'international united front' against imperialism, in which Third World Communists could play an influential and eventually a directing role.

Kennedy differed from John Foster Dulles, the architect of United States policy in the fifties, in accepting that genuine neutrality was a logical policy for the 'new nations' which had emerged from the progressive collapse of European colonial rule in the Third World. In the case of Algeria, for example, he had been an early supporter of the independence movement and had no reason to feel unduly concerned when France was obliged to enter into serious negotiations with nationalist leaders – which De Gaulle was preparing to do by mid-December 1961. What worried him was the fear that in some cases the transition from colonialism to independence might produce the type of revolution which could be exploited by local Communist Parties, and ultimately by Moscow and Peking. One such crisis had already arisen in the former Belgian Congo, where the conflict over the Katanga secession was still unresolved. Elsewhere in Africa the first moves were being made towards armed revolt against Portuguese colonial rule: that, too, presented a big opportunity for African Communists.

In this context Vietnam was the one case where an anti-colonial

independence movement *had* been completely taken over by
Communists – and had succeeded in gaining control of half the
country. And now, despite efforts to present itself to the world as a
genuinely nationalist organisation, the Communist-led NLFSVN
was seeking to absorb the rest of the country into a unified socialist
state.

Whilst Kennedy was bound to see the situation, at least partly,
in terms of the strategy of 'containment' which he had inherited
from Dulles, he also recognised it as an example of Communist
control over what might otherwise have been a genuinely nationalist revolution.

Whereas the Americans saw the attainment of independence by
a former colony as an end in itself – whether achieved through
armed rebellion or through a peaceful transfer of power –
Marxist–Leninists regarded that as merely one step in a country's
progress towards socialism. The sequence would be completed
only when the same country had passed through a two-stage
process of 'national-democratic revolution' under the leadership of
a Communist-led front, followed by 'socialist revolution' under a
proletarian Communist or Workers' Party. Thus countries which
the West regarded as already independent – including South
Vietnam – might be regarded as still subject to 'imperialist
domination' and therefore in need of 'liberation'.

The Americans were conscious also of parallels – actual or
potential – between Vietnam and Latin America. It was a measure
of American priorities in this regard that in mid-December 1961,
while Secretary of Defense McNamara went to Honolulu for a
conference on Vietnam, the President himself was preparing to
visit Venezuela and Colombia: two countries where it was still
possible for the United States, by cultivating friendly relations with
democratic governments, to demonstrate that the 'Alliance for
Progress' did not depend solely on right-wing dictatorships.

The most pressing American objective in Latin America was to
defeat (or at least tame) the revolutionary regime in Cuba.
Already in October and November, Kennedy's advisers had been
debating the possibility of clandestine operations against Castro;
and towards the end of November – almost simultaneously with
critical new decisions on Vietnam – the President had approved
'Operation Mongoose' in which an important role was assigned to
the Indochina veteran Edward Lansdale.[1] Meanwhile Castro
himself, on 1 December, proclaimed his life-long adherence to

Marxism – Leninism and confessed he had previously concealed his convictions in order to seize power. Whatever the circumstances and ambiguities of that speech, Castro was now clearly identified in American minds with the promotion of revolution – and ultimately Soviet influence – throughout Latin America. There was no direct connection between Cuba and Vietnam in the decision-making of either the Communist powers or the United States at this stage. But fears about Latin America were an important element in the background of Kennedy's decisions on Vietnam.

II

American policy in South-East Asia entered a new phase with the letter addressed by President Kennedy to President Ngo Dinh Diem on 14 December 1961, promising increased support against the insurgency now threatening the stability of South Vietnam. The following day McNamara flew to Hawaii to preside over a meeting of the American officials most concerned with implementing that promise; including Ambassador Elbridge Durbrow, Lieutenant-General Lionel McGarr (head of the MAAG in Saigon) and the commander-in-chief of US forces in the Pacific, Admiral Harry Felt.[2] A major debate which had been going on in Washington and Saigon for several months finally ended with a series of presidential decisions in November which amounted to the inauguration of a new doctrine of 'counterinsurgency' – with Vietnam as its most important test case. It would require an expansion of American military assistance to the armed forces of South Vietnam, together with the use of military advisers and logistic support teams; but there was to be no deployment of American combat troops to operate as whole divisions on the battlefield.

The question whether to deploy US infantry and armoured units to Indochina had already arisen the previous March, when Kennedy was considering his response to an offensive in Laos by Pathet Lao and neutralist forces recently re-equipped by North Vietnam. At a news conference on 23 March 1961 the President had threatened to intervene directly unless it proved possible to negotiate an immediate ceasefire; and we know now that he had consulted the JCS on the feasibility of implementing plans to put American ground troops into Southern Laos. Any decision to send troops to South-East Asia at that moment would in fact have stretched the United States strategic reserve beyond the point of reasonable security, leaving inadequate forces to deal with possible crises in other parts of the world. In the event, however, a ceasefire was agreed during April and a new Geneva Conference on Laos opened on 16 May. Kennedy thus adopted a policy of seeking the neutralisation of Laos by international agreement, and for the time being abandoned the alternative possibility of an Indochina strategy based on establishing and defending a continuous line across southern Laos and central Vietnam from the Mekong to the sea.

By early October, with no final settlement of the Laotian question in sight, the situation in South Vietnam itself had deteriorated to the point where some of Kennedy's advisers began to advocate the deployment of a SEATO force to defend its borders with both North Vietnam and Laos, and so prevent a possible expansion of external support for the armed struggle in the South. The JCS, obliged to accept that deployment to Laos was politically impossible once the Geneva talks were under way, urged unilateral military action by United States forces in South Vietnam. Kennedy himself appears to have vetoed both suggestions, and instead opted for the strategy of counterinsurgency.

Precise proposals for what was described at one point as a 'limited partnership' between Washington and Saigon were worked out by General Maxwell Taylor and Walt W. Rostow (respectively the President's special military adviser and his deputy assistant for national security affairs) during a mission to Saigon from 18 to 25 October. But even in that context a proposal to send an American task force of 8000 men – mainly composed of army engineers with the ostensible task of assisting in flood relief in the Mekong Delta – was turned down by Kennedy, who saw it as not only a risky violation of the Geneva Agreements of 1954 but also the thin end of a wedge which might eventually lead to American participation in a full-scale war. A Pentagon memorandum of 8 November, probably inspired by the Office of the Secretary of Defense rather than by the JCS, warned the President that if the Chinese chose to intervene in Indochina at some future point the number of American troops that would be needed for such a war might be as high as 200,000. Despite his willingness to call up a number of reserves at the time of the Berlin Crisis the previous July, Kennedy realised that a commitment on this scale would require a major military build-up and a complete reorientation of economic priorities of a kind he was not prepared to contemplate.

The actual programme approved by NSAM no. 111, dated 22 November 1961, was based on the principle of counterinsurgency as a form of military assistance. The United States would assist the government and armed forces of South Vietnam to defend themselves, by expanding training programmes, sending more advisers to work with Vietnamese officers in the field, and most important of all supplying a number of logistic support teams of helicopters and armoured vehicles manned by American troops. The first helicopter units arrived on 11 December and by the end of the year there were already 2600 American military personnel operating in South Vietnam; more would arrive during 1962.[3]

Even this limited deployment of American forces went far beyond the limits of external military support allowed to the Saigon government under the Geneva Agreement, as it had been interpreted by the Western powers since the French withdrew the last of their own forces in 1956. Washington sought to justify the expansion of military aid to Saigon on the grounds that, by resuming the armed struggle and reinfiltrating men and supplies from the North into the South, the Communist side had already broken the ceasefire agreement. Evidence of such infiltration, and of Hanoi's ultimate responsibility for the activities of the NLF-SVN, was published in a State Department booklet issued on 8 December 1961.[4]

Against that evidence the Communist side continued to insist that the new conflict had developed entirely inside South Vietnam, as a response to 'repression' on the part of the Diem regime. It was therefore an 'internal' revolutionary movement rather than action by one state against another. When challenged by the International Commission, established to supervise the original ceasefire in 1954, Hanoi brushed aside allegations about its own involvement with the assertion (on 11 December 1961) that 'the PAVN high command will resolutely reject all decisions taken by the International Commission relating to the so-called 'subversive activities' in South Vietnam, a question which has no relevance to the Geneva Agreement'.[5] Technically that was so: the Commission had no formal powers to investigate political opposition movements arising *within* either of the two zones of Vietnam. But in any case the presence of the Polish delegate at all deliberations of the Commission made it impossible to secure unanimous condemnation of any Communist infringement of the ceasefire. By persisting in its denials of direct involvement in the South, North Vietnam was able to focus international attention on more obvious violations of the 1954 agreement by the United States and Saigon; and, whatever the rights or wrongs of the affair, it was a propaganda battle the Americans seemed bound to lose. Their own intervention, even if the details remained secret, was inevitably more open and undeniable than Communist infiltration of men and supplies through Laos; and American processes of decision-making were always more public than those of the VNWP and its branches in South Vietnam.

One other course open to the United States seems not to have been seriously considered at this time, although it must have been discussed hypothetically at the Pentagon: namely military action against North Vietnam. It is true that certain clandestine operations north of the 17th parallel had been authorised in March 1961; but their purpose seems to have been merely intelligence-gathering and small-scale sabotage. They were on a far smaller scale than Communist infiltration of men and supplies into the South at this period and are unlikely to have had any deterrent effect on Hanoi.[6] Despite his conviction that Hanoi was entirely responsible for the southern revolutionary movement, and above all for re-activating guerrilla warfare, Kennedy had no desire to allow the conflict to spread significantly beyond the boundaries of South Vietnam. The purpose of counterinsurgency was to demonstrate that a 'national liberation movement' could be defeated *without* escalating the conflict into a wider war.

Vietnam was not yet the main focal point of conflict in the Third World which it was to become by the middle of the decade. It was, however, the country where a revolutionary armed struggle already under way, directed specifically against the United States, seemed most likely to succeed; and also the one point at which a victory for such a Marxist–Leninist revolution would breach the global frontier between the Communist countries and the 'free world'. Comparison between the situations in Germany and Vietnam was inevitable, since both were countries divided by earlier wars in which Communist and anti-Communist regimes confronted one another across heavily defended military borders. But despite that fundamental similarity, the differences between them were even more apparent.

The Berlin Crisis had arisen from a confrontation between two highly organised military alliances – NATO and the Warsaw Pact – whose long-standing arrangements included the stationing of Soviet troops in East Germany and American troops in the West. In principle a major conflict between them, over Berlin or any other issue, could easily escalate beyond the 'nuclear threshold' and become the starting-point for a Third World War. Yet precisely for that reason a crisis there could be handled as a finely calculated military – diplomatic game in which neither side was in serious danger of losing control. When Soviet and American tanks moved up to confront one another across the Berlin Wall at the end of October 1961, it was the signal that the crisis had reached its limit rather than the prelude to an actual exchange of fire. In such a context the principle of mutual deterrence was allowed to operate to the full: although one side or the other would have to back down, the underlying balance of power was maintained.

In Vietnam none of these factors applied. First, SEATO was very far from being the South-East Asian equivalent of NATO: only the United States was thoroughly committed to defending the independence of South Vietnam, and within the region it could rely only on the Philippines and Thailand as military allies. Nor, secondly, was the partition of Vietnam accompanied by the presence on either side of the 17th parallel of American and Soviet (or even Chinese) combat units. The MAAG which the United States had maintained in Saigon after 1954 was far from equivalent to the type of American presence that existed in South Korea or even Taiwan. As a result there was little scope for resolving the conflict in Vietnam through direct military confrontation between Washington and Moscow (or Peking), with each side keeping its own forces under tight control. The conflict in Vietnam was not a 'game', like that played in the claustrophobic circumstances of the West Berlin enclave. It was a more open-ended revolutionary struggle which could only be resolved to the advantage of the West if the government in Saigon was able to reassert control over the whole of South Vietnam. A true parallel in Europe would have been a military – political conflict over the status of West Germany itself, not merely of Berlin. It was thus impossible for Kennedy to meet the challenge to South Vietnam by sending two divisions along a road – and daring the Communist powers to object.

The Kennedy decisions on Vietnam in late 1961 did not change American policy towards the other two countries of Indochina – Cambodia and Laos – whose national unity and international neutrality had been formally guaranteed by separate agreements signed at Geneva in 1954. The agreement on Cambodia had been implemented remarkably smoothly, allowing ex-King Sihanouk to take effective control of the government and to develop peaceful relations with all the world's major powers. Despite several clandestine attempts to undermine his regime in the late 1950s, for which he blamed the United States or its clients in Thailand and South Vietnam, it was evident by late 1961 that the Kennedy Administration accepted Sihanouk's neutrality as a *fait accompli* and had no intention of undermining Cambodian stability. It was probably something of an embarrassment to Washington that relations between Phnom Penh and Bangkok had deteriorated to the point of a complete break in diplomatic relations in October 1961, following a dispute over the Preah Vihear Temple situated on the Thai–Cambodian border. On the other hand everyone recognised that Sihanouk's non-aligned strategy depended on the fact that Thailand and South Vietnam were both closely allied to the United States; whilst Cambodia had no common border with North Vietnam.

In Laos, by contrast, the situation was far more complicated. The neutralist Prince Souvanna Phouma – supported by the forces of Kong Lae since the coup of August 1960 – represented only one of three contending 'factions'. The main conflict was between the rightists, led nominally by Prince Boun Oum but effectively by General Phoumi Nosavan, and the Pathet Lao or 'Patriotic Front', led by Prince Souphanouvong and including the still secret People's Revolutionary Party under Kaysone Phomvihane. For the time being the rightists controlled the government in Vientiane and the neutralists and Pathet Lao were based at Khang Khay, whilst the traditional pattern of Thai–Vietnamese rivalry found expression in Thai support for Phoumi Nosavan (a relative of Sarit Thannarat) and North Vietnamese backing for the Pathet Lao.

The emergence of a neutral and unified Laos, most probably under the leadership of Souvanna Phouma, depended on his ability to achieve a measure of agreement between the 'three princes' and to persuade the other two 'factions' to join a coalition. Only when internal agreement was achieved would the 14-nation international conference convened at Geneva in May 1961 be able to bring an end to hostilities and guarantee the unity and neutrality of Laos. Conversely, however, only an international diplomatic framework of some kind would hold a Laotian coalition together, and so allow Souvanna Phouma's aspirations to be fulfilled. The King, living in the ancient capital of Luang Prabang, was constitutionally entitled to invite Souvanna Phouma to form a government – and did so on 18 October 1961; but there remained serious disagreements about the distribution of portfolios among the three 'factions'. Another meeting of the three princes at Ban Hin Heup on 14 December appeared to achieve further progress towards a coalition; and on that basis the Geneva Conference felt able to adopt (in principle) a declaration on Laotian neutrality at its meeting of 18 December. Unfortunately the situation deteriorated yet again after another meeting of the princes in Vientiane (on 27 December) at which the rightists resumed their 'hardline' position on the allocation of ministries in the coalition. Although the full Conference persuaded the factions to meet again in January, this time in Geneva, it was becoming evident that a new round of fighting was likely before an agreement finally emerged.[7]

Meanwhile the government of Sarit Thannarat in Bangkok feared that the neutralisation of Laos on terms acceptable to the Communist powers – and particularly the inclusion of the Pathet Lao in a national coalition – would in the long run threaten the security of Thailand. Consequently the Thais, with encouragement from at least some elements in Washington, continued to provide aid to Phoumi Nosavan's forces and urged him to take a firm line in negotiations between the three 'factions'. By late 1961 the rightists were making probes into Pathet Lao or neutralist territory and there was a serious danger that the May ceasefire would break down completely. Nevertheless the neutralisation of Laos remained central to Kennedy's whole approach to the South-East Asian region. If Laos and Cambodia could be made genuinely neutral, without any new danger of intervention from North Vietnam in their affairs, it would be possible to regard Thailand as relatively secure – and perhaps in the long run South Vietnam would become less important in United States strategy.

In examining Kennedy's reasons for military restraint it is

important to pay some attention to China. Memories of the Korean War were still sufficiently vivid to ensure that no American president would lightly embark on a policy that might culminate in another ground conflict with China on the Asian mainland. On the other hand, Washington had reason to fear that without some signal of American determination in Vietnam, Peking might encourage an escalation of revolutionary struggle across the whole of the Indochinese peninsula. Peking's encouragement of anti-imperialism, directed specifically against the United States, was likely to be strengthened further by the continued exclusion of the People's Republic from the United Nations, confirmed yet again by a vote in the General Assembly on 15 December 1961. The following day, at a meeting of the World Peace Council in Stockholm, the Chinese delegate disagreed openly with his Soviet counterpart in urging that body to place the national liberation movement on the same level as the disarmament movement as a contribution to 'world peace'.

Sino-Soviet relations were still tense, in the aftermath of Zhou Enlai's dramatic withdrawal from the 22nd Congress of the Soviet Communist Party in October. But in the circumstances of late 1961, Sino-Soviet rivalry offered little opportunity for the United States to draw China towards some form of Sino-American *détente*. In South-East Asia, Communist disunity merely served to multiply the problems with which the Americans had to contend, making it increasingly difficult to apply the Dulles doctrine of 'containment' – but at the same time making it all the more necessary for them to take positive action if they wished to defend their own interests and power.

Whether there was any direct communication between Washington and Peking at the end of 1961 is impossible to say, on the basis of the documentation so far available. We do know that at a press conference on 11 October – the same day the NSC decided to send Taylor and Rostow to Saigon and postponed further action until their return – the president had made a somewhat evasive reply to a question based on reports that the Chinese foreign minister was seeking talks with Washington at ministerial level. Kennedy noted the possibility of further exchanges at the periodic meetings of their respective ambassadors in Warsaw; but very little has been revealed about the progress or content of the latter series of encounters during the Kennedy period.[8] Nor have we any means of knowing whether the Chinese themselves reacted to American moves in Vietnam by changing previous plans. Conceivably there was some unspoken understanding that Peking would moderate its moves in Indochina so long as the United States refrained from deploying combat units on the Asian mainland.

It will be apparent from what has been said so far that Kennedy's decisions on Vietnam towards the end of 1961 involved an element of paradox. The President was deeply conscious of the global implications of the conflict there, both as an episode in the Cold War and as a test case for 'wars of national liberation'. He recognised that Indochina might become the focal point of a major East–West crisis at some time in the future. Yet he was determined to limit the immediate conflict to the purely 'national' arena of South Vietnam, and to prevent it from expanding into a larger international war which might interfere with the real objectives of his foreign policy. 'Counterinsurgency' was, above all, an attempt to resolve the paradox by demonstrating to the world at large that the United States had the means to achieve that end. The Vietnam story during 1962 and 1963 is essentially one of how and why the Kennedy strategy failed. But it is pointless to look for the explanation solely on the American side: the most important reason why the strategy failed was that the 'enemy' – that is, Hanoi and its allies – were able to defeat it.

3 Hanoi and its Allies

Each Communist Party is a workers' party functioning in its own country. Each Party wages the struggle in the light of its current national conditions and the tasks facing the workers. But at the same time the Communist Parties in the various countries are fighting for the same goal and in accordance with the same Marxist–Leninist principles. That is why the Communist Parties in the various countries have been endeavouring to coordinate their actions, to maintain close ties, exchange experiences, and to discuss among themselves the major problems of the development of modern society and the tasks facing Communists throughout the world.

The working class, the masses and the proletarian revolution in every country are part and parcel of the world socialist revolution. The achievements of the forces of socialism in any one country strengthen the entire international Communist movement. Conversely the failure of the forces of socialism in any country is bound to affect the movement as a whole. In view of this the Communist Parties cannot and will not confine themselves to definite national fronts. . . . But unity does not mean that the Communist Parties of the various countries have to accept instructions from a specific central organisation as capitalist propaganda maintains.

Commentary by Moscow Radio (in Chinese),
30 January 1962

Of course Parties like the CPSU and the CCP, standing at the head of the world's two biggest states, can go on with their work even if the polemics continue . . . (But we) have no right to fail to think of those detachments of the Communist movement which are forced to carry on the struggle against imperialism in extremely difficult and complex circumstances. Such Parties rightly consider that they require friendship with both the CPSU and the CCP. All Marxist–Leninist Parties draw strength from the unity and solidarity of the Communist movement for the overcoming of difficulties.

CPSU letter to CCP,
29 November 1963

I

On 19 November 1961 – three days before Kennedy put his signature to NSAM-111 – Ho Chi Minh returned to Hanoi from another visit to China and to the Soviet Union, where together with Le Duan and Xuan Thuy he had attended the 22nd Congress of the CPSU. As representatives of the VNWP they had avoided making a public stand at the Congress: when Zhou Enlai withdrew from the meeting to return early to Peking on 23 October, Ho and Le Duan had tactfully embarked on a week's tour of Byelorussia and the Baltic states. Later on, however, unlike the Chinese delegates, Ho had stayed on for further talks in Moscow before spending a week in China on the way home. An equally independent line was taken by other Asian Communist leaders; notably the Indonesian D. N. Aidit, in whose company Ho travelled from Moscow to Peking on 12 November. The fact that Ho was not obliged to 'choose' between the ideological positions of Khrushchev and Mao was reflected in the warmth of the reception he received from the Chinese leaders in Peking.[1]

Nevertheless, the Vietnamese Communist leaders were deeply conscious of their membership of the 'world socialist system' and of the 'socialist camp'; and their position at this and all other times must be understood in Marxist–Leninist terms. Ho Chi Minh's career as an international Communist is well known. Le Duan, who had emerged as the second-ranking leader of the Party in 1957, had had less experience outside Vietnam but was equally ready to take a position on international issues when the occasion arose. Marxist–Leninist decisions inside Vietnam could not be divorced from the common theoretical framework which all Parties shared, which was fundamentally international in scope and ambition.

Hanoi's relationship with Moscow had in fact been growing stronger rather than weaker during the preceding year, largely for economic reasons. As one of the least industrialised of all Communist countries at that time, North Vietnam was far more dependent than China on external economic support and could not afford to imitate the Chinese policy of 'self-reliance'. When Moscow had suddenly decided in the summer of 1960 to terminate its aid projects in China and had withdrawn all Soviet technical personnel, the Chinese had responded by a deliberate decision to seek only trade relations with other countries and to avoid dependence on external sources of aid or investment. Hanoi was in no position to adopt the same independent line. Its first Five Year Plan (approved at the VNWP Third Congress in September 1960) pre-supposed substantial levels of material and technical assistance from both China and the Soviet Union; to have abandoned it would have resulted in an economic catastrophe which Ho and his colleagues could not contemplate. During the summer of 1961 premier Pham Van Dong made a tour of almost all the 'fraternal countries' to secure both an expansion of economic aid and the consolidation of existing North Vietnamese debt arising from previous aid agreements.[2] His talks with Khrushchev in August also touched on the question of South Vietnam; and in that area, too, he was able to secure at least the verbal support of the Soviet leader for the revolutionary armed struggle there.

The ultimate responsibility of Hanoi for the revolution in the South after 1956 is no longer an issue for historians, as it once was for propagandists: the Vietnamese Communist Party has long since abandoned the pretence that the struggle for eventual reunification represented anything but a brilliant victory for its own political and military leadership. Nor need one doubt that victory would have been impossible without substantial material support from China and the Soviet Union. Until about the middle of 1961 Hanoi had probably been able to develop and support the southern revolutionary struggle from its own resources – including weapons and supplies captured inside the South. Material assis-tance from the fraternal countries could be used entirely for building up the defences and economy of the North itself, which had by that time reached the stage of socialist construction. But the American decision to expand military assistance to the Saigon regime meant that sooner or later the southern struggle would reach a point where it too depended on external aid – as had happened in the earlier Viet-Minh independence war, once the Americans began to provide aid to France in 1950. When that point was reached Hanoi would be obliged to strike a balance between its need to 'build the North' and its ambition to 'complete the national democratic revolution' in the South.

By August 1961 the North Vietnamese could rely on a measure of support from both Moscow and Peking for an intensification of the southern struggle. The Chinese role may have been especially important at that period. But Peking's strategy probably extended beyond the immediate goal of Vietnamese reunification, to the promotion of revolutionary movements across mainland South-East Asia. On his way home from Moscow, Pham Van Dong visited not only Peking but also spent five days (17–21 August) in the Yunnanese provincial city of Kunming – a place he had first visited when summoned there by Ho Chi Minh in spring 1940. Although firm documentary evidence is lacking, Kunming may still have been a meeting point for South-East Asian Communists, and it is not impossible that on this occasion the Vietnamese premier's visit coincided with some kind of conference to discuss regional strategy. Party histories written in 1977 tell us that the Thai Communist Party held its third congress in September 1961, at which it resolved to prepare for armed struggle; and also that (sometime during the same year) the Malayan Communist Party decided to return to the armed struggle line it had abandoned in 1957.[3] Neither of those decisions is likely to have been made without encouragement from the CCP. In the event, however, any plans for a wider regional struggle would appear to have been abandoned in the new circumstances which arose by the end of the year.

In September or October 1961 the VNWP reorganised its Southern Bureau (usually known by the English initials COSVN); and at a meeting shortly afterwards the latter approved a resolution calling for intensification of the anti-American struggle.[4] It envisaged a fairly rapid advance towards a 'general uprising' against the Diem regime, and predicted a 'high tide' in the southern revolution in the near future. Although it ruled out any return to the scale of fighting that had characterised the later phases of the resistance war against the French, the resolution called for equal emphasis to be placed on the military and political aspects of the struggle: a decision which found immediate reflection in a marked increase in the number of guerrilla 'incidents' reported during October – as many as 150, compared with only 50 in September. It was the resulting crisis for Saigon which occasioned the Taylor–Rostow mission and the Kennedy decisions of November and December.

II

When Ho Chi Minh returned to Hanoi on 19 November, therefore, he could feel confident of his own Party's relations with both the CPSU and the CCP; but he could not afford to be complacent. It was unlikely that the situation of 1954–5 would be repeated: there was little chance of North Vietnam being obliged to sacrifice the southern struggle yet again, in the face of combined pressure from both its principal allies. On the other hand, the moves now contemplated by Kennedy – soon to be implemented in South Vietnam – would make it difficult for the Communist side to win merely on the basis of the present level of armed struggle, which was designed to supplement a political revolution rather than to produce outright military victory. There was a danger that greater United States involvement would force Hanoi to rely more heavily on Chinese support than Ho would have wished, and that the Russians might revert to their policy of regarding Indochina as mainly a Chinese responsibility within the pattern of world revolution.

Such a solution may possibly have been considered during the second half of December, when a high-powered Chinese military delegation led by Marshal Ye Jianying was received in North Vietnam. Of all the senior military figures in Peking, Ye was perhaps the one most likely to favour a stronger Chinese commitment to South-East Asian revolutions. A native of Guangdong province, he had been associated with Zhou Enlai since the days of the Nanchang uprising of 1927 and together they had been in contact with Ho Chi Minh when he returned to southern China from Moscow in 1938–9. After 1949 Ye had been given responsibility for military affairs in South China before being appointed head of the PLA military inspectorate in 1954: the position he held in 1961. Ye was accompanied to Hanoi on this occasion by a number of other generals who had past or present associations with southern China, and in some cases also close ties with the commander of the Fourth Field Army, Marshal Lin Biao. Notable among them were Liu Yalou (commander of the PLA air force), Yang Chengwu (deputy chief-of-staff), Huang Yongsheng (commander of the Canton Military Region) and Xiao Hua (deputy head of the PLA political department).[5] Men of such seniority are unlikely to have been sent to Vietnam without a significant purpose: conceivably some plan to strengthen the PAVN to the point where it could resist an all-out American attack.

Yet reports of the activities of the Chinese delegation in North Vietnam suggest that its visit was less than a complete success; or possibly that its initial objectives were overtaken by other events towards the end of the month. The arrival of the generals in Hanoi, and their visit to the town of Vinh in Vietnam's fourth military region, were prominently reported by the *Peking Review* of 22 December 1961; but a week later the issue of 29 December made no mention at all of Vietnam. Instead it concentrated on China's exclusion from the United Nations and on Indonesia's claim to West Irian: despite the continuing American buildup in Saigon the question of South Vietnam was suddenly ignored by the Chinese media.

Also noticeable and perhaps even more surprising, was the fact that not all members of the Vietnamese Politburo appeared in public to greet the Chinese generals: Le Duan, Le Duc Tho and Nguyen Duy Trinh were not mentioned throughout the visit, and Nguyen Chi Thanh appeared only on the first day. On 29 December, when the Chinese ambassador He Wei gave a reception in their honour towards the end of the visit, only two Vietnamese Politburo-members were reported as attending: Vo Nguyen Giap (the delegation's principal host) and Truong Chinh. Even at the VNWP's own reception the following day several top leaders were still absent.[6] Whatever the reason, it seems clear that the visit did not produce a close military alliance between the PLA and the PAVN. Possibly the Vietnamese could not agree on a political realignment which would have offended the Russians; possibly there was some reassessment when it became clear that Kennedy was not after all going to place combat troops in Vietnam; or possibly there was a change of mind in Peking, where a continuing economic crisis made it difficult to think in terms of massive expansion of material aid for North Vietnam. For their own part, by early January the Vietnamese were again placing emphasis on the theme of restoring Sino-Soviet unity.

III

In the Communist world as a whole, the six weeks between late December 1961 and early February 1962 were a period of acute crisis. The 'Sino-Soviet dispute' was only one dimension of a more complex pattern of conflict, in which the most critical element seems to have been a major power struggle in Moscow itself. The Chinese leadership was also engaged in an internal reassessment, which was to lead to a temporary moderation of its attitude towards Moscow. We can be sure that Hanoi was following the course of both conflicts closely before deciding how to deal with its own problems.

One focal point of conflict in Moscow was the continuing problem of Albania, and the related question of Tito's position in the international Communist movement, which had been key issues at the CPSU 22nd Congress the previous October. Ought 'de-Stalinisation' to be carried to the point of completely reversing Stalin's verdict against Tito in 1948–9 and readmitting Yugoslavia to the status of a socialist country, despite its special relationship with the West? (The Chinese supported the Albanian line of total opposition to any such move.) Within the Soviet leadership, Suslov was probably fighting a rearguard action against a complete *rapprochement* with Tito; whilst others may have been willing to go even further towards 'de-Stalinisation' than Khrushchev himself.

In mid-December, as the USSR and Albania finally broke off diplomatic ties, there were signs of an improvement in Soviet–Yugoslav relations. Belgrade not only sent a delegate to a trade union conference in Moscow; his speech was reported in the Soviet press. Not long afterwards, however, an important Soviet conference on ideology – probably designed to establish a new consensus – generated new controversy leading to a serious crisis by the end of the year.[7]

The course of events during January 1962 remains obscure, but there are several indications of an acute conflict being slowly and painfully resolved. Unofficial suggestions that Molotov was about to be rehabilitated (8–9 January) were followed a week later by evidence of the final eclipse of his 'anti-Party group', in the form of a decree of 15 January against places or factories being named after Molotov or his allies. (At that stage Voroshilov also seemed to be included in the official condemnation of the group.) Meanwhile Khrushchev visited Byelorussia, where on 12 January he made a stinging attack on the agricultural failures of that region. After that, Khrushchev and Suslov both 'disappeared' until the end of the month and we cannot even guess what was happening behind the scenes. We know only that on 30 January Suslov reappeared in Moscow at a conference on social science, together with F. R. Kozlov; whilst Khrushchev was reported visiting Kiev. In early February, moreover, it became clear that the attempt to purge Voroshilov (which had first begun during the 22nd Congress) had

TABLE 3.1   *Communist relations, January 1962*

Soviet relations	Chinese relations	North Vietnamese relations
		10 Jan.: Vietnamese Party circulated letter calling for international Communist meeting to resolve differences.
		10–11 Jan.: Cadres conference in Hanoi; speeches of Nguyen Duy Trinh, Ho Chi Minh, on 1962 plan.
8–9 Jan.: Signs of possible rehabilitation of Molotov, followed by his final eclipse; decree on place-names, 15 Jan.	13 Jan.: Five Sino-Albanian agreements signed, strengthening ties with Tirana.	
10–12 Jan.: Khrushchev in Byelorussia; then disappeared until 28 Jan. Suslov also out of sight, 10–30 Jan.	13 Jan.: China signed agreements with Laos (i.e. Souphanouvong government) including that for building road from Yunnan.	18 Jan.: Hanoi reported creation of People's Revolutionary Party in South Vietnam.
15 Jan.: Moscow Radio broadcast (in Chinese) on need for unity in world socialist system.	20 Jan.: Sino-Vietnamese trade protocol signed in Hanoi.	20 Jan.: Nguyen Duy Trinh at meeting of Soviet specialists in Hanoi.
	22 Jan.: *Renmin Ribao*: 'The common militant task of the world's people is to oppose US imperialism.'	
29 Jan.: Collapse of Geneva three-power talks on banning nuclear tests.	30 Jan.: Mao spoke at conference of Chinese cadres to discuss the economic crisis; 'moderate' attitude towards Soviet Union, intellectuals, expertise, etc.	30 Jan.: *Nhan-Dan* carried Soviet message of greetings, including emphasis on aid projects under way and planned.
30 Jan.: Suslov reappeared at conference on philosophical questions in Moscow; Khrushchev reappeared in South.		

failed. Thus at least one important Stalinist survived, albeit stripped of his old power and influence; and the trend towards 'de-Stalinisation' lost some of its momentum. It appeared that a new balance had been struck within the leadership, which allowed Khrushchev to survive but excluded any closer relations with Tito for the time being.

The immediate effect of these events on East–West relations is not easily judged. At the end of January the Soviet side broke off the tripartite talks on banning nuclear tests, which had been going on in Geneva since 1958; no further progress was possible in that area for the remainder of 1962. During February there were again a number of incidents of Soviet interference with Western air traffic in the 'corridor' to Berlin. On the other hand secret negotiations permitted an exchange of Soviet and American 'spies' on 10 February (U-2 pilot Gary Powers in return for Soviet agent Rudolf Abel). Two days later Khrushchev wrote to Kennedy proposing a summit meeting in March, in the context of the wider Geneva conference on disarmament. Although American rejection of the specific proposal was inevitable, the mere fact of an exchange of letters seemed to keep the door open for further contacts.

Another major issue still dividing the Soviet leaders was the relative priority given to investment in the defence industries and in agriculture. Since early 1960 Khrushchev had been attempting to limit the size and expense of the Soviet armed forces and to devote more resources to improving agricultural production. Agriculture was still one of his foremost concerns in late 1961 and early 1962, and he clearly intended to carry through a large-scale reform of investment priorities at the next plenum of the CPSU Central Committee in early March. During February, however, the generals were pressing their opposition to his plan – possibly with support from Suslov – and their case was considerably strengthened when Secretary of Defense McNamara made a speech in Chicago, on 17 February, arguing the need to improve American capabilities for 'limited war'.[8] In the event, on 9 March the Central Committee reaffirmed the old pattern of investment priorities, which seems to have represented a further setback for Khrushchev.

Relations between the Soviet Union and China seem to have become a little less tense as a result of developments in Moscow during January and February 1962. Events in China itself may also have contributed to the slight amelioration which occurred.

To talk of *rapprochement* would be premature. The main issue in China was the state of the economy after 'three bad years' following the failure of the 'great leap' of 1958. Mao Zedong, who had suffered something of an eclipse during that time, was now beginning to reassert his influence. In January 1962 he was strong enough to force Liu Shaoqi – chairman of the People's Republic since 1959 – to submit plans of the Party bureaucracy to a large conference of 7000 cadres. But in practice Mao could not ignore the views of those – notably the economic expert Chen Yun – who favoured a return to 'learning from the Soviet Union' as the immediate solution to China's difficulties. Mao's own speech to the conference of cadres – on 30 January, coinciding with the end of the most acute phase of crisis in Moscow – was remarkably moderate in its attitude to the Soviet model. A month or so later, towards the end of February, a 'work conference' presided over by Liu Shaoqi adopted a series of more precise proposals by Chen Yun, to be formally ratified by the National People's Congress in April.[9] A new Sino-Soviet trade agreement was also signed in April, but there was to be no return to Soviet aid or investment in Chinese development projects.

Meanwhile on 22 February, following a brief visit to Peking by a Soviet delegation bound for Hanoi, the CPSU addressed a formal letter to the CCP urging it to abandon its 'special stand' and to reunite with other fraternal Parties in the interests of international solidarity. The Chinese replied on 7 April, reaffirming their ideological position but also speaking of the need for efforts to restore international unity: they called on the CPSU to seek a reconciliation with Albania.[10]

The North Vietnamese, who had never been sympathetic towards 'de-Stalinisation', must surely have been encouraged by events in Moscow during January and February 1962, as well as by the easing of Sino-Soviet tension. On 20 January Nguyen Duy Trinh presided over a meeting of Soviet experts working in North Vietnam which amounted to a signal that Soviet economic aid was still very much appreciated. Ten days later, on 30 January, *Nhan-Dan* published a message from Ambassador Tovmasyan expressing a desire for continuing friendship between the Soviet Union and the DRVN. He pointed out that since 1955 as many as 30 industrial projects had been completed with Soviet aid, and that 150 more were to be built under the new Five-Year Plan (1961–5). Supplies to North Vietnam in 1962 would also include tractors, trucks and chemical fertiliser in larger quantities than before.[11] In April the 7th Plenum of the VNWP Central Committee was able to define a new stage in its plans for economic development in the North. On the basis of Soviet assistance it was possible to envisage the continuing development of industry – with an emphasis, at least in principle, on the same primacy of heavy industry which characterised the Soviet Union's own economic line at this period.[12] In practice the industrialisation of North Vietnam was a remote long-term objective; but it was one to which Moscow would continue to pay lip-service until the early 1970s.

Continuing Soviet interest in maintaining good relations with North Vietnam – whatever might happen to Sino-Soviet relations – was reflected by the visit to Hanoi of a delegation including the senior Party officials B. N. Ponomarev and Y. V. Andropov, from 21 February to 2 March.[13] We know nothing about the talks which took place. But by 10 March it was evident that the Vietnamese leaders had reached their own consensus on a 'middle way' involving friendship with both Moscow and Peking. On that day the Vietnamese announced the expansion of both the Soviet and Chinese friendship associations in Hanoi. They also signed a treaty of friendship with Mongolia – whose line was 'pro-Soviet' and 'anti-Albanian' – which may have been intended to signal respect for Moscow without having to take their own stand against Albania.

IV

Developments in other parts of the world from February to April 1962 suggest that that period was a 'turning-point' of major consequence in the evolution of Communist global strategy – both Soviet and Chinese. In Soviet–American relations, it was the period when the 'Berlin Crisis' (which finally came to an end in April with the recall of Generals Konev and Clay) was superseded by a new focal point of tension, namely Cuba. Soviet statements of 18 and 23 February supporting the Castro regime against any threat from the United States marked the beginning of a new trend in Moscow's strategy. At about that time an internal conflict within the Cuban leadership – between the 'Castroites' and a faction led by A. Escalante – was entering its most critical phase. During March Castro was strong enough to purge Escalante,

TABLE 3.2 _Communist relations, February– March 1962_

Soviet relations	Chinese relations	North Vietnamese relations
8 and 23 Feb.: Soviet–Japanese agreements on bilateral trade in iron and steel, oil, etc.	9 Feb.: _Peking Review_ attack on Japan's economic offensive in S.E. Asia.	10–14 Feb.: Soviet trade delegation in Hanoi, negotiated Soviet–DRVN agreement for 1962.
10 Feb.: Exchange of R. Abel for G. Powers completed.		February: VNWP Politburo Resolution on situation in South; reaffirmation of existing strategy, despite US intervention.
12 Feb.: Khrushchev letters to Kennedy and Macmillan, proposing meeting in context of Geneva disarmament talks.	14 Feb.: Chen Yi appealed for international Communist unity.	16 Feb.: Opening (somewhere in S. Vietnam) of NLFSVN First Congress, lasting until 3 March.
14 Feb.: Kennedy's reply, suggesting that a summit meeting await progress in talks at foreign minister level.	16 Feb.: Chen Yi, speaking to Japanese journalists, was optimistic about Sino-Soviet relations.	18 Feb.: DRVN appeal to Geneva Co-chairmen.
	20 Feb.: Ponomarev visited Peking briefly.	21 Feb–2 March: Visit of Ponomarev and Andropov to North Vietnam; Le Duc Tho prominent in receiving them.
18 Feb.: Soviet statement supporting Cuba against threat from US.		
21 Feb.: _Krasnaya Zvezda_ criticised Chicago speech by McNamara on 'limited war'.	22 Feb.: Soviet letter to CCP, calling on Chinese to abandon their 'special stand'.	
23 Feb.: Khrushchev sent further letter to Kennedy.	21–26 Feb.: Liu Shaoqi presided over Central Work Conference, which adopted economic ideas of Chen Yun.	24 Feb.: Chinese statement supporting Vietnamese struggle against US 'armed intervention' in South.
late Feb.: Negotiation of increased Soviet aid to East Germany, followed by Mikoyan visit to Berlin in March.	26 Feb.: China warned India not to resolve border issue by using force.	2 March: Ponomarev and Andropov left Hanoi.

	3 March: Chinese NPC meeting postponed.	3 March: End of NLFSVN Congress in South; not yet publicly reported.
5–9 March: CPSU Central Committee Plenum: opened with report by Khrushchev on need for agricultural investment; ended by confirming policy of concentration on defence and heavy industry.	5 March: Li Fuqun attended Peking rally in support of North Vietnam.	
10 March: Cuba: start of Castro's campaign against faction of A. Escalante, who was forced out by end of month.		10 March: DRVN signed friendship treaty with Mongolia; also announced expansion of work of *both* Chinese and Soviet friendship societies in Hanoi.
	mid-March: Decision to replace He Wei as Chinese ambassador to North Vietnam.	

SOURCES As for Table 3.1. Additional sources indicated in notes to this chapter.

forcing him to withdraw to Prague by the end of the month. Finally on 11 April *Pravda* congratulated 'comrade' Castro on his success, and in effect recognised Cuba as having the status of a socialist country.[14] Not long afterwards Khrushchev began to consider installing nuclear missiles in Cuba.

Also during February the Sino-Indian border dispute began to enter a new phase. On 26 February China warned India against any attempt to resolve the issue by force. But relations continued to deteriorate during March, and on 13 April – two days after an alleged intrusion by Indian forces into territory claimed by China – Peking published a long series of documents to justify its own position in the eyes of the world.[15] This too marked the first stage of a conflict which, like that of the Cuba missiles, would come to a head the following autumn.

Another indication of growing Soviet interest in more distant parts of the world could be observed in Indonesia, where Admiral Gorshkov's visit of October 1961 was now followed up by further exchanges. A statement of 8 February reaffirmed Soviet support for the Indonesian claim to West Irian, and was the prelude to a visit to the USSR by the Indonesian air force chief Omar Dhani. He was received by Khrushchev in Sochi on 16 February. Soon afterwards a relatively low-level Soviet delegation, headed by the regional specialist Guber, visited Indonesia from 22 February to early March. These moves were not enough to prevent Sukarno from agreeing to a negotiated American solution of the West Irian question, worked out under American auspices between March and July. But they made it more difficult for Kennedy to draw Indonesia wholly into the Western camp. Moreover the Chinese made no immediate attempt to compete with the Russians in Indonesia; and the reduction of Sino-Soviet tension probably made it easier for the Indonesian Communist Party to resolve its own problems. On 10 April a PKI Central Committee Plenum, to be followed by a full Party Congress later in the month, adopted a 'united front' line of continued support for Sukarno – and the Party's statutes were changed accordingly.[16]

Indeed it is possible to see the days around 11–13 April as the point at which a new pattern of Communist relations and global strategy finally crystallised, assuming the shape it would take for the next six to eight months. The 'hard' line now prevailing in Moscow was compatible with an easing of Sino-Soviet tensions and the restoration of a loose form of international solidarity. However, it did not prevent a new Soviet initiative towards Yugoslavia – at least on the level of state-to-state relations. On 11 April it was announced that foreign minister Gromyko would shortly visit Belgrade for talks with Tito – perhaps in the hope of preventing any further friction which might interfere with Soviet policies towards India, Indonesia and Indochina. The effect of all these moves was that the global context of Communist strategy in South Vietnam underwent a significant change. But in the new situation it was still possible for Ho Chi Minh and his colleagues to continue their own struggle.

V

A new stage in the evolution of Communist strategy in South Vietnam had begun at a VNWP Politburo meeting in February 1962 – although its decisions were not publicly reported until many years later.[17] The resolution it approved was quite different in tone from the COSVN resolution of October 1961: there was no longer any talk of a 'high-tide' of revolution in the South, nor of early advance towards a 'general uprising'. Nevertheless, the Party's determination to continue the struggle remained unshaken. Although stronger intervention by the United States would lead to a fiercer armed conflict, the balance of forces between the two sides had not ultimately changed. It was still possible to force the Americans and the Diem regime onto the defensive and to destroy the 'Staley–Taylor plan' (as it was always called by Hanoi).

The VNWP Politburo meeting coincided with the convening of the first full congress of the NLFSVN, somewhere in South Vietnam, between 16 February and 3 March. But the absence of any report on that meeting until early April suggests that its decisions could not be finalised without further consideration in Hanoi; or perhaps until the international situation in the Communist world had become clearer. In the event it was only on 12–13 April that the Hanoi media finally published the names of the new NLFSVN Central Committee, together with the movement's declaration and a four-point 'appeal' to the population of the South. The latter called for an end to the war, an end to the pacification programme, the appointment of a coalition government, and the adoption by South Vietnam of a policy of peace and neutrality.[18]

Whilst leadership of the movement undoubtedly still lay with

TABLE 3·3   *Communist relations, April 1962*

Soviet relations	*Chinese relations*	*North Vietnamese relations*
5 April: Decision to postpone meeting of Supreme Soviet (on 10th): presumably new stage of crisis already beginning.	7 April: Chinese letter to CPSU, urging Soviet attempt to improve relations with Albania, as preparation for international Communist meeting.	
7 April: Yugoslavia: arrest of M. Djilas, to appease Moscow.		
	10–16 April: NPC completed its work; approval of Chen Yun's economic policy.	
10 April: CPSU decree condemning Leningrad Party Committee; followed by removal of Spiridonov (strong critic of Stalin).		
11 April: Announcement of Gromyko's visit to Yugoslavia on 16th. *Pravda* recognised Cuba as a socialist country; approved 'comrade' Castro's purge of Escalante.	11 April: First of series of 'incidents' on Sino-Indian border.	11 April: Vo Nguyen Giap formally protested to International Commission against US actions in South Vietnam.

12 April: General Clay's return to US, following end of Soviet harassment of Berlin air corridors.	13 April: China published texts of Sino-Indian exchanges and other documents on the border dispute.	12–13 April: Hanoi reported composition of new Central Committee of NLFSVN and published the appeal issued by the NLFSVN Congress.
20 April: *Pravda* reported recall of Konev from command in Germany; final end of Berlin Crisis.	13–20 April: Soviet trade delegation in Peking, leading to new agreement for trade in 1962.	mid-April: Start of new fighting in N. Laos, leading to Pathet Lao capture of Nam Tha in early May.
23–5 April: Supreme Soviet met; approved heavy industry policy, etc.	21 April: Chinese protest to India about border incidents since 11 April.	23 April: Soviet–North Vietnamese agreement on scientific and technical co-operation signed.
		'April': VNWP Central Committee 7th Plenum: decisions on development of industry, including heavy industry.

SOURCES   As for Table 3.2.

the Party and its COSVN, the line now being put forward wa.
ostensibly that of a purely southern 'united front' without any
reference to early reunification. The concept of a broad coalitior
was designed to appeal to non-Communist politicians opposing the
Diem regime, as well as to international public opinion; and the
fact that the role of Hanoi was completely hidden made it more
difficult than ever for the Americans to justify their own actions ir
terms of Communist 'aggression'. The importance of a coalitior
government – and therefore of the political as well as the military
struggle – was also emphasised in an internal COSVN document of
April 1962, later captured in the South, which again presented a
contrast with the COSVN resolution six months earlier. There was
no question of returning to political struggle alone, however. The
political balance in South Vietnam could only be changed by
force. A later Hanoi source tells us that in May 1962 the Party
Committee of Interzone V (southern Central Vietnam) decided or
the creation of three 'mainforce' regiments to operate in the
provinces of Quang-Nam, Quang-Ngai, Binh-Dinh and the
Central Highlands region.[19]

In this context decisions were almost certainly also taken about
the next phase of Communist strategy in Laos. By now there were
grounds for suspecting that Chinese, Soviet and North Vietnamese
views on Laos did not precisely coincide. At least some members of
the Vietnamese Communist leadership – probably including Le
Duan, but not necessarily Ho Chi Minh – regarded the revolution
in Laos (and also that in Cambodia) as contributing to an
integrated Indochinese revolution under Vietnamese leadership.
The Chinese perspective, by contrast, embraced the whole of
mainland South-East Asia and treated the Vietnamese, Laotian,
Cambodian, Thai and Malayan revolutions on much the same
level; each under the leadership of its own Communist Party –
which should have direct relations with the CCP. An underlying
tension between Chinese and Vietnamese ambitions may have
been reflected in the signing on 13 January 1962 of a number of
Sino-Laotian agreements (between Peking and the 'government'
in Khang Khay) including one for the construction of a road from
Yunnan into the Pathet Lao province of Phong Saly. Such a road
would link northern Laos directly with China, and thus relieve the
Chinese from the necessity of always communicating with the
Pathet Lao through Hanoi.[20]

But whatever the ultimate goals of either China or North

Vietnam, the period from February to April 1962 appears to have seen a temporary relaxation of the drive to expand the revolution into Laos and beyond. That too may have been a result of Kennedy's firm policies, which we must examine more fully in the next chapter.

4 The Kennedy Strategy Takes Shape

Wisdom requires the long view. And the long view shows us that the revolution of national independence is a fundamental fact of our era. This revolution cannot be stopped. As new nations emerge from the oblivion of centuries, their first aspiration is to affirm their national identity. Their deepest hope is for a world where, within a framework of international cooperation, every country can solve its own problems according to its own traditions and ideals. . . .

There used to be much talk a few years ago about the inevitable triumph of Communism. We hear such talk much less now. No one who examines the modern world can doubt that the great currents of history are carrying the world away from the monolithic idea towards the pluralist idea – away from Communism and towards national independence and freedom. . . .

We must seize the vision of a free and diverse world – and shape our policies to speed progress towards a flexible world order. This is the unifying spirit of our policies in the world. The purpose of our aid programs must be to help developing countries to move forward as rapidly as possible on the road to genuine national independence. Our military policies must assist nations to protect the processes of democratic reform and development against disruption and intervention.

President Kennedy, in speech at University of California,
23 March 1962

Our security and strength, in the last analysis, directly depend on the security and strength of others, and that is why our military and economic assistance plays such a key role in enabling those who live on the periphery of the Communist world to maintain their independence of choice. Our assistance to these nations can be painful, risky and costly, as is true in Southeast Asia today. But we dare not weary of the task. . . . A successful Communist breakthrough in these areas, necessitating direct United States intervention, would cost several times as much as our entire foreign aid program and might cost us heavily in American lives as well.

President Kennedy's last speech,
due to have been given in Dallas, 22 November 1963

I

The formal commitment to South Vietnam contained in President Kennedy's letter of 14 December 1961, whilst it was based on general principles already approved in NSAM-111, required a series of further decisions to be taken during the early months of 1962. The first 'Secretary of Defense Conference' at Honolulu in mid-December was followed by a second such meeting a month later, and by several more during the first half of the year. Another important conference – attended by American ambassadors in Asia and by Averell Harriman – was the Far East Regional Operations Conference held at Baguio (in the Philippines) from 10 to 14 March 1962.[1]

The pattern of American command responsibilities in South Vietnam itself began to take clearer shape with the creation on 8 February of the Military Assistance Command, Vietnam (MACV). Until that time, the Military Assistance Advisory Group (MAAG), which had grown out of the programme of American military assistance to the French before 1954 and had been permitted to continue under the Geneva Agreement, had provided advice, training and equipment to the ARVN. MAAG differed from a full-scale Command in that, although headed by a lieutenant-general, its military personnel worked within programmes run jointly by the State Department and the Pentagon, and were answerable to the 'country team' headed by the Ambassador. Now that actual American military units were being deployed to provide logistic support to the South Vietnamese army, a new arrangement was natural. But the creation of a new command gave rise to questions about its status within the regular military hierarchy, and its relationship to the existing structure. In the end it was agreed that MAAG would continue to have responsibility for advisory and aid programmes, but would in future report to the commander of MACV rather than directly to the Ambassador. MACV itself, however, was denied the status of a full unified command reporting directly to the JCS. A proposal to that effect had been vetoed by CINCPAC on the grounds that the defence of South Vietnam – or even of the Indochinese Peninsula – could not be treated separately from the security of the whole Far East, extending from Japan and Korea to Pakistan and the Indian Ocean. Nevertheless it was agreed that the commander of MACV, Lieutenant-General Paul D. Harkins, would take with him to

Saigon the responsibility for military planning which he had previously exercised under the Pacific Army Command in Honolulu: a responsibility which involved the defence of mainland South-East Asia not merely of Vietnam. In certain respects therefore, Harkins was the logical successor to Lieutenant-General Lionel C. McGarr (head of MAAG since mid-1960) who now resigned. But McGarr's former deputy, Major-General Charles J. Timmes, remained chief of MAAG until 1964 and in that capacity still exercised operational control over the programme.[2]

Underlying the American debate about these technicalities of command and control lay a fundamental difference of perspective. The advocates of counterinsurgency (including civilian officials and special forces officers) saw it as a new type of military assistance, and as an alternative to more direct military involvement. But the more orthodox military establishment, oriented towards planning the conventional operations that would be necessary in the event of a larger war, saw counterinsurgency as merely one of a number of possible military actions in a changing situation: in effect, the first rung on a ladder of 'flexible response'. Whilst Kennedy, as President, could insist that counterinsurgency was the immediate strategy in Indochina and elsewhere, he could hardly prevent the JCS – and under them CINCPAC and MACV – from continuing to plan for other possible contingencies beyond the scale of the insurgency actually under way in South Vietnam. Those plans were bound to include, at least as a theoretical possibility, the eventual deployment of American combat troops to South-East Asia.

Meanwhile in Washington a series of more general discussions was taking place under the direct auspices of the NSC. The Special Group (CI), created by NSAM-124 on 18 January 1962, was given responsibility for formulating the doctrine of counterinsurgency and overseeing its application in a number of designated countries: in the first instance, South Vietnam, Laos and Thailand.[3]

The military–political doctrine of counterinsurgency had emerged from a long period of analysis and debate going back to the late 1950s. It had begun to take clear shape as a policy option by the summer of 1961, notably in two important speeches of Walt W. Rostow and Roger Hilsman (in June and August) and in the more private deliberations of a secret committee presided over by the CIA Deputy Director for Plans, Richard Bissell.[4] Between January and September 1962 as many as fourteen NSAMs dealt with various aspects of the new doctrine, the most important being no. 182 (dated 24 August), which approved a highly classified report on 'US Overseas Internal Defense Policy'.[5] A national seminar for senior officials was convened in June and early July and received active encouragement – as did the US Special Forces at Fort Bragg – from the President himself. By then the programmes already devised for South Vietnam and Laos were well under way.

As practised in Vietnam during 1962–3, counterinsurgency embraced four main types of programme:

First: the development of a South Vietnamese capability for counter-guerrilla operations, through the provision of more US advisers (down to battalion level) and of helicopters and armoured vehicles to improve mobility in the field, as well as through the training of Vietnamese special forces in new tactics and methods of operation. The essential object was to defeat the Communist guerrillas whenever they sought to operate as organised units, and if possible to prevent them moving on from company-size to battalion-size operations. In the first instance, three helicopter companies were provided by the US army. But in mid-March 1962, after a certain amount of inter-service wrangling, it was decided that the fourth such unit would be supplied by the US Marines. Deployed initially to Soc-Trang in the Mekong Delta, it was later transferred (September 1962) to Danang. Thus began the division of labour within the United States armed forces which was to last throughout the war, with the marines playing the dominant role in the northernmost provinces of South Vietnam and the army being responsible for the rest of the country.[6]

Second: improvement of the civilian capabilities of the government of South Vietnam to police and administer rural areas, through the development of pacification programmes whose hallmark was the 'strategic hamlet'. This included the application to South Vietnam of lessons learned in Malaya during the 'emergency' (1948–60); and to that end Ngo Dinh Diem brought in a team of British advisers headed by R. G. K. Thompson, whose programme for the pacification of a number of provinces in the Mekong Delta was finally approved on 19 March 1962. Other programmes under the general heading of pacification included 'Operation Sunrise', inaugurated on 22 March in Binh-Duong province (on the very edge of an area controlled by the Communists); and the more successful 'Operation Sea Swallow' in Phu-Yen province starting on 8 May, which by August had brought under government control several districts conceded to the Communist side for most of the time since 1954. In July 1962 a CIA report on the progress of pacification indicated that about 2000 'strategic hamlets' had been established in various parts of the country, and another 7000 were planned.[7]

Third: the use of chemical herbicides to defoliate areas where Communist guerrillas might hide, and to deny them food by destroying crops in localities under their control. Kennedy himself wanted to move cautiously in this area. A defoliation programme approved on 30 November 1961 (NSAM-115) began to get under way during January; but crop destruction was not authorised until November 1962. In time both types of operation would become symbols of the American attempt to use superior technology as a means of overcoming the political and practical advantages enjoyed by the Communists on the ground.[8]

Fourth: the establishment of special forces camps in the upland and forest areas of Central Vietnam, particularly the Central Highlands populated mainly by non-Vietnamese ('montagnard') tribes. American special forces teams sent to that region had instructions to live among the tribespeople and train them to defend their villages. Starting with an experimental programme amongst the Rhadé tribe in Darlac province late in 1961, then making recruits amongst the Sedang further north, the special forces had established over 25 fortified camps in upland areas by the end of 1962.[9] The subsequent history of the Vietnam War would demonstrate the correctness of the judgement that this highland region must be prevented from falling into the hands of the Communist forces; but as time went on it would become evident that the special forces programme alone was not enough. It was there, if anywhere, that United States combat units would eventually be needed.

It lies beyond the scope of the present study to assess how far these American prorammes were effective on the ground. Certainly some progress was made during the spring and summer of 1962, which seemed to justify the Kennedy decisions and to encourage the consolidation of counterinsurgency as a general doctrine. One consequence for South Vietnam itself was that the role of the government armed forces (ARVN) was greatly strengthened, since the whole strategy of counterinsurgency required the existence of a Vietnamese military machine capable of receiving and applying whatever kinds of American military support were deemed necessary to counter Communist tactics for the time being. At the same time the Americans were becoming more committed than ever to the existing civilian government of Ngo Dinh Diem; a commitment that was strengthened even further after the President and leading members of his family survived an air attack on his palace in Saigon on 27 February 1962. But the result of that episode was to make Diem increasingly suspicious of the political ambitions of his military officers – and reluctant to permit the rationalisation of the South Vietnamese military command structure which the Americans believed necessary. Consequently, over the next two years, tension between the government and the armed forces in South Vietnam was almost inevitable.

II

In the wider international perspective, it is possible to see Kennedy's emphasis on counterinsurgency in South Vietnam as a means of dealing with the problems of that country in such a way that the conflict would not spread to the rest of South-East Asia. Whether that would continue to be possible in the longer term depended not only on events in Vietnam but also on developments elsewhere. An important element in Kennedy's Asian strategy was his desire for an international agreement on the neutralisation of Laos. The full intricacies of the military – diplomatic sequence leading to the Laos agreement of 1962 will be known only when all the archives become available to historians. But Kennedy's policy clearly involved combining patient diplomacy with the deployment of military force as a means of establishing both the aims and the limits of American military intentions. No agreement was possible at all unless he could reassure Bangkok that the creation of a new coalition in Laos would in no way diminish the American commitment to defend Thailand.

Early in February 1962 it was reported that 400 American

troops – engineers and other specialists – were to be sent to Thailand to improve communications and other facilities. But until he was completely satisfied about American intentions, the Thai prime minister, Sarit Thannarat, was likely to continue supporting the rightist Laotian faction of Phoumi Nosavan, whose 'extremist' position was itself one of the main obstacles to agreement on a new coalition. Sarit demonstrated his independence of the Americans by providing weapons and other assistance to allow Phoumi to reinforce his last remaining strong-point in northern Laos at Nam Tha. It would appear that the CIA gave clandestine support to this latter move; but American diplomats made known their official disapproval, and later in the month Kennedy ordered the suspension of cash-grant aid to Vientiane. In effect what happened at Nam Tha was a holding operation, to maintain an anti-Communist presence in the far north until Sarit was ready for serious negotiations. Meanwhile in talks between the rightists and Souvanna Phouma at Luang Prabang from 16 to 18 February, Phoumi Nosavan continued to take an unco-operative line and frustrated any immediate progress towards a coalition.

Kennedy's next move was to invite the Thai foreign minister to Washington. On 6 March a formal joint statement, issued by Thanat Khoman and Dean Rusk, established the principle that United States troops would defend Thailand even in circumstances where the other members of SEATO were reluctant to act. Although it fell short of a bilateral security treaty, this amounted to a more formal and specific American commitment than any so far made to South Vietnam. It was immediately followed, moreover, by the Baguio Conference mentioned above, which met from 10 to 14 March 1962. It was now possible for Averell Harriman to persuade both Sarit and Phoumi Nosavan of the necessity for an agreement on a new Laotian coalition, which he appears to have done at a meeting in north-east Thailand towards the end of March.[10]

By mid-April Kennedy was satisfied that a negotiated solution in Laos was possible in principle, although it would still be necessary for him to demonstrate the firmness of American resolve at every step. As early as 19 April he approved a decision, recorded in NSAM-149, to withdraw American special forces teams from 'forward positions' in Laos – but not until after 7 May.[11] In that interval the Pathet Lao (with North Vietnamese reinforcements) launched an attack on Nam Tha, which was finally abandoned by

TABLE 4.1   *South-East Asia: Diplomacy and Conflict, February–March 1962*

Laos, Thailand	South Vietnam	Indonesia
		4 Feb.: Robert Kennedy arrived in Tokyo at start of Asian tour.
4 Feb.: Report that 400 US troops will be sent to Thailand to assist aid projects. early Feb.: Sarit Thannarat provided aid to Phoumi Nosavan to reinforce Nam Tha.	8 Feb.: US MACV formally established.	8 Feb.: Soviet statement supporting Indonesian claim to West Irian. Indonesian air force delegation went to USSR
		13–18 Feb.: Robert Kennedy in Indonesia for talks with Sukarno.
16–18 Feb.: Souvanna Phouma visited Vientiane; talks with Phoumi Nosavan on a new coalition. 19 Feb.: Robert Kennedy in Bangkok.	16 Feb.: NLFSVN First Congress began; lasted until 3 March. (Not reported until April.)	
23 Feb.: Sarit alleged that Chinese troops had massed near the Laos border.	24 Feb.: Chinese statement supporting North Vietnam's denunciation of US actions in South Vietnam.	22 Feb.: Soviet delegation arrived in Jakarta (Guber). 24 Feb.: Sukarno proclaimed general mobilisation to recover West Irian.

27 Feb.: Abortive attack on Diem's palace in Saigon.

6 March: Rusk–Thanat Joint Statement, on US commitment to defend Thailand.

10–14 March: Baguio meeting: US Far East Regional Conference.

12 March: Netherlands agreed to US proposal as basis for negotiations on West Irian.

19 March: Diem approved pacification plan for provinces of Mekong Delta.

20 March: Malik and Van Roejen began informal talks near Washington.

22 March: 'Operation Sunrise' began in Binh-Duong province, north of Saigon.

24 March: Harriman met Sarit and Phoumi; persuaded latter to agree to new coalition in Laos.

SOURCES See notes to Chapters 3 and 4.

Phoumist forces on 6 May. But when the latter retreated to the banks of the Mekong and crossed over into Thailand, the move was dramatised in Bangkok as evidence of a direct Communist threat to Thailand's own security.

In retrospect it seems clear that neither the Pathet Lao nor the North Vietnamese had any intention of crossing into Thailand in hot pursuit. Nevertheless, in keeping with the Rusk – Thanat statement, the United States immediately sent 4000 marines to Thailand. The first units arrived on 11 May, followed by a formal announcement of the decision in Washington and Bangkok on the 15th. Simultaneously Britain, as a member of SEATO, sent a Royal Air Force squadron to Chieng Mai in Northern Thailand. Only then was it possible to embark on a serious attempt to achieve an actual diplomatic solution in Laos. Even on 24 May a presidential meeting approved contingency plans for the use of Thai and American forces inside Laos in the event of the failure of negotiations and a breakdown of the ceasefire.[12] But that contingency did not arise. The 'three princes', and other leading figures of the three Laotian factions, met in the Plaine des Jarres from 7 to 13 June and at last produced a detailed blueprint for a new coalition headed by Prince Souvanna Phouma. When the new government formally took office in Vientiane on 23 June, the stage was set for its participation in the final phase of the 14-nation conference in Geneva.

At that point, however, yet another Asian crisis seemed to be looming on the horizon, involving relations between the United States, Taiwan and the People's Republic of China. Already in March 1962 Nationalist leaders on Taiwan had returned to the theme of an eventual attack on the mainland, arguing that their forces must be ready to take advantage of the supposedly desperate economic situation then prevailing and the likelihood of a popular uprising against Communist rule. Despite official American attempts to discourage such thinking, Chiang Kaishek on a number of occasions talked publicly about his plans to invade the mainland, and by June it was evident that Peking was nervous. A concentration of PLA units was observed in Fujian province opposite the Taiwan Straits, accompanied by allegations of Nationalist intrusions into Chinese territorial waters.

The situation was discussed at a White House meeting on 20 June, at which Kennedy decided he must try to defuse the conflict before a serious crisis ensued. Three days later the American ambassador in Warsaw met his Chinese counterpart to reassure him that the United States had no intention of backing an invasion of the Chinese mainland. Then, in order to avoid any misunderstanding in Taiwan itself or amongst the American China Lobby, the President devoted part of his news conference on 27 June to a reaffirmation of the American commitment to defend Taiwan itself against attack.[13] It is impossible to assess the true significance of all this on the basis of the limited evidence so far available. Possibly it was a more serious crisis than the public was allowed to know; and possibly it was a turning-point in Sino-American relations. The only certain conclusion is that whatever happened was not allowed to stand in the way of finalisation of the agreement on Laos.

On 9 July the new Vientiane government issued a formal declaration of its future neutrality in world affairs, including a demand for the withdrawal of all foreign troops from the country. Two weeks later (23 July) the nations represented at Geneva issued a Declaration on the Neutrality of Laos, together with a Protocol promising the withdrawal of all foreign forces and reaffirming the responsibility of the International Commission to maintain the new ceasefire. One of the more remarkable aspects of this agreement was that both documents were signed by all fourteen delegations – including not only the United Kingdom and the Soviet Union (as Co-chairmen) but also the People's Republic of China and the United States.[14] The Kennedy Administration did not share the earlier opinion of John Foster Dulles that an American signature to such a document was tantamount to diplomatic recognition of Peking.

III

Kennedy's policy towards Laos was in keeping with his desire for friendship with other genuinely neutralist countries in the region. It is even possible that he was trying to improve relations with Burma early in 1962, and perhaps to promote closer ties between Rangoon and Tokyo. The Japanese premier Ikeda had included Burma in a tour of South and South-East Asian countries in November 1961 in the hope of reaching agreement on a revised figure for Japanese reparations. There was even talk in Washington of a possible military assistance programme for Burma.[15] But the government of U Nu was overthrown by a military coup on 2 March 1962 and General Ne Win embarked on a 'Burmese Road to Socialism' which precluded the acceptance of military aid or foreign investment from any quarter. Thereafter, although Burma was still sometimes mentioned by exponents of the 'domino theory' as one of the countries liable to be affected by an American defeat in Vietnam, it did not figure prominently in United States strategy during the remainder of the decade.

Elsewhere in South-East Asia, Kennedy's objectives included the improvement of United States relations with Indonesia, and also the promotion of greater regional co-operation. There too, he was inclined to encourage a Japanese role. Washington was no longer seeking to enlarge SEATO as a means of promoting collective security. Its aim was rather to bring about improved diplomatic and economic relations among all the countries of South-East Asia, and to stabilise its own relations with them. Some progress had been made towards cultural and economic regional co-operation with the creation in July 1961 of the Association of South-East Asia (usually known as ASA); but it included only Thailand, the Philippines and the Federation of Malaya. The Americans were conscious of the need for Indonesian participation in a larger grouping. Thus Indonesia was important to the Americans not only because Western oil companies had extensive operations in Sumatra but also because it held the key to South-East Asian regional co-operation.

President Kennedy had already embarked on a policy of improving Indonesian – American relations when he received Sukarno in Washington the previous April. Between 4 and 18 February 1962 – coinciding precisely with the establishment of MACV in Saigon – Attorney-General Robert Kennedy undertook a personal mission to Tokyo and Jakarta, followed by a briefer visit to Bangkok.[16] Relations between Japan and the United States were still good, despite the anti-American demonstrations which had forced Eisenhower to cancel a presidential visit 18 months before. But Washington could no longer afford to take its ally for granted: a recent agreement on final repayment of debts arising from American aid to Japan after 1945 had marked an important stage in the recovery of Japanese independence; and that impression was reinforced by a new Soviet–Japanese trade agreement, soon to be signed. Robert Kennedy's visit was both timely and remarkably successful.

In Indonesia, where he established a friendly relationship with Sukarno, his main task was to convince the Indonesian president that American-sponsored diplomacy offered a better hope than military action for securing a transfer of power in West Irian. In mid-February, at the very moment when Khrushchev was promising further military aid to an Indonesian air force delegation in Sochi, Robert Kennedy was reassuring Sukarno and his first minister, Djuanda, that the Dutch were now ready to enter into unconditional negotiations in the presence of a third party – perhaps the United States – and that UN Secretary-General U Thant was also willing to act as mediator.[17] A diplomatic solution was not guaranteed, but there was at least a possibility that these discussions would bear fruit.

There was still a danger that the West Irian problem might lead to more serious military action, which would allow the Soviet Union to increase its military influence in Jakarta. Sukarno's proclamation of general mobilisation on 24 February, taken shortly after the arrival of a Soviet delegation, was another step in that direction. There was a danger, too, that Indonesia's relations with Japan might be damaged if Tokyo continued to grant landing facilities to Dutch reinforcements bound for West Irian: anti-Japanese demonstrations occurred in some areas even while Robert Kennedy was still in Jakarta. However, on 12 March 1962 the Americans persuaded The Hague to negotiate with Sukarno, and a week later informal talks between Dutch and Indonesian diplomats opened at a house outside Washington. On 2 April the American intermediary Ellesworth Bunker formulated proposals which would eventually become the basis for a settlement – although there were further difficulties to be overcome and more fighting occurred before agreement was finally reached at the end of July.[18]

The firmest American ally in the region, the Philippines, was at this time seeking to play a more active diplomatic role under a new president. To that end, Macapagal was anxious to make a show of independence of the United States: for example, by moving the national day from 4 July to the anniversary of the Philippine Revolution of 1898; by placing greater emphasis on the heroes of national history; and also by introducing new regulations for foreign investment. Perhaps as an additional means of asserting this new regional role, the Philippine government also decided to take up the claim of the heirs of the Sultanate of Sulu to possession

TABLE 4.2 *South-East Asian Diplomacy, June – July 1962*

Laos	Vietnam	Maritime South-East Asia
	2 June: International Commission made a *Special Report* to the Geneva Co-chairmen, condemning both sides; but Polish member dissented from criticism of Hanoi.	June: Informal talks between Dutch and Indonesian representatives continued, in United States; no agreement yet.
7–13 June: Conference of 'three princes' led to final agreement on a new coalition.		
14 June: United States resumed financial aid to Vientiane government (suspended in February).		22 June: Philippines government announced its claim to Sabah, on behalf of heirs of sultan of Sulu.
23 June: Souvanna Phouma took office as prime minister of new coalition government in Laos.		24 June: Further landing of Indonesian forces in West Irian: last phase of fighting.
23 June: Warsaw: Sino-American ambassadorial meeting, including American attempt to defuse crisis over Taiwan threat to invade Chinese mainland.		
2 July: Geneva Conference reassembled.		12 July: Resumption of Indonesian–Dutch talks, to finalise an agreement on West Irian. Subandrio went to Washington on 18th.
9 July: Laotian government made formal declaration of its neutrality.		
	20 July: NLFSVN issued four-point manifesto, repeating call for US withdrawal and demand for a coalition government.	

23 July: Geneva Conference delegates signed Declaration and Protocol on Laos. All foreign forces to withdraw by 7 October.

23–5 July: Sixth Secretary of Defense Conference, Honolulu: McNamara authorised preparation of 'comprehensive plan' for South Vietnam, and looked towards eventual phased withdrawal of US support units.

27 July: Speech by Macapagal, calling for a 'Greater Malayan Confederation': initial impulse for development of 'Maphilindo' idea.

30 July: Indonesia and Netherlands reached agreement on transfer of West Irian; signed on 15 August.

31 July: London Agreement on creation of Federation of Malaysia by August 1963.

of the British colony of North Borneo (about to be included in the Federation of Malaysia): a claim which had been pressed by certain groups within the Philippines Congress since late 1961. In February 1962 the foreign ministry agreed to investigate it, and the following June – despite Britain's refusal to negotiate on the issue – Macapagal came out in favour of pursuing the claim as national policy.[19]

Britain, meanwhile, was concerned about the future of its possessions in Borneo; and about the status of Singapore, which had internal self-government under Lee Kuan Yew but was not yet fully independent. Basic agreement on the creation of a Federation of Malaysia had been reached during 1961 in talks between London and Kuala Lumpur, with the result that by February 1962 Lord Cobbold was embarking on an exercise to ascertain opinion in the various component areas. In principle there seemed no reason why the proposed new Federation of Malaysia (intended to embrace Malaya, Singapore, Sarawak and North Borneo, or Sabah) should not take its place in the evolving pattern of regional relations. On 31 July the London Agreement established the terms on which the Federation of Malaysia would come into existence at the end of August 1963.

July and August 1962 can now be seen to have been the high-point of Kennedy's diplomatic success in South-East Asia. A week after the Geneva declaration on Laos, the Dutch and the Indonesians finalised their agreement on the transfer of power in West Irian (formally signed on 15 August). The most serious threats to stability in the region, the conflicts over Laos and over West Irian, had thus been resolved on terms which Kennedy could accept and with the active participation of the United States. The stage was now set for further progress towards regional co-operation.

IV

The contrast between Kennedy's pursuit of counterinsurgency in South Vietnam and his willingness to seek diplomatic solutions elsewhere in South-East Asia is bound to appear something of a paradox. Why was he unable (or was he unwilling?) to find a diplomatic solution to the problem of South Vietnam? One answer might be to suggest that Kennedy himself would have preferred to do so but was obliged by 'hawks' in his Administration – especially in the Pentagon – to adopt a rigorously anti-Communist line in this one critical area of South-East Asia. More careful analysis, however, shows that to be an oversimplification.

There can be little doubt that a divergence of opinion about Vietnam did exist in Washington in 1962, and can be illustrated from documents reprinted in the *Pentagon Papers*. On the one hand, J. K. Galbraith, Kennedy's ambassador to India, submitted a memorandum on 4 April warning against the danger of a long-drawn-out and indecisive military commitment in Indochina. He called for greater efforts towards a political solution, on the assumption that 'the Soviets are not particularly desirous of trouble in that part of the world'. On the other hand, the JCS put forward a classic restatement of the 'domino theory' in a memorandum of 13 January 1962, and on 13 April wrote a detailed rebuttal of Galbraith's optimistic views.[20] It might be argued that Kennedy, faced with this conflict between 'moderation' in the State Department and 'extremism' at the Pentagon, was obliged by circumstance rather than conviction to allow the JCS to have their way: an interpretation which may appeal to those historians who study only American documents and are inclined to explain decision-making in Washington entirely in terms of a conflict between wisdom and folly on the American side.

It is not necessary to defend the 'domino theory' in its crudest form in order to recognise that Ambassador Galbraith's memorandum presents an equally oversimple view of the Vietnam conflict – one which might be characterised as the 'liberal illusion'. His proposals assumed that military restraint on the part of the United States would evoke corresponding restraint on the Communist side: that a standstill on the introduction of American troops and material into South Vietnam could realistically be bargained for a 'suspension of Viet Cong activity'. Galbraith also assumed that Hanoi and its allies would then accept a genuine political compromise within South Vietnam, leading to the establishment of a 'broadly based non-Communist government that is free from external interference' but which need not be 'militarily identified with the United States'. That amounted to taking the published demands of the NLFSVN at face value whilst ignoring the evidence that it was Hanoi – with at least the acquiescence of Moscow and Peking – that had gradually resumed the armed struggle in the South; and that its aim was not compromise but reunification. There was nothing at all at that time to suggest that Vietnamese Communist leaders would call a halt to the armed struggle unless they believed their essential aims could be achieved without further military action.

That is not to imply that Galbraith's initiative had no basis at all in the diplomatic situation of April 1962. It had almost certainly arisen from discussions with Indian officials, and took account of the fact that India still acted as chairman of the International Commission in Vietnam. In all probability this was a serious Indian attempt to revive the framework established by the Geneva Conference of 1954, even though the ceasefire itself had long since broken down; perhaps it was an attempt to revive the somewhat vague ideas about an eventual political settlement expressed in the Final Declaration. That may have been the principal reason why the International Commission made a *Special Report* to the Co-chairmen of the Conference on 2 June[21] – a move already anticipated by Galbraith in his memorandum. It sought a middle path between the two sides, insisting that both North and South Vietnam – recognised as the temporary administrative authorities of the two Zones – had violated specific articles of the ceasefire Agreement. But the fact that the Polish member of the International Commission refused to join in any condemnation of North Vietnam meant that the report as a whole was not unanimous. A minority statement by the Polish delegate supported all of Hanoi's claims and demanded action by the Co-chairmen to secure the immediate dissolution of MACV and a complete American withdrawal from Vietnam. Such disagreement left little room for diplomatic manoeuvre on the part of the Indian government, or for the report to become the basis of an agreed initiative by the two Co-chairmen.

Nor was there any realistic possibility of applying to South Vietnam the same formula which produced a diplomatic solution in Laos, though there were indications in the summer of 1962 that the idea was being considered in some quarters. The principle of a coalition government in the Southern Zone of Vietnam was certainly compatible with the programme of the NLFSVN, both in its original form and in the form approved by the First Congress of the Front. It became an explicit demand in the Front's 'four-point manifesto' issued on 20 July 1962. Likewise the principle of South Vietnamese neutrality (without, at this stage, any reference to reunification) was enunciated in detail by another NLFSVN statement on 18 August 1962.[22] That this was more than window-dressing is indicated by the activities of the North Vietnamese foreign minister in Europe in the month or so following the Geneva Declaration on Laos. On 22 August he had a meeting with the veteran South Vietnamese political exile Tran Van Huu (who in the early 1950s had served for a time as prime minister of the Associate State of Vietnam under Bao Dai) at which it was suggested that Huu might play a role in Vietnam comparable with that of Souvanna Phouma in Laos. A few days later Tran Van Huu himself appeared at a press conference to endorse the idea of South Vietnamese neutrality – including the proposal that reunification might be delayed for 15–20 years.[23]

There were, however, fundamental differences between the kind of coalition envisaged by Tran Van Huu and the NLFSVN, and that which had actually been brought into existence in Laos. The new government in Vientiane embraced all three political factions in Laos – including the rightist Phoumi Nosavan whose close links with the United States and Thailand were publicly acknowledged. There was also rough parity between the political and military forces of the rightists, the neutralists and the Pathet Lao. Whether such a government could work in practice remained to be seen; but in the diplomacy leading to its formation all the principal political elements inside the country were directly involved, and all interested international forces were represented in some way. Only on that basis was it possible to establish the international agreement on which internal reconciliation must depend. But in the case of the NLFSVN proposal for South Vietnam – whether it is seen as merely a propaganda exercise or as something more substantial – it was taken for granted that the existing regime in Saigon would be overthrown, and there was no question of the pro-American Ngo Dinh Diem being included in a new coalition. Nor did any significant neutralist element in South Vietnam possess the kind of power base enjoyed by Souvanna Phouma and Kong Lae; it was absurd to suppose that Tran Van Huu, as a former *collaborateur* of the French, could suddenly return from exile in Paris to play such a role. In the absence both of Diem and of American military support, which was to be withdrawn as part of an agreement, there would be an immediate political vacuum – enabling the Front (that is, in practice, the Communists) to dominate the coalition from the start. Such a prospect was hardly a satisfactory basis for international compromise.

All this points to the conclusion that in practice there was little possibility of a diplomatic solution to the problem of Vietnam at this stage. One might be tempted to go even further and suggest that without Kennedy's continuing commitment to firm action in South Vietnam (and also Thailand) the United States would have been unable to achieve even the degree of diplomatic success it did achieve in South-East Asia in the summer of 1962.

Since the Americans could see no immediate opportunity for a negotiated settlement in South Vietnam, they began to turn their attention to devising a long-term strategy to replace both their *ad hoc* implementation of NSAM-111 and also SEATO plans for military intervention (which had been overtaken by the commitment to Laotian neutrality). Remaining American forces in Laos were to be withdrawn by 7 October 1962, and thereafter it would be impossible to send in either American or Thai military personnel to operate openly as combat units. Contingency plans for major military involvement in the area were predicated on overt action by North Vietnamese and possibly Chinese forces. But the more immediate American concern was with the insurgency inside South Vietnam, and that was the main item on the agenda of the Sixth 'Secretary of Defense Conference' in Honolulu, which opened on 23 July within hours of the Geneva signing of the Declaration and Protocol on Laos.

The *Pentagon Papers* contain two detailed progress reports on the counterinsurgency programme in South Vietnam in mid-1962: one by the State Department Bureau of Intelligence and Research (18 June), the other by the CIA station chief in Saigon (13 July).[24] Neither could pretend that all problems had been solved or that anything but a long and difficult struggle lay ahead. But both reports were optimistic rather than pessimistic about the long-term prospect for success and sought to refute any suggestion that the situation was still deteriorating. In terms of individual incidents, the picture at that time included both successes and failures. The ambush of an ARVN convoy in Binh-Duong province on 16 June, which demonstrated the ineffectiveness of the first strategic hamlet programme in that area, could be balanced against a report in mid-July that in Phu-Yen province ARVN units had recovered control of a district which had been in Communist hands for most of the time since 1954. Later compilations of statistics suggest that from mid-1962 the American programmes initiated since the beginning of the year had begun to take effect; and that the immediate collapse of the Diem regime had been averted. But they had not yet made sufficient impact on the situation to force the Communist side either to seek a formal compromise or to abandon the struggle altogether. Nor did anyone in Washington expect that to happen in the next year or more.

Nevertheless at the Honolulu meeting McNamara proceeded from the assumption that victory was possible, and that it was realistic to plan for the eventual withdrawal of most American support units from South Vietnam, leaving the main responsibility for internal security in the hands of ARVN. The Secretary called on CINCPAC and MACV to devise a 'Comprehensive Plan for South Vietnam', looking ahead as far as 1968, on the assumption that the total number of American military personnel required in South Vietnam at any one time would not rise above 12,500 and that a 'phased withdrawal' could begin after the end of 1965.[25] These instructions reflected confidence in the ability of United States personnel to train South Vietnamese officers to take over most of the logistic and technical roles currently being performed by Americans. They did not amount to a prediction about how long the conflict itself would have to go on. But even this degree of optimism presupposed that Communist military activity would remain on roughly the same level – and that political stability could be maintained in Saigon and the other main urban centres. Above all, the whole Kennedy strategy assumed that the conflict could be fought out within the borders of South Vietnam and that North Vietnamese troops would not become directly involved.

APPENDIX TO CHAPTER 4

Extracts from the International Commission's *Special Report* to the Co-chairmen of the Geneva Conference, 2 June 1962: see note 21.

Having examined the complaints and the supporting material sent by the South Vietnamese Mission, the (Legal) Committee has come to the conclusion that in specific instances there is evidence to show that armed and unarmed personnel, arms, munitions and other supplies have been sent from the Zone in the North to the Zone in the South with the object of supporting, organising and carrying out hostile activities, including armed attacks, directed against the Armed Forces and Administration of the Zone in the South. These acts are in violation of Articles 10, 19, 24 and 27 of the Agreement on the Cessation of Hostilities in Vietnam.

... the (Legal) Committee has come to the further conclusion that there is evidence to show that the PAVN has allowed the Zone in the North to be used for inciting, encouraging and supporting hostile activities in the Zone in the South, aimed at the overthrow of the Administration in the South. The use of the Zone in the North for such activities is in violation of Articles 19, 24 and 27 of the Agreement on the Cessation of Hostilities in Vietnam....

The Commission accepts the conclusions reached by the Legal Committee that there is sufficient evidence to show beyond reasonable doubt that the PAVN has violated Articles 10, 19, 24 and 27 in specific instances. The Polish Delegation dissents from these conclusions....

Taking all the facts into consideration, and basing itself on its own observations and authorised statements made in the USA and the Republic of Vietnam, the Commission concludes that the Republic of Vietnam has violated Articles 16 and 17 of the Geneva Agreement in receiving increased military aid in the absence of any established credit in its favour. The Commission is also of the view that, though there may not be any formal military alliance between the Governments of the United States of America and the Republic of Vietnam, the establishment of a US Military Assistance Command in South Vietnam, as well as the introduction of a large number of US military personnel beyond the stated strength of the MAAG, amounts to a factual military alliance which is prohibited under Article 19 of the Geneva Agreement.

The Commission would also like to bring to the notice of the Co-chairmen a recent and deliberate tendency on the part of both the Parties to deny or refuse controls to the Commission's teams, thereby completely immobilising their activities and hindering the Commission in the proper discharge of its obligations to supervise the implementation of Articles 16 and 17 of the Geneva Agreement....

5 China's Asian Strategy: a New Phase

The contradiction between the people of the whole world and imperialism is the primary one. . . . There are also the contradictions between the people of all countries and revisionism, the contradictions among imperialist countries, the contradiction between nationalist countries and imperialism, internal contradictions within imperialist countries, and the contradiction between socialism and imperialism.

> Mao Zedong, speaking at CCP Central Committee's
> 10th Plenum, 24 September 1962

The contradiction between the socialist camp and the imperialist camp is a contradiction between two fundamentally different social systems, socialism and capitalism. It is undoubtedly very sharp. But Marxist–Leninists must not regard the contradictions in the world as consisting solely and simply of the contradiction between the socialist camp and the imperialist camp. . . .

The various types of contradiction in the contemporary world are concentrated in the vast areas of Asia, Africa and Latin America. These are the most vulnerable areas under imperialist rule, and the storm-centres of world revolution. . . .

In a sense, the whole cause of the international proletarian revolution hinges on the outcome of the revolutionary struggle of the people of these areas, who constitute the overwhelming majority of the world's population. Therefore the anti-imperialist revolutionary struggle of the people in Asia, Africa and Latin America is not merely a matter of regional significance but one of overall importance for the whole cause of proletarian world revolution.

> CCP Proposal concerning the General Line of the International Communist Movement, 14 June 1963

I

By the late summer of 1962 President Kennedy had reason to be pleased with the progress of his policies in South-East Asia. The pattern of relations that was beginning to emerge in the region was one which the United States could accept despite the continuing problem of Vietnam. Certain Asian countries were willing to ally themselves firmly with the West and to accept American military assistance as the basis of their own defence strategy: the chain of those 'defence support' countries extended across all of Asia from South Korea and Taiwan (and also the Philippines) in the east to Pakistan and Iran in the west; with Thailand and South Vietnam as key allies in the Indochinese peninsula. The importance of this first group of countries for American global strategy was emphasised in September when General Maxwell Taylor made a tour of East and South-East Asia, immediately before taking up his new appointment as Chairman of the JCS. (Malaya and Singapore, whose defence was a British responsibility, were less closely aligned with the United States.) A second group of countries preferred a policy of neutrality – or 'non-alignment' – towards East–West relations. They included Indonesia, Burma, Cambodia and, of course, India; and if the Geneva Agreement of 23 July 1962 meant anything, Laos was about to join their number. Kennedy's policy towards these countries was to cultivate good relations with them and to counter Soviet and Chinese influence through diplomacy and economic assistance.

In Indochina, Kennedy's determination to continue supporting the Diem regime in Saigon – and to stand by the Rusk – Thanat commitment to defend Thailand – did not prevent him from seeking also to improve American relations with the neutral governments of Cambodia and Laos. He recognised that as 'buffer states' between North Vietnam and Thailand those countries would need to maintain connections with both sides; and there is nothing to suggest that he was alarmed when (on 7 September) Souvanna Phouma established diplomatic relations with Peking and simultaneously broke off relations with Taiwan. Nor did he object to Cambodian neutrality: by this time he was even contemplating supplying T-28 planes to Cambodia's armed forces in order to strengthen their ability to counter any future incursions by Vietnamese Communist guerrillas. But before doing so, he had to come to terms with what in the end would prove an insoluble problem: how to maintain friendship with *both* Cambodia and Thailand at the same time.

Relations between the two latter countries had been deteriorating for some time. They became worse still when, on 15 June 1962, the International Court of Justice at The Hague gave its ruling on their territorial dispute over possession of the Preah Vihear temple. The Court's decision in favour of Cambodia produced an outburst of anti-Cambodian feeling in Bangkok, exacerbated by the failure of the Americans to side openly with Thailand on the issue. Sarit eventually intervened early in July, with a broadcast urging the Thai people to accept the ruling. But soon afterwards he expressed alarm at reports of possible United States military aid to Sihanouk and refused to accept assurances that it was not intended for use on the Thai–Cambodian border. Foreign minister Thanat reiterated the same objections in September.

On 20 August, perhaps with direct encouragement from Peking, Sihanouk made things still more difficult for Kennedy by issuing an appeal to the fourteen participants in the recent Geneva Conference on Laos to hold a similar conference to guarantee the neutrality and territorial integrity of Cambodia. Thailand, which had the longest border with Cambodia, rejected the idea out of hand. Washington replied cautiously, as did London; only Peking gave the proposal immediate endorsement.[1] In the end Kennedy's failure to secure the acquiescence of Thailand to a new American policy on Cambodian neutrality was to have consequences for Vietnam far greater than anyone appreciated at the time. But his own objectives in the second half of 1962 were wholly compatible with his wider Asian strategy.

There were signs that the Soviet Union, at least, might accept the new pattern of relations in South-East Asia and base its own strategy on the principle of 'peaceful competition'. Deputy premier Mikoyan, who seems to have had special responsibility for Soviet economic relations in East and South-East Asia at this period, visited Indonesia in the latter part of July 1962. His purpose was probably to ensure that the United States role in resolving the West Irian conflict did not lead to a complete shift in Indonesian foreign policy, and the virtual exclusion of Soviet influence. A little later it became apparent that the Russians were also making overtures to other countries in South-East Asia. On 20 September, the Thai prime minister Sarit told a press conference that his government had agreed to open trade negotiations with the Soviet Union–which might lead to an exchange of notes on future trade relations, although not a formal protocol.[2] On the same day the Singapore leader Lee Kuan Yew was being welcomed in Moscow, where he succeeded in persuading his hosts to adopt a more moderate attitude towards the planned Federation of Malaysia. Whereas on 22 August Moscow Radio had echoed remarks by D. N. Aidit, to the effect that British plans represented a new 'threat' to Indonesia, the tone of Soviet commentaries on that subject was modified later in the year.[3]

At this stage, however, Peking's Asian strategy began to diverge significantly from that of Moscow. The Chinese were in no position to risk a head-on clash with the Americans; nevertheless, the greater militancy of their anti-imperialist line became increasingly apparent that autumn. They expressed their disapproval of General Taylor's Asian tour by shooting down a Nationalist U-2 'spy-plane' over East China on 9 September, the day after his arrival in Taibei. The possibility of this leading to a new crisis was only averted by another Sino-American ambassadorial meeting in Warsaw on 20 September.[4] A more serious conflict was emerging on another front, however: China's Tibetan border with India.

That issue had, as we have seen re-emerged during the early part of 1962. The question of blame lies outside the scope of our present enquiry: it is beyond dispute that by July each side was establishing military posts in territory claimed by the other, creating a particularly complicated situation in the Thagla Ridge sector of the border in the north-east. The decision of the Indian defence leadership to 'evict' Chinese forces from territory claimed by India–taken on 9 September, while Nehru was in London–was the critical turning-point in the escalation of the conflict. Despite a further exchange of notes between 13 and 19 September, establishing a date for talks to open (15 October), a negotiated solution was becoming less and less likely. The first actual clash in the Thagla Ridge sector occurred on 20 September, by which time the Chinese had probably made up their own minds to fight.[5]

The diplomatic phase virtually came to an end on 10 October when the Indian army embarked upon 'Operation Leghorn' to drive Chinese forces back from the disputed frontier in the north-eastern sector. They met with stronger Chinese resistance than they expected; and four days later *Renmin Ribao* warned Nehru to 'pull back from the brink'. Later the Chinese would claim that until that point even Khrushchev had acknowledged the correctness of Peking's attitude and actions. But the Soviet leader clearly did *not* approve of the Chinese decision to embark on a major military offensive on 20 October. If the motives behind China's policy towards India in autumn 1962 remain a matter for speculation and controversy, one factor was almost certainly the growing rivalry between the two Communist powers for influence in the 'Third World' – and particularly among the non-aligned countries of Asia. India now appeared to the Chinese as an ally of Moscow in the efforts of the latter to be taken seriously as a leading power in Asia and Africa.

For their part the Chinese appear to have countered that trend by seeking to improve their own relations with Indonesia. China had played relatively little part in providing support for the campaign to recover West Irian, having left it to Moscow to supply weapons to the Indonesian armed forces during 1961–2. But now Peking began to see Indonesia as a potential ally in the anti-imperialist struggle; and the deterioration of Sino-Indian relations probably strengthened that idea. For the moment the Chinese were more concerned with establishing and sustaining an alliance with Sukarno than with enabling the PKI to seize power. Their first move was an invitation to Madame Hartini Sukarno to attend the national day celebrations that year: she arrived in China on 23 September and was given a place of honour at the Tiananmen parade on 1 October.[6]

One other aspect of China's emerging new strategy must also be mentioned, which had more to do with a desire for greater economic independence of the Soviet Union than with the pursuit of anti-imperialism. In September 1962 Peking attempted to revive the economic *rapprochement* with Japan which had begun to develop in the mid-1950s but had been thwarted by Taiwan (and its Japanese friends) in the spring of 1958. The new Japanese government of Ikeda appears to have been more favourably disposed to this idea than its predecessor, as well as slightly more independent of the Americans; also Kennedy was less likely than Eisenhower and Dulles to oppose a new initiative towards Peking. The delegation of Japanese Dietmen which visited Peking from 14 to 19 September 1962 included a prominent member of the ruling Liberal Democratic Party (Matsumura) and also two members of

prime minister Ikeda's own faction. The evident success of their
discussions with Zhou Enlai and Liao Chengzhi led to more
detailed talks, towards the end of October; followed by the
signature of the Liao–Takasaki Memorandum – a five-year
'private' trade agreement – on 9 November 1962.[7]

II

By September 1962 the apparent Sino-Soviet *rapprochement* of the
preceding spring had begun to evaporate. One factor is believed to
have been China's sharp reaction to Soviet willingness–indicated
in a message to Peking on 25 August – to enter into arms control
talks with the West which might culminate in a nuclear non-
proliferation treaty.[8] Also relevant was a revival of Soviet interest
in improving relations with Yugoslavia. An important meeting of
the CPSU Presidium in Moscow on 20 September, at which Khrushchev demonstrated his authority by forcing through his own plans
for reforming the Party Committee system, was followed a few days
later by the arrival in Belgrade of L. I. Brezhnev (at that time
Soviet head of state). Since the Chinese had only recently resumed
their attacks on Tito – for example in *Renmin Ribao* on 17 and 18
September – it can be assumed that they disapproved strongly of
the visit. These developments coincided, moreover, with the
worsening of Sino-Indian relations and with China's decision to
improve its relations with Japan and with Indonesia. On 18
September, too, they announced that Peng Zhen would soon visit
North Vietnam: an event to which we must pay more attention in
due course.

   Another probable indication of Sino-Soviet tension at this time
was the political crisis which erupted in Mongolia in early
September. On 10 September 1962 it was reported that the leading
'nationalist' figure in the Mongolian Party leadership, Tumur
Ochir, had been purged – thus removing a potential challenge to
the pro-Soviet Tsedenbal.[9] Having been promoted to high
positions in the Mongolian Party the preceding January, Tumur
Ochir was now accused of 'arousing national passions' and of
trying to carry too far the campaign against the Mongolian
'Stalinist' Choibalsan. In all likelihood the 'coup' was a Soviet-
inspired move designed to forestall any Mongolian temptation to

adopt a neutral line between Moscow and Peking, or even to side openly with the Chinese.

With the benefit of hindsight – including the CCP's own reinterpretation of its history following the death of Mao Zedong – this period can now be recognised as the start of a new phase in Chinese revolutionary strategy: a phase which would culminate in the emergence of 'Maoism' as a distinct political ideology. A series of high-level meetings during August and September ended with the 10th Plenum of the CCP Central Committee (24–27 September), which reaffirmed Mao's theories of class struggle and of the unchanging nature of imperialism. Having recovered the initiative Mao was strong enough to exclude from the plenum the 'rightist' supporters of Peng Dehuai, who had fallen from grace in August 1959 but who may have had hopes of rehabilitation following the partial *rapprochement* with Moscow the previous spring. Chen Yun too, whose financial expertise and 'pro-Soviet' ideas had been allowed to shape Chinese economic policy in April 1962, again lost much of his influence without actually being purged. On the other hand, Liu Shaoqi's continuing importance seemed to be indicated by the republication of his famous essay of 1939 on 'how to be a good Communist'. The new balance of forces within the Party was reflected in the promotion of three new people to the CCP Secretariat: Lu Dingyi, later identified as a protégé of Peng Zhen, the Party boss in Peking; Luo Ruiqing, PLA chief-of-staff since 1959; and Kang Sheng, who would emerge as a key 'Maoist' leader in the cultural revolution. Mao himself, although still dependent on a broad consensus of support for his new line, was already embarking on the course which would eventually bring him into collision with 'revisionism' both in Moscow and inside the Chinese Party.[10]

Mao's perception of the world revolution was completely different from that currently prevailing in the Soviet Union. To describe him as 'nationalist', however, would be to misunderstand what in Marxist–Leninist terms was a highly subtle approach to the pattern of global conflict. For the Russians the all-embracing 'contradiction' in world society was that between socialism and capitalism as global systems, with the 'world socialist system' steadily gaining in strength and coherence under Soviet leadership. Whilst Mao did not deny the importance of that perspective, he insisted on giving at least equal weight to the 'contradiction' between imperialism and the oppressed peoples of the world,

TABLE 5.1 *China and the rest of Asia, September 1962*

China and USSR	Relations with India	Relations with Japan, USA	South-East Asia
3 Sept.: China, replying to Soviet message of 25 August, rejected any agreement on non-proliferation of nuclear weapons.			
		4–20 Sept.: General M. Taylor went on tour of US allies in East and South-East Asia: China strongly critical.	
	5 Sept.: Nehru rejected idea of visiting Peking for talks on the Sino-Indian border dispute.		
			7 Sept.: Peking established relations with Laos; Vientiane broke off relations with Taiwan.
	8 Sept.: Nehru left for London; in his absence:	8 Sept.: Taylor arrived in Taiwan.	

9 Sept.: Indian government decided to 'evict' Chinese troops from border area, treating Thagla Ridge as the boundary.

9 Sept.: Nationalist U-2 plane was shot down over East China by PLA air force.

(10 Sept.: Thai foreign minister criticised US plan to supply T-28 planes to Cambodia.)

10 Sept.: Peking: republication of Liu Shaoqi's essay on how to be a good Communist, written in 1939.

10 Sept.: Mongolia: Purge of the 'nationalist' figure Tumur Ochir.

13 Sept.: Chinese proposal that border talks should begin on 15 October, without preconditions.

14–19 Sept.: Visit to Peking of Japanese LDP delegation, led by Matsumura, to discuss trade.

15–22 Sept.: Build-up of forces on both sides of 'Dhola Post', in N.E. sector of frontier.

17–18 Sept.: *Renmin Ribao* had sharp attacks on Tito.

18 Sept.: Announcement that Peng Zhen will visit Hanoi later in month (He arrived in Hanoi on 30 Sept.)

19 Sept.: India agreed to begin talks on 15 October.

TABLE 5.1 *China and the rest of Asia, September 1962*

China and USSR	Relations with India	Relations with Japan, USA	South-East Asia
20 Sept.: Moscow: CPSU Presidium approved Khrushchev's plans for reform of Party Committees.	20 Sept.: First actual clash between Chinese and Indian forces on Thagla Ridge.	20 Sept.: 114th Meeting of US and Chinese ambassadors, Warsaw; reference to 9 Sept. U-2 incident.	21 Sept.: Nguyen Duy Trinh arrived in Peking, 23 Sept.: NLFSVN delegation in Peking (for national day). 23 Sept.: Madam Hartini Sukarno arrived in China: given place of honour on national day (1 Oct.).
24 Sept.: L. I. Brezhnev began visit to Yugoslavia. 24–7 Sept.: Peking: CCP Central Committee 10th Plenum.			

SOURCES Monitored broadcasts; *Peking Review*; N. Maxwell, *India's China War* (Harmondsworth, Middx., 1972).

whose national liberation struggles would prove decisive in the current phase of world revolution.[11] The peculiarly Chinese version of an international united front which emerged from this argument allowed the Chinese to ally themselves with all political forces opposed to imperialism – whether 'socialist' or not – whilst rejecting any alliance with 'revisionists' like Tito and, by implication, even Khrushchev. The Chinese criterion for assessing any political movement was its behaviour towards the two global forces of 'imperialism' and 'anti-imperialism'. Thus 'revisionists' were condemned for being willing to compromise with American imperialism; but the Soviet Union as such was still seen as potentially anti-imperialist.

III

Peng Zhen's visit to Hanoi, which was announced on 18 September, took place between 30 September and 11 October 1962. In the interval, during the last ten days of September, the North Vietnamese planning chief Nguyen Duy Trinh went to China and was warmly received by Mao, Liu, Zhou and Deng.[12] More symbolic, but also significant, was the presence in Peking from 23 September until early October of a delegation representing the NLFSVN: one of several indications that the Chinese were much more ready than the Russians or East Europeans to recognise formally the independent identity of the southern movement.

A more practical aspect of Sino-Vietnamese relations at this period was not revealed until many years later. Only in 1979 did the Chinese, in an effort to refute Hanoi's complaints that Vietnam had received too little help from China during the anti-American war, admit that they had responded favourably to a request for arms as early as mid-1962. In summer of that year, they insisted: 'President Ho Chi Minh and Nguyen Chi Thanh came to China and requested military assistance for the people of South Vietnam. The Chinese government immediately provided 90,000 weapons for the people of South Vietnam.'[13] It may have been these Chinese weapons that were being secretly shipped southwards by North Vietnamese vessels a few months later. We know from a Hanoi source that 'Group 759' was responsible for transporting weapons, ammunition and equipment to the South by sea during

1961–2, and that their first successful run to Ca-Mau – a Communist base near the southern-most tip of Vietnam – began on 14 September 1962.[14] The fact that the Chinese referred in this context to the *South* Vietnamese people fits in with a growing impression that Peking sought to foster the idea of a separate struggle in the South: one which was both independent of the North – apart from a few arms shipments – and capable of developing its own military–political strategy without any large-scale intervention by the PAVN.

Coinciding as it did with a new phase of Sino-Soviet rivalry in Asia, Peng Zhen's visit probably had a dual purpose: to encourage the North Vietnamese to persist in their anti-American struggle, and to dissuade them from any temptation to condemn the new Chinese line established at the 10th Plenum.[15] Peng Zhen's own political background was very different from that of Ye Jianying and the other veterans of the Long March who had visited Hanoi in December 1961. He had first emerged as a Communist labour leader in North China in the 1920s. During the resistance war against the Japanese, and then the civil war, he had spent much of his time in the 'white' areas behind enemy lines as a specialist in united front work. In 1951, during the Korean War, he had been given charge of the campaign to mobilise the masses against American imperialism. His past experience and present ideas were both in tune with the new Party line approved at the CCP 10th Plenum. In South-East Asia his main concern was with promoting anti-imperialism through political mobilisation of the masses, in the cities as well as in rural areas, rather than with the intensification of armed struggles involving substantial Chinese military assistance.

Although he was an important Party figure in China, on this occasion Peng Zhen visited Hanoi as leader of a delegation from the National People's Congress – which meant that the Vietnamese leader assigned to act as his principal host, in his capacity as chairman of the DRVN National Assembly, was Truong Chinh. That was not entirely inappropriate. Although we have no firm evidence of any personal association between them, the respective roles of the two men in China and Vietnam in the early 1950s were so similar as to suggest that they at least had certain ideas in common. Truong Chinh's re-emergence to prominence early in 1951 had coincided with that of Peng Zhen; and his emphasis on mobilising the masses to conduct campaigns for rent reduction and land reform may well have owed something to China's example during the Korean War anti-American drive. It is possible too that, in the circumstances of 1962, Truong Chinh shared the Chinese belief that the struggle in South Vietnam should be based on a better combination of political mobilisation and guerrilla struggle, not transformed into a larger military conflict. These similarities may have contributed to the Western impression of Truong Chinh as leader of a 'pro-Chinese' or 'Maoist' faction in the VNWP leadership: it may have had some validity in this context but he cannot be regarded as supporting everything Chinese for its own sake.

To judge from the coverage given to Peng Zhen's visit by the *Peking Review*, it was more successful from the Chinese point of view than that of Ye Jianying and the generals. We know nothing, of course, about the actual content of his talks with Vietnamese leaders; nor about Vietnamese reactions to the Chinese 10th Plenum. But whatever Peng Zhen had to say in Hanoi, it does not appear that his advice was immediately rebuffed. The Vietnamese probably received sufficient encouragement from the Chinese to allow them to continue the southern struggle, despite the increasingly successful counterinsurgency campaign. Provided they could maintain a sufficient threat to Diem's control over the countryside, they might in due course be able to mount a political challenge within the cities, and so destabilise the 'rear area' on which the Kennedy strategy depended.

An equally important consequence of the new phase of Sino-Vietnamese relations was that it might eventually oblige Moscow to reaffirm its own support – and increase its material aid – for North Vietnam. By the end of the year that was how things would turn out; but for the moment the Russians were preoccupied with the new strategy they were pursuing in Cuba.

Part II
1962–3

6 The Missiles Crisis and its Aftermath

The United States government accuses Cuba of creating a threat to the security of the United States. But who is going to believe that Cuba can be a threat to the United States? If we think of the respective size and resources of the two countries, of their armaments, no statesman in his right mind can imagine for one moment that Cuba can be a threat to the USA or any other country.... With regard to the Soviet Union's assistance to Cuba, this assistance is exclusively designed to improve Cuba's defensive capacity.

Soviet Statement on Cuba, at United Nations, 23 October 1962

Let me make it absolutely clear what the issue of Cuba is. It is not an issue of revolution. This hemisphere has seen many revolutions, including the one which gave my own nation its independence.... The foremost objection of the states of the Americas to the Castro regime is not because it is revolutionary, not because it is socialistic, not because it is dictatorial.... It is because he has aided and abetted an invasion of this hemisphere – and an invasion at just the time when the hemisphere is making a new and unprecedented effort for economic progress and social reform. The crucial fact is that Cuba has given the Soviet Union a bridgehead and staging area in this hemisphere ... that it has made itself an accomplice in the Communist enterprise of world dominion.

Ambassador Adlai Stevenson, addressing the UN Security Council, 23 October 1962

On more than one occasion we have made it clear that we neither called for the establishment of missile bases in Cuba nor obstructed the withdrawal of the so-called 'offensive weapons' from Cuba.... What we did strongly oppose, still strongly oppose, and will strongly oppose in the future, is the sacrifice of another country's sovereignty as a means of reaching a compromise with imperialism.

Renmin Ribao editorial, 31 December 1962

I

Vietnam did not figure prominently in relations between the United States and the major Communist powers during the latter part of 1962. Nevertheless we must pay some attention to the broader pattern of international conflict during that period, in view of its consequences for East–West relations in general. The eventual escalation of the Vietnam War came about in a world whose assumptions had been significantly transformed by the Cuba missiles crisis and its aftermath.

The starting-point of that crisis was a decision by the Soviet Politburo to deploy medium and intermediate range ballistic missiles at sites in Cuba, well within reach of the principal cities of the Eastern seaboard of the United States.[1] It is impossible for us to know whether the decision was taken at one sitting in April or May, leaving only details to be worked out later, or took shape gradually during the summer and early autumn. But by mid-September the first medium-range missiles had begun to arrive in Cuba and sites for the IRBMs were under construction. The question at that stage was whether the Americans, whose U-2 'spy-planes' made regular flights over certain parts of the island, would discover the presence of the sites and the missiles before they became operational. Precisely how the Americans first began to suspect the true nature of Soviet intentions has never been revealed. We know only that in early October the Director of Central Intelligence, John McCone, was urging more careful reconnaissance by U-2 flights over an area of Cuba protected by anti-aircraft rockets; and that on the 10th Senator Keating claimed publicly to have intelligence that nuclear missiles were being installed there. Only on 15 October was it finally confirmed by a U-2 flight over the western part of the island that sites were indeed being prepared for intermediate range missiles; at which point the top leadership in Washington embarked on a highly secret, week-long debate about how to deal with what might shortly become a serious threat to the security of the American mainland.

A good deal has been written about the sequence of American decision-making which followed, both before and after the speech of 22 October in which Kennedy demanded a halt to the deployment of Soviet missiles and indicated a 'quarantine' on further shipments of military and strategic materials to Cuba by sea. Since the outcome of the crisis was seen as a 'victory' for the United States, the people most directly involved in those decisions have been relatively forthcoming in providing personal accounts of what actually happened.[2] (However, actual documentation on the crisis is still remarkably thin by comparison with the type and quantity of material available concerning decision-making on Vietnam, through the *Pentagon Papers* and the subsequent declassification of secret records.) For the Soviet side, of course, we have neither personal recollections nor access to internal documentation, and efforts by Western observers to analyse the Kremlin's reponse to Kennedy's actions have not always been entirely satisfactory.[3] However, it lies beyond our present task to attempt a detailed new assessment of events either before or during the missiles crisis. Our concern must be limited to its broader significance for understanding the general character of American and Soviet perceptions of the world at the time.

The deployment of offensive missiles to Cuba was undoubtedly a Soviet initiative, but its purpose and objectives are still to some extent a matter for speculation. Two quite different interpretations are possible: on one level the Russians may have been concerned with defending the revolution in Cuba itself; on another level their action, had it been successful, would have gone a long way towards changing the strategic balance of power between the Soviet Union and the United States. Both interpretations must be taken into account.

The fear that at some stage the Americans might make a new – this time more successful – bid to overthrow the Castro regime by force was probably genuine; especially following *Pravda*'s recognition the previous April that Comrade Castro was now engaged in 'building socialism'. Nor could it be denied that Kennedy was under continual pressure from right-wing opinion to remove Castro. We now know that in August the NSC had authorised the stepping up of 'Operation Mongoose': a covert action designed to undermine Castro's position. There were also plans for a military exercise elsewhere in the Caribbean that autumn in which 7500 US Marines and four aircraft carriers would 'liberate' a small island by force. In these circumstances it was logical for the Soviet Union to undertake a further programme of military assistance to Cuba, and that was the acknowledged purpose of Guevara's visit to Moscow at the beginning of September. Moreover the weapons actually installed in Cuba before the 'quarantine' were not all offensive in character. They included surface-to-air missiles (notably the SA-2 which brought down a U-2 plane on 27 October), coastal missile sites, guided missile patrol boats, and Mig-21 aircraft: all weapons whose purpose was defensive, although by that time their main task was to defend the Soviet missile sites, not just Castro's government.[4] The possibility cannot be ruled out that the Russians, afraid that even this array of weaponry would form an inadequate deterrent if Kennedy ever decided on a full-scale invasion, had reached the conclusion that the only effective long-term protection for Cuba lay in a formal American commitment to refrain from any military action against Cuba; and that the best way to achieve such a guarantee was to engineer a full-scale crisis which would end in some kind of compromise. Certainly if that *was* Khrushchev's principal objective, the whole operation can be said to have achieved its end; and there is plenty of evidence for that idea in Soviet public statements of the time.

Even so, it is impossible to ignore the strategic significance of the missiles themselves: that is, of sites which (when completed) would have allowed the deployment of 48 MRBMs and 24 IRBMs – of which 42 of the former actually reached Cuban soil; as well as 42 Ilyushin-28 bombers whose parts were being rapidly assembled, and 22,000 Soviet military personnel stationed in Cuba (by mid-October) to service both defensive and offensive missiles. Had the Americans failed to discover their true character before they became operational (from about mid-December), the presence of the missile sites in Cuba would have substantially changed the strategic balance of power in the world. That in turn would have placed Kennedy at a serious disadvantage when it came to the next round of discussions on such issues as Berlin or arms control. And already on 18 October, unaware that the American discovery had already taken place, Gromyko had indicated in a conversation at the White House that after the forthcoming Congressional elections the Soviet Union would renew its demand for a German peace treaty.[5] The notion that the Russians seriously intended such a transformation of the global balance of forces seems to be substantiated by remarks said to have been made on the subject by Mikoyan, speaking to Communist diplomats when he visited New York on his way home from Cuba at the end of November. To the extent that it *was* a serious Soviet objective, the outcome of the crisis must be regarded as a defeat for Moscow. But it was a setback in the sense of failure to secure a hoped-for expansion of military power, rather than the loss of any actual power they had enjoyed before. It was a gamble which had not paid off, but no premium had been paid; and the Americans were not even allowed to inspect the Soviet weapons that had to be withdrawn from Cuba. In that regard, the extent of Khrushchev's personal defeat ought not to be exaggerated.

In Kennedy's actual handling of the crisis, what mattered most was the skill with which he and his advisers combined diplomacy with the threat and use of force. It is important to recognise how little the outcome depended on the superiority of the American nuclear arsenal – except that it deterred even the hardest of Soviet 'hardliners' from seeking to transform the conflict into a nuclear war. What counted in practice was the American ability to deploy superior conventional forces in an actual theatre of operations: the western Atlantic.[6] Even on that level Kennedy and his civilian advisers were anxious to use only the minimum force required to make the Russians change their minds. The conflict between 'hawks' and 'doves' in the week of 16–21 October centred on the issue of precisely how much force was necessary – not how to conduct an actual war, which everyone hoped to avoid. Kennedy's problem was to find a course of action sufficiently firm to force his opponents to take account of their *knowledge* of United States military might, but sufficiently restrained to allow him to pull back from the brink as soon as it became clear that he had won.

Restraint was in evidence on the Soviet side too, although there were several anxious days before that became apparent in Washington. In the end, both sides agreed to accept the *status quo ante* mid-1962: Soviet missiles were to be withdrawn in return for an American promise not to take any future military action against Castro; and Khrushchev – in public at least – took the line that that had been his primary objective from the start. (Any tacit understanding there may have been that the removal of Jupiter missiles from Turkey was also part of the 'deal' did not emerge in public; there is evidence that those missiles were due to be removed in any case.) The complicated diplomacy required to persuade Castro to surrender the Ilyushin-28 bombers, which he claimed had been a gift to his own armed forces, went on until 20 November – and the 'quarantine' was not finally called off until then. In the end Castro was allowed to keep the defensive missiles supplied by the Soviet Union that summer; but his only effective guarantee against overt American attack was in the form of a promise by one superpower to another.

One aspect of the missiles crisis has special relevance for

Vietnam. In his televised broadcast of 22 October, challenging the
Russians to abandon the deployment of missiles, President Kennedy was careful to disclaim any intention of harming the Cuban
people. His argument was that the Castro regime was allowing

TABLE 6.1   *Two crises: the Cuba missiles crisis and the Sino-Indian war,*
September – November 1962

4 Sept.: Kennedy issued warning to Soviet Union not to place offensive missiles in Cuba.	
5 Sept.: U-2 photographs revealed Mig-21 planes in Cuba.	
7 Sept.: Kennedy obtained Congressional authority to call up 150,000 reserves.	
8 Sept.: First Soviet MRBMs arrived in Cuba; more arrived a week later.	9 Sept.: Indian decision to 'evict' Chinese forces from areas claimed by India in Thagla Ridge sector.
11 Sept.: TASS published Soviet denial of any intention to deploy Soviet missiles in another country such as Cuba.	15–22 Sept.: Build up of forces on both sides of disputed frontier in North-East.
	20 Sept.: First actual clash occurred.
25 Sept.: Castro announced plan for new Soviet port in Cuba, to explain construction work now going on.	
early Oct.: McCone urged U-2 reconnaissance of Western area of Cuba; not agreed until 9th.	3–6 Oct.: Further exchange of Notes failed to establish a basis for negotiations between China and India.
10 Oct.: Senator Keating claimed to have evidence of installation of Soviet offensive missiles in Cuba.	10 Oct.: Indian forces embarked on 'Operation Leghorn' to drive Chinese out of disputed area; stiff Chinese resistance.
	14 Oct.: *Renmin Ribao* urged Nehru to 'pull back from the brink'.
15 Oct.: U-2 photographs revealed, or confirmed, evidence of construction of sites in Cuba for MRBMs and IRBMs.	
16–21 Oct.: Secret meetings of NSC ExComm group in Washington to decide on US response.	17 Oct.: Chinese began preparations for major offensive along whole border.
	17–20 Oct.: Romanian delegation in New Delhi.

TABLE 6.1 *Two crises: the Cuba missiles crisis and the Sino-Indian war,*
September – November 1962

18 Oct.: Kennedy received Gromyko at White House; accepted continued Soviet assurances without revealing his knowledge of missiles.

18 Oct.: Ambassador Galbraith flew to Washington after meeting with Nehru.

20–3 Oct.: First major Indian offensive on both sectors of border; Indians forced to retreat, and to abandon Tawang on 23rd.

21 Oct.: Kennedy decided on his strategy to deal with the situation, and ordered necessary military preparations.

22 Oct.: Kennedy's televised speech on the discovery of the missiles, imposition of naval 'quarantine', etc.

24 Oct.: Naval blockade of Cuba began, to prevent arrival of Soviet ships already at sea.

24 Oct.: Chinese government statement, urging mutual withdrawal of forces, to allow peaceful settlement of dispute.

25 Oct.: *Pravda* too 'hard' line on Cuba, and supported Chinese position on border issue; Khrushchev out of sight.

26 Oct.: *Pravda* editorial, 'Reason must prevail'; Khrushchev reappeared that evening. Construction of missile sites continued, but a KGB man had informal conversations in Washington. Khrushchev sent private letter to Kennedy, offering a compromise and the withdrawal of the missiles.

27 Oct.: Soviet SA-2 missile brought down a U-2 plane over Cuba; in Moscow, *Krasnaya Zvezda* raised issue of US missiles based in Turkey and elsewhere around USSR. Khrushchev sent public letter to Kennedy proposing a tougher compromise than on 26th, to include the missiles in Turkey.

27 Oct.: *Renmin Ribao* reiterated Chinese proposals of 24th. Nehru sent letter to Zhou Enlai, proposing a return to the situation of 8 September 1962. China rejected that idea.

27–8 Oct.: Kennedy decided against retaliation for U-2 attack; and to answer Khrushchev's private letter of 26th, whilst ignoring that of 27th.

28 Oct.: Khrushchev broadcast a letter to Kennedy: virtual capitulation on missiles, in return for American promise not to attack Cuba. Castro broadcast 'five demands' as his own

TABLE 6.1   *Two crises: the Cuba missiles crisis and the Sino-Indian war,*
September – November 1962

basis for an agreement; unacceptable to Washington.

30 Oct.: NSC cancelled all American covert operations against Cuba, including 'Operation Mongoose'. U Thant flew to Havana, but Castro refused to allow any UN inspection.

1 Nov.: Castro refused to surrender the Ilyushin-28 bombers which he claimed were his own, as a result of Soviet aid.

2 Nov.: Soviet deputy premier Mikoyan began a visit to Cuba (till 25 November).

3 Nov.: *Pravda* published remarks by Voroshilov, praising Khrushchev for avoiding a World War.

5 Nov.: *Renmin Ribao* praised Castro's stand against UN inspection in Cuba; on 7th, Aidit and Pham Van Dong also praised Castro.

12 Nov.: *Renmin Ribao* denounced Tito's attitude to the missiles crisis.

15 Nov.: Castro complained to United Nations about continuing American U-2 flights over Cuba.

20 Nov.: Khrushchev informed Kennedy that the Ilyushin-28s were to be withdrawn. Kennedy called off the naval blockade.

29 Oct.: United States offer to supply military equipment to India, which was agreed.

31 Oct.: Nehru took over defence ministry from Khrishna Menon.

3 Nov.: American military supplies began arriving in India.

4 Nov.: Zhou Enlai's letter to Nehru, insisting on withdrawal to positions of 7 November 1959, as 'line of actual control'.

5 Nov.: *Pravda* called on both sides to bring about a ceasefire and settlement; but Peking saw this as taking Indian side.

11 Nov.: *Renmin Ribao* denounced Nehru for accepting Western military assistance.

14–15 Nov.: Further fighting on both sectors of border; Indians again retreated.

15 Nov.: Zhou Enlai's letter to Afro-Asian leaders, justifying the Chinese case against India.

18–19 Nov.: Final offensive by Chinese forces led to total collapse of Indian morale. Nehru made urgent request for aid to US and UK.

20 Nov.: Chinese forces proclaimed a unilateral ceasefire; began withdrawal by end of month.

SOURCES   E. Abel, *The Missiles of October: Twelve Days to World War III* (London, 1969); M. Tatu, *Power in the Kremlin: from Khrushchev's Decline to Collective Leadership* (London, 1969); N. Maxwell, *India's China War* (Harmondsworth, Middx., 1972); *Peking Review*.

Cuban soil to be used for military preparations whose real purpose had little or nothing to do with Cuba's own real interests. The same theme was taken up by Ambassador Stevenson in his speech to the UN Security Council the following day. But Communist statements, whether by Soviet spokesmen or by the Cuban President Dorticos, took precisely the opposite stand – insisting that the sole purpose of Soviet military aid to Cuba was to enable it to defend its territory against the American 'threat' to the Cuban Revolution. What danger, they asked, could a small country like Cuba present to the armed might of the United States? Whereas Kennedy was concerned about the consequences for the global balance of power of Cuba's alliance with Moscow, the Communists sought to limit the debate to the rights of a small country to pursue its own revolutionary path and to make whatever alliances it chose in order to defend its revolution.[7]

In South Vietnam, too, American policy was directed towards countering the global strategic consequences of a 'revolution' whose real inspiration came from outside South Vietnam; whereas the Soviet position was that only the South Vietnamese people (and their 'liberation front') were legitimately involved in the revolution against Ngo Dinh Diem, and that it was the Americans who, by seeking to oppose that revolution, were guilty of 'aggression' and of posing a 'threat' to Hanoi. But in the case of the Cuba missiles, Kennedy was able to prove his point beyond any doubt: the photographs presented by Stevenson to the Security Council showed that the USSR *was* using its alliance with Cuba to bring about a transformation of the global balance of power. In Vietnam it would be much less easy for the Americans to translate ultimate strategic anxieties into a precise justification for the actual policy being pursued, against a 'national liberation revolution' still in progress.

The possibility of a direct analogy between the missiles crisis and the situation in Indochina was in fact already present in some American minds towards the end of 1962. In a State Department memorandum of 28 November, which eventually reached the President, Walt Rostow drew attention to the continuing infiltration of military supplies and personnel from North to South Vietnam along the Ho Chi Minh trail through Laos. This, he insisted, was in violation of a clear Soviet undertaking given to Averell Harriman at Geneva that the Russians would make themselves responsible for bringing such infiltration to an end. The signed documents, of course, included no such formal undertaking;

but they did formally preclude the use of Laotian territory for
military purposes by any foreign country – including North
Vietnam. In view of the strain that continued infiltration would
place upon South Vietnam (and upon American counterinsurgency programmes), Rostow urged his superiors to take immediate
action – and if necessary, significant risks – to force the North
Vietnamese to respect the Geneva Declaration on Laos. If
Kennedy failed to act, he would be 'continuing to accept, on our
side of the truce lines of the Cold War, a serious illegal act at a place
where US prestige and interests are heavily committed'.[8]

In effect, Rostow was recommending the same degree of
determination in Indochina as Kennedy had demonstrated during
the missiles crisis. In practice the risk of an actual war in Laos was
too great for Kennedy to take, and in the immediate aftermath of
the missiles crisis the American public would have found it difficult
to bear yet another round of extreme international tension for the
sake of an area of the world which did not appear to have the same
importance as Berlin or Cuba. Rostow recognised the President's
good reasons for refusing to accept his advice. Nevertheless, writing
ten years later, he argued that the failure to act against the
infiltration routes in Laos at that point may have been the single
greatest mistake in United States foreign policy in the 1960s.

II

The impact of the missiles crisis in the Soviet Union – and in the
Communist world as a whole – is difficult to assess. Western
commentators who suggested that it led directly to a loss of
authority by Khrushchev himself – on the assumption that the
decision to deploy the missiles had been his and that the
monoeuvre had failed – were probably underestimating the
complexity of Soviet politics. In the end Khrushchev succeeded in
reasserting his influence, although probably on the basis of a
different balance of forces within the leadership from that existing
before the crisis began. For a short time in the middle of the crisis
(on 23, 24 and 25 October 1962) there may have been some doubt
whether Khrushchev would survive at all, or would be forced to
resign, as actually happened almost precisely two years later. He
was not referred to by name in the Soviet media on those three

days, and on the 25th there was a report that a town in the Ukraine would no longer bear his name. Another suggestion of imminent change in the Soviet line was the publication on 23 October of a new *History of the CPSU* compiled by a team under B. N. Ponomarev, which was strongly critical of Tito, and whose publication had been held up for some time.[9] Moreover, on 25 October *Pravda* not only took an uncompromising stand on the Cuba missiles but also supported the Chinese position on the Sino-Indian border issue. It is not inconceivable that if Khrushchev had been politically eliminated at that point some kind of Sino-Soviet *rapprochement* would have followed.

However, by the afternoon of 26 October it would appear that Khrushchev had survived the immediate threat to his leadership. That day's *Pravda* urged that 'Reason must prevail!'; and in the evening the First Secretary reappeared at a concert in the company of Kozlov and Brezhnev. Also that day – but some hours later, allowing for the time difference – a secret meeting between the American John Scali and the KGB resident in Washington (A. Fomin) opened up the possibility of a compromise along the lines actually agreed in the end. That move allowed Kennedy to reply along the same lines to a private letter from Khrushchev, also dated 26 October and to ignore indications on the 27th that Moscow was about to return to a 'hard' line. The result was that on the 28th the Soviet leader felt strong enough to take responsibility for a virtual capitulation on the question of the missiles; and a few days later to send Mikoyan to Havana to force Castro into line. These were not the actions of a man who had lost authority. Perhaps there is some justification for supposing that Khrushchev owed his own survival to Kennedy's relative restraint, first in not bombing Cuba immediately, and then in not escalating the conflict on 27 October.

For their part, the Chinese were by this time wholly absorbed in their war with India, where they had launched a full-scale offensive on 20 October. The initial phase of the fighting proved disastrous for the Indian forces, which had to abandon the important town of Tawang (in the north-eastern sector) on 23 October. The following day a Chinese statement called for a settlement of the conflict – on Chinese terms. But by then the

Chinese leaders must have been following the missiles crisis closely, and watching to see what would happen in Moscow. It is impossible to know what effect Khrushchev's re-emergence, and his subsequent communications with Kennedy, had on Chinese calculations. They appear to have left the next move to New Delhi.

The possibility of an Indian request for United States military assistance had probably already been raised by Nehru on 18 October, when Ambassador Galbraith suddenly left for Washington for consultations. If nothing more, the Indian government would have to consider the financial implications of an actual war if it became necessary to purchase new supplies of weapons and ammunition. The Americans, although preoccupied with Cuba for the next ten days, made an offer to supply equipment to India on 29 October; and by 3 November the first deliveries arrived. By then Khrushchev's survival meant that Nehru could still rely on a measure of Soviet sympathy. An article in *Pravda* on 5 November, appealing to both sides to agree to a ceasefire and a negotiated solution, was seen in Peking as a 'pro-Indian' move – which suggests that whatever new balance of forces may have emerged in Moscow was unlikely to produce a Sino-Soviet *rapprochement*.

China, after denouncing Nehru's willingness to seek Western military aid, began a new offensive on 14–15 November – leading to a complete collapse of the Indian army in the north-eastern sector by the 19th. In face of this renewed onslaught Nehru sent urgent appeals to both London and Washington for much more substantial military support. The Chinese, aware that they could not sustain the military campaign once India began to receive American and British assistance, called a unilateral ceasefire on 20 November.

As far as the South Asian subcontinent was concerned, the immediate crisis was over. China had scored a major success, the Soviet Union had suffered a setback, and the United States had gained some ground. China's principal aim in this later phase of the war seems to have been to cause Nehru to lose face throughout the Third World. On 15 November, at the start of the second Chinese offensive, Zhou Enlai circulated an open letter to other leaders in Asia and Africa justifying China's territorial claims and blaming India for the outbreak of hostilities.[10] In this context the Sino-Indian war appears as another important move in China's own bid to lead the Third World in the direction of anti-imperialism. In challenging Tito's attitude towards American imperialism, and in exposing India's claims to be truly non-aligned, the Chinese were trying to demonstrate that no 'middle path' was possible: that the only correct policy for all Asian and African peoples and governments was to take a stand against imperialism.

The Americans welcomed the possibility of a closer relationship with India – and perhaps an opportunity for new diplomatic efforts to heal the breach between India and Pakistan. Without some measure of agreement in that area, there was a danger that an expansion of Western military aid to the two countries would merely increase the danger of war between them rather than their ability to resist other enemies. On 21 November Averell Harriman left Washington for New Delhi accompanied by a team including Roger Hilsman and Paul Nitze (Assistant Secretary of Defense).[11] Other talks were going on at the same time with a British team which had flown in from London. Towards the end of the month, Harriman and the British defence minister Sandys went on to Karachi; and on 30 November the prime ministers of India and Pakistan issued a joint communiqué agreeing to new efforts to resolve their differences over Kashmir. But during December, despite the communiqué, it proved difficult to make further progress on this diplomatic front – especially since the Chinese were now withdrawing from their advance positions along the border and the threat to India was thus greatly reduced.

III

The plenum of the CPSU Central Committee which met in Moscow from 19 to 23 November 1962, coinciding both with Castro's decision to surrender the Ilyushin bombers and with China's announcement of a unilateral ceasefire in the Sino-Indian war, marked the end of the Soviet leadership crisis for the time being. The fact that the plenum approved Khrushchev's proposals for restructuring the Party committee system, which had been taking shape since August, indicates that the First Secretary himself was no longer under threat. The plenum also made three promotions to the CPSU Secretariat: Y. V. Andropov, V. N. Titov and L. F. Ilyichev, none of whom would appear to have been close to Khrushchev's principal antagonist M. A. Suslov. In addition the former KGB chief A. N. Shelepin was made head of a new

Party – State Control Commission.[12] If further evidence were required that Khrushchev's line was still being followed, it came early in December when Tito visited Moscow to carry the Soviet–Yugoslav *rapprochement* a stage further.

Another indication of the return to stability was the holding of several Party Congresses in Eastern Europe. From 5 to 14 November, Suslov visited Bulgaria to supervise a Congress which confirmed the 'pro-Soviet' Zhivkov in office whilst purging the 'pro-Chinese' prime minister Anton Yugov. Later the same month, Otto Kuusinen attended a Party Congress in Hungary; and in early December Brezhnev was present at that in Czechoslovakia. About the same time F. R. Kozlov went to Rome for the Italian Communist Party Congress.[13] The corresponding Congress in East Germany, held the following January, would be attended by Khrushchev in person.

By around 10–12 December, it would appear that a series of decisions had been taken in Moscow which together amounted to a coherent new global strategy. The *rapprochement* with Tito was by then all but complete; and on 10 December *Pravda* fired the opening shot in a new round of polemics with China by reprinting the 'anti-Chinese' speeches of Novotny and Togliatti at their respective Party Congresses. The Chinese reply came at the end of the month with a strong denunciation of Togliatti in *Renmin Ribao*. Meanwhile on 12 December Khrushchev's speech to the Supreme Soviet was remarkably conciliatory toward the West; he acknowledged that both sides had shown restraint during the missiles crisis, and expressed hopes for a further easing of East–West tension. He followed this up with a letter to Kennedy, which led by mid-January to serious talks on technical aspects of a tripartite test-ban treaty.

Thus far it is possible to see a logical relationship between the various strands of Khrushchev's strategy: restraint in Cuba and moves towards arms control fitted in well with a conciliatory line towards the 'revisionist' Tito, whilst the harsh Chinese reaction contributed further to the image of a 'moderate' Soviet leadership under attack from an 'extremist' revolutionary China. In South-East Asia, however, this simple picture begins to break down; there the issues at stake were not purely ideological but also strategic. Unless the Russians were willing to leave responsibility for the revolution in Asia solely in Chinese hands – which they were not – they needed to develop their own presence in the area and to treat the Chinese as rivals.

We have no means of studying the debate which must have been taking place within the Soviet leadership on the question of global strategy at this time. But such limited impressions as we have suggest a logical conflict between two schools of thought: one group preferred to concentrate solely on the defence of land frontiers and the continued build-up of conventional forces; the other believed that ultimately Soviet power would depend on a stronger capability for action across the globe – including a network of alliances and also a more powerful navy. This second school regarded the Cuban episode not as a reason for abandoning global ambitions but as a reason for acquiring greater strength. The advocates of the global strategy seem to have won during the power struggles of 1962–3.

Continuing interest in the global strategy was reflected in a Soviet announcement on 12 December 1962 that a military mission would shortly visit Hanoi. The visit took place shortly afterwards (15–29 December) and the delegation, led by the chief of staff of the Warsaw Pact forces General P. I. Batov, also included four army major-generals, an air force lieutenant-general and a naval captain: a group no less impressive than that which had accompanied Ye Jianying to Hanoi exactly a year before.[14] Coming so soon after the expansion of Soviet military aid to Cuba – much of which remained in place despite the withdrawal of the nuclear missiles and bombers – the mission seemed to imply a parallel willingness to help strengthen the defences of North Vietnam. It may have been intended specifically to counter Chinese insinuations that Moscow had been willing to 'sacrifice another country's sovereignty as a means of reaching a compromise with imperialism', and to reassure North Vietnam that Soviet aims in Cuba had been achieved.[15] There was no question of introducing sophisticated missiles, however, and certainly no question of employing nuclear weapons to resolve the issue of Vietnamese reunification. Ironically, although Ho Chi Minh (and perhaps some of his colleagues) commanded greater political respect than Castro as members of the international Communist movement, North Vietnam received far less military and economic aid than Cuba. Even so, the Batov mission represented a new level of Soviet commitment, which almost certainly strengthened ties between the PAVN and the Soviet armed forces.

Presumably it also amounted to at least tacit support of Hanoi's current line on the South. Shortly before Batov's arrival the VNWP Politburo had on 10 December reached a number of

TABLE 6.2 *Soviet relations with the West, China and Vietnam, December 1962 – January 1963*

East–West relations	Soviet Union, China	North Vietnam
1962		
2 Dec.: Mikoyan returned from visit to Cuba and United States.	3–18 Dec.: Tito's visit to Moscow.	
	2–8 Dec.: Italian CP Congress, attended by F. R. Kozlov.	
	4–8 Dec.: Czech Party Congress, attended by L. I. Brezhnev.	
	10 Dec.: *Pravda* reprinted anti-Chinese speeches of Togliatti and Novotny.	10 Dec.: VNWP Politburo Resolution on continuing the war in the South.
	11 Dec.: Tass reported arrest of Col. Penkovsky as a US spy; *Pravda* published a long article on this, 15 December.	
12 Dec.: Khrushchev speech to Supreme Soviet, reviewing the missiles crisis and proposing further reduction of tension; also included further attack on Albania.		12 Dec.: Announcement of Gen. Batov's forthcoming visit.
13 Dec.: Sino-American ambassadorial meeting in Warsaw; no details known.		
	15 Dec.: *Renmin Ribao* responded to Khrushchev's Supreme Soviet speech.	15–29 Dec.: Soviet military delegation led by Gen. P. I. Batov visited North Vietnam.
		17 Dec.: USSR handed over control of aircraft to Laotian government.
18 Dec.: Kennedy–Macmillan meeting in the Bahamas.		
19 Dec.: Khrushchev letter proposing negotiations to end nuclear tests.		
29 Dec.: Kennedy replied positively to Khrushchev's letter of 19th.		29 Dec.: End of Batov visit.
	31 Dec.: *Renmin Ribao* on 'The differences between Togliatti and ourselves'.	

1963

7 Jan.: Khrushchev agreed to preliminary talks, at expert level, on a test-ban.	7 Jan.: *Pravda* again attacked Albanians 'and those who support them'.	2–3 Jan.: Battles at Ap-Bac, Plei-Mrong.
14 Jan.: Test-ban talks opened, Geneva.		7 Jan.: DRVN government changes.
	15–21 Jan.: East German Party Congress, attended by Khrushchev; further Sino-Soviet polemics.	12–20 Jan.: Andropov's visit to Hanoi.
23–4 Jan.: *Pravda* criticised Franco-German Cooperation Treaty (signed on 22nd); formal protest made on 5 February.		22–6 Jan.: Novotny visited Hanoi.
	27 Jan.: *Renmin Ribao* denounced 'reversal of verdict' on Tito; urged Communist unity on basis of Moscow documents of 1957, 1960.	
31 Jan.: Soviet side broke off test-ban talks, as a separate exercise. Renewed emphasis on UN disarmament talks, due to resume on 12 February.		2 Feb.: *Nhan-Dan* had strong praise for Soviet victory at Stalingrad (1943).
8 Feb.: United States resumed underground nuclear tests.	10 Feb.: *Pravda* article urging Marxist-Leninist unity; still critical of Albania.	10 Feb.: VNWP Politburo statement, praising both CPSU and CCP and urging unity on basis of Moscow documents of 1957, 1960.

SOURCES   D. C. Watt, *Survey of International Affairs 1963* (London, 1977); M. Tatu, *Power in the Kremlin: from Khrushchev's Decline to Collective Leadership* (London, 1969); *Peking Review*; monitored broadcasts.

decisions about the next stage of the war. By this time there were over 10,000 American military personnel in South Vietnam and the Kennedy strategy of counterinsurgency was beginning to take effect. A classified State Department assessment of 3 December observed that 'the Viet Cong has had to modify its tactics and perhaps set back its timetable', but that it had not yet been fundamentally weakened and was unlikely to abandon the struggle.[16] The same report expressed some optimism about the progress of the strategic hamlet programme and concluded that a Communist victory in the next year or so was unlikely: in itself, a substantial change from the situation prevailing a year before. Nevertheless the Communist side reacted in precisely the way the American analysts expected: the effect of counterinsurgency was to force them to adopt a longer-term strategy, not to abandon the war altogether. The Politburo meeting of 10 December decided that the struggle in the South now amounted to an 'anti-aggression war', which must continue until it became possible to force the Americans and Diem into a more passive state. Militarily the emphasis would still be on guerrilla warfare and on greater co-ordination of forces, in order to destroy the strategic hamlets 'bit by bit'. It was also necessary to step up the political struggle in order to mobilise the population and gradually to expand the people's armed forces.[17]

What the Communist forces in the South needed, even in the short term, was some kind of victory on the battlefield which would be sufficiently spectacular to rally the faint-hearted both in Hanoi and in the South: a symbolic demonstration that in spite of their advanced technology the Americans were not invincible. Therein lay the importance of the engagement which took place at Ap-Bac in the Mekong Delta at the beginning of January 1963, in which an ARVN operation to mop up a supposedly small but important 'Viet Cong' force ended in a pitched battle against a well-prepared Communist battalion. Several helicopters were destroyed and three American advisers, as well as 66 government troops, were killed in action. Statistically it was not a major defeat for the government side; psychologically it was far more important. It was a battle which the PLAFSVN had carefully prepared and had wanted to fight, but which ARVN and its advisers had badly misjudged – perhaps mainly through faulty intelligence.

On the Communist side the victory was celebrated and publicised as proof that their forces could successfully counter

American helicopters. Later in the year the name 'Ap-Bac' was given to the first of a series of 'emulation drives' amongst recruits to the PLAFSVN. On the American side, despite the efforts of General Harkins to prevent it being reported in overdramatic terms, it became at one and the same time a symbol both of the uncanny ability of the 'Viet Cong' to outwit even the best American advisers, and of the tendency of MACV to try to hide that fact from the press.[18] At about the same time an almost equally important engagement took place in the Central Highlands, although it received less publicity at the time: a special forces camp at Plei Mrong (west of Pleiku) was over-run on 3 January 1963, demonstrating that another key element in counterinsurgency was not invulnerable.

We need not assume that these operations involved any element of Soviet direction. The most the Russians could hope to achieve by continuing to support Hanoi's struggle at this stage was an opportunity to influence its choice of strategy. Were Moscow to abandon its support for the revolution in Indochina the likeliest result would be to make North Vietnam and the Pathet Lao wholly dependent on China. In these circumstances the Vietnamese Communists had a good deal of freedom of action, and the Ap-Bac engagement proved that they could still keep the initiative.

IV

The international climate, as measured by East–West diplomacy, changed yet again towards the end of January 1963. The first effort to promote *détente* in the wake of the Missiles Crisis proved to be short-lived.

Following another Soviet letter to Kennedy on 7 January 1963, initial talks on a test-ban treaty opened a week later. Khrushchev still seemed to be in firm control at the time of the East Berlin Party Congress (15–21 January), which approved a series of reforms designed to make the German Democratic Republic a model of socialist industrialisation – with very little being said about a German peace treaty or the status of Berlin. (It was also an occasion for further polemical exchanges between Khrushchev and the leader of the Chinese delegation.) But then on 31 January the test-ban talks were suddenly broken off by the Soviet side. By

the time the larger Geneva conference on disarmament reconvened on 12 February it was evident that the atmosphere of
East–West relations had undergone yet another sudden change.

Two possible explanations – not necessarily incompatible – can
be offered for this change. One would concentrate on the impact of
the Franco-German Treaty of Co-operation, signed on 22 January
1963, which provided for regular meetings between their respective military leaders – and opened up the possibility that the two
countries together might develop an independent strategy which
could not easily be drawn into agreements worked out between
Moscow, Washington and London. Whether this represented a
serious danger or not is less important than the fact that
Khrushchev's opponents seem to have been able to use it as a basis
on which to resume their attack on his policies. *Pravda* carried
strong criticisms of the Franco-German treaty in the last week of
January.[19]

Alternatively it might be argued that at the end of January
Khrushchev was obliged to acknowledge the force of Chinese
criticism and to allow the consensus in the Soviet leadership to
move back towards the line of appearing to conciliate Peking. In
this context, Vietnam may once again have been an important
consideration. Even though real Sino-Soviet unity was no longer
possible, the one way to prevent China from gaining exclusive
leadership over other Asian Communist Parties – particularly the
Vietnamese and the Indonesian – was to make a token move
towards improving relations with Peking. In that way it might be
possible to head off China's proposal for a new international
meeting, and so ensure that it was not supported by other Asian
Parties.

Above all Moscow must prevent any ideological collaboration
between the Chinese and Vietnamese Parties against its own line;
which meant convincing Hanoi that the CPSU did not accord
higher priority to peaceful coexistence than to solidarity against
imperialism. This need to consolidate Party relations produced yet
another Soviet mission to Hanoi in January 1963, led by Y. V.
Andropov, now himself a member of the CPSU Secretariat. Like
Peng Zhen the preceding October, however, he went as head of a
Supreme Soviet delegation and was received principally by
Truong Chinh rather than by Le Duan.[20] Andropov was followed
by the Czech president Novotny, who arrived in Hanoi on 21
January after visits to Indonesia and Cambodia. The Novotny visit

provided the Vietnamese with an ideal opportunity to show that their primary concern was to unite the whole socialist camp behind their own struggle rather than to become enmeshed in the polemics of the Sino-Soviet dispute.

The effect of the two visits on Hanoi's attitude cannot be gauged precisely. But on 10 February, as if in unison, the VNWP Politburo and the PKI Central Committee both made appeals for greater international Communist solidarity. Five days later a sudden thaw in Sino-Soviet relations seemed to be signalled when Khrushchev – at a diplomatic reception attended by foreigners – suddenly greeted the Chinese ambassador with unaccustomed warmth and proposed a toast to friendship between the two countries.[21] It was not necessarily mere coincidence that he chose to make the gesture at a reception for the King of Laos and Prince Souvanna Phouma, who were completing a visit to Moscow on that day.

7 Laos: the Limits of Détente

We are taking a chance on all of Southeast Asia, and we're taking a chance in other areas. Nobody can make any predictions . . . on any matter in which there are powerful interests at stake. I think, however, that we have to consider what our alternatives are and what the prospects for war are in that area if we fail in our present efforts. . . . It is my judgement that it is in the best interests of our country to work for a neutral and independent Laos. We are attempting to do that, and I can assure you that I recognise the risks that are involved. But I also think we should consider the risks if we fail.

President Kennedy at a news conference,
15 January 1962

I am sure that you must be as disturbed as I am about the situation in Laos. Over the last fortnight there have been reported many breaches of the ceasefire; the armed forces of the Neutralist Party have been under serious military attack, and grave accusations have been made . . . about the presence of foreign military personnel.

British Foreign Secretary to Soviet Foreign Minister,
19 April 1963

I have the honour to bring to your esteemed attention that the situation in the Plain of Jars, in the provinces of Savannakhet and Thakhek, and most recently in the province of Vientiane, is daily becoming more serious because of the intensive and dangerous activities of the Pathet Lao and their allies. Besides many violations of the ceasefire committed by the afore-mentioned troops, observers have noted the arrival in Pathet Lao zones of North Vietnamese combat units, fully equipped with their basic weapons and therefore on a war footing. . . . There can no longer be any doubt that North Vietnamese forces are massively assisting the Pathet Lao by reinforcing them along the whole front. . . .

Souvanna Phouma, to the Geneva Co-chairmen,
20 June 1963

I

Laos was still the key to United States strategy in South-East Asia. With the benefit of hindsight, there has been a tendency for commentators to assume that the breakdown of the Geneva guarantees of 1962 was inevitable from the beginning and that the renewal of conflict there was merely a matter of time. In early 1963, however, that assumption was not entirely justified. A genuine neutralisation of Laos, based on the restoration of internal stability, might still have been possible if all the major powers concerned had continued to exert pressure on the three Laotian 'parties' to work together. The eventual collapse of the Geneva arrangements can be understood only by examining in detail the sequence of events in Laos during the critical months from February to June 1963; and setting them against the background of international developments, especially in the Communist world.

Souvanna Phouma's aim on resuming the leadership of a new coalition in mid-1962 was to imitate the success of Prince Sihanouk of Cambodia: that is, to use international pressures as a means to maintain the balance of political forces inside his own country. He had one advantage over Sihanouk, in that Laotian neutrality had been publicly guaranteed by the great powers – a degree of diplomatic formality which was to elude the Cambodian leader throughout the 1960s. The real basis of Sihanouk's success, however, lay in the fact that Cambodia's internal politics had never become so completely polarised as they were from the beginning in the case of Laos.

In Cambodia, 'rightist' military and bureaucratic leaders like Lon Nol or In Tam had acquired only a limited power base – partly because Sihanouk had restricted the role of American military and economic assistance since 1955. (The externally supported right-wing opposition forces of Son Ngoc Thanh, the Khmer Serei, did not represent a serious challenge.) On the left, the Viet-Minh oriented Khmer Issara had dissolved itself after the Geneva Agreement of 1954; whilst the clandestine Communist Party, or People's Revolutionary Party, decided in 1960 against reactivating the armed struggle. It would appear that the Communist leadership passed through an internal power struggle following the death (perhaps murder) of its secretary-general Tou Samut in July 1962, out of which the 'pro-Chinese' Saloth Sar (later known as Pol Pot) emerged on top. But the Communists continued to respect Sihanouk's role as national leader, at least for the time being. Returning from another of his frequent visits to Peking, in March 1963, Sihanouk even invited the leftist leaders to join in a new effort to resolve the country's problems. They declined to enter into a coalition, however, leaving the neutralist Sangkum as the only political party formally in power.[1]

By contrast, Souvanna Phouma faced the task of holding together a coalition in which important ministries were controlled by the Pathet Lao (with links to Hanoi) and by the Savannakhet faction of Phoumi Nosavan (supported from Thailand). Not only did those two 'factions' have their own armed forces. They also controlled substantial territory: the Communists in the North and East, along the Chinese and North Vietnamese borders; the Rightists in the lowland areas along the Mekong, which were of direct interest to Thailand. The only hope for lasting stability lay in the maintenance of an acceptable balance of power between the two extremes; and in the ability of the neutralist forces of Kong Lae to provide an independent power base for the prime minister and for the neutralist political party of foreign minister Quinim Pholsena. The need for a proper balance between the three military forces was recognised on all sides. On 27 November 1962 an agreement had been reached for their integration into a single national army on the basis of numerical equality: 10,000 Pathet Lao, 10,000 Phoumists, and 10,000 neutralists. It would not be easy to persuade Phoumi Nosavan to demobilise most of his existing force of 60,000 men; nor would it be easy to prevent the continuing participation of North Vietnamese advisers in the forces of the Pathet Lao. In the interim much would depend on the unity and coherence of Kong Lae's units, occupying as they did strategic positions in the Plaine des Jarres.[2]

Another complicating factor was the continued presence of the American CIA. The 660 American and 400 Filipino special forces sent to Laos during the fighting of 1961–2 had been withdrawn by the appointed deadline of 7 October. But Air America continued to supply clandestine assistance to groups it had recruited and armed in the upland Meo areas. It was unlikely that such activities would in themselves have completely undermined the restoration of stability if all other factors had favoured it; but they provided a legitimate ground for complaint if at any time the Pathet Lao chose to accuse the Americans of violating the 1962 agreement. On 5 January 1963 an Air America plane was shot down during a clandestine supply mission over Northern Laos. Two days later the Pathet Lao issued a statement strongly condemning both the Savannakhet Party and the United States, and on 15 January Souphanouvong formally urged Souvanna Phouma to complain to the International Commission about the illegal activities of Air America and to demand its withdrawal.[3] At that stage Souphanouvong's primary objective was probably to persuade neutralist elements to take an anti-American line; perhaps also to justify his own continuing relations with Hanoi. But the prime minister avoided the issue by pleading ignorance.

The decisive phase in Laos came during the weeks from 11 February to 31 March 1963 when Souvanna Phouma – accompanied by the King as well as foreign minister Quinim Pholsena and two other ministers – undertook a world tour of all the fourteen countries which had attended the Geneva Conference on Laos. Starting in Moscow, they proceeded to Western Europe and the United States, then to China and North Vietnam, finally to India, Thailand and Cambodia. Everywhere they were welcomed warmly and given promises of support.[4] This was the kind of global diplomacy at which Cambodia's Sihanouk had excelled; and if circumstances inside Laos had remained calm the tour might have given Souvanna Phouma the framework he needed to establish Laotian neutrality as a fact of international life. But the situation in Laos did not remain undisturbed: barely a day after the King and his ministers left Vientiane one of the leading neutralists, Colonel Ketsana, was assassinated; and during the following weeks the unity of Kong Lae's neutralist forces began to crumble. Ketsana had adopted a 'rightist' position, favouring continued acceptance of American aid, but had been opposed by Deuane Sunnalath who believed in close co-operation between the neutralists and the Pathet Lao. There now emerged a bitter struggle between Deuane and Kong Lae, with the result that the neutralist forces themselves became polarised between 'right' and 'left' factions. On 12 March Deuane accused Kong Lae of staging an ambush in the Plaine des Jarres (from which he himself had only narrowly escaped) and appealed to all 'patriotic' elements to protest against the incident; by the end of the month the situation there was extremely tense. Then on 1 April, immediately following the King's return to Vientiane, Quinim Pholsena was assassinated by one of his own supposed bodyguards.[5] Within a week a new battle was underway in the Plaine des Jarres between opposing groups of neutralists.

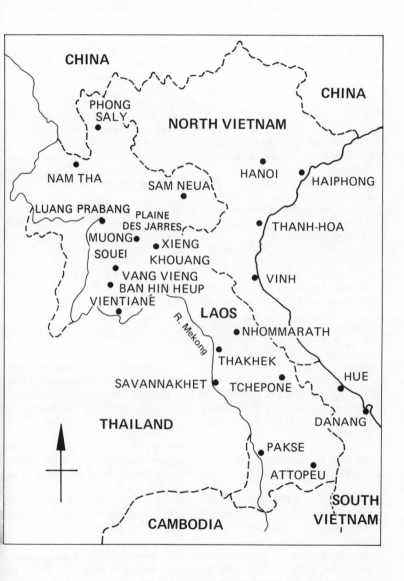

MAP 1 *Kingdom of Laos*

TABLE 7.1   *Events in Laos in the context of Communist relations, February–May 1963*

Communist relations	Laos: diplomacy and conflict
10 Feb.: *Pravda* article on internation-unity. VNWP call for unity.	11 Feb.: King of Laos, Souvanna Phouma, Quinim Pholsena, embarked on world tour – starting in USSR.
	12 Feb.: Assassination of Col. Ketsana.
	(12–18 Feb.: Prince Sihanouk of Cambodia had talks with Liu Shaoqi in Peking.)
15 Feb.: Khrushchev embraced Chinese ambassador at Laos reception in Moscow.	
21 Feb.: Soviet letter to CCP, urging an end to polemics, and bilateral meeting to resolve differences.	20 Feb.: Arrival in Hanoi of first Laotian ambassador to DRVN.
26–7 Feb.: *Renmin Ribao* again carried anti-revisionist articles.	26–7 Feb.: King of Laos (and delegation) in Washington.
5 March: Mao Zedong called on the PLA to 'learn from Lei Feng' (later an important 'Maoist' slogan).	6–10 March: King of Laos in Peking.
8 March: Khrushchev's speech on literature and art, marking the end of 'de-Stalinisation' in that sphere.	
9 March: Chinese reply to CPSU letter of 21 February, urging action to resolve differences, but indicating no change of line.	10–12 March: King of Laos in Hanoi.
	(11 March: DRVN minister of heavy industry began visit to China.)
10–13 March: Series of decisions on industry; creation of Supreme National Economic Council, headed by Ustinov.	12 March: Appeal by Col. Deuane for support among neutralists against Kong Lae.
	mid-March: Situation in Plaine des Jarres becoming extremely tense.
17 March: Khrushchev withdrew to Black Sea (until 20 April).	18–20 March: King of Laos in Cambodia.
27 March: Chinese PLA political work regulations approved by CCP (not yet published); gain for 'Maoist' line.	27–30 March: King of Laos visited India; delegation completed its tour at end of March.
30 March: Soviet letter to CCP, again indicating desire for talks, but no change of line. Invitation to Mao to visit Moscow.	30–1 March: Clashes between opposing neutralist factions in Plaine des Jarres.
	1 April: Assassination of Quinim Pholsena, followed by more intense fighting.

6–8 April: Signs of gain for 'hardline' group within Soviet leadership.

8 April: *Pravda* failed to count Yugoslavia as a socialist country.

8 April: Souphanouvong withdrew to Khang Khay, virtual breakdown of coalition in Laos.

10 April: US decision to assist forces of Kong Lae in Laos.

11 April: *Pravda* corrected its 'error' regarding Yugoslavia in issue of 8 April.

Disappearance of F. R. Kozlov; later said to have suffered a stroke.

15 April: Date of US–British letter to Khrushchev urging resumption of talks on a test-ban; delivered on 24 April.

12 April: Reported completion of Chinese road from Yunnan into Northern Laos.

17 April: *Pravda* welcomed two volumes of essays on agriculture by Khrushchev.

mid-April: Kong Le's forces obliged to retreat in Plaine des Jarres.

19 April: Phoumi Vongvichit left Vientiane for Khang Khay.

19–23 April: Exchange of letters between Geneva Co-chairmen (UK, USSR) failed to produce agreement on joint message to Laos.

20 April: Khrushchev back in Moscow.

21 April: Souvanna Phouma visited Khang Khay. Ceasefire agreed, to halt fighting in Plaine des Jarres.

25 April: Indication of loss of rank by M. A. Suslov; Mikoyan appeared above him in precedence at May Day parade.

26 April: Harriman met Khrushchev in Moscow; secured Soviet statement supporting Laotian neutrality.

28 April: Castro began visit to Moscow.

4 May: Kozlov's illness reported.

5 May: Letter from Souphanouvong to the Geneva Co-chairmen, blaming Americans for situation in Laos.

6 May: Soviet Note to Britain supporting complaints against Phoumi Nosavan and against the International Commission.

7–11 May: Trial and conviction of Col. Oleg Penkovsky and British spy G. Wynne.

8 May: Khrushchev letter to Kennedy, leaving open the possibility of further negotiations on test-ban issue.

9 May: Britain rejected any joint action on basis of Soviet allegations.

On 8 April Souphanouvong once again withdrew from Vientiane to the Pathet Lao stronghold of Khang Khay.

This turn of events was viewed with concern in Washington, where Laos was the subject of a meeting of the NSC on 10 April.[6] Whilst the scale of fighting was not great, it threatened the survival of Kong Lae's neutralist forces as a coherent element in the 'tripartite' pattern of Laotian politics on which the coalition – and ultimately the Geneva Declaration of 1962 – had been based. Kennedy and his advisers were willing to take what action they could to help strengthen Kong Lae's position, but they were anxious not to alienate Souvanna Phouma himself by over-reacting to the situation. Their main hope was that the Russians could be persuaded – perhaps by Britain – to bring pressure to bear on both Hanoi and the Pathet Lao to ensure a return to the situation that had prevailed before mid-February. But that raised the question whether Khrushchev was still prepared to co-operate in new efforts to restore stability in Laos.

II

The new crisis in Laos coincided with important developments in the Soviet Union and in Sino-Soviet relations during February and March 1963. The Moscow reception for the King of Laos on 15 February, at which Khrushchev suddenly embraced the Chinese ambassador, was followed by more substantive Soviet moves towards reopening a dialogue with Peking. A new Soviet letter to the CCP Central Committee, delivered personally to Mao on 23 February, had at least the appearance of a conciliatory

SOURCES FOR TABLE 7.1   *Annual Register;* M. Tatu, *Power in the Kremlin: from Khrushchev's Decline to Collective Leadership* (London, 1969); *Documents Relating to British Involvement in the Indochina Conflict 1945–1965* (London: HMSO, 1965), Cmnd 2834.

move. Mao responded by inviting the Soviet leader to visit Peking – safe in the knowledge that Khrushchev was certain to refuse. The Chinese replied formally to the Soviet letter on 9 March, but without yeilding any significant points of principle.[7] On the Chinese side Mao's thinking was probably just as distant from that of the Soviet 'hardliners' as Khrushchev's was from that of any 'pro-Soviet' element in the CCP. Nevertheless, the exchanges coincided with – and can be partly explained by – a distinct shift in Soviet internal politics: perhaps a more significant, albeit temporary, shift than had occurred immediately following the missiles crisis.

On 8 March Khruschev made a speech to a meeting of writers and artists which amounted to a complete reversal of 'de-Stalinisation' in that field. Even more important, a series of measures designed to reinforce the priority of industrial investment culminated in the appointment on 13 March of D. F. Ustinov to head a Supreme National Economic Council which greatly strengthened the link between industry and the armed forces. Shortly afterwards, Khrushchev himself withdrew to the shores of the Black Sea.[8]

The political trend in Moscow continued to move against Khrushchev, so far as one can tell, until a climax was reached around 8–10 April. On the 8th, in publishing the usual slogans for May Day, *Pravda* failed to count Yugoslavia as a 'socialist' country – which seemed to mark a return to the habits prevailing before Tito's visit to Moscow. On the 10th it was announced that a forthcoming plenum of the Central Committee, to discuss ideology, would be held on 28 May. Together these two things seemed to imply a decision to resume the attack on Tito's 'revisionism'. But then on 11 April *Pravda* 'corrected' its 'error' about Yugoslavia. On the same day Kozlov, who was later said to have suffered a stroke, suddenly disappeared from the top leadership. That this represented a significant change seemed to be confirmed a week later, when on Khrushchev's 69th birthday (17 April) *Pravda* was full of praise for the First Secretary's latest volume of speeches on agriculture. By the time he returned to Moscow on the 20th, Khrushchev was obviously in firm control. Even more striking was the fact that, for the first time since 1960, deputy premier Mikoyan again had precedence over M. A. Suslov in the official ranking for the May Day parade. Although

Khrushchev was unable to reverse the March decisions on heavy industry, which represented a major long-term gain for the 'military-industrial complex' within the Soviet system, he reaffirmed Party-State control over the Supreme National Economic Council.

It is impossible to trace a direct connection between the political crisis in Moscow and the situation in Laos. But following Khrushchev's reassertion of his own authority in mid-April, it immediately became possible to resume the dialogue between Moscow and Washington; and a significant easing of tension followed. On 19 April 1963 the British foreign secretary wrote to his Soviet counterpart (in their respective capacities as Co-chairmen of the Geneva Conference) suggesting that joint action be taken to restore the ceasefire in Laos.[9] Although exchanges between then and 23 April failed to produce agreement on a joint message to the government of Laos, it proved possible to impose a new ceasefire on the ground on 22 April. Laos was again discussed by the NSC at a series of meetings between 20 and 23 April, as a result of which Kennedy concluded that a diplomatic solution might be possible after all. He ordered the deployment of elements of the Seventh Fleet to the South China Sea, where their presence might be interpreted in Moscow as a threat to North Vietnam. But he also decided to send Averell Harriman to Moscow, where direct talks with Khrushchev elicited a statement on 26 April reaffirming Soviet support for the 1962 guarantee of Laotian neutrality.[10] But Pathet Lao intransigence prevented any inspection of the new ceasefire by the International Commission. Before long the Russians would begin to plead that they lacked sufficient control of events in Laos to prevent a further outbreak of hostilities. In reality, they could no longer afford to take a 'weak' line which would mean abandoning the initiative (and Hanoi) to the Chinese.

One other development of this period may be mentioned in passing. On 29 April the French government informed Souvanna Phouma of its intention to withdraw immediately from the Seno base, which it had been permitted to continue in being under the Geneva Agreements of both 1954 and 1962. The French agreed to maintain the security of the base until a formal transfer was possible, and it was not until 9 July that the Laotian armed forces (that is, the forces of Vientiane) announced their decision to proceed with the takeover.[11] The net result of the change was to make the Americans exclusively responsible for Western military support of the Royal government in Laos and to liquidate the last remaining element of French military presence in Laos or Vietnam. This would permit De Gaulle to play a more independent role in Indochina during the second half of 1963.

III

These political shifts in Moscow almost certainly had other consequences for East–West relations, as well as for the advice Moscow was inclined to give to more revolutionary-minded members of the socialist camp–particularly Cuba and North Vietnam. About the time of Khrushchev's apparent recovery of power, Kennedy and Macmillan sent another letter to Moscow (dated 15 April, but not delivered until the 24th) urging a new effort towards banning nuclear tests. This drew a grudging reply on 8 May. But, as we shall see, Khrushchev was obliged to continue the dialogue with China a stage further before he felt free to embark on direct talks with the United States and Britain.

In the meantime he also had to reimpose the line of peaceful coexistence on Castro; for without stability in the Caribbean any improvement in Soviet–American relations was out of the question. The Cuban leader visited Moscow from 28 April to 23 May 1963 and his talks with Khrushchev on that occasion appear to have cemented Soviet–Cuban relations, essentially on Soviet terms. Cuba was obliged to accept the principle that its security depended on Soviet–American *détente* and that further revolutionary activity in South America was therefore inappropriate. Castro also had to forego the possibility of independent industrial development and to accept continuing dependence on sugar production. In return he received massive Soviet economic assistance in other spheres.[12]

There was a remarkable contrast, however, between the line adopted by Cuba and the sequence of events in North Vietnam during the spring of 1963. In March the growing strength of the 'hardliners' in Moscow was no doubt especially welcome in Hanoi. On 13 March, coinciding precisely with Khrushchev's defeat on the issue of the Supreme National Economic Council, two important Vietnamese speeches marked the 80th anniversary of the death of Karl Marx.[13] Together they serve as a guide to current Vietnamese Communist thinking, which was by no means identical with the 'Maoism' of the CCP's 10th Plenum, and had much more in common with the line of the Soviet 'anti-Party group' defeated by Khrushchev in 1957 and 1961. Nguyen Chi Thanh, whose speech was immediately published, dwelt on the importance of both class struggle and anti-imperialism. He also spoke of the need to avoid rightist and leftist errors in applying a correct Marxist–Leninist line, although it is impossible to link his remarks to any specific elements or groups within the Party. Le Duan's speech in no way contradicted that of Thanh but dealt with a number of additional points at greater length. Particularly noticeable was his emphasis on revolutionary violence, although he fell short of actual criticism of peaceful coexistence. He also returned to the theme of the role of heavy industry in building an independent socialist economy in Vietnam. On the latter point, Vietnamese ideas were similar to the line taken by Romania at a CMEA meeting in mid-February, where Khrushchev's proposals for greater economic integration were opposed on the grounds that the 'international division of labour' would mean the end of Romanian industrial investment.

Ironically, however, the Soviet decision to concentrate resources on a further expansion of the 'military–industrial complex' implied new limits on what was available for external economic aid. The Vietnamese were therefore obliged to turn to China. From 11 March to the end of April their minister of heavy industry (Nguyen Van Tran) visited Peking, Shanghai and a number of other places – probably in the hope of securing additional assistance. But it was impossible to fill the gap completely. Nor was the situation eased after mid-April: Khrushchev's willingness to appease Castro by offering massive assistance to Cuba placed even greater restrictions on the funds available to help Vietnam. On 29 April the communiqué of the VNWP Central Committee's Eighth Plenum indicated a considerable revision of the Five-Year Plan (which still had nearly three years to run), and at a meeting in May to study the resolution of that plenum Le Duan found himself having to emphasise the virtues of 'self-reliance'. He sought to convince the assembled cadres that they could do without some of the 'luxuries' previously imported from abroad; meanwhile more emphasis must be placed on agriculture.[14]

Thus Cuba and North Vietnam were both obliged to accept some restriction of their economic ambitions – but in very different circumstances. Whilst Cuba became more dependent than ever on Soviet aid, the Vietnamese were still able to maintain a measure of independence by relying on China. This was even more evident in the sphere of revolutionary strategy, where Khrushchev's ability to force Castro into line had no parallel in Moscow's relations with Hanoi. Ho Chi Minh and his colleagues were determined to continue the struggle in the South, even if an economic price had to be paid; and the Chinese were more than willing to encourage them to do so, provided that there was no major expansion of military activity. The Vietnamese therefore continued to adhere to the principle of combining a low-level guerrilla campaign with an extension of the political struggle.

At this point Liu Shaoqi paid a state visit to Hanoi from 10 to 16 May 1963.[15] It would be a mistake, nevertheless, to see that visit as signalling a final North Vietnamese decision to align itself with China, to the exclusion of any continuing alliance with the Soviet Union. Ho's object was still to promote a restoration of Sino-Soviet harmony. He was no doubt encouraged by the fact that on 9 May, the day before Liu arrived, Zhou Enlai had received the Soviet ambassador in Peking and had formally accepted an invitation to send a CCP delegation to Moscow for bilateral talks. Five days later (while Liu was still in Hanoi) it was agreed that Deng Xiaoping, Peng Zhen and Kang Sheng would travel to the Soviet capital on 5 July. Thus Liu Shaoqi's talks with Ho took place against a background of optimism – albeit shortlived – about improved relations between the two principal Communist Parties. The Vietnamese situation, indeed, may have been a principal reason why Khrushchev could not afford, just yet, to abandon the dialogue with Peking.

The Chinese delegation to Hanoi, which also included Chen Yi, was welcomed with great warmth; and the whole Vietnamese Politburo took part in the official talks. A joint statement issued on 16 May was strongly anti-revisionist in tone, as was Liu's speech to the Nguyen Ai Quoc Party school the day before. But neither document made any reference to Sino-Soviet tensions, nor gave any hint of possible moves to create a schismatic Communist international organisation in Asia. Ho Chi Minh was probably still at pains to destroy any Chinese illusion that he might be willing to lead his own Party into rebellion against Moscow. His aim, as always, was to develop his own revolutionary strategy in Indo-china with support from both major Communist powers. If, for the time being, greater support seemed to be forthcoming from Peking than from Moscow, that might prove to be only a temporary phase.

IV

In these circumstances, it soon became clear to the Americans that there was little hope of resolving the renewed conflict in Laos merely on the basis of diplomatic exchanges between Washington, London and Moscow. The Pathet Lao, the North Vietnamese, the Chinese and the Russians were now united in blaming the United States for the deteriorating situation in Laos. Souphanouvong sent a letter to the Geneva Co-chairmen to that effect on 5 May, and the following day the Soviet foreign minister tried (unsuccessfully) to persuade his British counterpart to join in a message to Vientiane which would have virtually sided with the Pathet Lao against the other factions. Not until six weeks later did Souvanna Phouma come out with the open accusation that North Vietnam had itself been moving combat-ready troops into Laos from as early as March, and that they had begun to fight alongside the Pathet Lao.[16] By then the fighting had resumed, and conditions no longer existed for the kind of diplomatic solution which had worked the year before.

One last attempt was made to invoke the Geneva machinery as a means of establishing a framework for fresh negotiations: on 22 May the International Commission made a Special Report to the Co-chairmen on the growing seriousness of the situation in the Plaine des Jarres, and a week later the Co-chairmen agreed on a joint message to Laos urging the parties to allow the Commission itself to operate normally.[17] But nothing came of that initiative.

The Pathet Lao protested strongly when in mid-June the Indian and Canadian members of the Commission insisted on going to inspect the battlefield in Southern Laos without their Polish colleague, after the latter had refused to join them. It is by no means easy to obtain a clear picture of the fighting on the ground at that period, nor to decide who was to blame, in view of the charges and counter-charges levied by the two sides. But the most important areas of conflict were round Nhommarath (east of Thakhek), which the Pathet Lao captured on 15 June; and at Attopeu (in the far south) which they attacked less successfully on 13–14 June.[18] Both were areas whose incorporation into Communist-controlled territory was necessary in order to complete preparations for an eventual enlargement of their infiltration route to South Vietnam.

SEATO exercises in Thailand between 11 and 20 June provided some reassurance to Bangkok; in any case there seems to have been no immediate threat to Thai security. Whilst there was no overt American military action inside Laos at this stage, on 19 June (shortly before leaving on a European tour) Kennedy approved various State Department proposals for contingency planning embodied in NSAM no. 249, dated 25 June 1963.[19] He explicitly deferred any decision on action against North Vietnam. It was on 20 June, too, that Souvanna Phouma openly accused the North Vietnamese of military involvement in Laos: in so doing, he was re-establishing his own right to receive additional American support if it proved necessary. As Laotian politics became polarised, he and Kong Lae had little choice but to throw in their lot with the United States, at least for the time being.

In an attempt to explain why the Russians seemed unable to do anything about the deteriorating situation, the British opposition leader Harold Wilson suggested in the House of Commons on 2 July that perhaps 'their writ doesn't run in Laos'. But there is little to suggest either that the Chinese, despite Liu Shaoqi's visit to Hanoi, were prime movers in the new fighting in Laos, or that they had a great deal to gain from the collapse of the political balance that had existed a year before. A more likely explanation is that the North Vietnamese were becoming involved in Laotian affairs on their own account, and that neither the Soviet Union nor China (acting alone) was in a position to stop them. Moscow's determination to retain a measure of influence in Hanoi, which led it to support North Vietnam and the Pathet Lao in the diplomatic sphere, made it impossible to bring Laos within the scope of East–West *détente*. It is by no means clear how far all the ramifications of this complicated situation were apparent to American policy-makers at the time. Certainly Laos was not central to Kennedy's thoughts at a moment when he was

TABLE 7.2 *Laos in the context of East–West and Sino–Soviet relations, May–June 1963*

East–West relations	Communist relations	Laos
		6 May: Soviet proposal for draft message by Geneva Co-chairmen which would have supported Souphanouvong's accusations against United States.
8 May: Khrushchev letter to Kennedy, leaving open possibility of further test-ban talks.		
7–11 May: Trial of G. Wynne and Col. Oleg Penkovsky in Moscow.		9 May: Britain rejected this draft, and defended action of International Commission.
	9 May: Zhou Enlai told Soviet ambassador China was willing to send delegation to Moscow for bilateral talks. (Date agreed for Deng's visit (5 July) on 14 May.)	
	10 May: Liu Shaoqi arrived in Hanoi.	14 May: New fighting reported in Plaine des Jarres.
	16 May: Ho Chi Minh–Liu Shaoqi joint statement at end of Liu's visit to North Vietnam.	18 May: Souvanna Phouma letter to Geneva Co-chairmen, refuting Souphanouvong's letter of 5 May; insists he is ready for further talks in Luang Prabang.
	20 May: CCP Draft Resolution on Rural Work (Mao's 'ten points') circulated in China.	
21 May: Soviet–American memorandum on collaboration in peaceful uses of nuclear energy.		

22 May: Special Report of International Commission on rapid deterioration of situation in Plaine des Jarres.

23 May: Soviet–Cuban Declaration at end of Castro's visit to Moscow; accepted Soviet line.

27 May: New incident in Berlin, involving a US enclave in E. Germany.

29 May: Geneva Co-chairmen sent joint message to Government of Laos: appeal for end to hostilities and for co-operation with the International Commission.

29 May: Patriotic Front (NLHX) again called for end to US intervention in Laos.

30 May: Kennedy message to Khrushchev proposing visit by a Western delegation for talks on a tripartite test-ban treaty.

4 June: *Renmin Ribao* denounced US actions in Laos, supported Patriotic Front line.

4 June: Castro speech praising Khrushchev; ignored by Chinese media.

6–8 June: North Korean president in Peking.

6 June: China warned USSR against signing a treaty which would preclude development of nuclear weapons by China.

8 June: Khrushchev letter to Kennedy, agreeing to receive US–UK delegation in Moscow.

TABLE 7.2 *Laos in the context of East–West and Sino–Soviet relations, May–June 1963*

East–West relations	Communist relations	Laos
10 June: Kennedy's American University speech on world peace.		
		11–20 June: SEATO exercises in Thailand.
		13 June: Pathet Lao forces attacked town of Attopeu (Southern Laos).
	14 June: CCP 'Proposal Concerning the General Line of the International Communist Movement'; CPSU refused to publish it or allow it to circulate in USSR.	
		16 June: *Renmin Ribao*: 'US Aggression in Laos must be checked!'
	18–22 June: CPSU Central Committee Plenum: discussion of ideology; promotion to CPSU Secretariat of Brezhnev and Podgorny.	
19 June: End of Soviet jamming of broadcasts by VOA and BBC.		19 June: Kennedy approved contingency planning by State Department for possible future actions in relation to Laos; basis of NSAM no. 249 (25 June 1963).
20 June: US–Soviet agreement to establish a 'hotline' between Moscow and Washington.		20 June: Letter from Souvanna Phouma to Geneva Co-chairmen, accusing North Vietnamese of sending combat troops into Laos from March (1963) in support of Pathet Lao.

SOURCES   As for Table 6.1; or otherwise indicated in notes to text.

preoccupied with negotiations for a test-ban treaty. Perhaps he still assumed that a diplomatic solution would emerge with the passage of time, once the larger issues of East–West relations had been resolved.

The more general course of East–West diplomacy in the early summer of 1963, and its impact of Sino-Soviet relations, are subjects which lie beyond the scope of the present study; the broad outline of events is in any case well known.[20] On 8 June Khrushchev again wrote to Kennedy, indicating his willingness to receive a high-level American–British delegation in Moscow to discuss the content of a treaty banning nuclear tests. Kennedy responded immediately in a speech on world peace at the American University on 10 June, and after three more weeks of cautious manoeuvring by both sides Khrushchev agreed (2 July) to a treaty excluding the vexed question of underground nuclear tests. The Chinese reaction to this apparent breakthrough was the CCP's 'Proposal concerning the General Line of the International Communist Movement', addressed to the CPSU on 14 June, which became the first public document in the Sino-Soviet ideological dispute. By the time Deng Xiaoping arrived in the Soviet capital on 5 July to begin talks with a delegation headed by M. A. Suslov (not by Khrushchev himself), the possibility of *rapprochement* on the ideological plane seemed remote. On 14 July the CPSU produced a direct reply to the Chinese 'Proposal' in the form of an open letter to its own Party membership. The following day Khrushchev opened the talks with Averell Harriman and Lord Hailsham which culminated in the initialling of an actual treaty on nuclear tests on 25 July. Meanwhile the Deng–Suslov talks reached an impasse on 20 July and the Chinese delegation went home.

Even at the time there was a general recognition that these developments marked a watershed in international affairs. On the one hand the Moscow Treaty opened up at least the possibility of new ways of thinking in the West about the 'Soviet bloc'. Without weakening existing commitments in Europe and elsewhere – and without deliberately abandoning the strategy of 'containment' – the United States could now begin to regard '*détente*' as a significant option in its bilateral dealings with the Soviet Union. Almost simultaneously, on the other hand, it became evident – even to those who had previously refused to believe in a 'Sino-Soviet split' – that the same did not apply to China. Chinese rejection of the test ban and denunciation of Khrushchev as a 'revisionist' seemed to confirm the impression that the main threat to world peace now emanated not from Moscow – nor even from Havana – but from Peking. The consequence for American global strategy was that greater priority would be given in future to defending Asia against China's supposed revolutionary ambitions, especially in South-East Asia.

8 South-East Asia: the Regional Perspective

It must be recognised that the fall of South Vietnam to Communist control would mean the eventual Communist domination of all of the Southeast Asian mainland.... The military and political effort of Communist China in South Vietnam and the political and psychological thrust of the USSR into the Indonesian archipelago are not brushfire tactics, nor merely a campaign for control of the mainland area. More important, it is part of a major campaign to extend Communist control beyond the periphery of the Sino-Soviet bloc and overseas to both island and continental areas in the Free World, through a most natural and comparatively soft outlet, the Southeast Asian Peninsula.

> Joint Chiefs of Staff Memorandum,
> 13 January 1962

Vietnam occupies a strategic position in South-East Asia.... The Vietnamese Revolution exerted great influence in this area by its victory over the French colonialists and the US imperialists. The Chinese leaders attempted to get hold of Vietnam, and then the whole Indochinese peninsula, and later on to use Indochina as a springboard for expansion into South-East Asia. At the September 1963 meeting in Canton between the four Communist Parties of Vietnam, China, Indonesia and Laos, premier Zhou Enlai said: 'Our country is a big one, but we have no way out. Therefore we hope the Vietnam Workers' Party will help blaze the trail to South-East Asia.'

> 'White Book' on Vietnam–China relations,
> Hanoi, October 1979

The great weakness of US policy in Southeast Asia since the 1950s, which indeed may ultimately prove a fatal defect, is that we have never been quite sure how serious we are about the whole business. Are our interests in Southeast Asia really *vital* national interests? ... My own view is that we shall ultimately fail to secure the basic objectives of policy in Southeast Asia until our commitment to the region becomes unlimited, as it has not been until now.

> William Henderson, at an Asia Society Conference in New York,
> 10–11 May 1963

I

Liu Shaoqi's visit to North Vietnam (10–16 May), whilst it reflected growing Chinese interest in the struggle in South Vietnam, was only one aspect of Chinese strategy in South-East Asia in 1963. Liu himself had already made a series of visits to the non-aligned countries of the region, not in his capacity as a Communist leader but as president of the People's Republic of China. His visits to Burma (20–26 April) and Cambodia (1–6 May) represented a continuation and consolidation of Chinese diplomacy over the previous few years. That to Indonesia, on the other hand, from 13 to 20 April, was a significant new departure and must be counted as the most important Peking initiative in the region since Zhou Enlai's journey to Bandung in 1955.[1] At the very least the Americans were likely to regard Liu's 'tour' as a manifestation of Chinese anti-imperialism, and as such a threat to their own interests.

Even more worrying from the Western point of view was the complicated situation now emerging in British Borneo, in the wake of Sukarno's declared policy of 'confrontation' against the Federation of Malaysia. The earlier struggle to liberate West Irian, which had succeeded in mid-1962, had taken the form of an irredentist campaign to recover a part of Indonesia which the Dutch had refused to transfer in 1949. The essence of 'confrontation', however, was a demand that the British possessions in Borneo – which the Indonesians called 'North Kalimantan' – should be given separate independence rather than be absorbed into the Federation. That demand, in turn, created the opportunity for leftist participation in a 'liberation struggle'; perhaps even Communist leadership of a front organisation directly comparable with the NLFSVN.

The first phase of the struggle for an independent 'North Kalimantan' was a short-lived revolt in Brunei under the leadership of the nationalist Azahari, which broke out on 8 December 1962. It was quickly suppressed by British troops and by the end of the year had ceased to be a threat even to Brunei. Also in mid-December, the British foiled what looked like plans for a parallel revolt in North Borneo (Sabah).[2] It would appear that Azahari's main support during that phase came from Manila rather than from Jakarta – the Philippines government having already taken the position that sovereignty over North Borneo had never been completely ceded to Britain and still belonged to the heirs of Sulu. By January 1963, however, it was evident that the only hope of waging a long-term 'liberation struggle' lay in Sarawak and depended on the participation of the local Chinese population, as well as on support from Indonesia. The Sarawak Liberation League, with links to the Malayan Communist Party, was ready to play an active role. In Jakarta, as early as 17 December, Chaerul Saleh founded a 'Committee for Indonesian solidarity with the revolution in North Kalimantan' which was bound to attract PKI support. Azahari therefore moved his headquarters to Indonesia early in 1963, and is said to have cultivated close relations with Nasution.[3]

At that point, it would seem, Chinese involvement also began. *Renmin Ribao* had come out in open support of the 'people of Brunei' on 15 December – although it was not until late March that NCNA reproduced a statement of the Malayan Communist Party (also dated 15 December) which referred explicitly to 'North Kaliman-tan'.[4] Important, but highly secret, decisions are thought to have been made during a visit by Subandrio to Peking during the first week of January 1963. Ostensibly it was an occasion for expressing Sino-Indonesian solidarity against imperialism, and Chinese en-couragement was an obvious factor in the speech made by Subandrio on his return home which first mentioned the word 'confrontation'. But Zhou Enlai is also believed to have offered Chinese help in training recruits from Sarawak and providing them with weapons for an armed struggle. During the following three months such training certainly took place (although the Chinese role has never been proved) and the first small-scale attacks on Sarawak border posts occurred on 12 and 23 April 1963. Meanwhile on 5 April the 'Revolutionary Government of North Kalimantan' broadcast a programme and manifesto over its own radio station, which had gone on the air during March.[5]

If the question of Malaysia had been merely a diplomatic dispute between Kuala Lumpur and Jakarta, it is very likely that Sukarno would have found some means to work out a diplomatic solution. A 'national liberation struggle' for the independence of 'North Kalimantan', however, was more difficult for him to deal with in his own terms – especially when it already had the support of both nationalists and Communists in his own country. Moreover, some elements in the Indonesian armed forces appeared ready to support guerrilla activity on a small scale –

partly to justify further military procurements and partly perhaps because they were reluctant to see the issue become a PKI monopoly. There was little chance of actual victory for a low-level guerrilla struggle in Sarawak; but the mere fact of its existence might be sufficient to disrupt Western regional strategy in South-East Asia, and force the United States into a defensive position. Certainly it allowed the Chinese and the PKI to pressure Sukarno into a more uncompromising anti-imperialist stand against Malaysia. Whilst participating in diplomatic moves during 1963, the Indonesian leader could not afford to make final commitments which might look like surrender on an issue of principle involving national independence.

Indonesian politics during the late Sukarno period depended, as is well known, on the skill with which the national leader himself was able to draw support from a wide range of political forces and balance them against one another: the key elements being the armed forces, various religious groups, and the Communists. In these circumstances, the only possible line for the PKI to adopt was that of a 'united front from above', which would enable them to influence Sukarno's policies, rather than a strategy for the actual seizure of power. Whenever the government moved towards compromise with the American oil companies, with international financial institutions, or with the other countries of 'Maphilindo', Aidit would insist that American imperialism was the foremost enemy of the Indonesian people, that Malaysia was an 'imperialist plot', and that 'counterrevolutionaries' should be smashed. In time, he would also call for the establishment of a coalition government (NASAKOM) and the implementation of agrarian reforms.

The PKI had little potential for creating its own rural base area of the 'Maoist' type. Its main strength lay in Java, where the land was too densely populated and village society too tightly-knit to allow any substantial area to be 'liberated' in the sense of being able to defend itself against government forces. During the period of electoral politics before 1959, the PKI had organised itself as a legal party and had done well in elections. Since the inception of 'guided democracy' it had been free to develop its own mass organisations and to mobilise workers (for example in the oil fields and in communications) and peasants in certain areas, as well as its own associations of women and youth. But it had no armed units and in that respect was quite different from the Viet-Minh or from the NLFSVN. Its one opportunity to pursue an anti-imperialist struggle in the immediate future lay in the possibility of using its political influence to push Sukarno more and more deeply into the policy of 'confrontation'.

Liu Shaoqi made no reference during his visit to the issue of 'North Kalimantan'; nor did it figure in the joint statement issued at the end of the visit. The main purpose of his visit seems to have been to cultivate Indonesian non-Communist figures likely to be most friendly towards China: particularly Madame Hartini and foreign minister Subandrio, both of whom had been in Peking in recent months. It may have been more than a coincidence, too, that during his stay Liu was invited to attend celebrations for the 17th anniversary of the air force, whose senior officers would also be identifiable later as 'pro-Chinese' (whereas the navy was oriented more towards the Soviet Union).

From Washington's point of view, Liu Shaoqi's 'tour' represented a more serious threat to American interests in South-East Asia than Sukarno's opposition to the Federation of Malaysia. The United States was not committed to taking Britain's side in the latter dispute: it was still possible for Kennedy to pursue a policy of friendly relations with Jakarta. But if Sukarno began to move towards a more 'anti-imperialist' view of the world and to establish closer relations with Peking, he might eventually be led to challenge both American business interests in Indonesia and also Kennedy's political strategy in the South-East Asian region. A similar danger existed in the case of Cambodia, where Liu was equally warmly received by Sihanouk. The conflict between Phnom Penh and Bangkok was at present only an irritant for Kennedy; but if the Chinese encouraged the Prince to take a more uncompromising line towards his neighbours, as well as to cultivate better relations with Hanoi, the eventual result might be a crisis in American–Cambodian relations. Changes of that kind would affect the political climate of the region, and might ultimately transform the whole context of the insurgency in South Vietnam.

II

A new debate on American policy in South-East Asia had begun in February 1963 with the publication of a report on aid to the region, compiled by a Congressional group under Senator Mansfield.[6] It

recommended a thorough review of military assistance programmes and looked towards an eventual contraction rather than
expansion of United States involvement – especially in the war in
Vietnam, which ought not to be allowed to become primarily an
American responsibility. Coming from a senior figure, whose visit
to Saigon in 1954 had contributed much to the initial commitment
to Diem, the report commanded wide respect in Washington. But
other influences on American policy seemed likely to work in the
opposite direction. At a meeting of the Asia Society in New York
on 10–11 May 1963 the oil expert William Henderson strongly
criticised those who questioned the American commitment to
South-East Asia, whether in the economic or in the military
sphere.[7]

At a time when leading members of the business community
were looking for investment opportunities abroad, and when the
President himself was anxious to create conditions for an expansion
of world trade, South-East Asia was acquiring greater economic
significance than ever, both as an area for investment by the
Americans themselves and also as a source of raw materials (and a
market) for Japan and Western Europe. From the point of view of
American business – especially the oil companies with investments
in Sumatra and certain banks with interests in Japan – the most
critical country in South-East Asia was not Vietnam but Indonesia. During the first half of 1963 American policy towards
Indonesia had two principal objectives: to negotiate new oil
contracts following Sukarno's demand for a larger share of profits,
in his speech of 24 February; and to stabilise Indonesia's foreign
exchange position on the basis of an international loan, on terms
acceptable to the International Monetary Fund. The Dutch as
well as the Americans were willing to participate in the latter
operation, and a first move towards it was the restoration of full
diplomatic relations between Indonesia and the Netherlands on
13 March. (The final transfer of West Irian to Indonesian control
took place on 1 May.)

By mid-year the Americans could feel satisfied that events were
moving in their favour: first minister Djuanda, with Sukarno's
apparent approval, introduced a series of economic reforms on 26
May; new oil contracts were finalised in Tokyo in early June; and
in mid-June an IMF team arrived in Jakarta to begin a detailed
study of the measures necessary for financial stabilisation.[8]
However, failure to work out a satisfactory diplomatic solution of

the Malaysia question might in the end disrupt the negotiations for an expansion of Western economic aid to Indonesia; and the PKI was quick to recognise the connection between the two issues. Aidit spoke out strongly against Djuanda's policies, notably in a speech for the 43rd anniversary of the PKI on 26 May. From that point onwards battle was joined between the bureaucrats, who favoured economic stabilisation and aid, and the revolutionary activists, who rejected all compromise with the Americans.

Sukarno could only afford to ignore the PKI if he could resolve the problem of 'confrontation' within the framework of 'Maphilindo' diplomacy. A series of bilateral exchanges between Indonesia, Malaysia and the Philippines during May was followed by a summit meeting between Sukarno and Tengku Abdul Rahman in Tokyo at the beginning of June. The ground was thus prepared for a conference of all three foreign ministers in Manila, where on 11 June they signed the Manila Accord. The three countries agreed on greater mutual co-operation in future, including formal machinery for regular consultations. They also sought to define a basis for recognition of Malaysia 'provided the support of the people of the Borneo territories is ascertained by an independent and impartial authority' – a task to be entrusted to the United Nations Secretary General, U Thant.

This agreement had still to be confirmed by a summit meeting of the three heads-of-state, however; and Sukarno, who embarked on another international tour during June and July, refused to commit himself to attending until the very last minute. Nevertheless a 'Maphilindo' summit did finally take place in Manila at the end of July and a Declaration confirming the Accord was issued on 5 August. Shortly afterwards the Malayan prime minister, despite misgivings in London, agreed to delay the inauguration of the Federation of Malaysia (due on 31 August) to allow the 'ascertainment' of opinion in the Borneo territories to proceed.

The day on which the 'Maphilindo' Declaration was agreed in Manila and the test-ban treaty signed in Moscow – 5 August 1963 – would prove to be the high point of Kennedy's foreign policy; and indeed the final moment of international optimism during his administration. Despite continuing difficulties in Laos the President could still feel that his global strategy was paying off. If he could consolidate his achievements in these two spheres – of *détente* with the Soviet Union and regional co-operation in South-East Asia – he might yet succeed in restoring the global stability which had appeared to exist in the mid-1950s. At that point, it might be argued, Kennedy would have been able to create the necessary international conditions for a graceful withdrawal from South Vietnam and the neutralisation of Indochina – without any damage to American interests in the rest of South-East Asia or elsewhere in the world. That hope may indeed have governed the President's own thinking about South-East Asia. Certainly he was beginning by now to move away from the close analogy between South Vietnam and Berlin which had affected his decisions of 1961.

On the other hand, it might equally well be argued that the diplomatic achievements of mid-1963 depended entirely on Kennedy's proven ability to apply American military capabilities in various parts of the world – including Vietnam – during the preceding two years. Without such demonstrations of United States power in Berlin and in the Caribbean, would there have been a test-ban treaty at all? Without the decisions of late 1961 and 1962 in South Vietnam, would there have been any progress towards 'Maphilindo'? These are not questions which the historian can answer with confidence; but it is important to recognise the strength of such arguments among American decision-makers at the time.

Therein lay the significance of the Asia Society Conference in May. The essence of William Henderson's position was an assumption that the American commitment to South-East Asia must combine both economic and military measures; and that in certain circumstances military action in one part of the region might be the only way to guarantee the stability required by Western and Japanese investors elsewhere. In that context he went so far as to challenge the wisdom of Kennedy's decision to pursue a political rather than a military solution in Laos; if the neutralisation of Laos were to be extended to South Vietnam, he believed, the result would be catastrophic. That amounted to something more than the 'domino theory' advanced by Eisenhower and Dulles in 1954. If the protection of South-East Asia as part of the 'free world' depended most of all on economic progress – which in capitalist terms meant not only aid programmes but also a substantial increase in international investment in the region – that in turn required political stability. The purpose of military action in Indochina therefore was not *merely* to prevent the total collapse of other 'dominoes' at a later stage, but also to ensure sufficient stability in Indonesia and Malaysia – in the short as well as the longer term – to allow investment and economic growth to take place. The diplomatic successes of 1962 and 1963 were steps in that direction, but the situation would remain fragile for many years to come.

III

It was in this context that South Vietnam began to appear as a key link – to borrow a Chinese expression – in the chain of United States commitments across Asia. Not only the Americans themselves – especially those who thought along the same lines as William Henderson – but in all probability their enemies as well were beginning to measure the strength of the American commitment to South-East Asia in terms of the success or failure of Kennedy's policies in Vietnam. Within South Vietnam the situation had remained relatively unchanged during the first four months of 1963. The Communist victory at Ap-Bac had not led to an immediate escalation of the armed struggle: its significance was rather to demonstrate the feasibility of continuing guerrilla activity on the same level, despite the greater firepower and mobility of South Vietnamese government forces. No doubt there was a continuing debate in Hanoi about the correct timing of any further intensification of military effort. But for the time being the Communist line was summed up by the title of an article by Minh Tranh broadcast by Hanoi Radio on 19 March: 'The South Vietnamese revolution must be long-drawn out, arduous and complicated, but will certainly be victorious.' The same impression of a return to the strategy of protracted war (rather than a quick victory) is gained from Communist documents of this date captured by government forces in the South.[9]

These more cautious assessments on the Communist side lend a measure of credence to the relative optimism of the Americans and Ngo Dinh Diem during March and April 1963. A report by R. G. K. Thompson was cautiously hopeful about the progress of the strategic hamlet programme, which had now been under way for about a year; and a Washington intelligence estimate of 17 April claimed that 'Communist progress has been blunted and the situation is improving.'[10] It was in the same spirit of confidence that Secretary of Defense McNamara convened another conference in Honolulu on 6 May to review the 'comprehensive plan' which had been evolving since the previous July; and to discuss a proposal to withdraw 1000 United States military personnel from Vietnam by the end of the year. This was based not on an assumption that 'victory' was in sight; merely a belief that the existing level of struggle could be dealt with by South Vietnamese forces once they had been trained to handle more sophisticated equipment. Both sides recognised that the conflict was likely to continue for a long time. It was now that Hanoi began to explore possible new dimensions of the struggle; among them that of 'world opinion', especially opinion in the United States, Western Europe and Japan, where opposition to deeper American involvement might eventually influence actual decision-making. The beginning of North Vietnamese efforts in that area, which would become increasingly important in the late 1960s, can already be discerned in the early months of 1963. The first target for North Vietnamese propaganda of this kind was American use of toxic chemicals, which was the subject of a protest by Hanoi to the Geneva Co-chairmen on 25 February 1963. That letter described in detail the spraying of crops (and the alleged poisoning of 198 people) in twenty villages of the province of Ben-Tre in the Mekong Delta. A month later, on 22 March, the Soviet Union proposed to Britain that the Co-chairmen demand a full investigation by the International Commission; to which London replied that the Commission would investigate the allegations as a matter of course if they were made through the correct channels, and that it was unnecessary for the Co-chairmen to express an opinion.[11]

'Operation Ranch Hand' had been expanding during the latter part of 1962 and was certainly affecting some lowland areas by now as well as the Central Highlands. But the Americans responsible for the programme insisted that the chemicals being used were not 'toxic' in any sense that would have made them illegal under international law; and that they were being used only against crops, not against human beings. In the meantime the subject had surfaced in the American press in a series of articles in the *Washington Star* (and other newspapers) early in February, on the basis of which Congressman Kastenmeier wrote to President Kennedy in mid-March; questions were also asked in the House of Commons in London. The South Vietnamese government sought to defend the crop-destruction programme at a Saigon press conference on 20 March; but the subject continued to be discussed in Washington during April. For their part the North Vietnamese continued to focus opinion on the issue by holding a mass rally in Hanoi on 7 April.[12]

One effect of all this was to draw Kennedy's own attention to the problem. As well as calling for a general review of the existing programme, the President consulted R. G. K. Thompson (head of the British Mission in Saigon) who on 4 April advised against relying on either defoliation or crop-destruction by chemical means. In other circumstances Hanoi's concentration on the issue, and the attention given to it by the media, might have had the beneficial result of forcing Washington to abandon a programme which in the long run was not in its own interests to pursue. But the structure of Vietnam decision-making was already too complex to allow the President to determine such questions without reference to the military bureaucracy and the vested interests involved. The only effect of the 'review' was that new guidelines were issued on 7 May 1963, which by defining more clearly the hierarchy of responsibility actually established a basis for the programme to expand.[13]

The issue of 'toxic chemicals' was one of several where it was possible for the Communist side (both Hanoi and its allies in the socialist camp) to influence Western opinion directly – by drawing public attention to what was (allegedly) happening on the ground and encouraging those Americans and Europeans who chose to protest. A much more complex question was that of the relationship between public opinion and the general American commitment to support the Diem regime. Ideally the Communist side may have hoped to find some way of influencing American opinion there too, in the hope that the commitment itself would be openly challenged in the press and in Congress; eventually even within the Administration. Whether Hanoi's friends were at any stage directly responsible for stimulating the internal American debate on that issue is impossible to say. But the Communist decision of early 1963 to adopt a strategy of 'protracted war' in South Vietnam was bound to place increasing strain on the United States commitment to South-East Asia. Of even greater consequence in that regard was the political crisis which developed in Saigon during the summer of 1963; which obliged the Kennedy Administration to question its commitment to the regime of Ngo Dinh Diem.

9 Vietnam: the 'Buddhist Crisis'

My general view is that the US is trying to bring this medieval country into the twentieth century, and that we have made considerable progress in economic and military ways; but to gain victory we must also bring them into the twentieth century politically, and that can only be done by either a thoroughgoing change in the behaviour of the present government or by another government. The Viet Cong problem is partly military, but it is also partly psychological and political.

Ambassador Henry Cabot Lodge to State Department,
30 October 1963

Owing to the different conditions existing in the cities and in the countryside, and especially owing to the fact that the enemy concentrated its efforts on controlling the medium-sized and large cities, the struggle in the cities was clearly different from that in the rural districts. . . . Here, instead of revealing the identity of red organisations we had to be adept at combining work done secretly with that done in the open, illegal activities with legal ones. The structure of the Party organisations had to be simplified; they had to keep strictly to themselves and be adept at concealing their identity; at the same time they had to carry on work among the masses by all possible open and legal means. They also had to make their way into various mass organisations such as the yellow trade unions, the student unions, educational organisations, art and literary organisations, industrialists' and businessmen's organisations, religious bodies, etc. and conceal their identity in these organisations, carry out united front work there, and win over the masses. . . . Such were the main points of the correct tactical line of which Comrade Liu Shaoqi is the exponent and which our Party followed in our work in the cities.

Li Weihan, in *Red Flag*,
February 1962

I

Until the middle of 1963 the conflict in Vietnam was far from being
a central concern of the Kennedy Administration, and it received
much less attention in the Western press than areas where more
dramatic events were taking place. The crisis, when it came, had
very little to do with the course of the Communist-led armed
struggle or the American-backed counterinsurgency campaign
against it. What changed during that summer, making South
Vietnam suddenly the focus of world attention, was the emergence
of an essentially political opposition movement in Saigon and
other cities led by militant Buddhist monks and their lay
supporters.

On 8 May, in the imperial city of Hue, demonstrations against a
decree forbidding the flying of Buddhist flags at the annual
commemoration of Buddha's Birthday ended in tragedy when
troops allegedly opened fire on the crowd and killed eight young
people (six of them girls).[1] Two days later Buddhist leaders at Hue
issued a statement setting forth five demands to the government in
Saigon; and by the end of the month the protests had spread to the
capital itself. As time went on it became clear that the Buddhist
issue had the power to galvanise a broad opposition movement
amongst the urban middle classes of South Vietnam, bringing to
the surface latent grievances in many other spheres of national life.
It also forced the Americans to consider how far they could
continue providing military assistance to a regime which no longer
commanded the respect of its own people.

The incident at Hue was not immediately identified as a major
crisis in Washington. Kennedy was much more worried that day
about civil rights demonstrations at Birmingham (Alabama)
which had erupted into violence on 7 May. The Vietnamese
Buddhists began to make a more dramatic impact on the world at
large only when Thich Quang-Duc committed ritual suicide by
fire in a Saigon street on 11 June. By which time the American
embassy, temporarily in the charge of deputy chief of mission
William Trueheart, had indicated its opposition to further repressive measures, and Diem had been pressured into appointing a
commission to negotiate with Buddhist leaders. The outcome was a
formal communiqué, signed by government and Buddhist representatives on 16 June, which went some way to meeting the 'five

demands' of 10 May. But it remained to be seen whether the situation would return to normal.

As an organised religion, consisting of a number of different Mahayana sects, Vietnamese Buddhism had developed strongly during the preceding two decades after its development had received a stimulus from the Japanese presence during the Second World War. The first attempt to create a unified national organisation had been made at a Buddhist congress in Hue in 1951 at which the principal speaker was a young monk called Thich Tri-Quang. After 1954 the Buddhist Association in North Vietnam had been drawn into membership of the Fatherland Front, and like the Catholic Church was allowed to function only under the watchful eye of the Party. In the South, by contrast, groups originating from various regions of Vietnam had been allowed to build their own temples and schools and a number of monks had been trained abroad. A Buddhist youth association originally founded in the 1940s claimed 70,000 members. The most impressive of the new temples (or 'pagodas') was the Xa-Loi in Saigon, whose new bell-tower had been completed in 1961. Internationally, the Vietnamese Buddhists had links with Japan and with reformed Buddhist groups amongst the overseas Chinese communities of South-East Asia, as well as with co-religionists in India, Burma and Sri Lanka.[2] However, it was not true that Vietnam had ever been a Buddhist country in the same sense as the Theravada kingdoms of Burma, Siam and Cambodia; or even to the same extent as Japan. In Vietnam, Buddhism, like Christianity, was a religion of organised sects within a society whose predominant tradition was that of ancestral and village cults, held together by Confucian respect for Heaven; and in the eyes of many Vietnamese intellectuals, Diem's principal fault during the long summer of 1963 was not that he himself was Catholic, or that he ill-treated the Buddhist sects, but that he had 'lost the mandate of Heaven'.

Down to 1962 there was little evidence of active persecution of Buddhists, despite Diem's Catholic devotion and Nhu's desire to make 'personalism' the state philosophy. Nevertheless, the ruling family was likely sooner or later to become worried by the growth of a religious movement over which it could exert little or no direct control. The circumstances of the Hue incident – which grew from a regulation banning the display of Buddhist flags – suggest that

Diem himself may have made up his mind to force a showdown before the Buddhists became too strong. On the other hand the skill and persistence of the Buddhist leaders between then and late August might be taken as evidence of a deliberate intention on their part to provoke and sustain a political crisis.

Diem and Nhu alleged that the Buddhist movement was being used by the Communists, and that the deaths at Hue had occurred because a 'Viet Cong' agent threw a grenade, not because government troops opened fire. The truth about what happened may never be known – even 'eyewitnesses' do not always see everything – but it is a matter of record that the official South Vietnamese version of the incident was rejected out of hand by the United States consulate in Hue and by the embassy in Saigon. American officials with some experience of the Vietnam conflict were by now well aware of Communist leadership of the struggle in the countryside and of the relationship between the NLFSVN and its masters in Hanoi. But in the absence of any hard evidence they were reluctant to see the emerging crisis in the towns and cities in similar terms. It was taken for granted that what was involved was an essentially non-Communist opposition movement in which religious persecution was truly the central issue; and that the United States was in danger of becoming identified with a hopelessly 'unpopular' Vietnamese leader and a policy of religious repression.

Nevertheless the historian is bound to consider the possibility that Diem was right. Infiltration of the Buddhist movement, by 'agents' of various sides, almost certainly took place: the government and the CIA were just as likely to have had their own low-level informants within the movement as were Hanoi, the southern Communists, and perhaps also the Chinese. But whether the Communist side was in a position to influence the actual direction of the movement or to promote anti-Diem demonstrations on its own initiative is a more difficult question. It is difficult to believe that the Party had failed to analyse the religious aspect of the 'contradictions' in South Vietnamese society, or that they were taken completely unawares by the Hue incident and its sequel. Nor would a decision to exploit Buddhist organisations and their grievances have been incompatible with revolutionary thinking in Hanoi – or Peking – at this juncture.

Western studies of the Chinese revolution, both in its own terms and as a model for South-East Asia, have tended to focus on its

'Maoist' characteristics almost to the exclusion of other aspects of China's revolutionary experience. A useful corrective to that impression is to be found in an article (published in *Hong Qi* in February 1962) by a leading Chinese specialist on united front work, Li Weihan.[3] Inevitably most of its attention was given to the 'Maoist' form of the united front whose aim was to mobilise the various classes among the rural population, in order to create both a political mass movement and revolutionary armed forces under the leadership of the Party. Predominantly rural in character, such a front could operate relatively freely in many areas until the expanding 'liberated zone' under its control eventually encircled the cities and main lines of communication. But even Mao did not expect the cities to fall like ripe fruit without any effort by the Party to infiltrate and win over the population. Towards the end of his article Li Weihan drew attention to the special conditions of the political struggle in the 'white areas', for which Liu Shaoqi had been responsible during the civil war of the 1940s. There a quite different kind of front work was required, which often involved concealing the identity and ambitions of the Party in order to exploit every opportunity for legal activity, and so mobilise the urban masses against the government.

Apart from the fact that Liu Shaoqi himself visited Hanoi in May 1963, there is one fairly precise indication that the Communist leadership in Hanoi was ready to pay attention to the urban struggle at this time. A speech by Truong Chinh, made in April but not actually published until the following autumn, analysed yet again the experiences of the August Revolution of 1945.[4] Whilst acknowledging the primary importance of the rural base of that revolution, it went on to insist that 'the cities also played a very important role'. There were many places, indeed, where the general uprising had begun in the cities and spread to the countryside, rather than the other way round. In 1945 the armed strength of the Viet-Minh had not been great enough for an 'encirclement' of Hanoi and Saigon: the revolutionary movement had depended fundamentally on united front work done in those two cities long before the August Revolution took place. Perhaps there would have been no revolution at all without the network in Hanoi which Truong Chinh himself had done much to build up during the Japanese occupation. Applied to the South in 1963, this theme amounted to a proposal for more attention to be given to urban activity there too: not separately from the rural movement, but as a necessary prelude to any further expansion of the armed struggle. But if we bear in mind Li Weihan's article on the united front in China, that did not necessarily mean that organisational responsibility for a new struggle in the cities would be given to the predominantly rural and by now semi-overt NLFSVN.

A small piece of evidence that Hanoi was actually expecting the Buddhist issue to arise in the South comes from a broadcast monitored almost one month before the demonstrations at Hue, reporting a meeting of the Unified Buddhist Association of (North) Vietnam on 10 April 1963, which had called on the Saigon administration to release four monks (recently imprisoned) and to end its persecution of Buddhism.[5] Beyond that, it is impossible to speculate; there is unlikely ever to be any 'proof' of Hanoi's (or Peking's) involvement in the unfolding crisis.

One thing is certain: whatever its origins, an urban revolt against Diem was precisely the catalyst the Communist side needed at this stage of the conflict to break the impasse in South Vietnam. Whilst the NLFSVN still had the resources to carry on a protracted struggle, even without massive external support, it lacked the ability to gain outright victory in the foreseeable future; time might even be on the side of the Americans and of Saigon. If the armed struggle remained at its existing level whilst the techniques of counterinsurgency were gradually improved, the rural population might eventually accept as inevitable Diem's imposition of strategic hamlets and a more rigorous police system. As it turned out, the Buddhist revolt made it difficult for the Americans to consolidate the small advantage they had gained since late 1961. By creating new 'contradictions', both between Diem and his American allies and within the non-Communist elite of South Vietnam, the revolt presented the United States with a kind of challenge it was not well equipped to meet, which might even lead them to reconsider their whole commitment on Vietnam.

II

The immediate consequence of the the first phase of the Buddhist revolt (from 8 May to late June 1963) was to shake the confidence of many American officials in the ability of Diem and his brothers to continue providing effective leadership for South Vietnam. The regime still had its defenders: apart from Ambassador Nolting, whose brief since 1961 had been to get along with Diem, they included the British official R. G. K. Thompson and others who believed that the growth of effective administration would be threatened by any major upheaval in Saigon, whatever its cause. But by the end of June there was a growing body of opinion in the State Department ready to argue that Diem no longer enjoyed sufficient popularity to lead a nation fighting an internal war for the 'hearts and minds' of the masses.

Doubts about Diem had been expressed much earlier, notably by Ambassador Durbrow in autumn 1960 – before the abortive coup of 11 November that year convinced the Eisenhower Administration it must continue to support him despite his imperfections. Durbrow had been recalled early in the Kennedy period, and for the next two years it was generally accepted that Diem was the only possible president. Criticism of him nevertheless began to resurface towards the end of 1962, particularly among educated Vietnamese whose dissatisfaction or open disagreements with the regime had forced them into exile. As time went on the Americans found themselves listening more and more to these aspiring politicians and would-be advisers, based in Paris or in the United States itself. An especially articulate example of such criticism was an essay published in Manila in November 1962 by a former Saigon journalist, Nguyen Thai.[6] In essence he made three charges against Diem and his family, each calculated to make an impact on Americans who thought of Vietnam in terms of the problem of 'nation-building': first, as a Confucian – despite his adherence to Catholicism – Diem had an ideology which was inadequate in a revolutionary situation; second, as a mandarin he was unable to cope with the problems of modern administration; and third, as a dictator he had come to rely on an ever smaller group of supporters (especially his own family) which cut him off from the rest of the South Vietnamese élite. Much of this was undeniable, and such thinking inevitably conditioned the American response to the Buddhist crisis.

The Kennedy Administration was now obliged to face up to a dilemma it had hitherto been willing to ignore: how far, in circumstances of 'subversion' and 'internal war', did an international commitment to the independence of an allied country amount also to a personal commitment to protect its rulers for the time being? In theory that question ought not to arise: in a 'free world', composed in principle of constitutional states, each country's choice of government remains its own internal affair – to be decided by the course of domestic politics, even if those politics turn out to be only nominally democratic. But in South Vietnam the Communist-sponsored revolutionary struggle was directed simultaneously against Diem and against the independence of the South under any government at all. The Americans had responded by supporting the existing regime precisely because its survival was threatened by Hanoi. But what was to happen if the same regime was called in question by a middle class urban movement which could not be dismissed as the creature of Hanoi, and whose grievances appeared to be wholly legitimate in terms of Western political thinking? Should American support be made dependent on criteria other than the mere fact of an external threat? At what point should Diem be judged by democratic political criteria – and found wanting? And if that point had now been reached, ought the Americans to allow their former protégé to be overthrown regardless of the international consequences?

The American attitude to Diem was inevitably conditioned by awareness of the United States' role in 1954–5, in first establishing him in power as leader of an independent South Vietnam. Where leaders like Sarit Thannarat in Thailand or Macapagal in the Philippines – not to mention Sihanouk in Cambodia or Sukarno in Indonesia – had to be treated with respect because they had emerged from an independent political process, there was a tendency even in Washington to regard Diem as a 'puppet' who could not have become president without American aid. This in turn produced an assumption that the United States was responsible for Diem's actions; and consequently the Buddhist crisis was interpreted – especially by the press – as a challenge to the American conscience. On the other hand it was not easy to translate the principle of 'leverage' into effective pressure of a kind that would force the regime to change its policies. Diem was well aware that – in addition to still having some American friends – even his enemies in Washington could not afford to abandon the assistance programmes on which the war effort depended. Probably no item of aid that Kennedy could safely threaten to curtail would be sufficient to force Diem into line. At the same time Diem's own political network within the country was still strong enough to make a military coup a highly complicated and uncertain operation.

III

During May and June 1963, apart from the civil rights issue at home, Kennedy was preoccupied with what seemed like larger international issues than the Buddhist crisis in Vietnam. Following Khrushchev's letters of 8 May and 8 June, which seemed at last to open the way to progress in the field of arms control, the President was determined to translate the ideals expressed in his American University speech of 10 June into a solid diplomatic achievement. The effort to win over doubters on his own side, as well as the anxiety of waiting to see how Khrushchev would finally respond, left him little time to think about events in Asia; and when he did so he probably still devoted more time to Laos than to Vietnam. Only following his return to Washington from a tour of four European countries, at the beginning of July, was he free to pay more careful attention to the problems of South-East Asia.

In certain respects that moment appears as a watershed in the history of United States global policy. Khrushchev's acceptance of a test-ban treaty in a form that the West could accept was followed by a sudden – albeit temporary – improvement in Soviet–American relations, which opened the way to new perceptions of the 'Soviet bloc'. Almost simultaneously it became evident, even to those who had hitherto refused to recognise a Sino-Soviet 'split', that relations between the United States and China would not necessarily follow the same path: that China must be treated as an independent entity, capable of generating a threat to the peace of Asia which it was beyond Moscow's power to control. At that point South-East Asia began to command Washington's attention to an even greater extent than during the Laos crisis of spring 1961, or during the key period of Vietnam decision-making later that year. The President was under pressure to make a stronger American commitment to the region; he was also conscious of the dangers of becoming more deeply involved in the politics of countries he did not fully understand. But he could not avoid the immediate crisis now looming in South Vietnam, about which he was briefed at a White House meeting on 4 July.[7]

Already by then, supposedly under pressure from the State Department rather than from his own choice, he had appointed Henry Cabot Lodge to succeed Ambassador Nolting in Saigon. This may have been taken as a signal that he intended to impose changes on the Diem regime; but it seems clear that he had not yet made up his mind what to do. In the meantime Nolting was allowed to return to South Vietnam for another month (11 July–15 August) and one last effort to make the old policies work.

The communiqué of 16 June had resolved nothing, except perhaps to allow the older generation of Buddhist dignitaries to withdraw from the fray and leave more radical members of the younger generation to take over. Demonstrations continued in Saigon and in the towns of Central Vietnam–the movement did not extend to the provinces of the Mekong Delta–and on 14 July the 'United Committee for the Protection of Buddhism' inaugurated a new and more intense phase of struggle. Whether or not Diem was correct in his belief that they were acting under Communist influence, the Buddhist leaders – notably Tri-Quang – possessed considerable political acumen and were well versed in the techniques of mass mobilisation. They also went out of their way to cultivate foreign journalists.

Among the more remarkable aspects of the crisis which developed during the summer of 1963 was the emergence of the news media as an integral factor in the situation. As Buddhist demonstrations made the Western public increasingly aware of Vietnam, there was a demand for news stories of the kind that could only be provided by correspondents on the spot; and an opportunity for the latter to make their reputations by energetic reporting of the events and local background. Although still quite small in numbers the Saigon press corps already included a number of younger reporters whose names would become associated in the public mind with penetrating and often critical analyses of American policy in Vietnam.[8] Their approach derived from a tradition of journalism whose first principle was to doubt the official line and then go beyond it to find out the 'truth'. In American history in the late 19th and 20th centuries there had been a good deal of truth which contradicted what the authorities were saying, and Pullitzer prizes were not won by men who believed everything they were told. Harkins, determined to present an 'optimistic' view of the situation, was naturally unwilling to share secret intelligence information with the press; with the result that Halberstam and others came to depend more on direct contact with field-level advisers for their impression of how the war was going. But what they obtained were localised impressions rather than a picture of the overall strategy. As newsmen, that was what they most needed: a story.

In their search for more accurate information and more penetrating analysis than the officials were providing, the press corps inevitably concentrated on the American side of the story. Their critical approach did not mean that they were in any sense 'pro-Communist', as some right-wing journals would inevitably suggest. But they had less reason, perhaps less opportunity, to devote the same critical attention to the Communist side. A reporter sent to Saigon was expected to report what was happening there—or out in the field—not to concern himself with events in Hanoi or Peking, or with the decision-making of the NLFSVN. Nor was he concerned with the possibility that the other side might be misleading world opinion even more outrageously than anyone in the United States government would have dared to do.

The result was a gradual deterioration in relations between the press corps and the United States embassy, which was already a problem even before the Buddhist crisis broke in June. The rift was already too wide to be healed by the visit of Assistant Secretary of State Manning in July, explicitly for that purpose, and was merely exacerbated by the arrival on the scene of a few 'establishment' reporters towards the end of August. Ambassador Lodge would prove more adroit than his predecessor in handling the press, and he succeeded to some extent in bridging the gulf. But by then a pattern had already emerged which was to shape relations between the United States government and the news media throughout the following decade. As the war progressed, it proved impossible to recreate the sense of confidence between the military authorities and accredited war correspondents which had been taken for granted in the Second World War and in Korea. Things would get worse when the television cameras arrived.

Among the reporters in Saigon, several were sufficiently sympathetic to the Buddhist cause to be given advance information about newsworthy events, with the result that Quang-Duc's self-immolation was pictured in newspapers and magazines throughout the world.[9] Equally embarrassing for the United States was the attention paid to Diem's persecution of Buddhists by internationally far more significant Buddhist organisations across Asia, from Colombo to Tokyo, which led in due course to appeals to the United Nations and later on the dispatch of a UN inspection team to Saigon.[10]

The Buddhists alone, however, did not have the power to destroy the regime, which still had an effective security force in addition to the regular armed forces. The ability to mobilise a larger number of followers and to stage various forms of protest, from hunger-strikes to ritual suicides (of which there were five more during August), was sufficient to embarrass Diem in the eyes of the world and to drive a wedge between the regime and the United States government. But the only political element strong enough to force an actual change of government in Saigon at this time was the army.

Ever since the abortive coup of November 1960 Diem had been conscious of that danger and had done his best to place his own men in key positions in order to prevent the emergence of a unified command structure over which he himself had no control. For their part the generals were conscious of the action taken by the Americans themselves in 1954 to avoid the creation of a military regime, notably Eisenhower's threat to cut off aid in the event of a coup. The generals and colonels involved in any new coup attempt would need some measure of assurance that if their action succeeded now it would meet with American approval. American attitudes had in fact changed somewhat since 1954. The Draper Report of August 1959 had included praise for the 'role of the military' in the Third World; and even civilian officials with experience of Asian and African countries were now willing to see military participation in government as potentially contributing to 'nation-building'.[11] Men like Hilsman were not opposed in principle to seizure of power by a military regime; such an outcome might in the end prove the only way of resolving the problems which Diem and Nhu seemed to be creating with each passing day.

No full account exists of the many different conspiracies which developed within the armed forces from about the end of June. Despite the remarkably full coverage of the American side of the crisis and the extent to which the documents of Washington's decision-making have been made public, there remain some very large gaps in our knowledge and understanding of South Vietnamese politics during these months. Few if any, even among the Vietnamese participants themselves, had full knowledge of everything that was happening or knew which actor was ultimately responsible for each move in a highly complicated situation. Diem's own security chief Tran Kim Tuyen was said to have been behind one plot. Another active conspirator, then or later, was the notorious Pham Ngoc Thao–later revealed as a supporter of the Communist side all along. Amongst the generals, an apparently quite separate plot was being hatched by Tran Van Don and Le Van Kim, with Duong Van Minh as their nominal chief; whilst the names of Nguyen Khanh and Tran Thien Khiem were also mentioned at a slightly later stage.[12]

Possibly the announcement of Lodge's appointment was taken as a signal of American support for a coup; if so, the temporary return of Nolting on 10 July seems to have had the opposite effect. The following day Ngo Dinh Nhu held a meeting of senior officers and indicated that he knew what was going on; which put an end to the first round of coup-plotting. Not least among the considerations of the various groups may have been the realisation that, even together, they did not have direct command of enough troops to mount an operation that would be certain to succeed. The presence in the capital of Nhu's own special forces, commanded by Colonel Le Quang Tung, meant that even the commander of III Corps (the military region around Saigon) did not have control of all units within reach of the presidential palace.

As a further demonstration of his intention to stand firm, Diem chose this moment to put on trial a number of military officers and civilian politicians arrested after the 1960 abortive coup, together with other civilians who had been signatories of the 'Caravelle Manifesto' of April that year. Thirteen officers were sentenced to terms of imprisonment on 8 July, and 34 civilians on the 13th. The latter included several men who would become prominent national figures in the period after the overthrow of Diem: notably Phan Huy Quat, Tran Van Huong and Tran Van Do. Whilst their trial may have served as a warning to other potential coup-plotters, it also contributed to the alienation of elements in the Saigon political community which had never been closely associated with the Buddhist sects. Another event which made a significant impact, reported on 8 July, was the suicide in prison of the celebrated nationalist writer Nhat Linh (Nguyen Tuong Tam).[13] The intellectual community was in no position to stage its own coup; but some of its members had American contacts and were able to reinforce the growing impression that the regime was completely out of touch with the non-Communist élite whose loyalty it most needed to attract.

Nolting's final departure from Saigon on 15 August 1963 marked the beginning of the most acute phase of the crisis. On the same day Reuters' in Singapore claimed to have a 'solid tip' that disturbances (and possibly a coup) in Saigon were expected very soon. By that stage the Buddhist movement was in full flood, with frequent demonstrations liable to get out of hand at any time and three more fire-suicides occurring between 13 and 16 August. By then too, coup-plotting had gone a stage further and it was not inconceivable that severe disorders arising from more Buddhist demonstrations would provide the army with the excuse it needed to isolate Diem in his palace and take over the city on the pretext of restoring order. On 18 August the senior generals approached Diem and asked him to impose martial law, which he did two days later. But then, in the early hours of 21 August, before the army had time to act, Nhu sent his special forces to occupy the main pagodas in Saigon, Hue and other places and arrested many of the leading dissidents. The suddenness of the move caught everyone by surprise. That it was not what the Americans expected is evident from the speed with which Ambassador Lodge – at that moment consulting Hilsman in Honolulu – flew immediately to Saigon, to arrive on the evening of the 22nd.[14] The following day student demonstrations led to more arrests and it became clear that Nhu (rather than Diem) was now in control of the situation. If there was still to be a coup, the generals and colonels needed much more explicit backing from the Americans; and on 23 August Tran Van Don made the first (documented) approach of the ARVN generals to a CIA officer. Lodge himself clearly favoured a coup: he would find it all but impossible to work with Diem and Nhu. On 24 August a State Department cable gave him the authorisation he needed, and for the next five days CIA officers in Saigon seem to have collaborated closely with the generals to work out a plan.

By 29 August Lodge was cabling to Rusk: 'We are launched on a course from which there is no respectable turning back, the overthrow of the Diem government.' The previous day the CIA station chief had cabled to McCone: 'Situation here has reached point of no return.'[15] Yet by the 31st – perhaps already on the 30th – the projected coup was abandoned. The documentary record in the *Pentagon Papers* implies that it was the generals who changed their minds, because they could not trust the Americans; but it also provides glimpses of the conflict going on within the United States government both in Saigon and Washington, which suggests that the underlying reason for the reversal of policy was an explicit American decision. General Harkins, who all along had insisted that an effort should be made to persuade Diem to dismiss

Nhu, was probably not in favour of a coup at all; nor were senior officials in the Pentagon.

A showdown within the American leadership seems to have occurred at a meeting in the State Department on the morning of 31 August, which apart from the absence of President Kennedy amounted to a meeting of the NSC. The record of that meeting is one of the few published documents to indicate the full bitterness of the conflict now raging in Washington. Those who advocated continuing efforts to remove Diem (represented on this occasion by Hilsman and another State Department official Kattenburg) were obliged to accept that the 'principals' (Rusk, McNamara, McCone, together with Vice-President Johnson) were firmly opposed to any further moves against the regime in the foreseeable future.[16] On the same day, as a pro-government demonstration paraded through Saigon, Nhu released a large majority of the ordinary monks and nuns arrested ten days earlier. A few days later the pro-government newspaper *Times of Vietnam* openly alleged that the CIA had tried – and failed – to overthrow the regime.[17]

What was the reason for this volte-face? The simplest – perhaps, in the end, the likeliest – explanation is that Diem and Nhu succeeded in outwitting the CIA to the extent that it was literally impossible for a coup to succeed. But, as always, events in Vietnam must also be seen in a broader context. Conceivably, the 'principals' had access to secret intelligence of a kind which forced them to revise some previous decision on Vietnam and to abandon the idea of a coup, regardless of what happened in Saigon. It may have been the changing international situation which led Washington to decide that a coup was too risky a venture at this time.

Both China and France took new initiatives in relation to Vietnam towards the end of August. The Chinese move, which must be seen in the light of a further deterioration in Sino-Soviet relations, amounted to a reaffirmation of support for the 'South Vietnamese people' in their struggle against Diem. On 29 August, Mao Zedong received a delegation representing the NLFSVN and issued a formal statement endorsing their cause. The following day a mass rally in their honour was attended by the leading Chinese general Zhu De; and the presence of a prominent Chinese Buddhist personality on the same occasion reinforced the impression that the Chinese regarded the Buddhist movement in Vietnam as an integral part of the anti-American struggle.[18] On the same day, President De Gaulle made the first of a long series of published statements indicating French support for the eventual neutralisation of South Vietnam.[19] The combination of these two developments may well have been enough to make the Americans think twice before risking a major upheaval in Saigon, at least for the time being.

Part III
1963-4

10 Intensification of the Struggle

Assuming no great increase in external support to the Viet Cong, changes and improvements which have occurred during the past year now indicate that the Viet Cong can be contained militarily and that further progress can be made in expanding the area of government control and in creating greater security in the countryside. However, we do not believe that it is possible at this time to project the future course of the war with any confidence. Decisive campaigns have yet to be fought, and no quick and easy end to the war is in sight. Despite South Vietnamese progress, the situation remains fragile.

US National Intelligence Estimate,
17 April 1963

US imperialism is by no means invincible; it is stronger than the other imperialisms, but it is by no means more powerful than the forces of world revolution, of the world's peoples. If the proletarian revolutionary forces, if the peoples of the world fight against it resolutely, they are fully capable of driving it back step by step and storming its positions one after another. . . .

If we had been afraid of US imperialism, if we had lacked confidence in our ability to wage victorious resistance against it, we would have called on the South Vietnam people to wait, and 'peacefully coexist' with the US–Diem clique; we would thus have committed an irremediable mistake. . . .

Nguyen Chi Thanh,
July 1963

In the final analysis it is their war. They are the ones who have to win it or lose it. We can help them, we can give them equipment, we can send our men out there as advisers; but they have to win it, the people of Vietnam.

President Kennedy, in television broadcast,
2 September 1963

I

For the first time, in late August and early September 1963, it is possible to document expressions of doubt about the whole Vietnam enterprise at the highest levels of decision-making in Washington. Kattenburg's warnings of impending disaster, at the meeting of 31 August, were overruled by Rusk; but at an NSC session on 6 September Robert Kennedy himself, who had been associated with counterinsurgency from the beginning, raised the question whether South Vietnam – with or without a change of government – was ultimately capable of resisting a Communist take-over. If not, the time had come to consider a complete withdrawal.[1] He was not in fact advocating such a course; but his remarks focused attention on the equally important and related question whether the degree of progress so far made in the counterinsurgency campaign justified the optimism of official reports. Two years after the Administration's approval of the Staley Plan, followed soon afterwards by General Taylor's programme of 'limited partnership', the Americans were now looking for results.

The question how much 'progress' was being made in the war was all too often couched in terms of the statistical measurement of trends rather than the analysis of conflicting strategies on the ground. There was no shortage of data upon which diverse forms of statistical method could be brought to bear, and abundant room for controversy about the resulting tables and graphs of 'trends'. Table 10.1 presents some of the more useful of these 'measures', in quarterly sequence, from the beginning of 1962 to September 1963. They demonstrate the effectiveness of increasing US intervention from mid-1962, but they also suggest that a year later the Communist side was beginning to recover lost ground, despite the strategic hamlets. Statistics alone, however, could not prove conclusively that the character of the war and the prospects for eventual government success had fundamentally changed as a result of the Buddhist crisis.

On another level a trenchant (and critical) analysis of the state of the war was being made during the first nine months of 1963, by a group of American officers with direct experience of the fighting as advisers working alongside Vietnamese commanders in the Mekong Delta: notably Colonel Daniel Porter and Lieutenant-Colonel John Paul Vann, who had both written critical reports

TABLE 10.1 *Statistical measures of progress in South Vietnam, 1962–3*

	(1) Strategic hamlets: total at end of quarter	(2) Communist activity:		(3) Weapons captured:	
		Larger attacks	Terrorist attacks	By Communists	By ARVN/US
1962					
Jan.–March:	–	68	2112	1777*	1202*
April–June:	2559	88	2652	1884†	1526†
Oct.–Dec.:	4080	31	1867	1172	1451
1963					
Jan.–March:	5332	35	1533	1192	1319
April–June:	6872	37	1948	1862	1265
July–Sept.:	8095‡	34	1880	2598	1086

* Relates to January–April (inclusive).
† Relates to May–August (inclusive).
‡ Figure for August 1963.

SOURCES (1) R. G. K. Thompson, *Defeating Communist Insurgency* (London, 1966) p. 138; gives monthly figures.
(2) Calculated from monthly figures in State Dept. Research Memorandum of 22 Oct. 1963: *The Pentagon Papers: the Defense Department History of United States Decision-making on Vietnam: Senator Gravel Edition (Boston, Mass.: Beacon Press, 1971)* vol. II, pp. 773ff; figures end at 18 Sept. 1963.
(3) For January–August 1962: *PP* (Gravel), vol. II, p. 773; from Oct. 1962: Thompson (1966) p. 40.

after completing their tours of duty in February and April 1963. Vann in particular, on his return to Washington, had tried to influence opinion in the Pentagon by alerting his fellow-officers to what he saw as the true state of affairs in Vietnam. He almost succeeded in briefing the JCS on 8 July, but was prevented from doing so at the last minute. Vann's criticism (as presented by David Halberstam, one of the leading Saigon journalists) had little to do with statistics: it derived from experience of actual combat operations. During the months after Vann left, Halberstam continued to make his own assessment of counter-guerrilla operations and by September had reached the firm conclusion that the war was rapidly being lost in the Delta.[2] Most of all he was

concerned at the failure of Vietnamese officers to fight engagements to a finish; at their reluctance to take casualties; and at
their inability to co-ordinate decisions, where an operation
involved more than one ARVN unit. These attitudes were due, at
least in part, to specific instructions to avoid heavy casualties;
Diem is known for certain to have given such advice to Colonel
Huynh Van Cao, commander of the 7th Division, on 6 October
1962.

A rather different perception of the rural conflict emerges from a
report (also dated September 1963) by R. G. K. Thompson on the
progress of the strategic hamlet programme. By this time he too
was somewhat critical of the counterinsurgency effort, but his
essential faith in pacification as a strategy remained as strong as
ever. Perhaps the most remarkable tribute to that strategy was
contained in an article by the leading Vietnamese Communist
Nguyen Chi Thanh, published in *Hoc-Tap* in July 1963. He
described the American decision to 'isolate the adversary' by
setting up strategic hamlets as a 'relatively clear-headed conclusion'; but he added that 'unfortunately for them, they are
beginning to be assailed by serious misgivings about the correctness of this plan'.[3]

In fact, the misgivings related mainly to Diem's application of
the strategy. Thompson himself was disturbed by the speed at
which Diem and Nhu were establishing strategic hamlets throughout the country; and by their failure to consolidate centres of
strength from which pacified areas could gradually expand
outwards.[4] Where Vann's anxieties derived from his impression of
individual operations, Thompson was concerned with the larger
picture. Strategic hamlets seemed to have become an end in
themselves, where they were originally supposed to be one element
of a long-range programme whose objective was to increase both
rural security and the effectiveness of government. But before
Thompson could reassert his influence the regime was overthrown;
and in the aftermath of the November coup, the whole pacification
programme collapsed. Only then did it become clear how
remarkably well things had in fact been going, at least down to the
middle of 1963.

To some extent the contrast between Vann's perception and
Thompson's was a continuation of the differences that had existed
between Thompson and McGarr in the autumn of 1961. Vann
(like McGarr) was concerned with counter-guerrilla warfare,

whereas Thompson sought greater co-ordination between military operations and the pacification of villages. Indeed it is not impossible that Diem's advice to Huynh Van Cao (which Vann deplored) had been given in response to suggestions by Thompson himself. In his view it was more important to develop secure areas, and gradually to eliminate Communist sources of manpower and supply than to pursue individual units of the PLAFSVN at a heavy cost in ARVN casualties. Where Thompson might be criticised perhaps was in failing to recognise the difference in size between South Vietnam (or even the Nam-Bo alone) and Peninsular Malaysia, where the emergency of 1948–60 had been fought to a successful conclusion. The difficulties of applying the Malayan model to the whole of rural South Vietnam, in the time available and with existing trained manpower, were greater than anything Thompson had experienced in the earlier campaign.

II

It is impossible for the historian to reach his own conclusions about the course of the war during 1963 without a detailed military analysis of each operation, and a study of each phase of pacification area by area. In general terms, however, the question whether ARVN and the Americans were in real danger of losing the war in the Delta in September 1963 can be answered by looking at the probable pattern of Communist strategy, and the extent to which the PLAFSVN was able to attain *its* goals. Until late August 1963 Communist strategy may have depended actively on the continuing crisis in Saigon and other cities. Bearing in mind Truong Chinh's observations in April about the interdependence of urban and rural struggle, there may even have been a deliberate plan to co-ordinate operations in the Delta with further political destabilisation in Saigon – to the point where a pro-American coup might be quickly followed by a neutralist one, leading to a coalition that included the NLFSVN. If so, the American decision against a coup in late August may have (unwittingly) defeated that option.

If the Communists were obliged in the end to concentrate on an eventual victory through armed struggle, they would need to develop their military capabilities beyond the level of mere guerrilla warfare and to adopt a more ambitious strategy in the

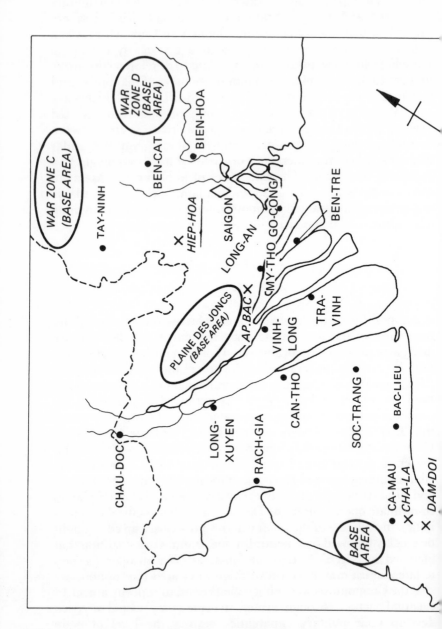

MAP 2   *The War in Nam-Bo, 1962–3*

South. Counterinsurgency and the strategic hamlet programme had had considerable success in some areas, especially in Central Vietnam; and the special forces camps were making it more difficult for the NLFSVN to operate among the montagnards of the Central Highlands. Only in the Mekong Delta was the PLAFSVN in a position to challenge ARVN and the pacification programme. It was there that some Americans felt the war was going badly. But a lasting military victory could not be won by the Communist side in the Mekong Delta alone: it would require a countrywide capability on the part of the PLAFSVN – which in turn meant greater reliance on external support of one sort or another. If that support was to come from North Vietnam, along the Ho Chi Minh Trail, the armed struggle would need to be reinvigorated and expanded in the Central Highlands and the upland areas further north.

At that stage of the war certain provinces would acquire special importance as points which the Communist side needed to control in order to link together its scattered base areas – or else as staging areas for absorbing more assistance from outside. Among the former may be mentioned the provinces of Hau-Nghia and Long-An, through which the PLAFSVN needed to pass in order to link base areas in the Delta with those north of Saigon. In the second category were the Ca-Mau peninsula, where the Communist forces might hope to land Chinese arms from the sea; and the Cambodian border area, which might eventually become the main point of entry for men and supplies coming down the Ho Chi Minh Trail. Later, when the war expanded, all those provinces became important areas of Communist activity – in the context of a long-term strategy far more ambitious than anything that can have been conceived before the autumn of 1963.

As an assessment of the actual military situation of spring and summer that year, therefore, the reports of Vann and Halberstam must in the end be regarded as unnecessarily alarmist. The more balanced assessments of General Krulak, and of Thompson in his own sphere, provided a better guide to the current realities of the war. On the other hand, a Communist decision to intensify the struggle would quickly transform the situation and might oblige the Americans to consider a further expansion of support for Diem. Such evidence as we have suggests that the Communist side made new moves in precisely that direction in early September 1963.

Mao Zedong's statement of 29 August, supporting Ho Chi

Minh's appeal of the previous day, was mainly addressed to the NLFSVN and may be interpreted as direct encouragement for them to embark on a new phase of struggle. On 3 September a plenum of the Front's Central Committee decided to launch their own appeal (broadcast on 16 September) calling for an intensification of the guerrilla struggle and of the campaign to destroy strategic hamlets.[5] The Americans were later convinced that in the first week of September, at a secret military conference held just across the Cambodian border opposite Darlac province, two North Vietnamese generals supervised the reorganisation of the PLAFSVN and inaugurated a new training programme. One of the generals was probably Tran Van Tra, a veteran of the revolution in Nam-Bo, who is known to have returned to the South sometime in 1963 and to have remained there until final victory was achieved in 1975.[6]

Several other things happened around 9–10 September, which may or may not have been co-ordinated by the Communist side. In Saigon, demonstrations by high-school students led to more arrests. In the Mekong Delta and further south, guerrilla attacks took place in Go-Cong province, at Soc-Trang airfield, and in the Ca-Mau peninsula. Also on 9 September, an unexplained incident occurred in Vientiane which the Pathet Lao insisted was a move by the rightists to tighten their control on the city, but which the government alleged had originated inside the Pathet Lao compound.[7] The timing of these events may have been related to Communist awareness of yet another 'debate' in Washington, where the Kennedy Administration was still in disarray.

III

All these developments must be seen against a background of continuing Sino-Soviet tension. Chinese bitterness about the test-ban treaty, expressed in public statements on 15 August and 1 September, was countered by Soviet criticism of China's attitude to the whole question of nuclear war. But that was only one dimension of a conflict which also included Soviet criticism of the 'people's communes' (in a _Pravda_ article of 24 August) and Chinese reactions to another visit by Khrushchev to Yugoslavia (20 August–3 September). On 6 September the first of a long series of

Chinese replies to the CPSU 'open letter' of 14 July 1963 traced the 'origins of the differences' between the two Parties back to the CPSU 20th Congress of 1956. (Other Chinese articles, later the same month, discussed the question of Stalin and the issue of Yugoslavia.) Relations were further soured by an incident at Naushki station, near the Sino-Soviet border, on 7–10 September.[8] Also about this time Khrushchev began to revive the idea of a new international conference of Communist Party representatives, which might end by rehabilitating Tito, reversing some of the tenets agreed in 1957 and 1960, and possibly even 'expelling' the CCP from the international Communist movement. By mid-October it would be obvious that Moscow could not command a consensus amongst other Parties for anything so extreme. In the meantime, nevertheless, it was important for the Chinese to try to win over other Asian Parties to their side of the dispute.

The North Vietnamese welcomed Chinese support for their anti-American struggle; but they were no more inclined than previously to join Peking in an open rebellion against Moscow. Their attitude to the test-ban treaty was cautious. A critical article in *Nhan-Dan* on 10 August had been seen as a firm indication that Hanoi would not add its signature to the treaty; and on 19 August Pham Van Dong sent a friendly (but not very precise) reply to the letter which Zhou Enlai addressed to heads of government throughout the world, urging an international conference to ban *all* nuclear weapons.[9] Whilst there is little evidence that the VNWP was shifting away from its long-standing principle of maintaining friendship with all members of the socialist camp, the marked increase of Chinese enthusiasm for the revolution in South Vietnam may at least have strengthened the hand of those Vietnamese who most valued friendship with China.

It is not easy to trace in detail the consequences of the Sino-Soviet debate for the struggle in South Vietnam: Chinese support may not have been the only factor in the decision of the NLFSVN, in early September, to step up its armed activities. But two conclusions may be tentatively drawn. First, it is clear that in the ongoing 'debate' in Hanoi, those who favoured an intensification of the struggle were becoming increasingly vocal during the summer and early autumn of 1963: the most striking example being Nguyen Chi Thanh's article in the July issue of *Hoc-Tap*, which seems to have been a reply to those North Vietnamese who doubted the possibility of ultimate victory against American military might.[10] Second, Chinese support for North Vietnam made it highly unlikely that the United States would succeed in negotiating its way out of Vietnam merely on the basis of *détente* with the Soviet Union.

Communist leaders in Vietnam probably also derived encouragement from events in maritime South-East Asia. The Chinese reaffirmed their support for the anti-imperialist cause there too, in late August and early September. On 28 August, the day before Mao's statement on Vietnam, the Indonesian Communist leader D. N. Aidit arrived in Peking after what appears to have been a somewhat frustrating month in the Soviet Union. As a senior Marxist–Leninist he was given a massive welcome at a Peking Rally, and also an opportunity to address the higher Party School of the CCP. His speeches on those two occasions (2 and 4 September) would later stand out as a major redefinition of Indonesian Communism, whose militant anti-imperialism was by this time close to – but not identical with – Chinese rather than Soviet theories of imperialism.[11]

Events were now moving rapidly in Indonesia itself. The British announced on 29 August that the Federation of Malaysia would be inaugurated on 16 September, come what may; which left Sukarno little choice but to adopt the hard line the PKI had been urging all along. When U Thant's ascertainment of opinion in the Borneo territories amounted to an endorsement of the Federation, Indonesia broke off relations with Kuala Lumpur and stepped up its 'confrontation'. The burning of the British embassy in Jakarta on 18 September was accompanied by direct action against British firms – until Sukarno stepped in to establish a form of control which stopped short of legal nationalisation. These actions put paid to the idea of an international stabilisation loan for the time being, and led the British to put pressure on Washington to end all military assistance to Indonesia; which, in turn, made it more difficult for Ambassador Jones to use American aid as a means of securing at least a measure of influence with Sukarno's regime.[12] Indonesia's decision not to sign the test-ban treaty, but to follow the Chinese line on the issue of nuclear weapons, was a further indication of this anti-Western trend.

Whether there was any attempt by the international Communist movement to co-ordinate the main anti-imperialist struggles in South-East Asia – in Indochina and in Indonesia and 'North Kalimantan' – is bound to remain a controversial question.

TABLE 10.2 *China and South-East Asia, August–September 1963*

Sino–Soviet background	China and other Asian parties	Vietnam and Laos	Indonesia and Malaysia
20 Aug.–3 Sept.: Visit of Khrushchev to Yugoslavia.		20 Aug.: Martial law in South Vietnam, after riots in Dan-ang and growing tension in Saigon.	
21 Aug.: Soviet reply to Chinese statement of 15 August on test-ban treaty.		21 Aug.: Ngo Dinh Nhu sent his own forces into Buddhist pagodas.	21 Aug.: Tengku A. Rahman agreed to delay inauguration of Malaysia.
		23 Aug.: University students demonstrated in Saigon; arrests.	23 Aug.: Indonesia willing to sign test-ban treaty.
24 Aug.: *Pravda* criticised Chinese communes.		24–9 Aug.: Cables indicate US encouragement of military coup in South Vietnam.	
	28 Aug.: D. N. Aidit arrived in Peking from Moscow.		28 Aug.: Indonesia changed its mind on test-ban treaty.
	29 Aug.: Mao Zedong's statement supporting people of South Vietnam	29 Aug.: De Gaulle's statement on peace and harmony in Vietnam.	29 Aug.: Britain and Malaya set 16 Sept. as date for inauguration of Malaysia.
	29–30 Aug.: NLFSVN delegation welcomed in Peking (Nguyen Thi Binn)	29 Aug.: DRVN protest to Geneva Co-chairmen on Buddhist issue.	

TABLE 10.2 *China and South-East Asia, August–September 1963*

Sino–Soviet background	China and other Asian parties	Vietnam and Laos	Indonesia and Malaysia
1 Sept.: Further Chinese statement denouncing test-ban treaty.		30–1 Aug.: Coup plot in South Vietnam collapsed. Nhu reasserted his own power.	
	2 Sept.: D. N. Aidit addressed CCP higher Party school.	3 Sept.: NLFSVN Central Cttee plenum (communiqué, 18 September).	
6 Sept.: *Renmin Ribao*: 'The Origin of Differences between the CPSU and ourselves.'	4 Sept.: Peking rally for Aidit.	First week of Sept.: PLAFSVN military conference, near border of Cambodia.	6 Sept.: Subandrio expressed doubts about UN Secretary-General's survey of opinion in Sarawak.
7–10 Sept.: Incident involving Chinese train at Naushki station, on Soviet border.		7–9 Sept.: School students demonstrated in Saigon; coincided with Krulak-Mendenhall visit.	
		9–10 Sept.: Guerrilla attacks in Go-Cong, Soc-Trang, Ca-Mau.	

11 Sept.: Sino-American Ambassadorial meeting, Warsaw.	11–16 Sept.: Aidit visited North Korea.	9 Sept.: Incident in Vientiane – Phoumists retained control there.	12 Sept.: UN Secretary-General completed survey of opinion in Borneo territories; Indonesia rejected it as superficial.
13 Sept.: *Renmin Ribao*: 'On the Question of Stalin.'	15 Sept.: Liu Shaoqi began a visit to North Korea (to 27 Sept.).		16 Sept.: Federation of Malaysia inaugurated; Indonesia refused recognition.
	16 Sept.: Aidit back in Peking; Lukman in Hanoi.	16 Sept.: NLFSVN appeal for intensification of struggle.	
17 Sept.: *Pravda* article indicated start of campaign for a new international Communist conference, to 'expel' China.		18 Sept.: Communiqué of NLFSVN plenum (3 September).	18 Sept.: Riots in Jakarta; British embassy burned. Action against British enterprises.
	21 Sept.: Zhou Enlai and Aidit flew to Guangzhou. Sept.: Zhou attended meeting of S.E. Asian Communist Parties in Guangzhou.	21 Sept.: Kennedy; instructions for McNamara–Taylor Mission to Saigon.	21 Sept.: Indonesia broke off trade relations with Malaysia; took control of British firms.

SOURCES   See notes to Chapters 9 and 10.

During the Sino-Vietnamese polemics of 1979, however, a long historical statement by Hanoi included one brief reference to a meeting at Guangzhou (Canton) in September 1963 – attended by representatives of the Communist Parties of China, Vietnam, Laos and Indonesia – at which Zhou Enlai talked about 'blazing the trail' to South-East Asia.[13] The Chinese themselves have not corroborated that reference. But information from broadcasts monitored at the time confirms that Aidit, having paid a visit to North Korea as well as to Peking, travelled to Guangzhou in the company of Zhou Enlai on 21 September. He left for home a week later, whilst Zhou himself reappeared in Peking on the 30th. Another senior member of the PKI, Lukman, was reported visiting Hanoi in mid-September; he too turned up in Peking at the end of the month.[14]

We do not know who represented the VNWP or the Lao People's Revolutionary Party at the Guangzhou meeting. Nor is there any reference to participation by Communists from Thailand or Malaysia. However, a later account of the history of the Thai Communist Party mentions that in August 1963 its Politburo 'adopted a resolution to start preparations for creating revolutionary bases in jungle areas'.[15] It seems highly probable that a meeting of some kind did take place in Guangzhou and that the Chinese were by this time seeking to devise a coherent regional strategy rather than merely to enunciate the ideological principle of opposing American imperialism.

IV

It is difficult to estimate American perceptions of Vietnamese Communist planning at this time. Nor is it certain that Kennedy yet appreciated that the crisis he was now facing in Asia was comparable with those he had had to deal with in Germany and the Caribbean in the two preceding years, although we know that in general terms he was aware of the Chinese 'threat' to South-East Asia. On 31 July 1963 a meeting of the NSC had discussed the possible implications of greater Chinese militancy in world affairs. But we have no access to the detailed record of American decision-making on China. Nor do we know whether anything of significance passed between the two countries at the 119th meeting of

Chinese and American ambassadors in Warsaw on 11 September.[16]

In relation to Vietnam Kennedy was acutely aware of the differing assessments of his advisers regarding the impact of the Buddhist crisis on the war, and he found it increasingly difficult to determine whether the public optimism of General Harkins and his staff was an accurate reflection of the situation on the ground. His dilemma was compounded by the tendency of those who wanted to replace Diem to offer as one of their arguments the 'fact' that the military situation was rapidly deteriorating; whereas those who believed Diem should continue in power were inclined towards an optimistic interpretation of the war. In an attempt to resolve that problem, the President sent General Krulak (currently in charge of counterinsurgency and special activities) and Joseph Mendenhall (of the State Department) to pay a flying visit to Saigon and to report back to the NSC on 10 September. But their respective assessments differed so much that Kennedy felt none the wiser.

A further NSC meeting a week later decided on a high-level visitation to South Vietnam by McNamara and Maxwell Taylor, who left Washington on 23 September and returned on 2 October. Their report, approved three days later, became the basis of NSAM-263, dated 11 October 1963.[17] There was no question of abandoning the commitment to Vietnam, even though it was not explicitly reaffirmed on this occasion. The principal concern of NSAM-263 was to demonstrate that the war was going well enough to permit continuation of the 'phased withdrawal' plan adopted earlier in the year. It held to the opinion originally put forward at Honlulu in July 1962 (and confirmed at the meeting there in May 1963) that the most important part of the military campaign against Communist forces in the field could be completed successfully by the end of 1965, perhaps earlier in some provinces. At the same time McNamara recommended stepping up the programme to train Vietnamese troops to take over all roles performed by American support units; and the NSAM reaffirmed the decision that 1000 of the now more than 16,500 United States military personnel in Vietnam would be withdrawn by the end of 1963.

Such a withdrawal, so long as it could be made without immediate repercussions on South Vietnamese morale, would mark the first step towards a return to the principle with which

Kennedy had begun and which he had reiterated on television as recently as 2 September: that this was a Vietnamese war which in the long run must be fought and won by the Vietnamese themselves. There was, of course, a possibility that the Saigon government might actually lose. But if most American advisers and support troops could be brought home before that happened, Kennedy would at least be free to accept it as a Vietnamese rather than an American defeat. Thoughts along those lines may explain why the President was so insistent, in early October, that an actual announcement be made about the 1000-man withdrawal. That move was strongly opposed by some of his advisers, on the grounds that any public reference to withdrawal at this stage might appear to weaken the American commitment; but the announcement was made.[18]

Behind that issue, however, there was a much larger one. In military terms the task of American support units in Vietnam was not *merely* to provide support for ARVN divisions but also to establish a framework within which it would be possible, should the need ever arise, to substitute United States for South Vietnamese combat troops on the battlefield. Perhaps Kennedy's moves at his point were governed by an unspoken determination to reverse a trend which might eventually lead to such deployments. But if so, he was bound to come into conflict with those who argued for expansion, not contraction, of the American commitment to South-East Asia.

It is impossible to tell whether McNamara and Taylor, as they inspected the situation in South Vietnam, had any knowledge of what was taking place in Guangzhou during that same last week of September. On questions of that kind the *Pentagon Papers* and other declassified documents relating to South-East Asia do not help us a great deal, since they include hardly any of the 'raw' intelligence data from which it might be possible to assess the ability of Kennedy and his senior advisers to follow Communist decision-making day by day. But there is little in the McNamara–Taylor report itself (2 October) to suggest that the Americans yet realised either the extent of Chinese determination to co-ordinate the revolutionary movements of South-East Asia; or the full significance of the Vietnamese decision to intensify their own armed struggle during the months ahead.

11 The Overthrow of Ngo Dinh Diem

I would suggest that we do not try to change horses too quickly. That we continue to take persuasive actions that will make the horses change their course and their methods of action. That we win the military effort as quickly as possible. . . . After all, rightly or wrongly we have backed Diem for eight long, hard years. To me it seems incongruous now to get him down, kick him around, and get rid of him. . . . Leaders of other under-developed countries will take a dim view of our assistance if they too were led to believe the same fate lies in store for them.

General Paul Harkins, in cable to General Taylor,
30 October 1963

The coup was a Vietnamese and a popular affair, which we could neither manage nor stop after it got started, and which we could only have influenced with great difficulty. But it is equally certain that the ground . . . was prepared by us and that the coup would not have happened as it did without our preparation. . . .

I believe the prospects for victory are much improved. . . . The prospects now are for a shorter war.

Ambassador Lodge, in cable to President Kennedy,
6 November 1963

The situation is very disturbing. Current trends, unless reversed in the next two to three months, will lead to neutralisation at best and more likely to a Communist controlled state . . . My appraisal may be overly pessimistic. Lodge, Harkins and Minh would probably agree with me on specific points but feel that January should see significant improvement. We should watch the situation very carefully, running scared, hoping for the best, but preparing for more forceful moves if the situation does not show early signs of improvement.

Secretary of Defense McNamara,
in Memorandum to the President, 21 December 1963

I

If anyone in Washington had time to notice, 22 October 1963 was the first anniversary of the broadcast in which President Kennedy had announced the presence of Soviet missiles in Cuba and had demanded their withdrawal. At that time it had taken only a week to force Moscow to back down; a month to force Castro to accept the Soviet–American *démarche*. One year later the Vietnam Crisis, approaching its first major climax, found essentially the same group of men (with different specialist advisers) sitting in Washington attempting to devise a solution to a very different and far more intractable problem. It was not merely a question of how to deal with a recalcitrant but economically dependent ally – a difficult enough issue in itself – but also a question of how deeply the United States should become militarily involved in South Vietnam. Kennedy himself was probably looking for the same middle path which he had taken in previous crises, using the minimum of force to obtain the maximum diplomatic and political advantage. But in the case of Vietnam, by contrast with Cuba, he lacked sufficient familiarity with the country and its politics; nor was he able to take for granted the ultimate superiority of United States conventional military strength in the actual area of the crisis. Some of his advisers might wish to prepare for greater future military involvement. But that was not the same as already possessing the capability required to handle an immediate crisis.

Events in Saigon during the last week of October 1963, leading to the overthrow and death of Ngo Dinh Diem and his brother Nhu on 1–2 November, have been described in detail numerous times.[1] Our main concern here must be with the decision-making that preceded the coup, and with its consequences for a rapidly changing situation. Some aspects of the story are by now very familiar; others may never be known at all. It has frequently been assumed that the removal of Diem followed from a deliberate decision in Washington, and certainly American power – as represented in Saigon by Ambassador Lodge – was a decisive factor when the crisis came to a head. But we should be careful not to overestimate the extent to which the political initiative lay, in all respects, with either the President or his ambassador. There is no documentary evidence which proves beyond all doubt that the coup plotting which resurfaced in Saigon at the beginning of October was inspired by a top-level American decision. The

TABLE 11.1   *The United States and South Vietnam, October–November 1963*

The war and the *NLFSVN*	The coup and its aftermath	United States decision-making
2 Oct.: McNamara–Taylor Report envisaged successful conclusion to war in central and northern areas of South Vietnam by end of 1964; in Mekong Delta by end of 1965.	2 Oct.: General Tran Van Don invited CIA officer Conein to meet him at Nha-Trang.	2 Oct.: McNamara–Taylor Report to President surveyed all aspects of policy; discussed possible coup, but recommended only exercise of pressure on Diem regime at this stage; no initiative for a coup.
	5 Oct.: Conein met with Duong Van Minh; discussed possibility of a coup.	5 Oct.: NSC accepted McNamara–Taylor recommendations. Some items of aid to South Vietnam were to be withheld.
		6 Oct.: Instructions to Lodge, cautious on question of a coup.
7 Oct.: Diem addressed National Assembly in Saigon; optimistic on progress of war.		7 Oct.: Lodge urged that US should not 'thwart' a coup if one materialised.
14 Oct.: US Mission subcommittee on province rehabilitation in Mekong Delta produced a pessimistic draft report, later accepted by Lodge and queried by Harkins.	mid-Oct.: Generals planning coup were given sufficient encouragement by Conein to continue with detailed plans.	17 Oct.: US Mission threatened to cut off funds for Le Quang Tung's special forces unless they left Saigon for Central Highlands.
19–20 Oct.: Series of four guerilla attacks in Mekong Delta suggested increased fire-power and effectiveness of PLAF-SVN.		

TABLE 11.1   *The United States and South Vietnam, October–November 1963*

The war and the NLFSVN	The coup and its aftermath	United States decision-making
22 Oct.: State Department (INR) Memorandum assessing statistical measures of progress in war; signs of deterioration.	22 Oct.: Remarks by Harkins to Tran Van Don, taken as discouraging coup originally planned for 26 October.	
23 Oct.: Lodge cable to Washington, also presenting pessimistic view of situation in field.	24 Oct.: Secret meetings of Tran Van Don and Conein indicated advanced state of plans for a coup before 2 November.	25 Oct.: White House anxious to avoid a coup which might fail; Lodge again urged 'no thwart' policy.
	26 Oct.: National Day, South Vietnam; last public appearance of Ngo Dinh Diem.	27 Oct.: Lodge and Diem had meeting at Dalat; no solution to deadlock.
	27 Oct.: Further Buddhist 'fire-suicide' in Saigon.	
	28 Oct.: Lodge, in brief conversation with Tran Van Don, assured him that Conein had full authority. Don again met Conein that evening.	
	29–30 Oct.: Coup planning in final stage, with Ton That Dinh in critical role. By this time, Nhu was planning his own counter-coup, which Dinh was able to foil. Special forces of Le Quang Tung were ordered to leave Saigon as part of Nhu's own plan.	29 Oct.: NSC met; decision to avoid direct US involvement in a coup, but to send a task force towards Vietnamese coast in case of emergencies.
30 Oct.: Following his return (on 29th) from a visit to Bangkok, Harkins criti-		30 Oct.: Cables indicated continuing disagreement between Lodge and Harkins

early Nov.: PLAFSVN forces took advantage of coup situation to make numerous attacks, destroy strategic hamlets, and extend control in Mekong Delta provinces.

1 Nov.: Coup took place. Key units occupied radio station, etc. in Saigon. Nguyen Huu Co secured control of 7th division at My-Tho, isolating IV Corps units loyal to Diem. At 4.30 p.m. the generals broadcast demand for Diem's resignation.

2 Nov.: Palace stormed and captured. Diem and Nhu killed, after surrendering at a church in Cholon.

5 Nov.: New government formed, with Nguyen Ngoc Tho as prime minister; Duong Van Minh became head of Revolutionary Council composed of generals and colonels.

7 Nov.: ARVN forces began series of new operations in areas of Cu-Chi and My-Tho, west and south of Saigon; not very successful.

8 Nov.: Date of NLFSVN statement setting forth 'six urgent demands'; broadcast, 16 Nov.

31 Oct.–1 Nov.: Admiral Felt paid a formal visit to Saigon; received by Diem. Lodge abandoned plan to visit Washington.

1 Nov.: Lodge avoided direct involvement; but in final telephone conversation (at 4.30 p.m.) he refused to help Diem.

3 Nov.: Lodge met with Tran Van Don and Le Van Kim; and with Duong Van Minh on the 4th; discussed new government.

7 Nov.: US recognition of new government.

McNamara–Taylor Report of 2 October explicitly opposed any immediate action to promote a coup, concentrating instead on the various forms of pressure which might bring Diem into line with American thinking. The most that report recommended was 'an intensive clandestine effort, under the ambassador's direction, to establish necessary contacts to allow the United States to continuously appraise coup prospects'.[2] That amounted to no more than contingency planning to create an option which Washington may or may not adopt at some later stage.

Moreover, the actual contact which occured in Saigon on the same day (but in fact, given the time zones, many hours before Kennedy first received the McNamara–Taylor recommendations) was allowed to appear and may truly have been an initiative on the part of General Tran Van Don. He and the CIA officer Lucien Conein 'accidentally' ran into one another at Saigon airport that morning, then met again at Don's house in Nha-Trang the same evening; three days later Conein was 'invited' to meet General Duong Van Minh in Saigon. Nor can it be firmly substantiated that the recall to Washington of the CIA station-chief (John Richardson), announced on 5 October, was intended as a 'signal' to the generals. Press reports at the time suggested it was due partly to a clash of authority between the station-chief and Ambassador Lodge, who wished to strengthen his control over the US mission in Saigon; and partly to a more general desire of the White House to limit the political role of the CIA in crisis situations.[3] Richardson was said to have been close to Ngo Dinh Nhu; but that had not prevented his whole-hearted participation in the coup-plotting of late August. His recall cannot be interpreted in itself as evidence that by this time Kennedy had already made up his mind about a coup.

One conclusion which is well-substantiated by the documentary record is that differences of opinion continued to plague United States decision-making throughout October. Lodge himself was inclined to favour a coup, having reservations only about whether it would succeed; whereas Harkins, as late as 30 October, was advising his own superiors at the Pentagon that it was neither necessary nor desirable. Lodge, moreover, wanted a coup which would succeed in removing Diem and Nhu once and for all – although he disapproved of their assassination – whereas some Americans may have preferred another abortive coup, like that of November 1960, which would clear the air and allow Diem to resume control under new conditions. Lodge and Harkins also disagreed about the progress of the war: in particular, the general challenged the pessimistic estimate contained in the ambassador's cable of 23 October.[4] Lodge was by then convinced that the war could not be won with Diem in power, whereas Harkins saw no military reasons for removing him. Another opponent of a coup at this time was CIA director John McCone, who told the President on 5 or 6 October that the US should adopt a 'hands off' policy towards internal Vietnamese politics. A suggestion that the United States might consider deliberately assassinating Diem as a possible solution was apparently abandoned at McCone's behest.[5]

Nevertheless the Vietnamese generals were given sufficient encouragement by Conein to go ahead with their plans, and Duong Van Minh eventually succeeded in drawing together at least two separate groups of officers into a single coherent scheme. A 'colonels' group, which included Pham Ngoc Thao and also the military intelligence chief Do Mau, is said to have had plans for its own coup on 24 October but was persuaded to wait. The 'generals' group included, apart from Minh and Don, Generals Le Van Kim, Mai Huu Xuan and Ton That Dinh. Since Dinh was in a position to order actual troop movements, his participation was central to the success of any coup. But he was also suspected by many of playing a double game, even of being ready to participate in a counter-coup devised by Ngo Dinh Nhu if the latter had looked like succeeding. In the end he joined in Tran Van Don's plot; and Don insists that he was throughout a loyal member of the group.

The most critical question of all was control over the 7th division, with its headquarters at My-Tho on the main route to the Delta, which until 31 October came under the command of IV Corps. The problem for the coup group was that the commander of IV Corps (Huynh Van Cao) was loyal to Diem and must at all costs be prevented from sending his own units to the capital to defeat the coup – as had happened in November 1960. In the event, Tran Van Don and Ton That Dinh succeeded in transferring command of the 7th division from IV to III Corps. They then used a subterfuge to circumvent the authority of the pro-Diem divisional commander and to give temporary operational control (on 1 November) to one of their own number, Nguyen Huu Co. Without that move, which may have determined the timing of the coup, the plan as a whole would have been in danger of collapse.[6] But it is by no means certain that the US embassy (even Lodge) realised its importance: the detailed planning of the coup was certainly done by the Vietnamese, and only they could have succeeded in lulling Diem and Nhu into a false sense of security whilst the necessary troop movements were under way.

A brief conversation between Tran Van Don and Lodge on 28 October seems to have amounted to the final go-ahead, and by the time Harkins returned from a short trip to Bangkok the following day it may already have been too late to prevent a coup; although, as we have seen, Harkins continued to argue against it on the 30th. What is not certain is that the President himself had already made up his mind and given any (presumably top secret) final instruction. Such limited evidence as we have suggests that he was still undecided. At a meeting of the NSC on the afternoon of 29 October (already the early hours of the 30th in Saigon), both he and Robert Kennedy are reported as taking the view that since pro-Diem forces were evenly balanced it would be folly to embark on a coup whose consequences for the rest of South-East Asia might be disastrous. A cable from McGeorge Bundy to Lodge following that meeting still urged the ambassador to discourage the generals, unless they could 'show a substantial possibility of quick success'.[7] The same meeting appears to have decided to send a naval task force to be ready off the coast of South Vietnam in case things went badly wrong: Kennedy's main anxiety at this late stage being fear that a coup would fail, rather than a positive desire to keep Diem in office. Nevertheless those present at the White House when news arrived that Diem and Nhu had been killed (in Cholon in the early hours of 2 November, Saigon time) say that Kennedy was deeply disturbed by it. His concern may not have been purely ethical: in his innermost calculations he may have needed Diem's survival for political reasons. Taken together, these various clues seem to point to the interpretation that the actual outcome of the coup was not precisely what Kennedy himself had planned. Afterwards, of course, he had no choice but to work with the results: on 7 November the United States formally recognised a new government in Saigon, with Duong Van Minh as head of a Revolutionary Council and Nguyen Ngoc Tho (formerly Diem's vice-president) as prime minister of a civilian cabinet.

II

There seems little doubt that, whether the United States actively instigated the coup or merely acquiesced in it, those who favoured

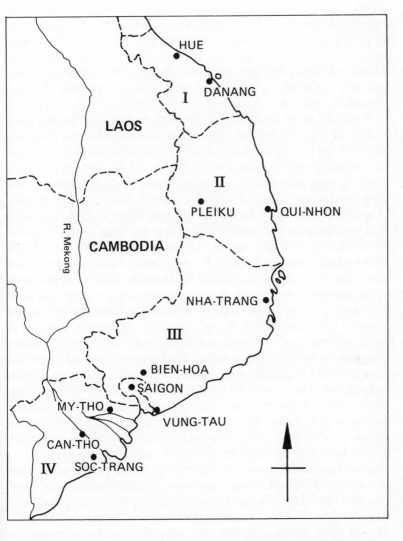

MAP 3 *South Vietnam, showing tactical zones of I, II, III and IV Corps, as reorganised in December 1962.*

action against Diem did so for essentially negative reasons rather than in order to place any particular general in power. In this respect the situation was very different from that of spring 1955, when Lansdale's purpose had been to defend Ngo Dinh Diem against his enemies. (It was different, too, from the circumstances of the CIA-sponsored coup in Iran in 1953, whose clearly defined objective was to put the Shah back in control.) The removal of Diem on 1 November 1963 opened a Pandora's box of political and military rivalries, which was very soon completely beyond American control.

Nor did Lodge, in advocating a coup, realise what an extensive upheaval it would involve. The opposition to Diem and Nhu was not directed merely at a few individuals: its aim was the destruction of a whole system – centred upon the Can–Lao – which had been built up over nine years and had exercised tight control over the government and armed forces of a state of twelve million people. The fall of Diem was followed not only by the release of many who had been imprisoned under that system but also by the removal from office of those who had been its loyal servants at various levels of the administration. By March 1964 it was officially reported that out of 41 province chiefs of South Vietnam as many as 35 had been replaced following the coup; indeed by that time some had been replaced twice. A similar change occurred at district level in many places.[8] Consequently by the middle of December the structure of local government was in chaos – and this in a country where programmes of counterinsurgency and civic action had depended above all on the effectiveness of grass-roots administration. Whilst subsequent American reports attempted to argue that the 'deterioration' of the military and security situation had already begun in July 1963, there can be little doubt that the principal factor in the deterioration (which certainly occurred by mid-December) was the coup itself and its political consequences.

The Communist side, moreover, was well-prepared to take advantage of this situation. Some American commentators suggested that the NLFSVN was actually taken by surprise by the coup, arguing that the Front made no public statement about it for more than a week afterwards; but they may have underestimated the subtlety of Communist strategy.[9] The coup itself offered no opportunity for the Front to seize power; nor even for serious efforts to create a coalition in which it might participate. The Party could at this stage do no more than observe the unfolding of new 'contradictions' within a 'ruling class' whose spirit was still anti-Communist; but whose personal ambitions and greed would lead inevitably to greater instability with the passage of time. The immediate task of the Front was to destroy the pacification programme in as many areas as possible, and to build up new strength in the countryside: not only in the Mekong Delta but also in the provinces north and north-west of Saigon, where base areas would eventually be required in order to link the Nam-Bo with other regions.

Having prepared the ground during the weeks since the military conference in early September, the PLAFSVN was ready to act – and would probably have staged a new offensive at this time in any case. The international conditions, as seen from Hanoi, were right for such a move in that Sino-Soviet rivalry had by this time passed beyond the point where either of the Communist powers could afford to allow the other to become Hanoi's exclusive ally. The Vietnamese took advantage of this to organise a meeting in Hanoi of the World Federation of Trade Unions' Committee for Solidarity with Vietnam, from 20 to 30 October, which as it turned out coincided with a further article in the series of Chinese replies to the CPSU 'open letter'. On 21 October *Renmin Ribao* returned to the theme of national liberation struggle, accusing the Soviet leaders of becoming 'apologists for neo-colonialism'. Khrushchev reacted, on 25 October, by again proposing an end to polemics and by signalling that the Russians had abandoned their idea of an international Communist conference.

In South Vietnam, as if to celebrate their ability to continue stepping up the armed struggle, the PLAFSVN made a series of four guerrilla attacks in various parts of the Mekong Delta on 19–20 October; and they seemed to the Americans to possess both greater firepower than before, and increased combat effectiveness. They were ready for a major offensive once Diem fell. During November, the number of guerrilla incidents rose to a record level, whilst an attempt by ARVN forces to return to the offensive in areas to the west and south of the capital, starting on 7 November, ended in failure. Moreover, participation in the coup by the ARVN 7th division (at My-Tho) created an obvious opportunity for Communist action in an area where the battle of Ap-Bac had been fought at the beginning of the year. This period of activity reached a climax on 23–24 November – the anniversary of the Nam-Ky rising of 1940 – with major guerrilla attacks on an

American special forces camp at Hiep-Hoa (between Saigon and the Cambodian border) and on a series of posts near Ca-Mau in the far south.[10] In many parts of the Mekong Delta the strategic hamlet programme broke down completely. In Saigon, the new government also faced economic difficulties, which stemmed only in part from the period of uneasy relations between Washington and Saigon during October. All these problems were discussed at a conference in Honolulu on 20 November, at which Lodge, Harkins and the Saigon country team met with Rusk, McNamara and Taylor. Whereas Lodge was still inclined to be optimistic about the prospects of the new government in Saigon, Harkins was beginning to recognise the dangers implicit in wholesale changes of personnel at the provincial and divisional level; he also noted the increase of guerrilla actions since the coup.

It was a measure of the new sense of urgency about the situation that the same meeting examined contingency plans – worked out earlier in the year by CINCPAC and approved by the JCS on 9 September – for systematic covert operations against targets north of the 17th parallel. One way in which the United States might choose to respond to any serious escalation of the conflict by Hanoi was to undertake action of its own against the North. It would appear, however, that few actual decisions were made at Honolulu – except to confirm that 300 of the 1000 men due to be withdrawn by the end of the year would actually leave on 3 December.[11] Instead of flying back to Saigon, Ambassador Lodge returned with Rusk and McNamara to Washington, where he intended to have further talks with President Kennedy on 24 November. As it turned out, his meeting on that day had to be with President Lyndon Johnson.

Whether President Kennedy would have found some means to recover control of the situation, had he not been assassinated on 22 November, is a question impossible to answer. We must postpone until the next chapter a discussion of the rumours that on the eve of his death he was looking for a 'way out' through diplomatic negotiations. What is certain is that the new president inherited a situation on the ground which was rapidly deteriorating, from the American point of view, not only in South Vietnam but also in Laos. Johnson himself was always at pains to emphasise the continuity between his own policy in Vietnam and that of his predecessor, claiming that his first NSAM on the subject (no. 273, dated 26 November 1963) did no more than reaffirm Kennedy's strategy. His critics would later argue that in reality NSAM-273 marked the beginning of the more 'hawkish' policy which led eventually to a larger war.[12]

As a statement intended to define the position of a new Administration, the document fulfilled a need which Kennedy himself would not have experienced at that moment; he had, after all, signed NSAM-263 only a few weeks before. Nor is it likely that Kennedy would have formally approved two of the points contained in the Johnson document: he would probably have been reluctant to make military victory for the South Vietnamese government the 'central objective' of United States policy in the area; and he may well have had doubts about authorising even contingency planning for military operations up to 50 kilometres inside Laos (under the control of MACV rather than that of the CIA, which had been responsible for all action in Laos hitherto). The latter decision implied an eventual willingness to extend overt military action across the frontier of a country whose neutrality had been guaranteed by international agreement. Kennedy, rightly or wrongly, regarded CIA operations amongst the Meo tribespeople as deniable – and in any case no worse than the degree of North Vietnamese involvement in support of the Pathet Lao. But to make certain areas of Laos an integral part of the South Vietnamese theatre of military operations involved a risk he would have preferred not to take.

That should not be taken to mean that Kennedy's approach to the problem was in any way naive. He was well aware that even a diplomatic solution depended on military and political effectiveness on the ground, and could not become an alternative to it. If he regarded the use of American combat troops as a 'last resort' measure, to be avoided if at all possible, he was not about to surrender South Vietnam immediately, nor to weaken the United States commitment to the region as a whole. The speech he was to have made in Dallas on the day he was shot makes that abundantly clear.

III

The period immediately following the death of Kennedy has been regarded, quite rightly, as one of the main turning points in the evolution of United States 'involvement' in Vietnam. One month after the Honolulu meeting of 20 November 1963, Secretary of Defense McNamara paid yet another visit to South Vietnam to reassess a situation which was again becoming critical. His report to President Johnson on 21 December stands in sharp contrast to the optimism of the memorandum which he and General Taylor had submitted to Kennedy on 2 October. There was no more talk of 'phased withdrawal', although McNamara did not recommend any new increase in American military personnel at this stage.[13]

The report focused attention on three aspects of the conflict. First, the political situation in Saigon was still very fragile and the performance of a new and inexperienced administration left much to be desired; nor did it help matters that there was still bickering among different personalities and groups within the American embassy. Second, the security situation had deteriorated alarmingly in certain key provinces of the Mekong Delta, where the Communist side was expanding the area under its own control. The Honolulu meeting had not reached any definite conclusions about the impact of Communist activity following the coup; but on 6 December Ambassador Lodge had forwarded to Washington a detailed report of the situation in Long-An province, where the US Operations Mission concluded that the strategic hamlet programme had broken down almost completely. McNamara's report confirmed this state of affairs and recommended immediate action to reverse the trend in the Delta provinces. Third, the report noted the continuing infiltration of men and supplies along the Ho Chi Minh Trail, and in that context discussed the need for new efforts in Laos and for covert action against North Vietnam.

Contingency planning for operations across the Laotian border and covert attacks north of the 17th parallel (by South Vietnamese troops) had been going on for some time, and further steps in that direction were authorised by NSAM-273. Johnson probably shared his predecessor's anxieties about the possible consequences of expanding the war. But as time went on he gave in to pressure from advisers who believed that operations of some kind against the North were unavoidable sooner or later – finding that course preferable to a decision to send ground combat troops to South-East Asia at the start of an election year. Thus a series of recommendations forwarded from Saigon in mid-December was passed to a special committee chaired by General Krulak, which in turn reported to the President on 2 January 1964.[14] After further refinement, the list of covert actions was given presidential approval two weeks later and the resulting OPLAN-34A was implemented from the beginning of February. Washington also approved U-2 flights over Laos as a preliminary to stepping up cross-border operations against the Ho Chi Minh Trail. McNamara admitted in his report of 21 December that whilst these actions were small enough to be concealed from the international news media, they were not sufficiently ambitious to make a significant impact on Hanoi. Nevertheless, in the jargon of 'escalation' theory, the implementation of these plans meant that a 'threshold' had been crossed. It remained to be seen whether the outcome would be of positive benefit to the strategy in the South which they were designed to assist.

There was no question, however, that American success depended most of all on the emergence of a new political order in Saigon following the overthrow of Diem. It soon became apparent that the coup had merely brought into temporary alliance a rather disparate group of officers incapable of working together once the target of their common hatred had disappeared. One group of senior generals did seem to be capable of acting in concert: Tran Van Don, Le Van Kim, Mai Huu Xuan, and perhaps also Duong Van Minh. But other generals and colonels, who may not have belonged to a single group in the first place, began to emerge as an opposing faction: notably Nguyen Khanh, Tran Thien Khiem and Do Mau. On 6 January a major reorganisation of military commands, together with a minor government reshuffle, increased the power of Don, Kim and Minh as a ruling triumvirate; whereupon the other group immediately began planning their own coup. They eventually secured American acquiescence by arguing that Don and Kim were close to the French and intended to co-operate in plans to neutralise South Vietnam.[15]

On 30 January 1964 Nguyen Khanh (at that time commander of I Corps in the northern provinces) seized control of Saigon and placed the three key generals under arrest. He decided to keep Duong Van Minh as titular head of state; but Don, Kim and Xuan were sent to the mountain resort of Dalat and held there under house arrest.[16] Ambassador Lodge does not appear to have had a hand in this second coup; nor do we find any reference to Conein or any other CIA officer. (It was the deposed group which had had close contacts with CIA.) The one American whom Khanh is said to have taken into his confidence was Colonel Wilson, the senior adviser to I Corps. In the new government announced on 8 February, Khanh himself became prime minister and there were three deputy premiers: a politician of the Dai-Viet party (Nguyen Ton Hoan, previously in exile in Paris); a Japanese-trained economist (Nguyen Xuan Oanh); and Colonel Do Mau. In addition Tran Thien Khiem became minister of defence; and Phan Huy Quat (another Dai-Viet leader from a different faction) foreign minister.[17] The Americans were confident that this would be a more effective government than the junta which had ruled since November. Only time would tell whether they were right.

12 Diplomatic Impasse

Present policy says that there is a war which can be won in South Vietnam alone. It says that the war can be won at a limited expenditure of American lives and resources somewhere commensurate with our national interests in South Vietnam. Both assumptions may be in error. There may be no war to be won in South Vietnam alone. There may only be a war which will in time involve US forces throughout Southeast Asia, and finally throughout China itself in search of victory....

... There may be a truce that could be won now in Vietnam alone, and eventually a peace throughout Southeast Asia at a price commensurate with American interests. That peace should mean in the end a Southeast Asia less dependent on our aid-resources and support, less under our control; not cut off from China but still not overwhelmed by China. If there is any opportunity of winning that kind of truce and peace, it would appear to involve initially the following actions:

a. It would involve an effort to strengthen the hold of the Saigon government on those parts of South Vietnam which it now controls....

b. It would involve an astute diplomatic offensive which would seek to enlist France, Britain, India and perhaps even Russia ... in a bonafide effort to bring about an end to the North–South Vietnamese conflict ... France is the key country.

c. It would involve US understanding, sympathy and sensible encouragement for the Cambodian desire to stand on its own feet without one-sided US aid. At this time Cambodia would appear to be the principal prototype of any eventual peace in Southeast Asia.... If Cambodia falls to its neighbors, or if it goes over to China, we may as well resign ourselves to an involvement of years in all of Southeast Asia, at great cost in resources and probably lives....

Memorandum from Senator Mansfield
to President Johnson,
7 December 1963

I

There are indications that before his death President Kennedy was beginning seriously to reassess the whole United States commitment to Vietnam. At least three people later recalled remarks in that vein: Senator Wayne Morse, White House aide Kenneth O'Donnell, and NSC staff member Michael Forrestal.[1] As a result speculation about his intentions has become an inevitable part of the story of American involvement in Indochina. Kennedy was aware of the political risks involved in any move to withdraw from South Vietnam without accomplishing the objectives he had set himself in 1961. What would amount to the first American retreat before a Communist challenge since the 'loss' of China might well produce a backlash comparable with Joseph McCarthy's 'witch-hunt' of 1950. Such a retreat could certainly not be contemplated before the election of 1964. Nevertheless, if withdrawal was to become a long-term presidential objective it was not too early to begin preparing the ground – and there are signs that Kennedy was already thinking along those lines in the autumn of 1963.

If nothing else, he was no longer inclined to emphasise the analogy between South Vietnam and West Berlin which had governed his policy two years earlier. During his visit to Germany he had impressed European opinion by his declaration: '*Ich bin ein Berliner!*' It is inconceivable that, had he lived to make a planned tour of Asia the following year, he would have addressed a Saigon audience with the slogan: '*Tôi là người Việt!*' But neither could he afford to regard Vietnam as a problem utterly apart from the rest of the world. Any long-term plan to withdraw from Vietnam under conditions short of military victory would require a strategy conceived in global, not merely bilateral, terms. The documentation on this question is inevitably thin. But fragments of evidence are available to sustain at least three hypotheses, each of which deserves to be taken seriously, even though it cannot yet be translated into a solid interpretation.

Hypothesis I

One line of speculation arises from an undated memorandum found in the Kennedy Library written sometime that autumn by one of the President's advisers, which suggested balancing an eventual American withdrawal from Vietnam against a Soviet military withdrawal from Cuba.[2] It is not known whether this memorandum had any influence on the President's own thinking. There is, however, independent evidence that the Administration was by now willing to consider *détente* with Cuba if certain basic conditions could be met. On 18 September 1963 an American official working at the United Nations, William Atwood, followed up indirect contacts with the Cuban delegation in New York by attempting to define those conditions in a State Department memorandum. They included the evacuation of all Soviet military personnel from Cuba; the adoption by Castro of a non-aligned foreign policy; and an end to Cuban revolutionary activities elsewhere in Latin America.[3] Further secret contacts at the United Nations eventually led Castro, on 31 October, to invite Atwood to pay a visit to Cuba sometime towards the end of the year. Meanwhile Castro used a television broadcast of 21 October to hint that he would welcome American assistance to repair damage inflicted by hurricane Flora. Three days later Kennedy himself had a meeting with a French journalist about to visit Cuba – perhaps looking for an additional channel of communication. Against this evidence, however, must be weighed other revelations many years later that (during this same month of October, and into November) the CIA was still actively conspiring to assassinate the Cuban leader. It is a measure of the ambiguity of American policy that Kennedy's last speech on the Cuban issue (18 November) has been interpreted by some to mean that he was ready for *rapprochement*, and by others as a secret signal to anti-Castro elements to go ahead with an assassination plot.

In the circumstances of late 1963, any attempt to change the political geography of the global balance of power in this way would inevitably have been opposed by the 'hawks', for whom South Vietnam was not merely another Third World country facing a revolution, comparable with Cuba, but a United States ally on the frontier of the Communist bloc. Kennedy would not have found it easy to persuade those in Washington who thought in such terms, despite his remarkable success during September in winning majority Congressional support for the test-ban treaty. Nor can we ignore the likelihood that Khrushchev would have experienced comparable difficulties on his side; whilst Castro was unlikely to accept without cavil the loss of the Soviet military umbrella established during 1962, merely in return for a resumption of 'normal' relations with the United States. Almost certainly

Castro had allies in Moscow, who would have opposed any idea of abandoning a military alliance with a country whose revolution had already been recognised as genuinely Marxist–Leninist and had reached the stage of 'building socialism'. It cannot have helped matters, either, that the main beneficiary of any American withdrawal from Vietnam would be China rather than the Soviet Union itself. The prospects for a settlement along the lines proposed in the anonymous memorandum were therefore very slender.

Hypothesis II

During the last months of the Diem regime it was frequently asserted that Ngo Dinh Nhu had established secret contacts with Hanoi and was willing in principle to negotiate a purely Vietnamese solution of the conflict, on the basis of a coalition which would have included both Diem's own entourage and the NLFSVN. After the coup Madame Nhu went so far as to accuse the Americans – but not President Kennedy himself – of bringing about the overthrow of the regime precisely in order to thwart such a negotiated solution. A Hilsman memorandum of 30 August 1963 also mentioned current rumours that Diem and Ho had made contact, suggesting – as one of several possibilities – that if this were true it would be a reason for going ahead with a coup at that time.[4] Attempts to bring about a Hanoi–Saigon solution on these lines were said to have been supported by the French ambassador in Saigon (Roger Lalouette), who was subsequently said to have been recalled to Paris because he had acted beyond his official instructions in taking the French consul from Hanoi to meet the South Vietnamese foreign minister.[5] In addition, an account by the Polish member of the International Commission at that time (Mieczyslav Maneli) indicates his own role in trying to persuade the French to act as mediators in this way. He suggests that by the summer of 1963 Ho Chi Minh and Pham Van Dong were willing to negotiate a compromise which would have allowed Diem to preside over a coalition, with firm guarantees of the independence and neutrality of South Vietnam. Maneli also argues that Hanoi's desire for a negotiated settlement was the reason why the Communists did not launch a major offensive to exploit the Buddhist crisis during July and August.[6]

Whether or not that was so, there is certainly evidence to justify the belief that contacts of some kind took place; and that they may have been the basis of De Gaulle's statement of 29 August. In all probability the initiative came from Hanoi – or perhaps from the Poles, which implies Soviet acquiescence – rather than from Saigon. What is less easily demonstrated is that the Communist side was sincerely willing to allow Diem to remain in power; or that any actual progress was made towards an agreement acceptable to Diem. At least equal weight must be given to the possibility that these moves were a ploy, designed to create yet another element of uncertainty in Saigon and perhaps to impress non-Communist opinion in the South.

On the American side there is no hard evidence that Kennedy himself was willing to entertain a solution negotiated independently by Diem and Nhu; but perhaps in the nature of things there could not be. There is every reason to believe that the 'hawks' in Washington would have responded to any firm knowledge of Saigon–Hanoi contacts by urging a coup. In any event, this hypothesis died with Diem. (A somewhat more Machiavellian interpretation would be that Hanoi deliberately allowed the Americans to believe secret contacts were being made, precisely in order to damage Washington's faith in Diem still further and so precipitate a coup. That would be to assume that Diem's removal was Hanoi's real objective.)

Hypothesis III

The idea of French participation in efforts to bring about a negotiated settlement need not itself depend on evidence of direct contact between Diem and Hanoi. Kennedy may ultimately have been willing to allow the French to resume the role in South Vietnam from which they had been deliberately excluded by Dulles in 1955. Franco-American relations had not yet deteriorated to a point which precluded such a *rapprochement*. It was true that De Gaulle had scuttled Kennedy's 'grand design' for Europe earlier in the year; also that the American president had failed to include Paris in his European tour in June and July; and that France had rejected any idea of signing the test-ban treaty. Nevertheless De Gaulle had accepted an invitation to visit Washington in February 1964, which if Kennedy had lived might have been an appropriate occasion for new diplomatic efforts towards a Vietnam settlement.

De Gaulle's remarks of 29 August 1963, as well as his conduct after Kennedy's death, demonstrated clearly his eagerness to become involved. Also relevant was his desire to improve France's relations with Peking – already apparent by the time of Edgar Faure's visit to China from 22 October to 5 November 1963 – which bore fruit in the announcement of formal diplomatic recognition on 27 January 1964.[7] A negotiated solution in Vietnam would certainly require Chinese approval, and Peking may have been ready to adopt a more conciliatory line if the outcome was to be a revival of French influence in Indochina following the departure of the Americans. The evidence we now have regarding Zhou Enlai's secret meeting with South-East Asian Communist representatives in Guangzhou in late September 1963 would seem to belie any impression that China was prepared to be conciliatory towards the United States. However, at the 119th ambassadorial meeting in Warsaw (on 11 September) followed by the 120th (on 14 November) there is reason to believe that one of the subjects discussed was the possibility of easing tension in the Far East.[8] Even so, it is unlikely that a 'solution' in Indochina could be found by negotiating with the Chinese alone. The stronger rhetoric of Chinese anti-imperialism did not alter the fact that North Vietnam still depended at least as much on Moscow as on Peking, and no new settlement was possible without Soviet participation.

Relations between Washington and Moscow had in fact begun to change for the worse by the middle of November. At a Kremlin reception for the October Revolution anniversary (7 November) the American ambassador asked the Soviet leader what had happened to the 'spirit of Moscow' of the previous summer. On the same day Khrushchev included in his speech a remark that Sino-Soviet *rapprochement* was inevitable sooner or later, and he was seen afterwards engaging in a conspicuously friendly conversation with the Chinese ambassador. At about the same time there were fresh incidents on the highway to West Berlin. A week later a small but ominous 'crisis' erupted over the disappearance in Moscow of an American academic, Professor Barghoorn, who was reported on 12 November to have been arrested on charges of spying. It took a direct protest by Kennedy himself to secure the professor's release three days later; and the affair cast a blight over Soviet attempts to celebrate the 30th anniversary of Soviet–American diplomatic relations on 15 November.[9]

Conceivably the Russians were attempting to influence Chinese policy just before the 120th Sino-American ambassadorial meeting, by retreating temporarily from their own *détente* with the West. If so, the Chinese response appears to have been ambiguous. On 19 November *Renmin Ribao* published another sharp attack on Khrushchev (its 'fifth comment' on the CPSU line). But it later became known that on the same day the Chinese delivered a note to the Soviet Union agreeing to talks on border issues between the two countries, even though they refused to allow publication of any announcement to that effect.[10] This slight lessening of Sino-Soviet tension did not, in the end, lead to a significant *rapprochement*: but it was a reflection of circumstances in which – at least in Asia – neither Moscow nor Peking could afford compromise with the West. As far as Vietnam was concerned, effective diplomacy leading to an American withdrawal depended on the achievement of some form of double *détente* with both major Communist powers simultaneously: an objective which probably lay beyond even Kennedy's reach in late 1963.

II

Nor were the prospects very bright for South-East Asian regional diplomacy at this time. In so far as South Vietnam represented a diplomatic rather than a purely military problem, it could not be divorced from the problems of Laos, of Cambodia, and of Indonesia's 'confrontation' of Malaysia. During the next year or so the various conflicts of the region would become even more closely intertwined, creating a far more complex situation than that envisaged by the 'domino theory' of the 1950s. Any United States decision to negotiate military withdrawal from South Vietnam depended to some extent on the solution of those other problems. Putting it another way, only when the remainder of the region was relatively stable would the 'domino theory' be shown to have no validity as a basis for policy towards Vietnam. Unfortunately regional stability in South-East Asia was to prove just as elusive as 'double *détente*' on a global scale

The question of Laos remained central to any long-term settlement in Indochina. Despite the impasse which appeared to have been reached there by mid-1963, hopes for new progress towards an agreement were revived during another international tour by Souvanna Phouma in late October and early November. In particular, Khrushchev's remarks during Souvanna's visit to Moscow led the Laotian leader to believe that the Russians would now support his efforts towards *rapprochement* with the Pathet Lao. At first that optimism seemed to be borne out by the willingness of the Pathet Lao to agree to a ceasefire between their own and Kong Lae's forces in the Plaine des Jarres on 16 November. But that failed to halt fighting on the ground for more than a couple of days; and another meeting between Kong Lae and the Communist general Singkapo could not prevent further attacks by both sides on 21 November.[11] More talks would be held in December and January, but the situation on the ground was far from encouraging.

Meanwhile a new crisis was looming for the Americans in their relations with Cambodia. In speeches of 12 and 15 November, Sihanouk announced his intention to nationalise certain economic enterprises and also to do without further economic and military aid from the United States. On 21 November he broke off all except diplomatic relations with Washington, obliging the Americans to begin withdrawing both their military (MAAG) and economic (USAID) mission from Cambodia. In another speech (on 19 November) the Prince called for the reconvening of the 1954 Geneva Conference on Indochina, to approve an international agreement guaranteeing Cambodia's neutrality within its existing borders. On 24 November he formalised that proposal in letters to the Geneva Co-chairmen.[12]

On the face of things, this might not appear to present any serious difficulty. Compared with Laos, Cambodia had no problems of national unity to worry about and its neutrality was an accepted international fact. The snag was that Sihanouk was also seeking the legal recognition of existing borders which were still disputed by both Thailand and South Vietnam. He was also demanding, in many of his speeches, an end to his neighbours' support for the right-wing Khmer Serei movement led by his rival Son Ngoc Thanh; and in particular the silencing of two radio stations believed to be broadcasting from Thai and Vietnamese territory. The Americans were faced with the dilemma that they must either reject the proposal for a conference on Cambodia, or persuade Bangkok and Saigon to come to terms with Cambodian demands. Failure to resolve this problem might lead Sihanouk to move closer to Peking, which continued to give full support to his

TABLE 12.1 *Indochina diplomacy, November 1963–February 1964*

France and China	Laos	Cambodia
1963		
	11 Nov.: Phoumist forces in Central Laos started offensive to recover ground lost in April.	12–15 Nov.: Sihanouk speeches on economic reforms, and desire to end American aid to Cambodia.
14 Nov.: 120th Sino–American ambassadorial meeting in Warsaw: discussion of tension in S.E. Asia.	16 Nov.: Kong Le and Singkapo agreed on Pathet Lao–Neutralist ceasefire in Plaine des Jarres, but it broke down by 19 November, and further meeting that day produced no agreement.	
19 Nov.: Chinese Note to USSR, agreeing to talks on border issues; also *Renmin Ribao* article on question of war and peace, attacking Khrushchev line.		19 Nov.: Sihanouk speech calling for an international conference to guarantee Cambodia's borders and neutrality. 21 Nov.: Cambodia and US exchanged formal notes on aid issue. 24 Nov.: Sihanouk, in notes to Britain and USSR, formally requested reconvening of Geneva Conference of 1954. 27–30 Nov.: M. Forrestal visited Phnom Penh; met Sihanouk on 30th.
25 Nov.: China and Cambodia signed civil aviation agreement.	29 Nov.: Souvanna Phouma proposed the neutralisation of Luang Prabang, in message to Souphanouvong.	

TABLE 12.1   *Indochina diplomacy, November 1963–February 1964*

France and China	Laos	Cambodia
early Dec.: Chinese technical missions in France.	3 Dec.: Further meeting of Kong Le and Singkapo: no progress.	11 Dec.: Soviet note to Britain, supporting Sihanouk's call for a new conference.
12 Dec.: Reports in Paris of French desire to improve cultural and economic relations with China.	12–13 Dec.: New clashes in Plaine des Jarres.	12–14 Dec.: Sihanouk recalled ambassadors from US and Britain.
13 Dec.: Zhou Enlai left for African and Mediterranean tour.	13 Dec.: Souphanouvong accepted Souvanna Phouma's proposal to neutralise Luang Prabang.	18 Dec.: Britain agreed in principle to a conference on Cambodia, stressing need for careful preparation.
mid-Dec.: Dean Rusk visited Paris.	20 Dec.: Representatives of Pathet Lao and Souvanna Phouma agreed on neutralisation of Luang Prabang.	22 Dec.: Flight from Cambodia of head of Bank of Phnom Penh.
1964		4–6 Jan.: Messmer visited Phnom Penh.
4–6 Jan.: French defence minister Messmer visited Cambodia; agreements on new aid.	5–6 Jan.: Clashes between neutralist and Pathet Lao forces north of Nhommarath.	
11 Jan.: Franco–Chinese contracts for construction of chemical plant in China.	16 Jan.: Souvanna Phouma protested to the International Commission about Pathet Lao attacks of 5–6 January.	

18–20 Jan.: S. Phouma in Sam Neua for talks with Souphanouvong; agreement in principle on eventually moving capital to Luang Prabang.

23 Jan.: New Pathet Lao offensive began.

31 Jan.: Souvanna Phouma protested to Geneva Co-chairmen about Pathet Lao attacks earlier in the month; unwilling to meet Souphanouvong again at this point.

18 Jan.: Soviet note to Britain, urging reconvening of 14-nation Geneva Conference to discuss Cambodia.

28 Jan.: Britain (in *aide-mémoire* to USSR) agreed in principle to a 14-nation conference on Cambodia; but was unwilling to fix a date at this stage.

4 Feb.: Incident on Cambodian–South Vietnamese border (at On-Dac).

7 Feb.: Sihanouk protested to Geneva Co-chairmen regarding On-Dac incident.

27 Jan.: Communiqué on France's formal recognition of Peking, and Franco-Chinese diplomatic relations.

30 Jan.: De Gaulle proposed neutralisation of Vietnam; idea rejected by Pres. Johnson on 1 February.

5 Feb.: Zhou Enlai returned to China.

11 Feb.: North Vietnam categorically rejected idea of neutralising its own territory.

policies. At the same time, if the Geneva Conference *were* reconvened to discuss Cambodia there was an additional danger (from the American point of view) that it might generate pressure for the immediate neutralisation of South Vietnam. The situation regarding both Laos and Cambodia was thus extremely delicate at the time of Kennedy's death.

A further indication of greater tension in mainland South-East Asia came from Burma, where a government communiqué on 15 November announced the abandonment of talks with the Burmese Communist Party.[13] These had begun in August, following an invitation by Ne Win in June, and are believed to have stemmed from Liu Shaoqi's visit to Burma in late April 1963. The talks were a logical move at a time when Peking was encouraging 'united front' tactics; their collapse might suggest a shift back to the line of armed struggle, at least in Burma. But there was no sign that Ne Win's government would seek outside help in order to contain any resumption of fighting by the Communist side. Burma, therefore, was not an American problem.

The situation in maritime South-East Asia was even less encouraging. On 6 November Sukarno had returned to the attack, with an order for the seizure of Malaysian-owned rubber mills in Sumatra and a speech alleging that his 'enemies' (by implication, the British and Americans) were trying to overthrow him. That same evening, the sudden death of First Minister Djuanda Kartawidjaja deprived Ambassador Jones of his most important potential ally within the Indonesian government. In the reconstituted cabinet, announced on 13 November, the new leading minister was the strongly anti-imperialist Subandrio.[14] Shortly afterwards, defence minister Nasution left for another visit to Washington and Moscow. Since the United States remained reluctant to provide weapons which might be used against the British troops supporting Malaysian forces in Sarawak, any new intensification of the fighting in Borneo would make it difficult for the Americans to continue the policy of using military and economic assistance to maintain good relations with at least some sections of the Indonesian armed forces. Kennedy probably still hoped to draw Sukarno away from the policy of 'confrontation'. As late as 19 November, when he received Ambassador Jones at the White

House, he was contemplating a personal visit to Indonesia sometime in 1964. But circumstances were far less favourable for an American mediating role than they had been at the time of the West Irian talks eighteen months before.[15]

At about this time, too, Thailand began to play a more active role in regional diplomacy. Foreign minister Thanat Khoman sought to use the occasion of a Colombo Plan ministerial meeting, which opened in Bangkok on 11 November, to bring the three 'Maphilindo' countries closer together. In that context he masterminded separate talks between the foreign ministers of Malaysia (Tun Razak) and the Philippines and of the Philippines and Indonesia (Lopez and Subandrio), and in each case secured promises of future co-operation. (Malaysia and the Philippines were still in dispute over the Sulu claim to Sabah.) But no progress was possible towards restoring direct contact between Malaysia and Indonesia, and the danger of open war between the two countries was now very great.[16]

What seems abundantly clear is that in the immediate situation of 20 November 1963, as his secretaries of state and defence conferred with the Saigon 'country team' in Honolulu, Kennedy could not possibly consider a complete withdrawal from South Vietnam in the next few months. His whole strategy in South-East Asia was under threat: its survival depended on the continuation – if necessary the reinforcement – of the combination of military, political, economic and diplomatic measures on which he had embarked in 1961–2. Those who have argued that in the end Kennedy would have been obliged to take many of the same decisions in Vietnam as his successor can at least point to the fact that what changed in November 1963 was not merely the occupant of the White House but also the complexity of the situation with which he had to deal. Given Kennedy's record of firmness in dealing with earlier crises, it is arguable that he might have been even tougher than Johnson in handling this new situation.

III

We have already seen that during his first month in office the new president found it necessary not only to reaffirm the United States commitment to Vietnam, but also to respond to a deteriorating situation in the Mekong Delta – and to take the first tentative steps towards direct action against North Vietnam. That did not mean that he immediately gave up all efforts to restore stability in other parts of the region, however. The period from late November 1963 to late February 1964 was one of intense diplomatic activity in South-East Asia which merits greater attention than it has usually received. Had more progress been made towards resolving the various conflicts at that time, it is possible that further escalation of the war in Vietnam might have been avoided.

Johnson's first task was to find some means to handle the problem of Cambodia without damaging relations with Thailand. To that end he sent Michael Forrestal (then on the staff of the NSC) to Phnom Penh and Bangkok at the end of November and the beginning of December.[17] He may still have been hoping to avoid a break in United States–Cambodian relations and to restore some of the aid programmes Sihanouk wished to cancel. Forrestal's approach to Cambodia was essentially similar to that of Ambassador Jones in Indonesia; and Sihanouk began to respond. But in Bangkok Forrestal soon became aware that the Thai government – as represented by Thanat Khoman and Pote Sarasin – was implacably opposed to any concession to Cambodia. Ambassador Graham Martin was inclined to take their side. It is not clear whether Sarit himself would have taken such a strong line at this point; but on 28 November he became seriously ill and his death on 8 December left Thanom Kittikachorn and Thanat Khoman in charge. As if to reinforce Thai independence, the King granted an audience on 3 December to Khrushchev's son-in-law, A. I. Adzhubei (editor of *Izvestiya*), who was then attending an Asian Editors' Conference in Bangkok.[18] By the end of the year Washington was forced to acknowledge that any compromise with Sihanouk or encouragement of his proposal for a new Geneva Conference would provoke an unacceptable deterioration in relations with Bangkok. A complete realignment of Thailand's international position was hardly likely; but strain of any kind in Thai–United States relations might prejudice SEATO contingency planning at some future date.

On 12 December Sihanouk embarrassed the Americans even more by announcing the withdrawal of his ambassador from Washington; two days later he made a similar move against Britain, whose attitude towards his conference proposal had so far been unsympathetic. In addition Sihanouk's policy of nationalising private banks caused alarm in at least one quarter: on 22 December the director of the privately owned Bank of Phnom Penh fled to Saigon, having diverted to his own use substantial funds which had originated as Chinese aid to Cambodia.[19] The incident may have sharpened even further Sihanouk's resentment against both the Americans and his immediate neighbours.

It would appear that a political shift was now taking place inside Cambodia, with the Prince relying increasingly on his director of the national bank Son Sann: a Japanese-trained economist with good contacts in Peking, who as recently as 1 October 1963 had been accorded a place of honour (alongside former Japanese prime minister Ishibashi) at the national day parade in Tiananmen Square. Sihanouk now made up his mind to seek closer relations with China, and also with France. Early in January the French defence minister, Pierre Messmer, an old Indochina hand, was warmly received in Phnom Penh and promised the Cambodians a number of items of military equipment, thus reviving an earlier military relationship between the two countries.[20]

To the extent that it implied a willingness on Sihanouk's part to maintain some kind of relations with the West, rather than becoming totally dependent on the Communist powers, the Americans welcomed the Messmer visit. They were less enthusiastic about rumours that France herself was planning to improve relations with Peking, perhaps even to the point of formal recognition. A visit to Paris by Dean Rusk in mid-December failed to dissuade De Gaulle from that course. Economic negotiations with the Chinese were already under way, and secret contacts at a higher level may have taken place between Chinese and French officials during Zhou Enlai's visit to North Africa in the second half of December. On 27 January 1964 it was finally announced that Paris and Peking were to establish diplomatic relations. French efforts to solve the problem of South Vietnam on the basis of neutralisation were thus based on a Peking–Phnom Penh–Paris triangle.

Any long-term solution of the Vietnam problem would sooner or later require direct contact between China and the United States. We know very little about whatever moves Johnson made to follow up the 120th ambassadorial meeting of 14 November. (Some contact there must have been, between then and the 125th meeting in November 1964; but the intervening sessions took place without publicity.) On 13 December 1963, in a carefully prepared speech in San Francisco, Assistant Secretary of State Hilsman denied that the United States had any aggressive intent towards Peking and spoke of 'keeping the door open to the possibility of change'. Although not immediately recognised as an olive branch, the speech allowed for the possibility of a responding signal – had Peking chosen to interpret it favourably. In the end the Chinese withheld comment for over two months: not until 19 February did *Renmin Ribao* deliver a sharp attack on Hilsman's position – thus effectively closing the door he had tried to keep open.[21]

In the meantime De Gaulle's attitude to Vietnam itself, even more than his policy towards China, caused increasing irritation in Washington. Where Kennedy may have seen French diplomacy as potentially contributing to an eventual solution of the Indochina conflict, Johnson came to resent it as an unwelcome intrusion into an area where the Americans had now assumed primary responsibility for defending the 'free world' against Communist ambitions. Both the President and Ambassador Lodge were particularly concerned about the effects of De Gaulle's public statements on political stability in Saigon; and we have already seen how that became a factor in the American attitude to Nguyen Khanh's coup at the end of January. On a personal level Johnson did not inherit his predecessor's admiration for the French leader, and an informal exchange between them at the Kennedy funeral in late November did not go well. By February the plan for a state visit by De Gaulle to Washington had been abandoned. Instead there was a return to the tense relations which had characterised the Dulles era, at least on the question of Vietnam.

The new crisis in United States–Cambodian relations, together with concern about French policy, somewhat overshadowed events in Laos at this period. During December fresh attempts to find a basis for compromise between Souvanna Phouma and the Pathet Lao led to a proposal to make Luang Prabang a neutral city, and perhaps eventually the seat of a reconstituted coalition. Agreement on neutralisation of the royal capital was reached on 20 December at a meeting between Phoumi Vongvichit and a representative of Souvanna Phouma. Despite further fighting early in the new year, Souvanna himself went up to Sam Neua for talks with Souphanouvong from 18 to 20 January, and a decision in principle was made about moving the government. This trend towards a new agreement was interrupted, however, by another Pathet Lao–North Vietnamese offensive towards the end of that

month, which occasioned a formal protest by Souvanna Phouma
to the Geneva Co-chairmen on 31 January.[22] But by then Laos
had been overtaken by Vietnam as the main focal-point of United
States policy in Indochina: from that point onwards any progress
towards a Laotian settlement would depend on events in Vietnam,
rather than the other way round.

IV

The early part of 1964 was also a period of intensive diplomacy
surrounding the conflicts in maritime South-East Asia. A significant 'escalation' of the fighting in Borneo occurred in late
December 1963, when Indonesian-trained guerrillas moved into
eastern Sabah and began an assault on the small but expanding
timber centre of Kalabakan. Had that move succeeded, the result
might have been to destabilise an area which made an important
contribution to the Malaysian economy. In the event British forces
were able to repulse the attack and by mid-January they had
forced the guerrillas to withdraw.[23] At that point the Americans
again intervened, sending Robert Kennedy to undertake a new
peace mission in the hope of achieving a ceasefire and a new round
of negotiations. At a meeting in Tokyo on 17 January 1964,
Sukarno accepted Kennedy's suggestion that if Kuala Lumpur
and Manila would agree to hold talks he himself would announce a
ceasefire in Borneo. Thereupon Kennedy paid short visits to the
Malaysian and Philippine capitals before meeting Sukarno again
in Jakarta on 22–3 January. The ceasefire was duly announced,
and Kennedy then went to Thailand to finalise arrangements for a
meeting in Bangkok of the foreign ministers of the 'Maphilindo'
countries and Thailand early in February.[24] Thanat Khoman
agreed to continue the role of 'honest broker' which he had taken
on in November, and there was a possibility that Thai forces might
be sent to monitor the ceasefire during the negotiations.

From about 20 January, however, this Bangkok-oriented pattern of regional diplomacy was complicated by the intervention of
Cambodia. On that day Sihanouk announced his own plan to
mediate between the 'Maphilindo' countries, with whose leaders
he still had good personal relations. Already in early January
Macapagal had offered to mediate between Cambodia and the
United States; and Sihanouk appeared willing to take up that

TABLE 12.2   *South-East Asian regional diplomacy, November 1963 – February 1964*

Thai diplomacy	Cambodian – Philippine diplomacy	United States diplomacy
1963 11 Nov.: Opening of Colombo Plan Meeting in Bangkok; attended by Tun Razak. 13–15 Nov.: Thanat Khoman attempted reconciliation between Malaysian and Philippines foreign ministers. 15–18 November: Thanat–Lopez–Subandrio talks in Bangkok led to statement on more co-operation. 19 Nov.: Subandrio, back in Jakarta, said no basis existed for negotiations about issue of Malaysia. 26 Nov.–3 Dec.: Editor of *Izvestiya*, A. I. Adzhubei, visited Bangkok for Asian Editors Conference. 28 Nov.: Prime Minister Sarit Thannarat became ill; taken to hospital. 6 Dec.: Thanat made strong attack on Sihanouk, and opposed idea of conference on Cambodia.	8–22 Nov.: Chinese general He Long in Indonesia, for GANEFO meeting. 19 Nov.: Sihanouk severed all except diplomatic relations with US: formal note delivered on 21 November. 21 Nov.: Chinese statement supporting Sihanouk's policy.	27–30 Nov.: M. Forrestal in Phnom Penh to discuss aid issue. 27 Nov.: Macapagal and Nasution met in Washington. early Dec.: Forrestal visited Bangkok; Thanat opposed any concessions to Sihanouk.

8 Dec.: Death of Sarit.

9 Dec.: Cambodian 'rejoicing' at death of Sarit.

12–14 Dec.: Sihanouk withdrew ambassadors from Washington and London.

13 Dec.: Hilsman's San Francisco speech on US attitude to China.

20–22 Dec.: Nasution visited Manila and Bangkok, on way home from USSR, US and Europe.

22 Dec.: Head of Bank of Phnom Penh fled to Saigon.

26 Dec.: Pote Sarasin warned US that relations would deteriorate if US pursued conciliatory policy towards Cambodia.

1964

early Jan.: Macapagal offered to mediate between Cambodia and USA.

7 Jan.: Thanat expressed concern at Messmer visit to Cambodia; possible French aid.

7–11 Jan.: Sukarno–Macapagal talks in Manila.

11 Jan.: Thanom Kittikachorn promoted to field marshal, establishing him as successor to Sarit.

11–14 Jan.: Sukarno in Cambodia: talks with Sihanouk.

15–18 Jan.: Sukarno in Tokyo.

17 Jan.: Philippines sent draft statement to Sihanouk, on normalising Cambodia–US relations.

17–18 Jan.: Robert Kennedy in Tokyo: talks with Sukarno, on Malaysia ceasefire.

19 Jan.: Sihanouk statement on US aid: some personnel still remain, may stay.

20 Jan.: Sihanouk offered to mediate in Malaysia's disputes with Indonesia, and Philippines.

20–1 Jan.: Robert Kennedy met Macapagal in Manila.

20–2 Jan.: Sihanouk in Kuala Lumpur.

21–2 Jan.: Robert Kennedy in Kuala Lumpur.

TABLE 12.2   *South-East Asian regional diplomacy, November 1963–February 1964*

Thai diplomacy	Cambodian–Philippine diplomacy	United States diplomacy
		22–3 Jan.: Robert Kennedy in Jakarta: persuaded Sukarno to proclaim ceasefire in Kalimantan (which lasted till 19 February)
		23–4 Jan.: Kennedy in Bangkok.
23–4 Jan.: Robert Kennedy in Bangkok, to discuss Thai role in an Indonesian–Malaysian ceasefire.	23–7 Jan.: Sihanouk in Manila: secured agreement on a meeting of Macapagal and Tengku A. Rahman in Combodia.	
		28 Jan.: Robert Kennedy back in Washington; reported to President Johnson.
	29–9 Jan.: Sihanouk in Jakarta: more talks with Sukarno.	
31 Jan.–1 Feb.: Thanat Khoman visited Jakarta to ensure Indonesian participation in:		
5–11 Feb.: Bangkok meeting of foreign ministers of Thailand, Malaysia, Philippines and Indonesia.	8–13 Feb.: Macapagal in Cambodia.	
	10–12 Feb.: Tenku A. Rahman there; Sihanouk arranged meeting at Angkor.	
mid-Feb.: Second Bangkok foreign ministers meeting postponed from 25 February to 3 March.		19 Feb.: *Renmin Ribao* renewed attacks on United States policy.
20 Feb.: Ceasefire in Kalimantan (Borneo) broke down; thereupon Malaysia insisted that there could be no discussion of other issues until it was restored. (3 March meeting in Bangkok failed to resolve this issue.)	22–9 Feb.: Macapagal in Indonesia; refused to support Sukarno in new phase of 'confrontation'; failed to bring about a reconciliation with Malaysia.	26 Feb.: Hilsman's resignation.

offer. Then, during the second week of January, Sukarno visited
Manila and Phnom Penh on his way to Tokyo. At that stage it was
possible to envisage a pattern of relations in which Cambodia,
Indonesia and the Philippines were all on good terms with one
another – and with Japan – without directing any antagonism
against Peking. Sihanouk's plan seems to have been to draw
Malaysia into the same fold; and on that basis to create a
framework within which the disputes over Borneo/North
Kalimantan might be contained if not actually resolved.

Between 20 and 29 January Sihanouk visited Kuala Lumpur,
Manila and Jakarta, in succession, and he appears to have made
some progress towards reconciliation.[25] The first step, as he saw it,
was to secure a *rapprochement* between Malaysia and the Philippines;
and to that end he announced in Manila that both Tengku Abdul
Rahman and Macapagal had accepted invitations to join in a
summit meeting in Cambodia early in February. If that worked,
Sukarno might come in later. There can be little doubt that in
taking this initiative Sihanouk was deliberately trying to outman-
oeuvre Thanat, whose antipathy towards the Cambodian ruler
was well known. Indeed, there was now some danger that the
projected meeting of foreign ministers in Bangkok might become
superfluous. It was probably in order to ensure continued
Indonesia participation in his own conference that Thanat himself
visited Jakarta on 31 January.

The net result of all these moves was that the Bangkok meeting
(involving Thanat Khoman, Tun Razak, Lopez and Subandrio)
did take place from 5 to 11 February; but was immediately
followed by a meeting of the Tengku and Macapagal (with
Sihanouk) at Angkor on 11–12 February.[26] But around the
middle of the month the momentum towards compromise – under
whatever auspices – seems to have been lost. Worse still, on 19–20
February the ceasefire in Sarawak broke down, with disastrous
consequences for further diplomacy. Macapagal visited Indonesia
from 22 to 28 February, only to find himself under pressure from
Sukarno to add his own support to the policy of 'confrontation';
whilst for their part the Malaysians insisted that no more talks on
general issues were possible until the ceasefire was reimposed. A
second Bangkok meeting of foreign ministers, after being postponed for ten days, did take place on 3 March; but it immediately
produced deadlock.[27] Perhaps by this time Sukarno was under so
much pressure from the PKI – and even from the armed forces –

that he found it impossible to agree to a new ceasefire without securing actual political concessions from Kuala Lumpur.

By late February, therefore, the various diplomatic initiatives which in November had seemed to offer at least the possibility of easing tension in South-East Asia had all run into difficulties. Contacts between Paris and Peking had failed to produce an opening for improved Sino-American relations, as a first step towards compromise in Indochina; and it had proved impossible to bring together the diverse strands of regional diplomacy. Meanwhile in Vietnam itself the PLAFSVN had embarked on a new guerrilla offensive in early February, with attacks as far afield as the Mekong Delta, the Central Highlands and the coastal area of Central Vietnam. Coinciding as it did with a new offensive in Laos at the end of January, this left the Americans with little choice but to make some kind of military response.

President Johnson would later be criticised for failing to negotiate a way out of Vietnam whilst there was (supposedly) still time; and also for assuming that a greater military commitment in Indochina was the only way to avoid a major defeat in the rest of South-East Asia. It is not necessary to espouse the 'domino theory' in its crudest form to recognise that both criticisms were based on an overoptimistic assessment of political realities. Johnson probably appreciated as clearly as his predecessor that the main interest of the United States lay in achieving stability in the maritime areas of South-East Asia, particularly Indonesia; and so long as there was still hope of restoring that stability by diplomatic means, he shared Kennedy's reluctance to become deeply involved on the Indochinese mainland. But until that stability was secured, he could not afford to abandon either South Vietnam or Laos to an uncertain future. Johnson's critics have still to demonstrate that there was any specific point in the sequence of events, between late November and late February, when the United States could have withdrawn from Vietnam on any terms save those of abject surrender to Hanoi. The consequences for the rest of South-East Asia of such a defeat must remain a matter for speculation; Johnson himself believed they would have been catastrophic.

13 Hanoi and Moscow: the 9th Plenum

The session holds that the final objective of the international Communist movement remains as always the overthrow of imperialism as a whole, the abolition of all regimes of oppression and exploitation in human society, and the building up of socialism and communism in every country of the world. To achieve this aim it is necessary to strengthen the cohesion and unity of the socialist camp and the international Communist movement....

Our Party draws a clear political distinction between the Tito revisionist clique, lackey of imperialism, and people within the international Communist movement who commit the error of revisionism or right-wing opportunism. Our attitude with regard to the Tito revisionist clique is to expose and oppose them consistently; and with regard to the mistaken people . . . to struggle for the sake of unity and to achieve greater unity through struggle.

> Communiqué of VNWP Central Committee's 9th Plenum,
> *Nhan-Dan*, 20th January 1964

The resolution [of the 9th Plenum] declared that 'We must be capable of restraining the enemy in the "special war" and of defeating them in that kind of war;' that we must 'fully understand that the motto of protracted conflict also means taking advantage of opportunities to win victory in a relatively short period of time,' and must 'flexibly combine political struggle with armed struggle, with both political and military struggle playing a basic, decisive role' – but with military struggle playing the direct decisive role in smashing the enemy's military forces . . . and enabling the revolution to win victory. In order to fulfil that requirement, 'the most important, decisive matter in all cases is to continue to strengthen our forces (especially our military forces) in all respects.'

> *The Anti-US Resistance War for National Salvation*
> (Hanoi, 1980)

I

In the evolution of Vietnamese Communist strategy the 9th Plenum of the VNWP Central Committee, which met sometime in December 1963, occupies a place at least as significant as that of Johnson's early decisions in the growth of United States involvement in the war. An official communiqué published on 20 January 1964 dealt mainly with the question of international Communist unity and confirmed the anti-revisionist line of the Party – without supporting the anti-Soviet polemics of the CCP.[1] A separate resolution calling for an intensification of the struggle in the South was kept secret. Its existence became known several years later, when a copy of it was captured by the Americans, but its authenticity was not confirmed by Hanoi until after the end of the war.[2] Taken together, the two resolutions make this Plenum one of the most consequential in Party history – even more important, perhaps, than the 15th Plenum (of the second Central Committee) which in effect had determined the resumption of armed struggle in the South in 1959.

Hardly anything was said about the South in the published communiqué of the 9th Plenum, apart from an injunction to 'extend active support to the patriotic struggle of our South Vietnamese compatriots'. Reference was also made to the need to strengthen political education in the Party, in order to eliminate 'rightist ideologies' and to inculcate a 'better comprehension of the Party's line on the Vietnamese revolution' – which fits in with subsequent reports of a political campaign (starting on 20 December 1963) to change the attitude of the people of the North towards the war in the South.[3] But we must rely on the captured text of the secret resolution – whose authenticity seems by now well established – for a full picture of the deliberations of the Plenum.

What we find is a blueprint for the intensification of both political and armed struggle, couched in terms sufficiently precise to dispel all remaining doubt about the extent to which the revolution in the South – and the line of the NLFSVN – was determined by the Party Centre at Hanoi. In defining 'immediate tasks' in the South, the resolution listed eight specific objectives and analysed the means for their implementation:[4]

(1) Actively participate in combat, to wear down and destroy one by one the elements of the enemy's forces (i.e. ARVN and its American advisers). In order to create favourable conditions

for the eventual 'general offensive and uprising' it was necessary first of all to 'disintegrate the lackey army' by making one attack after another as the opportunity arose.

(2) Destroy the enemy's strategic hamlets – an essential preliminary to mobilising the rural population.

(3) Develop the armed forces (i.e. the PLAFSVN). It was 'now one of our most important missions' to expand both their numbers and their fighting ability, under the leadership of the Party. (But there is nothing in this passage to justify the American belief that the 9th Plenum itself took the final decision to send whole units of North Vietnamese troops into the South.)

(4) Intensify the political struggle movement, consolidate political forces, and broaden the NLFSVN. This was a necessary preliminary to mobilising the people (in order to recruit more armed forces) and to developing the Front into something like a revolutionary administration for 'liberated areas'. It also covered attempts to win over elements in the population which might otherwise side with the Saigon government, through the formation of new political organisations to attract their support. Other tasks included proselytising among the religious movements to prevent them from being used against the NLFSVN; and planting agents in the Saigon government and armed forces who would then work for the Front.

(5) Intensify the task of troop proselytising (among ARVN troops), in order to persuade ordinary soldiers that their true interest lay in supporting the revolution against the Americans.

(6) Build up base areas and intensify economic and financial work; at present the base areas in the South were still small and weak. Particular mention was made of the need to develop activities in the mountain regions. Once developed, base areas must be self-reliant and capable of producing food as well as of fighting.

(7) Continue efforts to win international sympathy and support, both amongst other Third World countries and amongst the masses in the United States, Britain and France.

(8) Strengthen the leadership of the Party over the movement as a whole, and especially the role of the revolutionary youth associations. The most important task of the Party was to co-

ordinate the many different aspects of the expanding struggle within a single plan for the whole of South Vietnam. There was no suggestion here that 'the Party' meant anything but the one and undivided Vietnam Workers' Party.

One of the first results of the new policy decided by the plenum would appear to have been the Second Congress of the NLFSVN, held 'somewhere in South Vietnam' from 1 to 8 January 1964, whose new appeal to the people of the South was broadcast on the 15th. On 22 January the Vietnam News Agency (in Hanoi) put out a report of the speech made at that Congress by Tran Nam Trung as representative of the PLAFSVN.[5] He referred to the 'see-saw struggle' which had been going on since the spring of 1962; but the liberation forces had now gone onto the offensive, since mid-1963, and he predicted that the 'all-out, protracted resistance war' against the Americans would eventually win complete victory. The main import of the 9th Plenum resolution on the South was thus published in disguised form at the same time as the communiqué on international issues.

By early February the new strategy had begun to be reflected on the ground. In the Mekong Delta the defeat of ARVN operations in Ben-Tre province in the second half of January was followed by a one-day assault on the town of Ben-Tre on 6 February. There were also terrorist bomb attacks in Saigon on 9 and 16 February. By now, too, it must have been evident that a higher level of American activity in the Delta would sooner or later force the PLAFSVN in Nam-Bo to depend on support from other regions – perhaps ultimately from North Vietnam. The armed struggle as a whole would succeed only if Communist forces were also able to operate effectively in Central Vietnam, the Central Highlands and the provinces immediately to the north of Saigon. The most ominous aspect of the mini-offensive which developed in early February was that it included actions in all of those areas: an attack on the American advisers' compound at Kontum (2–3 February); attacks on a number of strategic hamlets in Tay-Ninh province (5–6 February); resistance to American-sponsored ARVN operations in the vicinity of Ben-Cat; and an attack at Ba-Long, in Quang-Tin province (9 February).[6] Another indication of the widening geographical scope of the war was the report in March that a significant number of strategic hamlets in the provinces of Binh-Dinh and Quang-Ngai (in southern Central Vietnam) had been destroyed or damaged in recent weeks.[7] During 1963 there

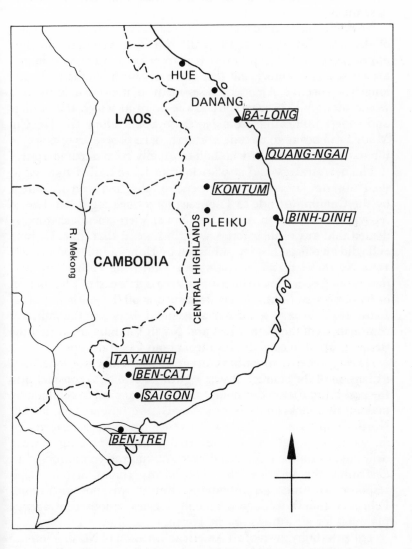

MAP 4 *South Vietnam, showing location of Communist attacks, February 1964*

had been relatively little activity in those areas; but in the anti-French war (before 1954) they had been an important Viet-Minh base area.

No single one of these incidents would have transformed the face of the war. But in the light of the 9th Plenum resolution they appear as the initial steps towards a larger and better co-ordinated armed struggle, embracing the whole of South Vietnam. In the longer perspective, American assessments of the course of the war would identify February 1964 as the point at which the soldiers and cadres infiltrating from North to South along the Ho Chi Minh Trail began to include northern-born people, as opposed to the natives of the South who had originally gone north in 1954.[8]

The new strategy had implications for Laos. Earlier fighting in the Plaine des Jarres, towards the end of 1963, had been attributed by the Communist side to Phoumist forces helping Kong Lae to recover ground lost in April. The North Vietnamese vehemently denied that any of their forces were in Laos at that time. Only in 1980 did an official history published by Hanoi admit that in early 1964 North Vietnamese 'volunteers' joined the Pathet Lao in a month-long operation to liberate an area north-east of Thakhek, in order to prevent rightist forces from cutting off the southern part of Laos. In February a formal agreement between the military commissions of the Pathet Lao and North Vietnam permitted the stepping up of joint activities throughout Central Laos.[9]

Having decided to embark upon such a deliberate long-term expansion of the conflict, it was logical for Hanoi to consider also the possibility that in due course the Americans might retaliate by making air attacks on the North. As early as 9 January 1964 an All-North People's Air Defence Conference discussed arrangements for setting up local organisations to dig shelters, hold air defence drills, and train the militia in simple anti-aircraft techniques.[10] In describing this meeting, the 1980 history claims that it was a response to American intentions. But it was not until mid-February that Washington actually began serious contingency planning for air attacks on the North.

The possibility even of an American invasion of North Vietnam was raised in a comprehensive analysis of the war contributed to the February issue of *Hoc-Tap* by General Nguyen Van Vinh.[11] It was seen as one of three options open to the United States at this point, albeit the most unlikely; the other two being immediate withdrawal, or the introduction into South Vietnam of substantial numbers of troops (perhaps tens of thousands) to carry on the war for a few more years. The latter course would still lead to an American defeat, because they would find it difficult to use conventional tactics in a guerrilla war and nuclear weapons would be completely irrelevant. If the Americans attempted to launch a general counteroffensive, they would have to throw all ARVN's strategic reserves into one main battle area, and would still not have enough troops to completely encircle and annihilate all the forces of the PLAFSVN. They would also face problems if they sought to revive and extend the strategic hamlet programme, since that would require them to disperse many of their troops to village posts which could then be attacked one by one. Yet if they failed to create more strategic hamlets, they would steadily lose control of the rural population. The article defined with remarkable clarity what was to become the main principle of Communist strategy over the next four or five years: to sustain a level of activity which, at each stage, would stretch South Vietnamese and American forces beyond the point where they could operate with equal effectiveness in all spheres and all geographical areas simultaneously.

II

In the pursuit of the armed struggle, therefore, we find a remarkable coherence in the sequence of Communist thought and action between mid-December 1963 and mid-February 1964. Then, however, the sequence appears to have been interrupted. The impression that the 9th Plenum marked the start of a *continuous* escalation of the war by the Communist side throughout 1964 is probably mistaken. Moreover the actual date of the captured text of the secret resolution (1 January 1965) seems to indicate a long interval between the 9th Plenum itself and the final confirmation of the resolution prior to its full implementation on the ground. At the very least, we may assume that further debate took place in Hanoi between mid-February and the end of 1964.

To understand the reasons for that hiatus in North Vietnamese decision-making, in so far as we can hope to understand it at all, we must look once again at the international Communist dimension – and the continuing saga of Sino-Soviet relations. Some American commentators interpreted the outcome of the 9th Plenum as a victory for a supposed 'pro-Peking' group over a 'pro-Moscow' group within the VNWP leadership.[12] Enough has been said in earlier chapters to demonstrate that such thinking derived from a misunderstanding both of the politics of North Vietnam and of the nature of the 'split' between the Soviet and Chinese Communist Parties. It is true that the tone of the communiqué published on 20 January was thoroughly 'anti-revisionist', as was that of an article in November's issue of *Hoc-Tap* which had criticised certain comrades in fraternal Parties who wanted to abandon the Moscow documents of 1957 and 1960, and to make 'dogmatism' (rather than 'revisionism') the main enemy of the international Communist movement.[13] The same themes emerged more fully in the published version of Le Duan's speech at the 9th Plenum itself, which appeared in *Hoc-Tap* in February 1964. It was noticeable too that on this occasion Le Duan acknowledged the importance of the Chinese revolution as a model for other Asian Communist Parties. But these Vietnamese documents all stopped short of an open attack of Khrushchev or the CPSU, confining their attention solely to Tito as the chief exponent of 'revisionism'. In that respect they stand in sharp contrast to the virulent anti-Soviet polemics of the Chinese fifth, sixth and seventh 'comments' on the CPSU line, published in *Renmin Ribao* on 19 November, 12 December and 4 February.

Even more striking was the fact that at one point the 9th Plenum communiqué referred specifically to 'the convening of the conference of representatives of Communist and Workers' Parties': a project which had been put forward by Moscow in the late summer of 1963 but which even Khrushchev had abandoned by November. There can be little doubt that the Vietnamese were no more willing now than formerly to join the CCP in an open revolt against the CPSU: their aim, as always, was to restore Sino-Soviet unity on the basis of a strongly anti-imperialist line. Ho Chi Minh seems to have left Le Duan, Truong Chinh and Hoang Van Hoan to argue about the precise formulation of the correct line; but that central principle must not be abandoned. Moreover, the fact that Le Duan (accompanied by Le Duc Tho and To Huu) led a delegation to both Peking and Moscow in late January and early February provides further evidence that Hanoi still wanted good relations with the CPSU as well as with the CCP.

Sino-Soviet relations themselves had entered a new phase around the end of November 1963, after the Chinese agreed to start border talks. On 29 November the CPSU delivered a new letter to the CCP, urging both an end to the ideological confrontation and also the resumption of economic co-operation – in accordance with an agreement signed in May 1962 but still not implemented.[14] The Chinese rejected the latter proposal, having already decided to pursue the goal of an independent modern economy on the basis of improved relations with Japan and Western Europe, especially France. But on the question of ideology there were signs of a continuing division of opinion within the CCP, with some key figures willing at least to enter into a new ideological dialogue with Moscow.

Although the debate within the CCP was not carried on openly, there are a number of indications that it was going on: the most important being a conference on social sciences convened by the Academy of Sciences in Peking in late October and November. Only one of the reports to that conference was widely disseminated: a long analysis of the history of revisionism by the theoretician Zhou Yang, which was delivered on 26 October, and finally published two months later. However, an unofficial version of Liu Shaoqu's speech to that conference (circulated some years later when Liu was under attack) implies a rather more orthodox attitude than that usually associated with 'Maoism'. For example, he placed greater emphasis on unity with other Communist Parties in Asia than on the unity of all anti-imperialist forces throughout the Third World.[15] Possibly his ideas also influenced the 'sixth comment' on the Soviet line, published by *Renmin Ribao* on 12 December, which was still sharply critical of peaceful coexistence but nevertheless ended with a suggestion that it was 'not yet too late for the CPSU leaders to rein in at the brink'.

The fact that Liu's speech remained unpublished is itself evidence of continuing disagreement. But so did certain other key documents of this period; notably Mao's instruction of 12 December on the role of art in the revolution, which would later be recognised as one of the starting-points of the 'cultural revolution'.[16] Mao's determination to establish a distinctively Chinese revolutionary ideology also found reflection in a PLA conference on political work, held sometime towards the end of the year, which set the tone for a campaign to 'learn from the PLA' during the first half of 1964. Another area of debate concerned the socialist education movement in the countryside, which Mao had inaugurated in May 1963 and which had been outlined in a ten-point Central Committee circular in September; but whose final character had still to be precisely defined. There, too, it is possible to see a growing conflict between Liu Shaoqi and some other leaders.[17]

On the Soviet side, the letter of 29 November to the CCP coincided with the publication in the press of a series of articles commemorating the anniversary of the birth of the economist N. A. Vosnesensky, whose ideas had been out of fashion since his purge from the top leadership by Stalin in 1949. Among current Soviet leaders, the man most closely associated with the purge of Vosnesensky – as well as with the denunciation of Tito in 1948 – was M. A. Suslov; but Suslov disappeared completely from public view between mid-September and early January 1964.[18] His temporary absence may have reflected a continuing Soviet debate on ideology in which he may have been losing ground. Identified with a form of international unity based on strict ideological discipline, Suslov was by this time as strongly opposed to 'Maoism' as he had previously been to Tito's 'revisionism'. His attitude to other issues of Soviet policy is not known; but it should be noted in passing that during the period of his 'eclipse', a plenum of the CPSU Central Committee held from 9 to 12 December 1963 approved a number of decisions in line with Khrushchev's ideas about the relative investment priority of agriculture, the chemical industry and the defence industries. The state of ideological flux in the Soviet and Chinese Parties must have presented serious problems for the Vietnamese; which may explain why their own communiqué was not published until 20 January 1964. By then it would appear that a new consensus had begun to emerge in Moscow, embracing both Suslov's emphasis on international discipline and Khrushchev's pursuit of *détente* with the West.

Khrushchev's interest in easing tension with the United States was reflected in the attitude taken by the Soviet leadership during a visit to Moscow by Fidel Castro between 13 and 22 January. The joint statement issued at the end of that visit implied that Cuba was now willing to moderate its line on supporting revolution in Latin America, in return for another substantial increase of Soviet aid.[19] (The Chinese, at this point, seem to have attempted to influence Castro in the opposite direction by emphasising their own support for the struggle in Latin America: on 12 January Mao issued a public statement designed to fan the flames of anti-American unrest in Panama, where riots were then taking place; and about the same time the Chinese media reprinted an article by Che Guevara on guerilla warfare which had appeared in *Cuba Socialista* the previous September. But Castro was unmoved, and accepted the Soviet line.) Another small indication of progress towards *détente* occurred at the Geneva disarmament talks which resumed on 21 January: both the American and the Soviet delegates put forward constructive proposals which might eventually lead to a treaty preventing the 'proliferation' of nuclear weapons.

The new Soviet consensus did not, however, call for the same policy of restraint imposed on Cuba to be applied to the revolution in Indochina; nor did it preclude continuing friendship between Moscow and Hanoi. Le Duan's form of anti-revisionism was not in itself anti-Soviet: so long as it was directed only against Tito, it was probably in accord with Suslov's own unexpressed thoughts.[20] Nor did *détente* between Moscow and Washington in the sphere of arms control necessitate any immediate change of strategy in South Vietnam. On the other hand the Russians probably still wanted to maintain the image Khrushchev had succeeded in creating in the West: of themselves as the voice of 'moderation' in the Communist world and of the Chinese as the more 'extreme' wing of the international Communist movement. Out of this impression grew the logical assumption – among at least some American specialists on Communist affairs – that North Vietnam's anti-imperialism and anti-revisionism amounted to a 'pro-Chinese' stand; and conversely that whereas the Chinese were probably encouraging Hanoi to step up the war, the Russians were more likely to exercise a restraining influence – to the extent that they had any influence in Hanoi at all. Subsequent developments, especially the revelations of 1979–80, suggest that that was not necessarily the case.

The Chinese were in fact remarkably restrained in their pronouncements on Vietnam during the early part of 1964. If one may take the pages of the English-language *Peking Review* as a guide to issues on which a consensus existed among Chinese leaders, it is notable how little that journal had to say about Indochina during the early weeks of the year. In January, especially, the theme of 'anti-imperialism' was pursued with reference to Latin American – and sometimes the Congo – rather than to Vietnam or Laos. The turning-point came with the article

TABLE 13.1   *Vietnam and the Communist world, November 1963–February 1964*

CPSU	CCP	VNWP *and* NLFSVN
		December:: VNWP Central Committee, 9th Plenum: precise date not known. Resolutions on international Communist questions, and on the question of the South.
26 Nov.: CPSU urged Japanese CP to restore good relations with Moscow.	19 Nov.: *Renmin Ribao*, 'Two Different Lines on the Question of War and Peace.' (China agreed to border talks with Soviet Union.)	
29 Nov.: CPSU letter to CCP urging end to polemics, resumption of economic relations.	28 Nov.: Japanese CP delegation received in Peking.	
1 Dec.: *Pravda* and *Izvestiya* carried articles on Vosnesensky.	30 Nov.: Date of Liu Shaoqi's unpublished speech.	
	4 Dec.: *Renmin Ribao* on need to build independent, modern economy.	
9–13 Dec.: CPSU Central Committee Plenum. Khrushchev seeking to limit military budget and to expand chemical industry.	12 Dec.: *Renmin Ribao* article on peaceful coexistence.	
	12 Dec.: Mao's 'instruction' on Party's line on art.	
	13 Dec.–15 Feb.: Zhou Enlai's tour of African countries (and Albania).	
		20 Dec.: Start of political campaign to change attitudes towards Southern struggle among people of North Vietnam.
	26 Dec.: Publication of Zhou Yang's anti-revisionist report of 26 October.	
31 Dec.: Soviet press carried interview with Khrushchev, indicating desire for peaceful collaboration with United States.		

Jan.: Reappearance of Suslov: first mention since mid-September 1963.

13–22 Jan.: Castro visited Moscow; accepted Soviet line on peaceful coexistence.

21 Jan.: US proposal for non-proliferation treaty tabled at Geneva Disarmament Talks.

29 Jan.: *Pravda* published Soviet proposals on disarmament, also allowing for nuclear non-proliferation agreement.

1–10 Feb.: Le Duan's delegation was in Moscow; received by Khrushchev on 8th.

12 Feb.: CPSU distributed statement on its position *vis-à-vis* CCP, but refused to send a copy to Peking.

10 Jan.: *Peking Review* carried article by Che Guevara on guerrilla warfare.

12 Jan.: Mao's statement supporting the people of Panama against US imperialism.

21 Jan.: Report of recent PLA political work conference: strong emphasis on Mao's thought.

27 Jan.: Sino-French diplomatic relations announced.

30 Jan.: Mao received Le Duan's delegation in Peking.

4 Feb.: *Renmin Ribao* article accusing CPSU leaders of being 'the greatest splitters of our time'.

1–8 Jan.: NLFSVN Second Congress; major speech by Tran Nam Trung. Appeal to people of South, published 15 January.

9 Jan.: All-North Air Defence Conference met in Hanoi.

20 Jan.: *Nhan-Dan* carried communiqué of VNWP Central Committee 99th Plenum, relating to international questions.

22 Jan.: VNA reported Tran Nam Trung's speech to NLFSVN Congress.

27 Jan.–15 Feb.: Le Duan and Le Duc Tho visited Peking and Moscow.

2–10 Feb.: PLAFSVN offensive under way attacks in Ben-Tre, Tay-Ninh, Kontum and Quang-Tin provinces.

11 Feb.: *Hoc Tap* article by Nguyen Van Vinh, analysing US difficulties in South Vietnam and predicting their defeat.

TABLE 13.1　*Vietnam and the Communist world, November 1963 – February 1964*

CPSU	CCP	VNWP and NLFSVN
14 Feb.: CPSU Central Committee plenum: decisions on industry and agriculture; Suslov reported on the international Communist movement.	14–18 Feb.: Zhou Enlai in Rangoon.	15 Feb.: *Nhan-Dan* editorial on the need to strengthen Soviet–Vietnamese unity on the basis of proletarian internationalism.
15 Feb.: CPSU agreed not to publish Suslov report; to allow Romanian attempt to resolve Sino-Soviet problems.	15–18 Feb.: Deng Xiaoping, Kang Sheng and Zhu De had talks with Japanese CP delegation (Miyamoto) in Guangzhou.	
	17 Feb.: Mao agreed to receive Romanian delegation, in effort to avert Sino-Soviet split.	
	19 Feb.: *Renmin Ribao* article rejected ideas put forward in Hilsman's speech of 13 December 1963.	

of 19 February in *Renmin Ribao*, criticising the United States' attitude towards China and virtually ending the possibility of a reduction of tension through early Sino-American contacts.[21]

III

In the first half of February 1964, Sino-Soviet relations were in fact approaching a crisis. On 4 February the Chinese 'seventh comment' accused the leaders of the CPSU of being 'the greatest splitters of our time'. The CPSU replied by circulating a statement of its own (dated 12 February) explaining its attitude towards the Chinese line. Copies were sent to all Parties deemed sympathetic to the Moscow line; but none was given, then or later, to the CCP. Then on 14 February Suslov delivered a long report to a plenum of the CPSU Central Committee, which set forth a comprehensive case against the Chinese from the point of view of 'proletarian internationalism'.[22] Although it was decided not to publish his report – at least until the Romanians had a chance to undertake one last attempt at reconciliation – the February plenum marked the point at which the Sino-Soviet 'dispute' began to develop into an irreconcilable 'split'. That same CPSU plenum also reversed some of the economic decisions taken the previous December, by restoring priority to investment in the defence industries.[23]

During this critical period, the Vietnamese had an opportunity to observe developments in both the CCP and the CPSU at first hand. At the end of January, Le Duan and Le Duc Tho left for Peking, where they were received by Mao Zedong on the 30th, and then the Soviet Union, where they spent the first ten days of February.[24] Given the long-standing involvement of both men in the affairs of the South, going back to the early 1950s, it is likely that their principal objective in Moscow was to persuade Khrushchev (whom they met on 8 February) to endorse the resolution of the 9th Plenum on the southern struggle. Some Western observers believed that they asked for substantially increased military assistance, and that they left empty-handed. But whilst it is likely that the Russians did refuse to support any immediate expansion of the military struggle – to an extent that would provoke direct United States involvement – they probably, offered sufficient assistance and approval to preserve Soviet–Vietnamese friendship.

The Soviet–Vietnamese talks were in any case not confined to the question of South Vietnam: the fact that Le Duan's delegation was seen off from Moscow by Suslov (together with Kirilenko, Andropov and Ilyichev) suggests that the visit was primarily an occasion for Party and ideological discussions, in which the Soviet side may have again succeeded in dissuading the Vietnamese from moving closer to the Chinese line. Hanoi's attitude was reflected by an editorial in *Nhan-Dan*, on 15 February, entitled 'Struggle to strengthen Soviet–Vietnamese Unity!'[25] About the same time, *Hoc-Tap* published Le Duan's speech to the 9th Plenum.

However, in the second half of February and during March, the situation changed yet again – for reasons which must remain obscure. We have already noticed the sudden return to a sharply anti-American line in Peking, represented by *Renmin Ribao's* article of 19 February 1964. Following that, there would appear to have been a slight easing of tension between Moscow and Peking during the last ten days of the month. Despite a series of acrimonious exchanges between 20 and 29 February, the Chinese finally sent a reply on the latter date to the Soviet letter of 29 November 1963. They suggested a resumption of bilateral talks, to begin the following October (1964); and the subsequent convening of a meeting of 17 Communist Parties (as opposed to the 25 named by the CPSU) to prepare for a full-dress international conference comparable with those of 1957 and 1960. The Soviet response (dated 7 March 1964) proposed a speeding up of the timetable to allow bilateral talks to begin in June followed by the preparatory meeting in October. The Chinese did not reply immediately; but on 31 March their 'eighth comment' on the CPSU line, devoted to an explanation of certain aspects of the position taken by the CCP at the Moscow meetings of 1957 and 1960, was less bitter than earlier (and later) articles in that series.[26] Meanwhile the border talks which had been promised the previous November actually got under way at the end of February.

It is impossible to tell how far, if at all, the Romanian attempt at mediation had been responsible for averting a total 'split' between the CPSU and the CCP. Nor can we be sure whether it meant that Suslov's fortunes had suffered another setback as a result. The publication of his February report in *Pravda* on 3 April was not necessarily a victory for his own views: it was even published in Peking towards the end of the same month.

By late March, too, it would seem that Liu Shaoqi was again

becoming influential in Peking. Since late November 1963, when the Chinese media had failed to publish his speech to the Academy of Sciences conference, he had not been very prominent. Now he began to re-emerge; and, also in late March, Mao began to listen to the views of Wang Guangmei (Mrs Liu) on the issue of socialist education in the countryside.[27] But Mao was careful to strike a balance by also encouraging the campaign to 'learn from the PLA', launched in February 1964. During the following months there would seem to have been intense rivalry between the Party secretariat (led by Liu and Deng) and the PLA generals for control over the next stage of the revolution. From our point of view, however, it seems likely that both sides of that conflict were interested in giving greater support to the struggle in South Vietnam.

During the last ten days of February there was a gradual return towards Chinese emphasis on the revolution in South-East Asia; and in particular on the struggle in Vietnam. On 27 February the DRVN foreign minister Xuan Thuy again appealed to his Chinese counterpart for support against the Americans; and on 2 March Chen Yi sent a favourable reply. Two days later (4 March) *Renmin Ribao* warned the Americans they were 'heading for complete defeat' in Vietnam.[28] The recrystallisation of China's anti-American line was also reflected in maritime South-East Asia. It may have been no more than coincidence that the ceasefire in Borneo broke down precisely on 20 February 1964. But by late March there was no doubt that the Chinese had committed themselves to support for an escalation of the struggle there too. Having for some time been content merely to reprint PKI statements on the issue, *Renmin Ribao* produced its own editorial on 27 March praising the 'struggle of the North Kalimantan people'.[29]

One other development of mid-February may have had some relevance to the change of mood in Peking. From 15 to 18 February 1964 Deng Xiaoping was in Guangzhou (Canton) in the company of Zhu De and Kang Sheng, for talks with the Japanese Communist Party leader Miyamoto.[30] It is not known whether any South-East Asian Communists were present on that occasion, or whether Vietnam figured specifically in Sino-Japanese Party talks. Certainly there were a number of other occasions during the next two years when the Japanese Communists sought to promote a spirit of 'united action' in support of the Vietnamese struggle, both for its practical value and as a symbol of anti-imperialism. We do know, however, that another international Communist figure was present in Guangzhou at that time: on 18 February the New Zealand Marxist–Leninist, V. G. Wilcox, delivered a report to the Guangdong Party School, which amounted to a new formulation of the 'pro-Peking' line and was widely disseminated in Chinese publications a month later.[31]

Towards the end of March, the situation again became clear enough for the Vietnamese Communists to re-establish unity among themselves. To that end Ho Chi Minh took the unusual step on 27 March 1964 of convening a 'special political conference' – which he did in his capacity as president of the DRVN under the 1960 constitution.[32] It drew together the leading cadres of the Party secretariat, the council of ministers and the national assembly, to endorse a political line set forth in a formal report by Ho himself. It was noticeable that Truong Chinh and Hoang Van Hoan again assumed leading roles, whilst Le Duan retired to the background for a while. No reference was made to any dramatic intensification of the armed struggle in the South. In that sense, perhaps, the North Vietnamese leaders were retreating from the full implementation of the 9th Plenum resolution. But their commitment to continuing the southern struggle was as firm as ever, and the main purpose of the conference seems to have been to reaffirm national unity in the face of any new threats from the United States. For the next six months – and especially from June to September 1964 – Chinese support was again the key factor in North Vietnam's calculations. Only in the autumn, when discussion of the 9th Plenum resolution was revived, did the consequences of the Hanoi decisions of late 1963 begin to take effect.

The above analysis cannot claim to have disposed of all the questions the historian must eventually ask in studying the relationship between the war and the international Communist movement in this critical period. It ought, however, to dispose of the American fallacy that at the Ninth Plenum the VNWP adopted *both* a 'pro-Chinese' ideological stand *and* a more aggressive strategy in South Vietnam. The little information we have about United States intelligence assessments of Communist intentions at this period suggests that Washington failed completely to understand what was happening on the Communist side. In a cable to Ambassador Lodge on 20 March 1964, President Johnson himself observed that 'we expect a showdown between the Chinese and Soviet Communist Parties soon, and action against the North will be more practicable after than before a showdown'.[33] In the event, no 'showdown' occurred. But in any case there was never a point at which Hanoi became so completely cut off from Soviet support that it was likely to yield to any but the most extreme form of American military pressure.

Part IV
1964

14 Coercive Diplomacy

The Joint Chiefs of Staff are convinced that, in keeping with the guidance in NSAM-273, the United States must make plain to the enemy our determination to see the Vietnam campaign through to a favourable conclusion. To do this we must prepare for whatever level of activity may be required....

Currently we and the South Vietnamese are fighting the war on the enemy's terms. He has determined the locale, the timing and the tactics of the battle, while our actions are essentially reactive.... We have obliged ourselves to labour under self-imposed restrictions with respect to impeding external aid to the Viet Cong. These restrictions include keeping the war within the boundaries of South Vietnam, avoiding the direct use of US combat forces, and limiting US direction of the campaign to rendering advice to the government of Vietnam. These restrictions, while they may make our international position more readily defensive, all tend to make the task in Vietnam more complex... and in the end more costly.

JCS Memorandum 46–64,
22 January 1964

US Military Action Against North Vietnam: ... Basic to this course of action is that it is a military course of action only in support of a political objective, and requiring consideration at every stage of political factors. We would expressly not be trying to conquer North Vietnam.... Rather, we are aiming to do three things: (a) get North Vietnam to stop, or at least sharply cut down, its supply of key items to the Viet Cong; (b) stiffen the Khanh government, completely assure it of our determination, and discourage moves toward neutralism in South Vietnam; (c) show all of Southeast Asia, including Sukarno, that we will take strong measures to prevent the spread of Communism... in the area.

Best action possibilities: ... the best way to start might be through a blockade of Haiphong–not because the short-term effect would be major, but because this is a recognised military action that hits at the sovereignty of North Vietnam and almost inevitably means we would go further....

Draft Memorandum by William Bundy,
Assistant Secretary of Defense, 1 March 1964

I

Whatever conclusions historians may reach about President Johnson's first three months in office, it is clear that by the second half of February 1964 the United States was facing another crisis in South-East Asia. There could be no going back to the situation of the late Diem period, or even to the circumstances which had prevailed at the time of President Kennedy's death. The Chinese had by now decided against any compromise with the American presence in the region, as was demonstrated by the *Renmin Ribao* article of 19 February; and there was no longer much reason to hope that a new settlement in Indochina would emerge from Sino-French diplomacy. The ceasefire in Laos was disintegrating and Communist forces had embarked on a new phase of armed struggle in South Vietnam. About the same time (20 February) the ceasefire in Borneo also broke down, and the PKI resumed its campaign to dissuade Sukarno from negotiations which might lead to recognition of Malaysia.

At this point Vietnam seemed to be the one area of South-East Asia where the Americans had the opportunity to counter the Communist challenge by means of direct action. By turning the tide of conflict there, they might hope to succeed in recovering the initiative in the region as a whole; if they failed to respond effectively in Vietnam their influence elsewhere seemed likely to decline even further, perhaps to nothing. Therein lay the importance of the Washington 'debate' on Vietnam – the first of many – which unfolded from mid-January to mid-March 1964 and which culminated in NSAM-288 (dated 17 March).[1] Everyone recognised that the most important aspect of the war was still the military–political campaign inside South Vietnam. But for the first time a president was willing to concede that it might, in the end, prove impossible to win that campaign without additional military actions beyond the borders of South Vietnam. The framework of American thinking thus began to develop along lines very different from those which had governed the Kennedy strategy.

Already by the last week in January it was becoming obvious that a larger American effort was needed if South Vietnamese government forces were to avoid defeat and recover control of the situation. At this point the JCS, whose chairman was still Maxwell Taylor, came forward with a set of proposals which amounted to a blueprint for escalation. JCS Memorandum 46–64, dated 22 January 1964, took as its starting point the overall commitment contained in NSAM-273 but then went on to argue for a wholly new strategy to win the war as quickly as possible. This would require not only air action over Laos and against North Vietnam but also a completely new approach to the war on the ground, with responsibility for all US programmes in Vietnam (and if possible direction of the whole war effort) vested in the commander of MACV. It might eventually require the deployment of additional American ground troops in a combat role in South Vietnam.

Such a sweeping change proved to be impracticable, in terms of South Vietnamese as well as United States political considerations. But the JCS were now clear about the direction they wished to take, and their analysis of the situation implied profound dissatisfaction with the conduct of the war up till then. They reiterated these views in a further memorandum on 18 February.[2]

On the issue whether to allow the war to expand beyond the borders of South Vietnam, Johnson had already taken the first step when he signed NSAM-273; and subsequently he had authorised the first phase of the Krulak plan (OPLAN-34A) for a series of clandestine operations north of the 17th parallel which began on 1 February 1964. What the JCS were proposing, however, was something far more ambitious involving overt United States participation in a war against North Vietnam. They were doing so against a background of increasing diplomatic frustration in South-East Asia, and of a hardening of determination in Hanoi.

President Johnson's own concern about this deteriorating situation may explain his remarks in a speech at Los Angeles on 21 February, when he warned 'those engaged in external direction and supply' of the insurgency in South Vietnam that they were playing 'a deeply dangerous game'. The Soviet agency TASS responded three days later with a counter-warning that American plans to extend the war to North Vietnam would have 'the most serious consequences'. By early March, Johnson was inclined to play down the impression of a direct and immediate threat to Hanoi. Nevertheless at a meeting of the 'principals' on 21 February (reinforced by members of the Vietnam Committee of William Sullivan), the President decided to speed up contingency studies of the feasibility of an overt campaign against the North.[3] A report assessing various possibilities for action – and the likely Communist response – was completed by 1 March and incorporated into a larger draft memorandum prepared for Secretary of Defense McNamara by William Bundy.[4]

Certain passages of this memorandum were later incorporated

into the recommendations submitted by McNamara to the President on 16 March. But a section dealing with military pressures against North Vietnam, which was considerably toned down during the course of later discussions, represents the clearest statement so far of the case for employing military threats to coerce North Vietnam. A rapidly escalating series of military actions, starting with a blockade of Haiphong harbour and the interdiction of rail links with China, would culminate (if necessary) in direct strikes against industrial and other targets – but not population centres – in the heart of the northern zone. The draft memorandum of 1 March also discussed the need for 'the strongest possible factual document' to justify such action by the United States; and for a Congressional resolution along the same lines as those which had assisted President Eisenhower in handling crises in the Taiwan Straits and the Middle East in the mid-1950s. But to begin with, planning must take place in secret at the highest level of the Administration, in the same way Kennedy had planned his successful response to the Cuba missiles in October 1962. Bundy was well aware of the great differences between the two situations; he was nevertheless thinking in terms of trying to repeat the 'miracle of the Cuba crisis'.

If it were indeed the President's policy *not* to accept neutralisation of South Vietnam, William Bundy's suggestions were remarkably cogent both then and later in the spring. They were not, however, adopted as policy. The strategy eventually recommended by McNamara, and authorised under NSAM-288, continued to give most attention to the war in the South and attached higher priority to 'border control' actions in Laos (and possibly Cambodia) than to immediate action against North Vietnam. Only at the very end of a long list of recommendations did McNamara include contingency planning for 'retaliatory actions' against the North (on 72 hours' notice) and for 'graduated overt military pressure' (on 30 days' notice). This was the framework within which William Bundy was to work in carrying out the responsibility assigned to him for co-ordinating the actions authorised by NSAM-288; which was his first task on taking over from Roger Hilsman as Assistant Secretary of State for Far Eastern Affairs in mid-March. He co-operated closely with his own successor at the Pentagon, the new Assistant Secretary of Defense for International Security Affairs, John McNaughton.[5]

The 'debate' did not, of course, end with NSAM-288. During

TABLE 14.1 *United States decision-making in the Asian perspective, February–March 1964*

USSR, China and North Vietnam	South Vietnam, Laos, Cambodia	Washington 'debate' on Vietnam	Indonesia–Malaysia–Philippines
	18 Feb.: Report on cross-check of previous security assessments; Harkins rejected 'pessimistic' interpretation of this.	18 Feb.: JSS Memorandum on need for more comprehensive war effort, including action against North Vietnam.	18 Feb.: *Harian Rakyat* (PKI organ) criticised Sukarno's economic policies.
19 Feb.: *Renmin Ribao* article criticising US attitude to China.		20 Feb.: Presidential decision to speed up contingency studies of possible action against North.	20 Feb.: Ceasefire in Borneo broke down.
		21 Feb.: Johnson's Los Angeles speech warning North Vietnam.	
21 Feb.: Soviet Note to UK urging reconvening of Geneva Conference to discuss Cambodia.	21 Feb.: Saigon meeting of Lodge, Harkins, Felt (CINCPAC) and Nguyen Khanh: discussion of US advisory role, pacification plan, mobilisation.		22 Feb.: Macapagal began a visit to Indonesia (to 28th), to persuade Sukarno to abandon confrontation. 22–23 Feb.: Aidit speeches calling for national front against Malaysia.
24 Feb.: Start of Sino-Soviet border talks.			

TABLE 14.1   *United States decision-making in the Asian perspective, February–March 1964*

USSR, China and North Vietnam	South Vietnam, Laos, Cambodia	Washington 'debate' on Vietnam	Indonesia–Malaysia–Philippines
24 Feb.: Soviet warning that extension of the war to North Vietnam would have 'most serious consequences'.			
		25 Feb.: State Department recommended deployment of F-100 fighter planes to Thailand.	25 Feb.: Bangkok Foreign Ministers' meeting due to take place; postponed.
		26 Feb.: JCS Memorandum urging integration of Laos into South Vietnam theatre of operations. Hilsman resignation reported.	26 Feb.: Agreement on meeting in Bangkok on 3 March; but now Malaysia insisted on restoring ceasefire as priority.
27 Feb.: Xuan Thuy's letter to Chen Yi, seeking reaffirmation of Chinese support.			28 Feb.: Macapagal said the Philippines will stay out of confrontation in future.
29 Feb.: CCP letter to CPSU indicating modification of earlier attitude to bilateral Party talks.		29 Feb.: CINCPAC telegram on possible deployment of ground troops to Thailand.	
1 March: Romanian delegation arrived in Peking to promote Sino-Soviet reconciliation.		1 March: William Bundy Memorandum; also report of interagency study group, both recommending military action against North Vietnam.	

2 March: Chen Yi's reply to Xuan Thuy, confirming Chinese support.	2 March: Souvanna Phouma visited Phnom Penh (to 7th), for talks with Sihanouk.	2 March: Further JCS Memorandum urging action against North.	3 March: Bangkok Foreign Ministers' meeting; broke down after Subandrio left for home.
	2–3 March: State Department considering proposal for quadripartite agreement on Cambodia's borders (Cambodia, Thailand, South Vietnam and USA).	3 March: Final preparations for McNamara–Taylor visit to Saigon.	
4 March: *Renmin Ribao*: 'US aggressors heading for defeat in Vietnam'.			
7 March: CPSU letter to CCP, urging speeding up of sequence of bilateral and multilateral meetings.			
		8–12 March: McNamara–Taylor visit to South Vietnam; discussion of all aspects of war with Nguyen Khanh.	
	11 March: Attacks on American and British embassies in Phnom Penh.		

SOURCES   See notes to Chapters 13 and 14.

the first two weeks of April the JCS pressed ahead with those planning tasks which had been authorised, and on 17 April they gave approval to OPLAN 37–64: a sequence of possible military actions against the North, to be implemented as and when required. Bundy and McNaughton, in the same period, were concerned with refining a possible scenario for political and diplomatic actions, combined with military threats, in case the President finally decided to go ahead with the idea of putting pressure on Hanoi.[6]

At this point it is necessary to recognise a distinction, at least in theory, between two quite different concepts for the employment of air power beyond the borders of South Vietnam. The ideas put forward in the memorandum of 1 March implied the use (or at least threat) of air strikes against vital targets in North Vietnam as a means to coerce the leadership in Hanoi: that is, to force them to withdraw material support from the war in the South by threatening destruction of their own half of the country. Within the Pentagon that would appear to have been the thinking primarily of the air force chief of staff, Curtis LeMay, with some support from commanders of the navy and the marine corps. The army generals (including Earle Wheeler, army chief of staff) and also McNamara himself favoured a quite different concept, requiring the use of air strikes as a means to defend the approaches to South Vietnam: that is, against targets in Laos and the southern provinces of North Vietnam, to limit or prevent the infiltration of men and supplies. If that was the aim of bombing, there was room for controversy over the precise extent of infiltration from the North as well as the extent to which the Communist forces in the South actually depended on it.[7]

In practice, as the 'debate' continued, the two concepts began to merge into one another, to produce scenarios for action which attempted to take account of both aims simultaneously. The result was that by the end of the year – well before the actual bombing campaign got under way – much of the clarity of Bundy's analysis had been lost.

II

A second major question to be raised during the Washington 'debate' of February–March 1964 was whether American military involvement on the ground, or even American-supported operations by Saigon government forces, should be allowed to extend beyond the borders of South Vietnam. In particular, ought the United States to take steps to counter increasing North Vietnamese use of the 'Ho Chi Minh Trail', which was a clear violation of the Geneva guarantee of the 'territorial integrity' of Laos? The military course contemplated by Kennedy in 1961, but then rejected in favour of a diplomatic solution, would have involved sending American (possibly SEATO) ground forces into North-East Thailand – and if necessary, into Laos. They might even have been instructed to link up with American units deployed to Central Vietnam, in order to create a defence line across the whole of Indochina. But once the Geneva Declaration of 1962 had been signed, such a course was impossible without some basis for alleging – and demonstrating – that North Vietnam or China had violated that agreement to an extent justifying retaliation.

At least one proposal along these lines was made, in a memorandum of 13 February from Walt Rostow to Secretary Rusk, arguing that some means must be found to enforce North Vietnamese compliance with international guarantees of Laotian neutrality. In late February, CINCPAC also raised the question of moving ground combat troops to Thailand. But in early March, Rostow found himself reprimanded by Johnson after a television commentator had suggested that the President was about to implement 'Rostow's Plan Six'.[8] Another recommendation to deploy troops to Thailand, ready for action in Laos if required, was made by Hilsman in one of two memoranda he wrote on 14 March. (The other was a vindication of existing policy in South Vietnam, and together they amount to a comprehensive outline of the original Kennedy strategy for Indochina.[9]) But Hilsman's resignation from the State Department had already been announced on 26 February, and these valedictory statements were unlikely to exert great influence.

Johnson had by this time made up his mind against any move to dramatise the situation. His dilemma was expertly set out by the American Ambassador in Vientiane, Leonard Unger, in a telegram of 1 March.[10] Either he could accept the policy of Souvanna Phouma, who was not yet ready to go along with the 'crisis' approach and still hoped for a diplomatic solution; or he could embark on a major United States intervention, leaving the Geneva agreements behind, which might lead to a large-scale war on the Asian mainland. Determined to avoid a larger war, the President chose accordingly.

Laos did, however, figure in the February–March 'debate' in a more limited way. A JCS Memorandum of 26 February argued that, even if action against North Vietnam was politically unacceptable, cross-border operations into Laos from South Vietnam and also low-level reconnaissance flights over Laos were necessary without further delay.[11] When NSAM-288 was finally approved it went a long way towards meeting that proposal, although the full range of proposed operations in Laos was to be planned only on a contingency basis. The President also insisted that actions of any size beyond the borders of Vietnam must depend on good relations with the governments of Laos and Cambodia.

This decision to work within the framework of the Geneva guarantees of 1962, despite the breakdown of the coalition government on which they originally depended, meant that any cross-border military actions in Laos, on the part of South Vietnamese or American forces, must first be cleared with the government of Souvanna Phouma. Relations between Vientiane and Saigon had been disrupted by the Buddhist crisis during 1963; but on 18 March 1964 it was reported that they had been restored following discussions in Dalat between Phoumi Nosavan and Nguyen Khanh. As far as Laos was concerned, provided the Americans and South Vietnamese moved carefully, there was now a good chance of keeping diplomatic and military objectives in harmony with one another.

In the case of Cambodia, things were very different. Sihanouk had been disappointed by the failure of his proposal for a new Geneva conference on Cambodian neutrality; particularly the refusal of Thailand to enter into any arrangements guaranteeing existing borders. He was willing, nevertheless, to entertain the possibility of a less ambitious arrangement leading to a quadripartite guarantee of Cambodia's borders in the form of a declaration by his own country, the United States, Thailand and South Vietnam. That idea was under discussion early in March; but the Thais remained intransigent, and the American attitude was ambiguous at best.[12]

Even Souvanna Phouma, who held talks with Sihanouk in Phnom Penh from 2 to 7 March, was reluctant to agree to a joint approach to the border question. Frustrated again, Sihanouk made another strongly anti-American speech on 9 March; and two days later he allowed a mob to attack the embassies of both the United States and Britain. Cambodian–American relations were now worse than ever.

The one possibility that remained was for some kind of *ad hoc* arrangement between Phnom Penh and Saigon for the policing of the Cambodian–Vietnamese border. The PLAFSVN had long been in the habit of using neutral Cambodia as a 'sanctuary' when its units were under pressure inside South Vietnam; and ARVN troops (together with their American advisers) were forbidden to engage in 'hot pursuit'. By early 1964 the danger of border incidents was increasing, and Sihanouk was becoming worried. For their part the South Vietnamese authorities – and presumably the Americans – would have liked some kind of arrangement under which 'hot pursuit' was allowed. On 19 March a South Vietnamese government delegation arrived in the Cambodian capital hoping to hold talks on the subject. But almost immediately a serious new incident occurred in which it was alleged that ARVN units had attacked the border village of Chantrea (inside Cambodia). Sihanouk protested and the diplomatic initiative foundered.[13] As the war expanded, further incidents occurred; but Sihanouk felt he had no choice but to allow increasing use of Cambodian territory by Vietnamese Communist guerrillas.

III

The main burden of Johnson's decisions of March 1964 was that the war must be fought primarily in South Vietnam. Nevertheless, by this time the doctrine of counterinsurgency, at least in the form in which it had been implemented since late 1961, had begun to be called in question. An extensive cross-checking of past data on rural security, authorised on 16 January 1964, produced a report a month later which cast doubt on the validity of 'optimistic' assessments made during the second half of 1963.[14] The main target of criticism was a system of reporting which had allowed the South Vietnamese authorities, at province and district level, to file misleading information; but doubts also arose about the effectiveness of the whole pacification programme.

Johnson was unwilling to accept the proposal of the JCS in their memorandum of 22 January, that full responsibility for the war effort should pass to the commander of MACV. Instead, on 14 February NSAM-280 established a new interagency team to supervise actual operations in South Vietnam, under the chairmanship of William Sullivan of the State Department.[15] Nevertheless the Pentagon became increasingly influential in the formulation of policies; and the military command structure established in 1962 was gradually reorganised. The latter subject was discussed during the visit of McNamara and Taylor to Saigon on 8–12 March 1964, and new arrangements came into effect the following May.[16] Thus MAAG was finally dissolved and its role taken over completely by MACV; Timmes was recalled. Another casualty was the British Advisory Mission of R. G. K. Thompson, although a group under the British embassy continued to play a part in police training. By mid-year Harkins himself was obliged to leave; his successor being General William Westmoreland, who had taken over as deputy commander of MACV on 27 January.

These changes did not immediately alter the basic assumption, inherent in the Kennedy strategy, that the war must be fought primarily by the Vietnamese armed forces with the Americans in an essentially supportive role. The principal recommendations of the McNamara Memorandum of 16 March (and therefore of NSAM-288) concerned ways in which the Vietnamese war effort might be improved on the basis of increased military assistance. A national mobilisation plan was envisaged, together with another 50,000-man increase in the size of ARVN; economic aid would also be strengthened and more equipment provided. (A proposal for land reform, although it had been mentioned by the JCS on 18 February, did not appear in the final recommendations.)

None of this necessarily implied more direct participation in the conflict by United States troops, and it is clear that Johnson was opposed to further deployments of ground forces to South-East Asia at this stage. Even so, the long term effect of organisational change was to prepare the ground for greater American involvement, should the need for it arise. Most important of all – though the point is a psychological one not easy to document – the expansion and streamlining of MACV's role in the war made it easier to think of counterinsurgency as the first rung on a ladder of 'flexible response', whose logic was eventual escalation. Kennedy had seen counterinsurgency as a new form of response to a new type of threat: a necessary (and hopefully sufficient) *substitute* for the deployment of American combat units to a country facing revolutionary armed struggle, not a prelude to other forms of involvement. Under Johnson that hard-and-fast line began to disappear.

Likewise, Johnson's decisions about contingency planning for action against North Vietnam and cross-border operations in Laos opened up the possibility that at some future stage the plans would be implemented. Whereas Kennedy had treated South Vietnam as a self-contained problem, and had regarded the situation in Laos as one affecting Thailand more than Vietnam, Johnson was moving in the direction of creating an Indochinese theatre of operations which would embrace Laos, North Vietnam, and potentially Cambodia – with South Vietnam as the focal point of an expanding war. A change of that order made sense only if the United States was willing to fight such a war to the limit of its capabilities, should it ever become a reality. But there was already a profound discrepancy – as the authors of the *Pentagon Papers* remarked – between the extent of the United States commitment contained in NSAM-288 and the extreme caution of the actual military preparations it approved.

The next stage of substantive decision-making came on 19–20 April 1964, at a conference in Saigon attended by Secretary Rusk, with General Wheeler standing in for McNamara. Both of them had had meetings with Nguyen Khanh in the previous few days, and had heard him argue the case for 'carrying the war to the North'. But the conference again preferred the more cautious strategy implicit in the March decisions. Ambassador Lodge appears to have played an important role on this occasion, urging the adoption of a 'carrot and stick' approach to North Vietnam: namely an offer of economic aid in return for restraint in the South, balanced by threats of punitive air strikes if Hanoi persisted in its present policy. The ambassador even suggested offering to withdraw some American troops if that would make a deal more acceptable to Ho Chi Minh. It was agreed that a message along these lines should be conveyed secretly to Hanoi by a 'third party'; and at the end of the month Rusk visited Ottawa to enlist the help of the Canadian member of the International Commission for Vietnam.[17] The 'scenarios' were once again placed on the back-burner. But it was taken for granted by this stage that there would be no progress towards a compromise without at least some threat to use military action.

Rusk himself was almost certainly influenced at this point by the apparent willingness of the Soviet Union to begin a new round of *détente* with the West. It was on 20 April that a Soviet–American understanding was reached permitting a reduction in the output of fissionable materials: a small but significant step towards agreement on the peaceful control of nuclear energy. Two days later, another small indicator was the exchange between the Soviet Union and Britain of the Russian agent Lonsdale in return for Greville Wynne (who had been involved in the Penkovsky affair). Negotiations were also under way for a consular treaty between Moscow and Washington which was actually signed on 1 June 1964, although not ratified until several years later. But an improvement in relations between Moscow and Washington would not in itself resolve the conflict in Vietnam.

IV

The American 'debate' of the months from January to April 1964 can be better understood when it is related to its intellectual context. What might be characterised as the theory of 'coercive diplomacy' is well represented in the literature of international relations by the writings of political scientists like Thomas Schelling and Herman Kahn, who were becoming increasingly influential in the years 1963–4.[18] The idea of playing politico-military games – based on an analogy with war games, using computers to assess the vast range of 'variables' involved – had been developed by the RAND corporation in the late 1950s and taken up by the Pentagon in 1961. The fashion then spread to private research consultancies associated with the 'military–industrial complex'. Among the foremost exponents of the art, Professor Schelling attempted to distil from it a conceptual theory which might be applied to actual conflicts among the great powers. Meanwhile Kahn, at the Hudson Institute, had developed an equally abstract representation of the stages that might be involved in the gradual escalation of a crisis involving the superpowers, both before and after they crossed the 'nuclear threshold'. He it was who invented – or at least propagated – the idea of basing actual decisions on the study of possible 'scenarios' of action and response.

The doctrine of 'coercive diplomacy' derived much of its appeal from the example of Kennedy's handling of the missiles crisis: an event which could very easily be represented as an international power game played by two teams of leaders in Washington and the Kremlin, each making its own move then waiting for a response, and each appearing to exercise precision control over the massive military machine at its command. The reality, even of the missiles crisis, was more complex than that; and the situation in Indochina in 1964 was more complicated still. Nevertheless in view of the continuity in American thinking, it may help us to understand the Vietnam Crisis more clearly if we attempt a detailed comparison between the two cases.

The first, perhaps most important, difference to emerge is that on the Communist side the immediate adversary was in this case not Moscow, nor even Peking, but Hanoi and the Vietnamese Communist network throughout Vietnam. North Vietnam's membership of the socialist camp (or the world socialist system) did not mean that its decision-making was subject to detailed Soviet or Chinese control. In 1964 its leaders enjoyed considerably more independence than Castro had been able to exercise when he had been obliged to surrender 'his' Ilyushin bombers on 20 November 1962. Above all the conflict in South Vietnam – which Hanoi was now pursuing with increased material support – was not merely a military–diplomatic challenge, initiated by Moscow, which could be switched on and off at will. It was a revolution.

Nevertheless North Vietnam's ability to step up the armed struggle in the South did depend to some extent on the approval of Moscow and Peking. Hanoi might perhaps be restrained if *both* its major allies were willing to exert their combined influence to dissuade the Vietnamese from continuing the war – as they appear to have done in 1954. After ten years, however, Soviet and Chinese leaders were unwilling to co-operate to that end; and their ideological dispute and diplomatic rivalry offered Hanoi an opportunity to play off one against the other. Johnson was therefore somewhat unrealistic in supposing – as his cable of 20 March to Ambassador Lodge implied – that the Sino-Soviet conflict might eventually make it easier to coerce North Vietnam.[19] The fact was that 'coercive diplomacy' could only succeed if the United States was able to apply pressure simultaneously to all three of the Communist countries involved in the conflict, or at least demonstrate by military means that Hanoi's persistence could only work to the disadvantage of all three. The one escape from that dilemma lay in the possibility (or hope) that Peking might be willing to enter into its own *détente* with Washington: a possibility utterly remote in 1964.

A further difference between 1964 and 1962 relates to the nature of American power in Vietnam, which depended on the very limited freedom of action of the government in Saigon. By this time the Khanh regime was even more dependent on the United States than either of its predecessors (the Diem regime, and then the 'junta'). But its own political stability was so fragile, and its control over the provinces so restricted, that even if it was no more than a 'puppet' it was no longer a reliable instrument of United States action. It could be argued that air strikes against the North – even the threat of them – might help boost the morale of the government and population of the South. But it might also be interpreted in Hanoi as a signal of desperation rather than confidence, especially if it took place at a time when the South was in imminent danger of collapse.

In the missiles crisis, success had depended to a great extent upon the conventional military superiority which the United States had been able to muster, at very short notice, in the Caribbean and the Western Atlantic. Given the weakness of the government's military position in South Vietnam, and the relatively small American military presence on the ground, the only way in which military superiority could be deployed quickly in South-East Asia was through the use of tactical air-power against North Vietnam. Therein lay the attraction, for the 'hawks', of a strategy which would shift the main arena of conflict away from the South towards North Vietnam and the Gulf of Tonkin. But given the fragility of the southern situation, it would still be much more difficult for Johnson to bluff his way through the crisis than it had been for Kennedy in 1962. It might well prove necessary to use ground troops in the end.

Yet another difference between 1962 and 1964 had special relevance for the theorists. In the missiles crisis the confrontation was between two nuclear powers. This made it more alarming in the short-term; but it also obliged both sides to consider immediate actions in the light of a *potential* escalation which might at some stage reach the 'nuclear threshold'. In 1964 North Vietnam itself was the only possible target for immediate American action, so there was no question of approaching the 'nuclear threshold'. (Any decision to use the full might of American military power against Hanoi would almost certainly have provoked retaliation by Moscow; but in practice nuclear weapons remained irrelevant to the Vietnam conflict throughout the Johnson period.) A scenario for escalation in Indochina, therefore, did not involve the ultimate stage of nuclear war, entailing equal risks for both sides in terms of 'mutually assured destruction'. A more likely ultimate risk was a large-scale ground war on the Asian mainland, which was a more daunting prospect for Washington than for Hanoi or Peking – or, since it would not be directly involved, for Moscow.

Ironically, therefore, the Americans found that instead of concentrating on measures to increase the adversary's awareness of risk – the 'dangerous game' of Johnson's 21 February speech – they became obsessed with the risks to themselves if they embarked on immediate strikes against the North: risk of Chinese involvement, risk of immediate collapse in the South, risk of a large-scale ground war. But delay itself created yet another risk. In principle 'coercive diplomacy' was supposed to force the adversary to negotiate on Washington's terms; at which point, as in the missiles crisis, a compromise would become both possible and necessary. But if the conflict dragged on, there would be increasing pressure on the United States to seek a negotiated 'solution' long before Hanoi was willing to make significant concessions. In such circumstances the Communist side might succeed in delaying American military action even further by appearing ready to negotiate, at some critical juncture, and simply playing for time. If Washington became too obviously conscious of the 'risk' factor, it would be very vulnerable to such tactics. Perhaps for that reason the Bundy Memorandum of 1 March opposed negotiations of any kind, at least for the time being. But there too the Administration was unwilling to adopt a forceful line.

Finally, one other difference from the missles crisis must be observed. Military action, or the threat of it, must always be justified to the satisfaction of the world at large; or at least that of the principal allies of the United States. In October 1962 it had been possible to produce actual photographs of missile installations in Cuba at a meeting of the UN Security Council: the facts of the situation were not in doubt, and Kennedy's decision to force

Moscow to withdraw was completely intelligible. In Indochina, by contrast, there was little opportunity for the Americans to establish clear-cut evidence of North Vietnamese violations of Laotian neutrality or of the Geneva ceasefire in Vietnam. Hanoi vehemently denied both charges, whilst Moscow and Peking had done nothing at all that could be shown to be improper in international law. Each new move by the Communist side had amounted to only one small step beyond the limits established by previous moves; the situation thus always remained ambiguous. The resulting dilemma for the Americans was aptly described by Rostow's allusion, in a memorandum of 23 April 1964, to the 'salami tactics' which allowed the United States no 'lucid basis' for an effective response.[20] Those tactics continued throughout the spring and summer of 1964.

15 The Third Laos Crisis

Our policy of delaying decision or action to force Hanoi's conformance with the 1962 accords risks posing us with a dilemma in both Laos and Vietnam, of either accepting a major setback or acting vigorously to salvage the situation from a base of apparent political disarray, if not disintegration. . . . We must reckon that Hanoi, Peking and (I would guess) Moscow all understand well that in Southeast Asia they have a game of salami tactics going which has a fair chance of denying to us the lucid basis for reaction we had in the other great postwar crises from Berlin to Korea to Cuba.

Memorandum of Walt W. Rostow (to Secretary of State),
23 April 1964

From the foregoing account of military developments it is evident that large portions of territory in Laos have recently changed hands. . . . Because of . . . persistent Pathet Lao denials of ready access to Pathet Lao controlled territory, the Commission is unfortunately not able to produce irrefutable evidence to show where responsibility lies for violations of the ceasefire. It is difficult, however, to avoid the inference . . . that the Pathet Lao has something to hide.

Report of Indian and Canadian members of the
International Commission for Laos,
20 June 1964

If we do not seek a Congressional Resolution, the international disadvantages are obvious, in that we may seem to have a relative lack of freedom of action and will not have built the major new base of commitment which, in the best of cases, such a resolution with its attendant debate might provide. On the other hand, if we do not have a Resolution we do not have the risks of a contest at home; nor do we pin ourselves to a level of concern and public notice which might be embarrassing if, in fact, we do not find it wise to take drastic action in the months immediately ahead. Thus we need to consider how much our course of action may be limited if we do not seek a Congressional Resolution.

Memorandum of William Bundy,
10 June 1964

I

There had been trouble in Laos almost every spring since 1959. Kennedy had had to deal with two major crises there; now, in spring 1964, a third Laos crisis was about to erupt. Against all the odds Souvanna Phouma was still attempting to restore the tripartite balance of forces on which the Geneva Declaration had been based, and to that end he made a new journey to Hanoi and Peking in early April. The Chinese still favoured a solution along those lines, and the Sino-Laotian communiqué of 8 April was couched in sympathetic terms. His visit to Hanoi was much less encouraging: it was probably the occasion on which he finally became convinced that the Vietnamese Communist leaders would not be satisfied until the Pathet Lao dominated completely the internal politics of Laos. That objective was certainly implicit in the action programme adopted by the Lao Patriotic Front (NLHX) at its second congress on 10 April 1964. Although it too emphasised the idea of national unity, the Front spoke of a unity of the whole people based on an alliance between the Patriotic Front and the 'patriotic neutralists' and an all-out struggle against the American imperialists.[1] It was a programme which had more in common with the principles of the NLFSVN – a front organisation completely under Communist control – than with the Souvanna Phouma's ideal of national unity and international neutrality, based on the ability of a strong neutralist element to reconcile politicians of both right and left. In such circumstances it is not surprising that the leaders of the three 'factions' failed to make significant progress towards a new compromise when they met on the Plaine des Jarres on 17 April.

Two days later, taking advantage of the absence of Ambassador Unger at the Saigon conference convened by Rusk, two rightist generals ordered units under their command to seize control of Vientiane in the early hours of 19 April and placed Souvanna Phouma under arrest.[2] The details of the affair remain obscure; there is even doubt as to whether Phoumi Nosavan, still the leading rightist general, was himself behind the coup or was taken by surprise. The attitude of the United States was also ambiguous at first; some Americans may have liked the coup to succeed. But by 20 April it was clear that Rusk himself was unwilling to countenance a right-wing military government in Vientiane. In common with the Geneva Co-chairmen and the other governments involved, the United States insisted on Souvanna Phouma's remaining premier. Ambassador Unger, accompanied by William Bundy, immediately flew back to Vientiane to enforce that decision. The King then intervened, summoning the prime minister and the coup leaders to Luang Prabang, as well as holding talks with the ambassadors of Britain, the USSR, the USA, Canada, India, Australia and France. As a result, Souvanna Phouma was restored to the premiership and announced that he remained head of the same government of national union as before.

In practice, however, it was impossible to pretend that nothing had changed. Souvanna Phouma, although not reduced to the status of a mere figurehead as some alleged, was now under pressure to accept closer collaboration between rightist and neutralist forces, which by early May had been achieved through the formal dissolution of the 'Savannakhet group' of Boun Oum and Phoumi Nosavan.[3] Phoumi, indeed, was the principal loser by the coup: he was obliged to return the defence portfolio to Souvanna Phouma and also appears to have lost the effective control he had previously enjoyed over the finance ministry. The new commander-in-chief of the army was his former subordinate – but now rival – Ouane Rattikhone.[4] Internationally the affair seems to have worked mainly to the disadvantage of Peking, whose statement of 22 April accused the Americans (despite appearances) of being the real authors of the coup.

The chances of restoring the coalition as a genuinely tripartite arrangement were now more remote than ever, and it would be difficult for Souvanna Phouma to avoid moving closer to the Americans as time went on. His last hope of retrieving the situation lay in making the neutralist forces of Kong Lae (in the Plaine des Jarres) less dependent on the support of the Phoumist battalions which had gone to their aid a year earlier. But his attempt to move units around towards the end of April merely created an opportunity for the Pathet Lao to exploit tensions between neutralist and Phoumist forces, and between the different groups of neutralists. The 'patriotic neutralists' of Deuane Sunnalath were now ready to join the Pathet Lao, as had been foreshadowed in the Patriotic Front programme of 10 April; which left Kong Lae little choice but to side with the rightists. Even then he might find it difficult to withstand a serious Pathet Lao attempt to drive his units off the Plaine des Jarres altogether.

The first indication that that was now the Pathet Lao objective came on 27–28 April when they seized the uplands of Phou San to the north of the Plain. Further probing activities on 13 May were followed by a full-scale Pathet Lao offensive on the 16th, forcing Kong Lae to abandon key positions in the area.[5] In addition to destroying Souvanna Phouma's plan for strengthening the neutralist military position, the new offensive would enable the Communist side to consolidate its own 'liberated zone' by establishing control over the main highway across the Plain (leading eastwards into North Vietnam), and by linking up its base areas in Sam Neua province and in southern Laos. This in turn made it difficult for the Americans to undertake secret cross-border operations from Laos into North Vietnam, as well as affording additional protection to areas traversed by the Ho Chi Minh Trail.

The new stage of conflict in Laos coincided with further developments in the sphere of both Sino-Soviet and Soviet–American relations. The possibility of a resumption of the trend towards Soviet–American *détente* (noticed in the last chapter) may have been one factor in the renewed deterioration of Sino-Soviet relations which became evident in late April and early May. On 7 May the Chinese rejected the timetable for inter-Party consultations put forward by the Russians two months earlier, proposing instead that the full-scale conference of Communist and Workers' Parties be put off for several years.[6] The Soviet response came on 15 May, in a statement by Suslov insisting that an early conference was absolutely necessary. His main concern was probably with Eastern Europe, where ideological discipline was an essential preliminary to any significant relaxation of East–West tension. But there were consequences for Asia too.

As had often happened in the past the worsening of relations between Moscow and Peking was accompanied by new Soviet efforts to appease Hanoi – although there was no high-level mission to North Vietnam on this occasion. On 21 April, perhaps alarmed by new signs of Soviet–American *détente*, the VNWP again issued an appeal for international Communist unity. Shortly afterwards a French Communist Party delegation arrived in Hanoi for talks with Le Duan, Truong Chinh and other Politburo leaders; which demonstrated once again their determination not to become isolated from other Parties by siding with Peking.

On 15 May, coinciding precisely with Suslov's remarks about an international Communist meeting – which the VNWP was unlikely to attend in the form proposed – Ambassador Tovmasyan held a press conference in Hanoi at which he reaffirmed Soviet support for North Vietnam's struggle against American imperialism.[7] This would suggest that the Pathet Lao onslaught of the following day, in which the North Vietnamese undoubtedly participated, had tacit Soviet approval. As if to turn a blind eye to what was happening at this point, the Polish delegate withdrew completely from the proceedings of the International Commission (in Laos) on 20 May; also a move which presumably had Moscow's blessing.

In South Vietnam the Communist side was not yet ready for another major effort. The PLAFSVN made a number of successful guerrilla attacks in the Mekong Delta in April, including an attack on the administrative centre of Chuong-Thien province which they temporarily occupied on 12 April. But for the most part their energies were devoted to consolidating the 'liberated areas' in preparation for the next phase of conflict. They also stepped up their terrorist campaign: its most spectacular achievement being the sinking of the American carrier ship *Card* in the port of Saigon on 2 May. Later the same day Ambassador Lodge narrowly avoided being on the scene of another bomb explosion; and McNamara himself was the target of an unsuccessful assassination attempt when he visited Saigon again on 12–13 May. Meanwhile in Hanoi the Party leadership was probably by now debating whether to send regular North Vietnamese (PAVN) units to the South later in the year. Soldiers of the 95th Regiment of the PAVN 325th Division, captured in the South in 1965, told interrogators that their unit had originally been recalled from duty in Laos during April 1964 in order to begin special training for infiltration down the Ho Chi Minh Trail.[8] But the final decision had not yet been taken.

II

Faced with what seemed to be a major new challenge in Laos, which he could not ignore, President Johnson assigned the task of working out an appropriate American strategy to an Executive

Committee ('ExCom') of the NSC – the type of body which had advised his predecessor during the Cuba missiles crisis.[9] By the middle of May, following yet another McNamara–Taylor mission to Saigon, concern about the lack of progress in South Vietnam under the Khanh regime probably constituted a second reason for asking whether the time had come to abandon the constraints implicit in NSAM-288 and to authorise military action against North Vietnam after all. The fact that the reorganisation of the United States command structure in Vietnam was also completed on 15 May suggests that in any case this would have been a time for considering possible new actions in the South. It was the moment, indeed, when the doctrine of coercive diplomacy might have been put to the test, had the President so determined.

The choice open to the United States was still essentially what it had been earlier in the year. On the one hand lay the policy of continuing to concentrate on the war in South Vietnam whilst looking for an eventual diplomatic solution in Laos; which meant expanding the American programmes in the South and undertaking very limited military action in Laos. On the other hand, a sequence of military actions and threats against North Vietnam might be devised in the hope of forcing Hanoi to change course – or at least reducing its capability for intervention in the other two areas. Either strategy would involve a measure of escalation; the second would produce a major international crisis which the Americans would then have to 'win'. During the nine days from 21 to 29 May 1964 these options were the subject of intense debate in Washington, Honolulu and Saigon.

Discussion of the former strategy raised questions about the extent to which American advisers, civilian and military, should take over effective responsibility for the war by working alongside their Vietnamese counterparts at every level. A policy of 'encadrement' of civilian American advisers into the Saigon administration was advocated by William Sullivan in a memorandum of 21 May; and on the same day the JCS sought Harkins' opinion on a parallel suggestion in the sphere of counterinsurgency operations. This latter request drew forth objections from the MACV commander, which were overruled. In the event, the principle of 'encadrement' was not pursued. Nevertheless this debate marked the beginning of a more active phase of United States involvement in the South, including the use of American advisers at lower levels of the Vietnamese armed forces than before.[10]

The strategy of direct action against Hanoi was even more controversial. The deliberations of the 'ExCom' during the week from 22 to 29 May can be only partially discerned from the available evidence, but they may well have been almost as dramatic as those of October 1962 – even though their eventual outcome was negative. On 23 May, under the pressure of continuing crisis, William Bundy produced the most concise and forthright in his series of 'scenarios' for action against North Vietnam: a 30-day programme which would have culminated in actual air strikes, to take place on the same day as a call for new international negotiations on Indochina.[11] This strategy was designed to force upon Hanoi a policy of restraint in both Laos and South Vietnam, treating those areas as two halves of a single problem. In the diplomatic sphere it would have implied more than merely reconvening the earlier conferences in Geneva. The boldness of the strategy was admirable, but its consequences were too unpredictable for President Johnson to risk during an election year. Already by 25 May it was clear that the most he would approve at this stage was a policy of 'graduated pressure' on Hanoi; and even that would be postponed if at all possible.

In the meantime, the British government – without Soviet concurrence – had responded to a request by Souvanna Phouma to convene a meeting in Vientiane under an article of the 1962 Declaration providing for 'consultations' in the event of a new crisis.[12] Souvanna Phouma himself made it clear (24 May) that he would attend a reconvened Geneva conference only if it was preceded by a ceasefire; and that he was now ready to accept military and political assistance from the Western powers, as well as to permit US reconnaissance flights over Pathet Lao territory. At this point (on 27 May) the Polish foreign ministry produced a new formula for negotiations which proved more attractive to the Americans than the French proposal to reconvene the 14-nation conference in Geneva without prior conditions. The Polish suggestion for a meeting of representatives of the three Laotian parties, the members of the International Commission, and the two Co-chairmen, had two advantages: it would not require the presence of both China and the Soviet Union in the same forum; and it would be confined to a discussion of Laos, without bringing in other Indochinese issues.[13] It so happened that on 28 May the funeral of the Indian prime minister Nehru occasioned the simultaneous presence in New Delhi of Secretary of State Rusk,

TABLE 15.1 The Laos crises of May–June 1964

Events in Laos	Diplomacy		United States decisions
	Communist moves	Moves of Souvanna Phouma and of Britain	
16–17 May: Start of main Pathet Lao offensive against Kong Lae's forces in Plaine des Jarres.		16 May: Souvanna Phouma protested to Geneva Co-chairmen about the Pathet Lao offensive.	
17 May: International Commission team forced to withdraw from area.			
	18 May: *Renmin Ribao* warned US against extending the war in Vietnam.		
		19 May: Further letter from Souvanna Phouma to Co-chairmen, proposing consultations in Vientiane under Article 4 of 1962 agreement.	19 May: JCS urged more vigorous application of OPLAN 34A covert operations against North Vietnam.
	20 May: Polish delegate withdrew from International Commission.		
21 May: Souvanna Phouma authorised US to conduct low-level reconnaissance flights over Laos.	21 May: Soviet suggestion to Britain, to reconvene full Geneva Conference on Laos; already proposed by France.	21 May: British decision to pursue idea of ambassadorial consultations in Vientiane.	21 May: Rusk cable to Lodge expressing concern about fragile situation in South Vietnam.

22 May: Souvanna Phouma announced intention to seek military and economic aid from France, Britain and United States.

24 May: Souvanna Phouma expressed willingness to attend 14-nation Geneva conference on condition it was preceded by a ceasefire, and return to the status quo of 16 May.

26 May: Britain issued invitation to 14-nations to attend Vientiane consultations.

22 May: Rusk speech on South-East Asia, intended as 'signal' to Hanoi and Peking.

23 May: Bundy's 30-day scenario for combining military action against Hanoi with call for new negotiations.

25 May: NSC 'ExCom' decided not to adopt 30-day scenario but to recommend 'graduated pressure' against North Vietnam, following a diplomatic warning.

26 May: Lodge cable to Rusk: only action against Hanoi will change situation in South Vietnam.

27 May: Recall of Harkins to Washington, following differences over scale of US participation in South Vietnam.

24 May: Souvanna Phouma defended his request for reconnaissance flights, on ground that Pathet Lao was conducting offensive.

26 May: Chinese foreign minister criticised Souvanna Phouma's plan to merge rightist and neutralist 'factions'; neutralist forces must have separate existence.

26 May: Chinese letter to Geneva Co-chairmen urging reconvening of 14-nation conference, without any conditions.

27 May: Polish proposal for meeting of representatives of Geneva Co-chairmen, International Commission and the three Laotian parties.

TABLE 15.1 *The Laos crises of May–June 1964*

Events in Laos	Diplomacy		United States decisions
	Communist moves	Moves of Souvanna Phouma and of Britain	
	28 May: Kosygin attended Nehru's funeral in New Delhi.	28 May: Rusk and Douglas Home attended Nehru's funeral: talks with Kosygin?	29 May: US decision to respond to Polish proposals, as preferable to diplomatic alternatives; decision to treat Laos and South Vietnam as separate problems.
			30 May: Draft 'outline' for message to North Vietnam, via Seaborn.
1 June: Souphanouvong declared he no longer accepted Souvanna Phouma as legal premier in Laos; desired to withdraw remaining personnel from Vientiane.			1–2 June: Honolulu Conference, attended by Rusk, McNamara, and Saigon country team. Debate on military action against North, still favoured by JCS (but not by Taylor, their chairman).
		2 June: Start of Vientiane consultations, not attended by Communist side. Main concern was with question of new ceasefire.	
4 June: Lao Patriotic Front made appeal for unity against American imperialism.			5 June: G. Ball visited Paris for talks with De Gaulle.
7 June: US reconnaisaance plane shot down over Pathet			

9 June: US planes retaliated by striking Pathet Lao positions.

10–11 June: Souvanna Phouma withdrew authorisation for US flights, then changed his mind again.

11 June: Khang Khay bombed by Laotian planes; Chinese building hit.

13 June: China protested against bombing of Khang Khay; again urged 14-nation conference on Laos.

mid-June: Vientiane consultations still in progress (to 29 June).

10 June: McNamara rejected JCS proposals for action against North Vietnam at this stage.

12–15 June: 'ExCom' discussed a Congressional Resolution on Indochina, but decided against it.

SOURCES *Documents Relating to British Involvement in the Indochina Conflict 1945–1965* (London: HMSO, 1965) Cmnd 2834; *Select Documents on International Affairs:* no. 16, *Laos* (Canberra: Department of External Affairs, April 1970) pp. 141–7; A. J. Dommen, *Conflict in Laos: the Politics of Neutrality*, 2nd edn (London, 1971) ch. xii; *Peking Review*, 19 June 1964.

British prime minister Douglas-Home and Soviet deputy premier A. N. Kosygin. It is not known whether they had any direct exchanges on the Laos question; but the event may well have provided an opportunity to take some of the heat out of the situation.

On 29 May the 'ExCom' decided that the Polish proposal was worth pursuing, and also that the problems of Laos and South Vietnam should still be treated separately; which amounted to a decision in favour of continuing a military strategy centred on South Vietnam. The JCS, however, had not yet given up hope of persuading the President to authorise overt air strikes of some kind against North Vietnam; they continued to recommend such action in memoranda of 30 May and 2 June, even though their own Chairman (still Maxwell Taylor) had reservations about it. The issue was debated at another Honolulu conference – again attended by Rusk as well as by McNamara – on 1–2 June 1964.[14] But the outcome remained the same. Nor did the loss of the first United States naval aircraft over Laos on 6 June affect the issue more than marginally. Retaliatory strikes were conducted against Pathet Lao gun positions on the 9th; and on 11 June planes of the Royal Laotian air force (but probably in reality Thai) bombed the Chinese compound at Khang Khay. But no further escalation seems to have been contemplated at that time.

The one element in the Bundy strategy which was still under consideration by the second week of June was a Congressional Resolution, which the President might still have decided to request sometime in the second half of the month as a signal of the United States' determination not to back away from commitments in South-East Asia. William Bundy was allowed to go as far as drafting such a resolution, and submitted a memorandum to justify the need for it. But at a further meeting of the 'ExCom' on 15 June, even that measure was set aside in favour of various less spectacular actions which the President was free to authorise without special Congressional approval.[15]

As far as warning North Vietnam was concerned, Rusk decided to go ahead with the plan to transmit an oral message through the Canadian representative on the International Commission (J. Blair Seaborn) when he visited Hanoi on 18 June. This amounted to the 'carrot and stick' principle put forward by Lodge two months earlier. An expression of American determination to protect the independence of South Vietnam was combined with a hint that military restraint might produce economic benefits for North Vietnam, although the message did not include any direct offer of aid. For his part Pham Van Dong refused to make a formal reply, merely reiterating Hanoi's earlier demands for an American withdrawal and the establishment of a coalition government (including the NLFSVN) in Saigon.[16]

The question of overt military action against North Vietnam thus appeared to have been settled for the time being. Preparations went ahead for the intensification of OPLAN 34A attacks on coastal installations in the North, using South Vietnamese naval craft: the first of them took place against the islands of Hon-Me and Hon-Ngu at the end of July.[17] But this fell far short of what the JCS had been recommending, and the 'scenario' was left in limbo. Its main contribution to later thinking was that it had established in the minds of officials a range of possible actions against North Vietnam which in the event would be applied *ad hoc* rather than as elements of a coherent strategy. The result was to make it appear in retrospect as if the United States was slowly and perfidiously implementing a long-term plan carefully worked out in advance – when in fact the plan had been thrown to the winds and the initiative virtually sacrificed to the Communist side.

III

It is impossible to judge whether the Bundy scenario would have worked had Johnson been willing to implement such a bold strategy. The policy he did adopt at this critical stage of the war certainly gave the United States the worst of all worlds. In making a deliberate decision not to dramatise the crisis the President had nonetheless allowed an imperceptible escalation of the war, based on the minimum action required to prevent the immediate fall of South Vietnam to Communist forces. This left the United States in a vulnerable position, as well as allowing the Communist powers time to prepare more thoroughly for an eventual confrontation. The historian can only speculate as to whether all this seriously reduced the chances of an eventual American victory once the 'real' Vietnam War began. But it probably made that larger war more likely rather than less. The essence of 'coercive diplomacy' lay in using military pressures to bring about the right conditions for effective diplomacy on American terms. Unfortunately from spring 1964 until the end of his Administration the level of military pressure which Johnson deemed appropriate was never adequate, at any given time, to force Hanoi to negotiate on terms he could accept.

The wider consequences of American restraint at this point are also difficult to assess. His reluctance to dramatise the American commitment to South-East Asia may have created the impression among leaders elsewhere in the region that, in the final analysis, Indochina was not sufficiently important to justify a direct military confrontation between the United States and China; and that in the long run the Americans would have to accept defeat in South Vietnam. The attitude of the neutralist leaders of Cambodia and Indonesia provide an acid test in this regard. It was on 20 June 1964 that Sihanouk, for the first time, approached the NLFSVN (as opposed to the government in Saigon) with a proposal for discussions about the Vietnamese–Cambodian border.[18] On the same day Sukarno – having previously responded to an initiative by Macapagal for a second 'Maphilindo' summit in Tokyo, and having even agreed to a token withdrawal of 'volunteers' from Sarawak – walked out of the meeting itself soon after it began. As a result 'Maphilindo' was virtually finished, until its resurrection in the post-Sukarno period in the guise of the Association of South-East Asian Nations. The fighting in Borneo immediately entered a new phase and the possibility of a diplomatic solution became more remote than ever.[19] It is impossible to demonstrate beyond all reasonable doubt that either of these developments followed directly from Washington's apparent 'weakness' in handling the third Laos crisis; but the coincidence should not be ignored.

In the case of Indonesia, the Russians were quick to seize the opportunity which appeared to have arisen from the sudden collapse of the 'Maphilindo' summit. Mikoyan paid another visit to Indonesia from 22 June to 1 July 1964, and in a bid to wean Sukarno away from support for the Chinese line in the Afro-Asian world, Moscow was now willing to offer additional military aid as well as more support for 'confrontation'. Negotiations continued when Subandrio and General Yani paid a return visit to Moscow (7–17 July) and received a promise of Soviet helicopters and other equipment which would permit a more efficient campaign against Malaysia.[20] They did not, however, acquire a military capability to actually defeat British and Malaysian forces in Sarawak, which may have been one reason for Sukarno's decision to move even closer to China in the autumn of 1964.

President Johnson himself, preoccupied with the politics of an election year, may not have been fully conscious of these possible longer term implications of his June decisions. It was during May 1964, in speeches in Atlantic City and Ann Arbor, that he first used the phrase 'great society' to sum up his ambitions for social and economic reform during a second presidential term. The Civil Rights Act was already moving through Congress and would come into effect on 2 July. A reminder of the urgency of the problems which most concerned him was to come two weeks later, when an incident in New York led to serious rioting in that city from 18 July, spreading to other urban centres before the end of the summer.

But perhaps an even more important factor in the President's thinking about South-East Asia at this time was an assumption that, given the massive military and economic capabilities of the United States, he could choose his own time to force a showdown with North Vietnam. In one sense, he may have been concerned about the short-term limitations of American military capacity – limitations which he knew would be made good within a year or so by McNamara's programmes at the Pentagon. The state of preparedness for 'limited war' was already much greater than it had been three years before, when Kennedy had been unable even to contemplate direct intervention in Laos. But a number of planned innovations relating specifically to warfare in tropical areas like Indochina, especially areas at a great distance from the American mainland, were not yet complete. For example, the testing of 'airmobility' by the 11th Assault Division (activated in February 1963) continued until late 1964 before being pronounced a success. Also the new C-141 transport plane (Starlifter) had had its first flight towards the end of 1963 but would not be ready for service until October 1964.[21] In an emergency, of course, the United States could have fought a war without these refinements; or could have speeded up their development. But Johnson may have decided that, if deployment of ground forces did become necessary and if he had a choice as to its timing, it would be logical to postpone that level of commitment until late in 1964 at the earliest: that is, until after the presidential election.

IV

In South Vietnam itself the Americans attempted to make a fresh start in late June and early July. Westmoreland, due originally to take over from Harkins on 1 August, officially became commander of MACV on 20 June. Three days later it was announced that Maxwell Taylor would replace Lodge as ambassador, with U. Alexis Johnson as his deputy also enjoying ambassadorial rank. During the first half of July, Ambassadors Taylor and Johnson then proceeded to reorganise the US mission and to make suggestions for a new system of liaison between the embassy and the Vietnamese government. The results fell short of the joint command which the JCS had been asking for; nor was there to be any 'encadrement' of American officers and officials alongside Vietnamese counterparts. But with a general as ambassador, and a more coherent relationship between Americans and Vietnamese, it was possible to believe in the illusion of progress. Towards the end of July it was also announced that the number of United States military personnel would be increased by about 5000 before the end of the year.[22]

These changes took place against the background of a new guerrilla offensive in South Vietnam, starting in June and becoming more intense in early July, which was Hanoi's effective response to the Seaborn 'warning'. Activity in the Mekong Delta culminated in an attack at Vinh-Chau on 10–11 July, whilst a growing campaign in the highlands of Central Vietnam threatened both US Special Forces camps and the main highways in that region. A major ambush on the road from Qui-Nhon to Pleiku, on 1 July, was followed a few days later by attacks on the camps at Polei Krong and Nam Dong; and in the latter engagement (inland from Danang, in Central Vietnam) it was claimed that the attackers included regular soldiers of the PAVN who had just infiltrated from the North.[23] If it was true, they were fighting alongside southern forces and not as a distinct unit. Hanoi was probably still debating whether to send whole units of PAVN troops into South Vietnam to supplement the campaign of the PLAFSVN.

Meanwhile the situation in Laos remained fragile. Souvanna Phouma's government in Vietiane now had the support of both rightist and neutralist (Kong Lae's) military units, but they were not yet strong enough to recover lost ground in the Plaine des

Jarres. By late June the American military mission in Laos was worried about the threat to Muong Soui posed by a build-up of Pathet Lao and North Vietnamese forces in the surrounding hills. Having abandoned the idea of using direct pressure against North Vietnam as a means of countering further moves by the Communist side, Washington was now faced with the question how far to become involved in support of the Vientiane government on the ground. There was no question of abandoning the Geneva framework entirely by putting in United States combat units. But it might be possible to authorise a small expansion of covert American (and also Thai) military involvement – violating only marginally the ceasefire lines guaranteed in 1962. During the last week of June, after another round of debate between the Pentagon and the State Department, it was decided to go ahead with a plan to strengthen the position of neutralist forces in the area north of Vang Vieng and then to advance into the hills around Muong Soui.

The resulting 'Operation Triangle' required the use of American logistic support to move reinforcements into Central Laos from Attopeu in the South, as well as the participation of (disguised) Thai aircraft and artillery units; CIA-trained Meo units were also involved. Preparations went ahead during the middle weeks of July and the operation finally got under way on 19–20 July.[24] Compared with the previous record of Kong Lae's forces, it was remarkably successful: a vital road junction between Muong Soui and Luang Prabang was recaptured, and by 6 August government forces had taken a significant part of Phou Kout mountain. For the time being, Muong Soui was secure. But by then the situation in Indochina as a whole had been transformed by the 'Gulf of Tonkin' crisis.

16 The Gulf of Tonkin Crisis

Aggression by terror against the peaceful villages of South Vietnam has now been joined by open aggression on the high seas against the United States of America. The determination of all Americans to carry out our full commitment to the people and to the government of South Vietnam will be redoubled by this outrage. Yet our response for the present will be limited and fitting. We Americans know – although others appear to forget – the risk of spreading conflict. We still seek no wider war. . . . It is a solemn responsibility to have to order even limited military action by forces whose over-all strength is as vast and awesome as those of the United States of America. But it is my considered conviction, shared through-out your government, that firmness in the right is indispensable today for peace.

> President Johnson, in his television address,
> 5 August 1964

In fact the so-called second Tonkin Gulf incident of 4 August never occurred. That night the Democratic Republic of Vietnam did not have a single war vessel on the waters where the US ships were. . . . The spokesman of the DRVN pointed out that the so-called second Tonkin Gulf incident was sheer fabrication. . . .

The Government of the People's Republic of China hereby solemnly declares: the flames of a war of aggression against the DRVN were lit by the United States. Since the United States has acted in this way the DRVN has gained the right of action to fight against aggression, and all the countries upholding the Geneva Agreements have gained the right to assist the DRVN in its fight against aggression. The DRVN is a member of the socialist camp, and no socialist country can sit idly by whilst it is being subjected to aggression. . . . Aggression by the United States against the DRVN means aggression against China.

> Chinese Government statement,
> 6 August 1964

I

The extent to which the United States had lost the initiative in Indochina became apparent during the first week of August 1964. In so far as they occasioned the first overt military action by the United States against North Vietnam, the 'Gulf of Tonkin' incidents have been seen by Americans as the beginning of their own Vietnam War. They also led to the Congressional Resolution of 7 August – on which, as it turned out, all subsequent American actions were based. That, in turn, led to a major controversy over the circumstances in which the Southeast Asia Resolution was approved, and to bitter conflict about what exactly happened in the Gulf of Tonkin on the night of 4 August. The official version of events was seriously challenged during the Hearings of the Senate Foreign Relations Committee in February 1968, and the constitutional issues which then emerged affected the whole question of the legality of United States military involvement in Vietnam.[1] Our present concern is not with that domestic constitutional debate, however, but with understanding the actual situation of 2–7 August 1964 as an international crisis – perhaps comparable with those about Berlin and the Cuba Missiles.

The bare facts, as seen from the United States, are well known and can be briefly summarised. In the afternoon of 2 August (local time) the United States destroyer *Maddox*, sailing off the North Vietnamese coast, was attacked by three 'PT' (motor torpedo) boats and forced to withdraw from the area. The following day the *Maddox*, accompanied this time by a second destroyer (the *C. Turner Joy*) was ordered to continue its patrol in the Gulf and again sailed close to DRVN territorial waters. After dark on the 4th (still morning in Washington) the two destroyers reported that they were again under attack by PT boats. In spite of subsequent confusion about precisely what had happened, President Johnson decided to retaliate on 5 August by sending American planes to bomb North Vietnamese naval installations at Quang-Khe and an oil depot at Vinh (Operation 'Pierce Arrow'). Simultaneously he authorised the forward deployment to South Vietnam and North-East Thailand of a number of fighters and bombers normally based in the Philippines and Japan.[2] On 5 August, too, he sent to Congress the message which resulted in the Joint Resolution on South-East Asia, passed almost unanimously two days later.

This combination of moves, intended as a warning that the

United States had both the capability and the determination for much more powerful action against Hanoi if it became necessary, was made in the same spirit as that which had inspired the Bundy scenarios of May and June. But it fell far short of what Bundy had proposed, both in coherence and in intensity; nor was the text of the actual Congressional Resolution the one he had drafted at that time.[3] The question inevitably arises: was this sequence of American actions deliberately devised by Washington, on the basis of initial moves intended to provoke the Communist side? Or was it a hastily improvised response to a genuine crisis whose timing had been decided in Hanoi or, conceivably, Peking?

There can be no question that an attack on the US destroyer *Maddox* did take place on 2 August, even though the accounts of the two sides differ in certain details. The initial United States version, as reported in the press, said that the destroyer had been attacked 30 miles out to sea. Only later did it become known that although the attack itself probably occurred there, the *Maddox* had earlier been much closer to the North Vietnamese coast (well within the 12-mile limit claimed by Hanoi although outside the 3-mile limit recognised by the United States); also, that it was no ordinary destroyer but was engaged in a highly secret intelligence patrol (code-named DESOTO) using electronic devices for surveillance of Communist activities onshore. Nevertheless, both Hanoi and Peking acknowledged that, on this first occasion, North Vietnamese PT boats did take action to drive away an American warship which they claimed had entered Vietnamese territorial waters. Only the second incident was dismissed as an American 'fabrication'.[4]

Regarding that second incident (on the night of 4 August) the evidence elicited during the Hearings of early 1968 leaves little doubt that top officials of the Johnson Administration had told less than the whole truth before the Senate Foreign Relations Committee three and a half years before. The outcome of the later Hearings convinced most critics of the war that the second incident, which President Johnson had used as his pretext for bombing North Vietnam, had not in fact involved a North Vietnamese torpedo attack on United States naval vessels in the international waters of the Gulf. Important questions remain unanswered about what actually did happen that night, when the two destroyers – operating with faulty equipment in rough seas–seriously *believed* they were under attack. But since the only hard evidence so far

TABLE 16.1   *The Gulf of Tonkin incidents: the American perspective*

OPLAN 34A operations: air strikes	DE SOTO patrol	Washington decisions
30–31 July: Night attacks by S. Vietnamese craft, against islands of Hon-Ngu and Hon-Me, off North Vietnamese coast.	31 July: *Maddox* moved along North Vietnamese coast, to begin its surveillance patrol.	2 Aug.: 10.15 a.m.: Pentagon statement to press, reporting the incident. That morning, Johnson met Rusk, Ball, McNamara and Wheeler; decision to continue the patrol, without retaliatory action.
31 July: PAVN made official protest to the International Commission regarding these attacks.	1 Aug.: *Maddox* moved steadily northwards.	
	2 Aug.: Early hours: *Maddox* twice changed course after radar contact and radio intercepts.	
	Afternoon (approx. 2.40–3.30 p.m.): *Maddox* was attacked by North Vietnamese PT boats; called on support from carrier *Ticonderoga*.	3 Aug.: President held further meetings, of which no details have been revealed.
	3 Aug.: *Maddox* joined by *C. Turner Joy*, to continue its patrol. Aircraft carrier *Constellation* left Hong Kong to join the *Ticonderoga*.	4 Aug.: Report of second incident came in around 10.00 a.m. McNamara held discussions throughout the day; at some point, he ordered deployment of US fighters and bombers from Japan and Philippines to Thailand and South Vietnam (taking place from 5 August).
3–4 Aug.: Further night attack by South Vietnamese craft, this time at Cap Vinh-Son.	4 Aug.: Instruction to *Maddox* to continue the patrol until 7 Aug.	
	Late evening (9.50 p.m. till after midnight): *Maddox* reported second attack, after radio intercepts; situation became confused.	

Noon: First of two NSC meetings that day; followed by President's 'Tuesday Lunch' with senior advisers.

6.00 p.m.: Pentagon spokesman gave brief report of second incident: details 'scanty'.

6.00 p.m.: Second NSC meeting decided on retaliatory air strikes; followed by meeting between president and Congressional leaders.

11.37 p.m.: President began television address, announcing retaliatory air strikes.

5 Aug.: Exchange of letters between Khrushchev and Johnson. Drafting of presidential message to Congress and text for a Joint Resolution.

6 Aug.: Rusk and McNamara appeared before joint meeting of Congressional Committees.

7 Aug.: Joint Resolution passed by Senate and by House of Representatives.

5 Aug.: 10.40 a.m.: US planes took off from carriers *Ticonderoga* and *Constellation*. 1.15–2.00 p.m.: Bombing attacks on Vinh, Quang-Khe and Hon-Gay installations: North Vietnamese torpedo boats destroyed.

7 Aug.: DESOTO patrol due to end.

SOURCES J. C. Goulden, *Truth is the First Casualty: the Gulf of Tonkin Affair, Illusion and Reality* (Chicago, 1969) pp. 253–61; G. Porter (ed.), *Vietnam: the Definitive Documentation of Human Decisions* (London and Philadelphia: Heyden, 1979) vol. ii, pp. 486–95 and 302–4; *The Pentagon Papers: the Defense Department History of United States Decision-making on Vietnam: Senator Gravel Edition* (Boston, Mass.: Beacon Press, 1971) vol. iii, pp. 128–30; A. Austen, *The President's War* (Philadelphia, 1971).

cited consists of still secret intercepts of messages between Communist naval units, it is impossible for the historian to be sure that
an actual attack occurred – even though North Vietnamese PT
boats may at one stage have contemplated it.

Further doubts about the sincerity of official American
statements arose from the revelation that the surveillance patrol on
which the *Maddox* was engaged happened to coincide with two
covert operations by ships of the South Vietnamese navy against
the offshore islands of Hon-Ngu and Hon-Me. Those other
engagements – part of the intensified OPLAN-34A programme –
took place on the nights of 30–31 July and 3–4 August. Also on 1
August, a North Vietnamese post at Nam Can near the border
with Laos was attacked by planes coming from the direction of
Laos. The coincidence of timing between these other attacks and
the surveillance patrol does not in itself prove that the Americans
intended to provoke a North Vietnamese response. But in the
atmosphere of distrust which prevailed in Washington by early
1968 many members of Congress – as well as journalists and anti-
war activists – found it easy to believe in such a connection; and an
interpretation along those lines has been implicit in much
American writing about the Gulf of Tonkin Incidents ever since.
The possibility that the *Maddox* had a genuine intelligence mission
which could only be conducted close to the North Vietnamese
coast has not been taken seriously.

In all this, it is not impossible that the commander of the Pacific
Fleet (Admiral Thomas Moorer) responded to a situation created
by the first incident by actively seeking to provoke a second attack.
On the morning of 4 August he ordered the *Maddox* and *Turner Joy*
to continue the patrol longer than had originally been planned,
knowing that further North Vietnamese action within the next few
days would provide the pretext for an air strike.[5] It will be recalled,
too, that in March the Pentagon had been ordered (under NSAM-
288) to be ready to undertake retaliatory actions against North
Vietnam on 72 hours notice. It so happens that the length of time
between the incident of 2 August and the bombing raids of 5
August was almost precisely that interval. It might be argued that
CINCPAC, despite the President's decision against retaliation,
made his own preparations for an air strike; even that he gave
Washington an oversimplified picture of events on the night of 4
August in order to force the President's hand. But an interpreta-
tion along those lines – which cannot in any case be substantiated

by firm evidence – still would not demonstrate a deliberate American intent to provoke an incident on 1 or 2 August. Moreover, the fact that the US Navy was not prepared for a strike immediately the first incident occurred, but had to order the carrier *Constellation* to sail from Hong Kong to join the *Ticonderoga* before it could take place, seems to confirm the impression that both the President himself and his senior military commanders were taken by surprise on the 2nd. The historian who wishes to argue otherwise and to insist that the whole affair was an American provocation from beginning to end has an obligation to produce new and stronger evidence for that interpretation. Even conclusive proof that the second incident was a complete fabrication by the American side would not be sufficient to challenge the prima-facie conclusion that the first attack represented a deliberate decision taken by Hanoi for its own reasons.

It would seem, therefore, that the historian is faced with two critical questions:

(1) Why *did* Hanoi attack the *Maddox* on the afternoon of 2 August?

(2) Why did Washington decide, on the afternoon of 4 August, to use the report of a second attack as pretext for retaliation?

Whilst the second question still requires us to look closely at decision-making in Washington, the first implies a need to re-examine the whole affair in the light of international Communist strategy in the period leading up to the first attack.

II

The documentary record so far available suggests that American officials themselves found it difficult to assess Hanoi's motives for the decision to fire on the *Maddox* on 2 August 1964.[6] A State Department intelligence memorandum of 6 August linked the attack to evidence of closer co-ordination between Hanoi and Peking during the preceding weeks; and such evidence as we have suggests that Sino-Vietnamese relations had indeed become warmer than at any time since the VNWP 9th Plenum at the end of 1963. Some indication of the change could be gleaned from public statements. On 6 July, replying to another letter from his North Vietnamese counterpart, Foreign Minister Chen Yi was more forthright than on any previous occasion in offering Chinese support in the event of an American decision to extend the war. Three days later *Renmin Ribao* made the same point in an editorial entitled 'A Stern Warning to US Imperialism'. The degree of military support the Chinese could provide was, of course, very limited; but the credibility of the warning was increased a little by the completion – noticed by American intelligence experts on 12 July – of an ostensibly civilian airfield at Phuc-Yen, north-west of Hanoi, which could now take Chinese (or Soviet) Mig-17 jet fighters. That was not all: the CIA was also convinced that a high-level Chinese delegation, probably led by Zhou Enlai himself, had paid a secret visit to Hanoi between 6 and 9 July.[7]

One reason for this apparent shift in the Chinese attitude towards Vietnam may have been a growing dissatisfaction with events in Laos; especially the conduct of Souvanna Phouma, who since his visit to Peking in April seemed to have moved very much closer to the United States position. Some of that dissatisfaction was expressed openly in *Renmin Ribao* on 6 July.[8] By then the Chinese may already have been aware of the preparatory moves for 'Operation Triangle', which represented a significant – albeit 'covert' – increase in both Thai and American involvement in the Laos fighting. In the long term that might have been a reason for renewed Chinese interest in negotiations which would reaffirm Laotian neutrality. Peking's strategy in the Indochinese peninsula probably remained what it had always been: to support North Vietnam with aid; to promote the revolution inside South Vietnam, without encouraging a major war; and to develop friendly relations with a neutral Laos and Cambodia.

During the three weeks from the end of June to 20 July 1964 – the tenth anniversary of the Geneva Agreements – it is possible to interpret both Chinese and American activity in terms of what the theorists of coercive diplomacy would recognise as a sequence of warning 'signals' (see Table 16.2). Even before Chen Yi's letter (and possibly Zhou's visit) to Hanoi, a minor incident on 29 June had led Peking to issue its '300th serious warning' to the United States: on this occasion, an American submarine had intruded into Chinese territorial waters off the coast of Guangdong. Two days later, commenting on the same incident, *Renmin Ribao* also brought up the question of Indochina and warned the Americans not to underestimate the strength of the Chinese people. A week after that (at a time when Zhou himself may have been in North Vietnam) the PLA shot down a U-2 plane belonging to Chiang Kaishek as it

TABLE 16.2 *Chinese and American 'signals' relating to Vietnam, July 1964*

China and North Vietnam	Washington and Saigon
29 June: China's 300th 'serious warning' to the US, following intrusion of submarine into Chinese waters off Pinghai (Guangdong).	
1 July: *Renmin Ribao* editorial on incident, including passage about Indochina: 'What is your intention?' Warning that US will 'court disaster' if it underestimates China.	
7 July: PLA air force shot down third U-2 plane (of Chiang Kaishek) over East China.	
6 July: Chen Yi's letter to Xuan Thuy: China will not 'look on with folded arms in the face of any aggression against the DRVN'.	
9 July: *Renmin Ribao* editorial on Chen Yi's letter: 'A stern warning to US imperialism'; also commentary on the 7 July U-2 incident.	9 July: Saigon allegation that regular PAVN troops took part in a battle south of the 17th parallel on 5–6 July; not confirmed.
	9 July: Press leak in Saigon about US contingency plans for air strikes against North, leading to Beichman story in *Washington Post* (10 July).
	10 July: Danang display of S. Vietnamese air power.
13–20 July: China staged 'week of common struggle' to commemorate Geneva anniversary.	
14 July: NCNA reported Pathet Lao statement denouncing American use of Thai troops in Laos, and denying any threat to Muong Soui.	
14 July: Chen Yi speech at French embassy in Peking, accusing US of open military intervention in Laos.	
19 July: Chinese government statement for 10th anniversary of Geneva Agreements: US has introduced tens of thousands of troops into Indochina; 'there is a limit to everything'; Chinese 'will not sit idly by,' etc. Guo Moruo in Hanoi for anniversary rally. *Nhan Dan* carried article by Vo Nguyen Giap: 'The South Vietnamese People will win.'	19 July: Nguyen Khanh and Nguyen Cao Ky both made public references to the idea of a 'March to the North'; Ambassador Taylor, in private, indicated disapproval.

flew over East China. On 9 July *Renmin Ribao* publicised both that incident and the Chen Yi letter.[9]

At that point the Americans and South Vietnamese responded with three 'signals' of their own. A press leak in Saigon, which cannot have been accidental, allowed Arnold Beichman to file a story about United States contingency planning for air strikes against North Vietnam in retaliation for Communist actions in the South.[10] On 10 July, at the newly constructed base at Danang, South Vietnam held what amounted to a display of its growing air power. On the 9th, too, the official Saigon news agency published a story alleging that during a battle just south of the 17th parallel on 5–6 July a unit of PAVN regular soldiers had been identified on the Communist side.[11]

Further Chinese warnings came during a 'week of common struggle' in support of North Vietnam, held from 13 to 19 July. On the 14th, as the New China News Agency reported Pathet Lao denunciations of the covert use of Thai forces in Laos, Chen Yi celebrated Bastille Day at the French embassy and accused the Americans of blatant military intervention in Laos. On 19 July the Chinese propagandist Guo Moruo, in a further gesture of solidarity, attended an anniversary rally in Hanoi. On the same day an official government statement on Indochina pointed out that the Chinese had thus far not reacted to the introduction of 'tens of thousands' of American troops into South Vietnam and Laos, but that 'there is a limit to everything'. A warning that China would 'not sit idly by' if the United States extended the war may have been calculated to evoke memories of the 1950 warnings which had preceded Chinese intervention in Korea.[12] But that need not mean that Peking actively favoured an intensification of the armed struggle at this stage; possibly the Chinese were divided on that issue, as on so much else during the summer of 1964.

In South Vietnam the PLAFSVN commemorated the Geneva anniversary by attacking the district town of Cai-Be in the Mekong Delta on 19–20 July. But although they scored another spectacular success, it was not the start of a general offensive. By this time a major debate was probably going on in Hanoi on the question of the 9th Plenum resolution and its implementation. Should the Party step up the military struggle? If so, should it send regular PAVN units into the South in the hope of a quick victory? An article published by Vo Nguyen Giap in *Nhan-Dan* on 19 July implied a negative decision on the second point: it emphasised the protracted nature of the conflict and referred to the 'spirit of self-reliance' of the South Vietnamese people.[13] But the failure of either Hanoi Radio or the VNA to broadcast the article immediately – there was a précis of it on 27 July – suggests that this was still a controversial theme. Possibly Nguyen Chi Thanh would have preferred a stronger military policy along the lines of that actually implemented later in the year. The absence of both Vo Nguyen Giap and Le Duan from the Hanoi rally of 19 July suggests they may have been somewhere else at that time: possibly abroad; or, conceivably, making a secret inspection tour in the South or in Laos.[14]

In Saigon, Nguyen Khanh also chose the Geneva anniversary to make his first public speech advocating a 'march to the North'; and although Ambassador Taylor let it be known that the Americans disapproved, it too can be interpreted as a 'signal' to the North. The situation was thus already tense two weeks before the Gulf of Tonkin Incident.

III

The complexity of Chinese internal politics in the summer of 1964 makes it difficult to penetrate the background of Chinese decisions relating to the conflict in Indochina. Several distinct revolutionary campaigns were under way inside China. Certain spheres of activity, particularly industry and the bureaucracy, were affected by the movement to 'learn from the PLA' which had begun in February 1964 and was led by the general political department of the armed forces. In many rural areas, and to some extent amongst the urban masses, a long-term campaign for socialist education (based on the slogan of 'four cleanups') had been under way since September 1963.[15] More recently, in June–July 1964, a festival of Peking Opera on revolutionary themes had begun to focus attention on the question of art and literature. All three campaigns were controversial; and behind the intellectual debate there probably lay a fundamental rivalry between the PLA and the Party bureaucracy for the leading role in the next stage of the revolution. Also lurking in the background were radical figures like Chen Boda, who after 1966 would set his stamp on the 'cultural revolution' in opposition to established figures in both the Party and the armed forces; but that crisis lay in the future.

By July Mao was willing to throw his weight behind those who insisted that the drive against corruption and conservatism in rural areas had so far been pursued too superficially. He thus supported moves by Liu Shaoqi and his wife Wang Guangmei, who gave the main report at a conference in Shanghai in mid-July, to deepen the socialist education movement across the country. Liu seems to have remained powerful in that sphere for the rest of the year – which probably meant that he had less time to concern himself with Vietnam. Simultaneously Peng Zhen was playing the dominant role in the movement to reform Peking Opera, despite the efforts of Mao's wife Jiang Qing to make her mark in that field.[16] Both developments might suggest that the Party machine was holding its own against the PLA. But it was the latter which came to the fore on such occasions as the shooting down of the U-2 plane on 7 July – which Mao praised at a PLA ceremony on 23 July – or the development of a crisis in the Gulf of Tonkin. The possibility cannot be ruled out that some elements of the PLA – especially in South China – had a hand in encouraging the Vietnamese to respond aggressively to the 'provocations' of the *Maddox* at the beginning of August.

Meanwhile relations between Moscow and Peking seemed to be deteriorating rapidly. On 10 July – although his remarks were not reported in the Chinese media – Mao told a group of visiting Japanese that China sympathised with Japan's loss of territory to the Soviet Union, and linked it to Russian territorial imperialism at the expense of China. A few days later (14 July) *Renmin Ribao* produced its 'ninth comment' – perhaps the most biting of all – on the line set forth by the CPSU precisely one year earlier: it accused Khrushchev personally of being a 'phoney Communist'.[17] By the end of the month, when it became clear that Moscow intended after all to go ahead with plans for a new international Communist conference (starting with a preparatory session in December), the Chinese reacted very sharply indeed. Since one of the principal issues between the two leading Communist Parties concerned the nature of imperialism and the question of *détente*, this would seem to imply continuing disagreement between them on the question whether it was possible in any area of the world to arrive at a negotiated solution of essentially revolutionary conflicts. On 3 August, moreover, *Renmin Ribao* published an article by Luo Ruiqing which took as its slogan Mao's injunction to 'draw a sharp line between ourselves and the enemy'. Whilst praising Stalin, the article accused Khrushchev not only of failing to oppose the enemy but of 'joining hands with them against the revolution'.[18]

In general the Gulf of Tonkin Incident served to strengthen those people in the Chinese leadership – notably Luo Riuqing – who favoured a more vigorous Chinese commitment to North Vietnam and who opposed any compromise with either Khrushchev or the United States. Liu Shaoqi and Peng Zhen also supported a stronger commitment there, but probably favoured political and diplomatic action in South-East Asia rather than an escalation of armed struggle. It would be wrong, however, to see any one leader or group completely dominating Chinese decision-making at this period. A consensus within the leadership depended very much on the logic of the situation rather than on the preferences of individuals. It was unlikely that a consensus would emerge in favour of a massive military commitment to Vietnam unless the Americans attacked China itself.

Against this impression of growing Chinese militancy on the eve of the Gulf of Tonkin crisis must be weighed indications that both Communist powers might be willing to participate in another round of diplomacy on Laos – which would make sense in view of their anxieties about 'Operation Triangle'. The first move was made by Moscow, in a Note to all the Geneva Conference participants delivered on 27 July calling for the urgent reconvening of the 14-nation conference on Laos and threatening that the USSR might withdraw from the Geneva Co-chairmanship altogether if the proposal was rejected. A few days later, Laos was among the subjects discussed when Khrushchev and Gromyko held talks in Moscow with the British foreign secretary R. A. Butler from 28 July to 1 August. Meanwhile the Soviet proposal received favourable replies not only from Hanoi (29 July) and the Pathet Lao (31 July) but also (2 August) from Peking.[19]

The fact that Souvanna Phouma's own position had been strengthened by the fighting of late July may explain his willingness, too, to attend a conference. After consultations with Ambassadors Unger and Alexis Johnson in Vientiane on 3 August, his cabinet met on the following day and it too endorsed the Soviet proposal.[20] Washington seems to have been less enthusiastic, insisting that the United States would not attend a new conference

TABLE 16.3 *Laos diplomacy, July–August 1964*

Great power diplomacy	Laos	North Vietnam
25 July: Soviet Note (delivered, 27 July) urging reconvening of 14-nation conference on Laos; implied threat to withdraw from role as Co-chairman if demand was ignored.	late July: 'Operation Triangle' in progress – significant gains for Kong Lae and Royal government forces, with American and Thai assistance.	27 July: VNA precis of article by Giap implied acceptance of protracted war and South Vietnamese self-reliance.
28 July: British foreign secretary (Butler) in Moscow for talks with Gromyko and Khrushchev; Laos was one of issues discussed.	28 July: Soviet chargé d'Affaires visited Khang Khay to meet Souphanouvong.	29 July: *Nhan-Dan* editorial supported Soviet proposals; 14-nation conference on Laos should meet urgently.
30 July: United States insisted on a ceasefire in Laos before a conference met.	31 July: Souphanouvong welcomed proposal for a conference on Laos.	1 Aug.: Nam-Can incident, in which planes bombed a post on Laos–North Vietnam border.
1 Aug.: Communiqué on Moscow talks; press conference by Butler, before leaving for home.		2 Aug.: *Nhan-Dan* editorial opposing idea of UN 'interference' in Indochina (relating specifically to Cambodia–Vietnam border).
2 Aug.: Chinese government statement approved Soviet proposal for 14-nation conference.		

5 Aug.: Exchange of letters between Khrushchev and Johnson about situation in Gulf of Tonkin; veiled Soviet warning to US?

5 Aug.: U Thant supported call for 14-nation conference on Laos.

3 Aug.: Souvanna Phouma met Amb. Unger and U. Alexis Johnson (from Saigon) for lunch; discussed Soviet proposal.

4 Aug.: Vientiane Cabinet approved Soviet proposal for 14-nation conference on Laos.

4–5 Aug.: Fear of revolt in Vientiane; nothing happened.

5–6 Aug.: Kong Lae and Royal forces made successful assault on Phou Kout.

7 Aug.: US deferred approval of plans for air and ground action in Laos 'panhandle'.

9 Aug.: Report that Souvanna Phouma and Souphanouvong have agreed to 'tripartite' talks in Paris.

2–5 Aug.: Crisis over Gulf of Tonkin Incidents: see Table 16.1.

5 Aug.: VNA reported DRVN's formal note to Moscow, supporting a conference on Laos.

until there was an enforceable ceasefire. Nevertheless, further diplomatic moves were a distinct possibility at that stage; which may have been the principal reason for President Johnson's reluctance to retaliate against the initial attack on the *Maddox* on 2 August.

One further piece of evidence suggests that some Chinese leaders would have preferred to reduce rather than to heighten tension in Indochina at this point. An article in the Austrian journal *Kurier* on 1 August, based on interviews with foreign minister Chen Yi and with an unidentified 'highest level' member of the Chinese government who may possibly have been Zhou Enlai, was remarkably optimistic on the subject of future relations between China and the United States.[21] Chen Yi implied that Peking was willing to hold talks with Washington immediately, if the Americans would only abandon their hostile policy towards China and withdraw their military personnel from Taiwan; he also looked towards a negotiated settlement in Indochina. His more senior colleague went even further, recognizing that the problems of Taiwan, Macao and Hong Kong would not be resolved for at least another two decades and denying that China had any need of territory beyond its own borders. The Chinese could not fight a modern, large-scale war – and did not want one. Their objective in Indochina was a conference which would produce formal treaties on Laos and Vietnam.

The failure of the Johnson Administration to respond to this 'signal' – if such it was – does not alter the belief that at least some key figures in the Chinese government were as anxious as Johnson himself to avoid the kind of confrontation that had occurred in Korea. But we cannot assume that the whole Chinese leadership was united behind a 'moderate' line.

IV

In all probability the decision to attack the *Maddox* was taken in Hanoi itself rather than in Peking, sometime between the early hours of 1 August and midday on the 2nd (Hanoi time). The North Vietnamese version of events claims that the destroyer was already taking provocative action near the coast of Ha-Tinh province on the night of 31 July, and that a further provocation occurred south of Hon-Mat island (off Vinh) early in the afternoon of 1 August.[22] Hanoi therefore had at least one whole day, possibly two, in which to decide whether to take any retaliatory action of its own. Nor should it be supposed that the North Vietnamese were responding to this type of surveillance mission for the first time. In late February and early March 1964 a previous surveillance patrol had approached within four miles of the North Vietnamese coast, and had later continued along the South China coast, without drawing any more serious reaction than to be shadowed by Communist vessels for part of the way.[23]

There was ample time, if the Vietnamese leaders so wished, to consult with Chinese and Soviet military attachés in Hanoi; and Soviet claims to be wholly ignorant about what was going on need not be taken seriously. What is certain is that Hanoi's decision was not taken on the spur of the moment or in the heat of battle. It was a deliberate act on someone's part. We can only speculate about possible reasons for such a decision. The hypothesis which springs most readily to mind is that whoever was responsible had an interest in preventing any reduction on international tension in South-East Asia at that moment.

Once the attack had occurred, both Hanoi and Peking seem to have played a waiting game. On the evening of the 2nd, the VNA put out an official statement denouncing the air attack on the Nam-Can post; and on 3 August *Nhan-Dan* carried an editorial warning the Americans against repeating such action. But it was not until around 8.45 a.m. on 5 August (Hanoi time) that VNA published the PAVN high command's account of the incident on the 2nd.[24] By then (6.00 a.m. Hanoi time; 6.00 p.m. on the 4th, Washington time) the Pentagon had put out its first tentative statement about the alleged *second* attack on the *Maddox*. As for Peking, no official report or comment about even the first incident appeared until several hours after the American air strikes on 5 August. An article in the pro-Communist Hong Kong newspaper *Wen Wei Pao* on the 4th, accusing the United States of provocations designed to 'test the patience of the Vietnamese and Chinese peoples', may have reflected the views of the leadership in Guangdong.[25] But Mao himself and his most senior colleagues had probably waited to see what the Americans would do next before making any move of their own.

Meanwhile in Laos, as we have seen, the trend towards negotiations was not seriously interrupted by the first incident.

TABLE 16.4 *The Gulf of Tonkin incidents: the Communist perspective*

Soviet Union	China (Peking time)	North Vietnam (Hanoi time)
1 Aug.: End of Butler's talks with Gromyko and Khrushchev.	2 Aug.: Chinese government statement on Laos, responding affirmatively to Soviet proposal for a new conference (put out by NCNA, 8.48 p.m.).	2 Aug.: 2.40–3.30 p.m.: Engagement arising from North Vietnamese torpedo attack on the *Maddox*.
		8.00 p.m.: VNA carried DRVN statement on air attack at Nam-Can, on NVN–Laos border.
	3 Aug.: *Renmin Ribao* had articles on 'revolutionary successors'; and (by Luo Ruiqing) on Mao's essay of 1939, including new denunciation of Khrushchev.	3 Aug.: *Nhan-Dan* editorial warned US not to use Laos territory for attacks on North Vietnam.
4 Aug.: Khrushchev in Saratov: speech on agriculture, including announcement of forthcoming CPSU Central Committee plenum in November (reported in *Pravda*, 5 Aug.).	4 Aug.: In Hong Kong, *Wen Wei Pao* commented on incident of 2 August and accused US of a 'provocation'.	

5 Aug.: TASS statement on the US strikes against North Vietnam: seen by the Americans as relatively mild in tone. No public comment by Khrushchev, but he wrote privately to Johnson urging US restraint and emphasising joint US–Soviet responsibility for maintaining peace in the world.

6 Aug.: Soviet delegate Morozov spoke at UN Security Council meeting on the Incident; same position as TASS statement. (NCNA criticised his failure to assert that the second incident was a US invention.)

5 or 6 Aug.: Zhou Enlai and Luo Ruiqing sent message to Pham Van Dong and Van Tien Dung, after the US air strike, proposing 'counter-measures in preparation for action' (revealed, 1979).

6 Aug.: *Renmin Ribao*: 'US must immediately stop armed aggression against North Vietnam' (broadcast at 6.30 a.m.).
9.40 a.m.: NCNA put out Chinese government statement on US action against N. Vietnam: 'Aggression against the DRVN is aggression against China.'

5 Aug.: 6.00 a.m.: Hanoi presumably aware of Pentagon statement on 'second incident' in Gulf of Tonkin.
8.45 a.m.: VNA put out PAVN statement giving its version of incident of 2 August, and of Hon-Me and Hon-Ngu attacks and Nam-Can attacks.
11.30 a.m.: Hanoi Radio accused Americans of inventing the 'second incident' as part of a 'new scheme of provocation'.
1.15–2.00 p.m.: US air strikes on Vinh and Quang-Khe.
9.45 p.m.: Hanoi Radio reported PAVN statement on US air strikes; very brief. evening: VNA reported DRVN official reply to Soviet Note of 27 July, supporting a conference on Laos.
6 Aug.: 11.00 a.m.: Hanoi Radio carried DRVN statement, again denying any incident on night of 4 August. *Nhan-Dan* editorial: 'The provocateurs got the blows they deserved.'

TABLE 16.4 *The Gulf of Tonkin incidents: the Communist perspective*

Soviet Union	China (Peking time)	North Vietnam (Hanoi time)
	6–7 Aug.: China moved 36 Mig-fighters to Phuc-Yen, North Vietnam. Also, by 97th, a whole PLA air force headquarters was moved from E. China to S.W. China, as part of general strengthening of defences close to Vietnam. 6–9 Aug.: Mass demonstrations in Peking and other Chinese cities. Big rally on 9th was attended by Zhou Enlai; speech by Liao Chengzhi.	7 Aug.: PAVN High Command held ceremony to honour those involved in events since 2 August.
8 Aug.: Khrushchev's first comment on the Incident, in speech at Ordzhonikidze: warned that if US starts a war, capitalism will be destroyed.		

SOURCES Monitored broadcasts in *SWB/FE/* 1621–1626; *Peking Review*, 7 and 14 Aug. 1964; CIA Memorandum on 'North Vietnam Crisis', 6–11 Aug. 1964, in Johnson Library, National Security File, Country File Vietnam, Box 48; Telegram from US Consul, Hong Kong, to State Department, 6 Aug. 1964, in NSC Histories, Box 38; text of Khrushchev–Johnson exchange of letters, 5 Aug. 1964, in G. Porter (ed.), *Vietnam: the Definitive Documentation of Human Decisions* (London and Philadelphia: Heyden, 1979) vol, II, pp. 302–4.

Note Hanoi time is precisely 12 hours ahead of Washington time; Peking time is 1 hour ahead of Hanoi time.

Souvanna Phouma consulted with American diplomats on the 3rd, and on the morning of 4 August his cabinet decided to respond positively to the Soviet initiative. But that evening the atmosphere in Vientiane was extremely tense; and the following afternoon it was reported that rumours of another revolt had been responsible for unspecified military activity during the night.[26] There is nothing to indicate whether the government feared action by the right or by the left at that time; but a new crisis may have been only narrowly averted.

The question what precisely happened in the Gulf of Tonkin on the night of 4 August will not be resolved finally until much more evidence becomes available. The fact of confusion on board the *Maddox* and the *C. Turner Joy*, which seems by now incontrovertible, does not in itself refute the official American claim that the confusion had as its starting-point some form of hostile or provocative action on the part of the PAVN navy. Although the official version of the second attack depended on communications intelligence of a kind which still cannot be released, it is impossible for the historian to dismiss it out of hand. Moreover, if the first attack on the *Maddox* had indeed been a provocation by the *Communist* side, then whoever was responsible for it may have been deliberately seeking to draw forth an aggressive American response. That interpretation makes a second Communist-initiated incident highly credible. Although the North Vietnamese (and also the Chinese) insisted that the second incident was an American 'fabrication', they did not begin to do so in radio transmissions until the equivalent of 11.30 p.m. (4 August) Washington time: that is, several hours after the Americans first mentioned it.[27] By that time United States aircraft had already taken off from the carriers *Ticonderoga* and *Constellation* and were heading for target areas in North Vietnam; and despite American efforts to ensure an element of surprise, it is possible that Hanoi already knew what was coming.

Perhaps the key question at this point is not whether the second attack did or did not occur, but why the Americans refused to ignore what they believed to be a second attack, as they had ignored the first. Their decision to embark on retaliatory action, taken sometime during 4 August (Washington time) was an

American move which must be explained in American terms. That was the moment, it would seem, when the 'hawks' were able to exert significant influence on United States decision-making.

We know that Ambassador Taylor, in a cable from Saigon to Washington on 3 August, expressed disappointment that the President had refused to act more vigorously following the first attack. He did not go so far as to recommend an air strike, but he urged consideration of naval action against the type of North Vietnamese craft responsible for the attack – including, if necessary, mining the approaches to their harbours.[28] Taylor was mainly concerned about the effect on South Vietnamese morale if no action at all was contemplated. Later the same day, he expressed even greater anxiety about the possible effects on morale of any Chinese decision to deploy its own Mig fighters and Ilyushin bombers inside North Vietnam. (Ironically it was the American air strikes on the 5th, rather than any earlier action, which actually occasioned such Chinese deployments.) CINCPAC was presumably also recommending stronger action on 3 August, as he gave the order for the *Constellation* to move from Hong Kong towards the Gulf.

It needed only a very small incident on the 4th to tip the balance in favour of the 'hawks'. In Washington that day a long series of meetings at the Pentagon and the White House eventually resulted in a precise plan of action, which was approved by the President and then by the NSC in the late afternoon. Only then, at 6.00 p.m. Washington time, did the Pentagon issue a public statement about the second attack. The 'scenario' decided upon included four elements: a presidential broadcast; followed immediately by air strikes against the PT boats and against oil installations at Vinh; followed by a message to Congress and a joint resolution empowering the President to take any further action he saw fit; and finally another message to Hanoi, to be communicated through Seaborn, signalling the limited objectives of United States action but also the possibility of more serious measures if the North Vietnamese continued on their present course.[29] Also at this point, following a visit to the White House on 6 August, U Thant embarked on his own peace initiative – making contact with Hanoi through a Soviet diplomat at the United Nations by the end of the month, but to no avail.

Nothing that has been said thus far has eliminated completely the possibility that the Gulf of Tonkin affair was, after all, a provocation initated by the American side: if not by the President and his top advisers, then by 'hawks' within the military hierarchy who were determined to force Washington to act. The President himself may have had his own motive for such a move. In the perspective of domestic politics, perhaps he had something to gain by deliberately staging a crisis (and responding to it) in order to outflank his electoral opponent. It enabled him to prove that he himself could be just as tough as Barry Goldwater if the need arose. Certainly in that respect the outcome of the actual crisis worked to Johnson's advantage. But to make such an allegation without at least some evidence drawn from the memories of those involved in Johnson's electoral strategy would be to go beyond the normal limits of historical research, in a field where access to official documentation and personal revelation is remarkably open. The allegation also assumes a high degree of cynicism on the President's own part, and a willingness to allow domestic political considerations to override his normal caution in the international sphere. The onus of proof is on those who would argue that case.

The possibility that the United States needed a crisis at this point for international reasons is slightly more plausible. In general, it must have been clear by now that the only way in which the situation in Indochina could be made to fit the pattern of crisis diplomacy which had evolved under President Kennedy was for the Americans themselves to provoke a crisis to which both Moscow and Peking would have to respond. Only then would it be possible to use all the pressures of a crisis situation to force Hanoi to retreat. It might be argued, too, that intelligence showing greater Chinese support for North Vietnam during July had made such a move more necessary than it had seemed in June. By creating an incident and then bombing the DRVN, the United States would demonstrate that neither Moscow nor Peking was ready to take significant risks in order to protect Hanoi against the consequences of a larger military struggle. But if that *was* the American objective, the crisis was not pursued with sufficient vigour, once it had broken, for the objective to be attained.

If it could be shown that North Vietnam was in fact deterred from carrying out some specific plan it had devised for the period between early August and the American presidential election on 3 November, that interpretation might make some sense. But in that case we are still dealing with a situation in which the Communist side had the initiative and the Americans were making a necessary response. There is little to suggest that Washington had anything to gain by choosing this moment to embark upon a major crisis of the proportions that would be required to force a long-term settlement of the conflict in Indochina. Nor did they follow up their initial actions against North Vietnam by continuing to raise the level of tension. The JCS may have wished to do so. The President himself was satisfied that he had done enough to contain the crisis and to prevent it from interfering with other, more immediate concerns.

V

Once the air strikes had taken place, and when it became clear that that was all the Americans intended to do, it was possible for Hanoi and Peking to make up their minds about their own next moves. On the military side the Chinese strengthened their defences in South-West China, transferring a whole PLA air force headquarters to that region from an area near the Taiwan Straits. They also moved 36 Mig fighters to the newly built airfield at Phuc-Yen in North Vietnam.[30] It was later revealed that, immediately following the air strikes, Zhou Enlai and chief-of-staff Luo Ruiqing sent a message to their counterparts in Hanoi (Pham Van Dong and Van Tien Dung) proposing closer military collaboration between the two countries to meet the American threat.[31] It is not clear whether this referred to the known movement of planes or involved contingency planning for some larger action.

On 6 August *Renmin Ribao* came out with an editorial attacking the American move and supporting Hanoi's claim that no 'second attack' had occurred. A few hours later (at 9.40 a.m. on the 6th, Peking time) an even more strongly worded government statement for the first time used the expression 'Aggression against the Democratic Republic of Vietnam means aggression against China'. It is possible that that statement was the subject of a major debate on the Chinese side. Meanwhile in Peking and other major cities there were mass demonstrations in support of North Vietnam, culminating in a rally on 9 August at which Liao Chengzhi delivered another denunciation of the United States. For its part Hanoi also issued an official statement on 6 August; and on the 7th held a meeting to honour the PAVN units which had taken part in the various incidents of the previous week.

The Russians were far more cautious than the Chinese. A TASS statement of 5 August was remarkably moderate in the circumstances; and a speech by the Soviet delegate at a special session of the UN Security Council the following day was criticised by Peking for failing to insist that the 'second attack' had been invented by the Americans. Khrushchev himself, preoccupied with an agricultural tour, made no comment on any of the incidents until 8 August. He then made a tough speech at Ordzhnikidze, but by then the worst of the crisis was already over. (Khrushchev had done much the same thing six years earlier at the time of the Taiwan Straits Crisis of September–October 1958, when his promises of support for China had come only at the very end of the sequence of actual military moves.) In private the Soviet leader sent a message to Johnson on 5 August, emphasising their joint responsibility for maintaining peace in the world and urging him to show restraint.[32] In practice, one might argue that both the Chinese and the Soviet responses were designed – each in its own way – to dissuade the Americans from taking further action. Khrushchev may even have been content to allow Vietnam to become mainly a Chinese problem (as it had been in 1954), which may have been the principal reason why Hanoi now had to rely more closely on Peking than some Vietnamese leaders would have wished.

Soviet restraint at this point left open the possibility that diplomacy relating to Laos would continue unaffected by the incidents in the Gulf of Tonkin. On 7 August the State Department informed the embassy in Vientiane that it would defer approval for American ground and air action against the Ho Chi Minh Trail in order to avoid provoking a Communist escalation in Laos.[33] That in turn made it possible, by 9 August, for Souphanouvong and Souvanna Phouma to reach agreement on a further round of 'tripartite' talks in Paris, which began towards the end of the month. Thus the Gulf of Tonkin Crisis did not, in itself, eliminate the possibility of a further Geneva Conference on Laos if other circumstances had favoured its success.

President Johnson and his advisers appear to have believed that their controlled response of 5–7 August was adequate to the immediate situation. In terms of domestic American politics their handling of the crisis was undoubtedly brilliant. As a Senator himself for more than two decades, Johnson had been remarkably adept at winning over individual colleagues to ensure a majority for any measure to which he was committed. Now, as President, he used all his skill to establish a national consensus behind the immediate course of action he believed to be right. He thus eliminated any danger that the situation might be exploited by the Goldwater camp for its own purposes in the forthcoming presidential campaign.

In the international context, however, what mattered were the consequences of his actions for the global and regional power struggle. It is less certain that Johnson's handling of the crisis was successful from that point of view. The air strikes of 5 August were restricted not only in physical scope but also in terms of their stated purpose. Whereas William Bundy's scenarios of late May and early June would have linked the bombing of North Vietnam directly to Hanoi's support of the struggles in South Vietnam and Laos, the first actual strikes north of the 17th parallel were linked only to incidents involving American ships in the Gulf of Tonkin, not to events inside Vietnam. It soon became clear that, despite his apparent firmness, Johnson had failed to recover the initiative for the American side. His response to the Gulf of Tonkin crisis was too restrained to counter a growing impression in the region that the United States would ultimately lose the struggle for Indochina.

The contrast between the Gulf of Tonkin Crisis of August 1964 and the Taiwan Straits Crisis of autumn 1958 is instructive. In the 1958 crisis the United States, by demonstrating its military power and determination without going beyond certain limits, may be said to have 'won' in the sense that it forced Peking to back down militarily and at the same time secured a renewal of diplomatic contact through the ambassadorial talks in Warsaw. Washington was not yet ready to follow up that advantage with magnanimity – for example, by agreeing to Peking's membership of the United Nations. But the net effect of the crisis was a lessening of tension between the United States and China. But in 1964 the Americans were unwilling to exercise more than token military power; and certainly they did not achieve any significant reduction of tension, either in bilateral relations with China or in South-East Asia. It might not be going too far to say that they 'lost' the Gulf of Tonkin Crisis.

In itself the crisis did not amount to an escalation of the war in Vietnam. But its failure to avert a more general intensification of revolutionary conflicts in South-East Asia made an eventual escalation in Vietnam all but inevitable. It is to the period immediately following the crisis that we must turn if we wish to understand that process of intensification and escalation more fully.

17 'The Focal Point of World Contradictions'

The situation in South-East Asia varies between countries, but all the peoples are engaged in anti-imperialist and anti-feudalist struggles. Fierce armed struggles are being carried on in South Vietnam, Malaya, Singapore, North Kalimantan and Laos. Burma, Cambodia and Indonesia are engaged in the struggle against imperialists and domestic reactionaries.... The Philippines and Thailand have to free themselves from US imperialist domination.... South-East Asia was in the past the 'lifeline' of British, Dutch and French imperialism; now it is the 'lifeline' of US imperialism.... Bung Karno has said that South-East Asia 'has become the focal point of world contradictions.'

Speech by Njoto at PKI meeting in Jakarta, 25 September 1964

This being said, about basic factors which would exist whatever the regime in China, I think it is still true that Communist ideology as such is the single most vital element in dealing with present-day China.... Because of that ideology, Peiping's assertiveness is greatly strengthened, and extended to virtually every contiguous area and beyond: down into South-East Asia all the way to Indonesia, to Tibet and at least to the point of wishing to neutralise a permanently weakened India....

I have characterised the designs of Communist China as basically militant and aggressive, and I think this applies particularly to South-East Asia at the present time.

Speech by William Bundy at Oxford, September 1964

I

Ambassador Taylor's hope that the air strikes of 5 August 1964 would have a beneficial effect on the political climate in Saigon were quickly disappointed. On 7 August Nguyen Khanh proclaimed a state of emergency in Saigon and at first it seemed as if he might succeed in making the larger crisis a justification for increasing both his own powers and the general effectiveness of his regime. But when he attempted to impose a new political 'charter' on 16 August, under which he was to become president with wide emergency powers, he precipitated a far more serious crisis than that which had confronted Ngo Dinh Diem almost exactly one year earlier.[1] By this time, indeed, the American embassy in Saigon was beginning to look back on the years before 1963 as a golden age of stability, and to appreciate more fully Diem's political skill in holding South Vietnam together.

The sheer complexity of the overlapping conflicts which had developed within South Vietnam during the first half of 1964 makes it impossible to do justice to the chaos which now ensued. Three strands of conflict can, however, be identified with some confidence.

First, there was a continuing conflict between militant Buddhists and the remnants of Diem's Can-Lao, who were mainly Catholics. Already in June, Buddhist demonstrations had called for action against former Can-Lao members still in office; in their turn, Catholic groups protested against direct American aid to Buddhist organisations.[2] By mid-August this 'religious' tension was again becoming acute.

Second, there was by now a serious conflict within the government coalition which Nguyen Khanh had formed in February, as well as within the officer corps of the armed forces. On one side stood Khanh himself together with a number of officers close to him, notably Nguyen Chanh Thi (the commander of I Corps) and Nguyen Cao Ky (Commander of the air force). On the other side the civilian politicians of the Dai-Viet party – particularly the group led by the Catholic Nguyen Ton Hoan – also had allies within the officer corps, who appear to have included Nguyen Van Thieu. By mid-August Khanh's principal aim seems to have been to purge the Dai-Viet element altogether.

Third, at the highest level of the armed forces there appears to have been intense rivalry between Nguyen Khanh, Duong Van

Minh and Tran Thien Khiem for the position of commander-in-chief (currently held by Khiem). As we shall see, Khanh would not rest until he had taken that post for himself and had driven his two rivals into exile. In mid-August he was not yet strong enough to do that.

The new crisis began on 21-22 August – the anniversary of Ngo Dinh Nhu's 'pagoda raids' – with Buddhist and student demonstrations calling for action against surviving members of the Can-Lao, as well as for early elections and various guarantees of political freedom. Within a matter of days the situation in Saigon was out of control; yet Khanh refused to suppress the riots, on the grounds that Diem's repressive measures in similar circumstances had led directly to his downfall. On 25 August the other generals forced him to rescind his 'charter' and to restore the system that had existed before. Two days later (on the 27th) a stormy meeting of the Military Revolutionary Council ended by appointing a 'triumvirate' under which power was supposed to be shared between Khanh, Minh and Khiem. Amid mounting disorder Khanh then withdrew to Dalat, leaving the armed forces to restore calm to the capital by the end of the month. In the meantime a group of Dai-Viet officers were plotting a coup, although on 24 August they were dissuaded from action by Tran Thien Khiem, whose support they needed. When eventually they made their move, on 2 September, they were not strong enough to counter the officers and units which still supported Khanh. Nguyen Khanh himself secured a reaffirmation of American support, and on 3 September he returned to Saigon to resume the premiership. Next day the Dai-Viet leader Nguyen Ton Hoan was obliged to leave for Japan. Duong Van Minh, still formally head of state, now agreed to appoint a 'High National Council' which would write a new constitution and so pave the way for return to civilian rule. The Dai-Viet officers – probably facing a purge if they did nothing – did attempt a coup on 13 September, only to be defeated by Nguyen Chanh Thi and Nguyen Cao Ky. By early October Khanh was strong enough to supplant Tran Thien Khiem as commander-in-chief and to send him as ambassador to Washington; he then forced Duong Van Minh into exile in Bangkok.

Nguyen Khanh's own role in this crisis is impossible to assess. Many years later he would admit that by early 1965 he was in direct contact with the NLFSVN, having become bitterly anti-American in a way that Diem and Nhu had never been.[3] Yet in the crisis of August–September 1964 there can be little doubt that Khanh owed his survival to positive American support against his rivals on all sides. It is difficult to imagine that Ambassador Taylor still believed, as some American officials had claimed earlier in the year, that Khanh was 'the ablest man in the country'. The main reason for Washington's reluctance to abandon him was probably the fear that to do so, having once selected him as their 'strong man', would be to invite even worse chaos. But among American officials the crisis left an enduring impression that no two Vietnamese generals or politicians were capable of working together. And certainly the price of Khanh's remaining in power was a remarkable wastage of military talent: in January he had overthrown three of the most able senior generals (Tran Van Don, Le Van Kim and Mai Huu Xuan); now, in September, he added to the list Tran Thien Khiem, Nguyen Van Thieu (who was forced out as chief-of-staff, although he would return as minister of defence six months later) and Do Cao Tri (formerly commander of II Corps). The impact of repeated crises on the conduct of the war must have been considerable. In particular a new pacification programme, due to begin on 12 September under the code-name *Hop-Tac*, had to be postponed when the units responsible for it became involved in the coup of the following day.[4]

Also difficult to estimate is whether the Communists had any direct part in the crisis. We noted earlier the possibility that in the spring and summer of 1963 they had infiltrated the militant Buddhist movement; and the student organisations certainly included a leftist element by now. If the disintegration had continued the Communist side might well have had an opportunity to press its own political struggle, even to the point of installing a regime willing to talk to the NLFSVN. But they must have realised that the Americans were not yet ready to acquiesce in such a change, and that it would merely lead to another coup. In so far as they had power to influence the course of events directly at this stage, their immediate interest probably lay in convincing Washington (and American opinion) that the government in Saigon was too fragile a base from which to embark on the systematic bombing of North Vietnam. That, indeed, was certainly the outcome of the crisis. The principle that the Americans were in Vietnam to assist in the process of 'nation-building' suffered a damaging blow from which it would not recover until after the emergence of the 'second Republic' under Nguyen Van Thieu (1967–75).

Whether or not it had played any significant role in the Saigon crisis, the NLFSVN awaited the outcome before making its own next moves. On 14 September, immediately after the abortive Dai-Viet coup, the Front appealed for a new offensive in the South – and also for greater co-ordination between the rural and the urban struggles.[5] By 21 September another guerrilla offensive was under way, principally in the provinces of the Mekong Delta. On that day, too, a series of strikes and demonstrations in Saigon served as a reminder that the Front was now capable of mobilising the urban proletariat as well as the rural peasantry.

It is impossible to tell whether the NLFSVN also had a hand in one other event which occurred at that point: the 'montagnard' revolt which broke out at Ban-Me-Thuot on 20 September, under the leadership of the 'Front Unifié de Libération des Races Opprimés' (FULRO). By this time a number of dissident leaders of various tribal groups had taken refuge in Phnom Penh, and there is some evidence that the revolt was engineered from there – perhaps with Sihanouk's blessing.[6] The immediate conflict between FULRO and the Saigon authorities was resolved fairly quickly, through American mediation. But the incident demonstrated the fragility of the South Vietnamese government's hold on the Central Highlands, which were to become an increasingly important military arena in the months ahead.

In Laos, too, another significant turning-point seems to have been reached in mid-September. The proposed tripartite talks between Laotian leaders had been brought another step closer on 28 August, when Souvanna Phouma and Souphanouvong had another meeting – this time at Saint-Cloud, near Paris. At that point it looked as though the Pathet Lao might be willing to rejoin the coalition and to accept a ceasefire, on the basis of a return to the military situation of mid-June 1964. They also held out the possibility of restoring a neutralist presence on the Plaine de Jarres, in a form Souvanna Phouma could accept. But such proposals amounted to a reversal of the rightist-neutralist gains of 'Operation Triangle' north of Muong Soui. At a meeting on 16 September, Ngon Sananikone (now representing the rightist 'faction') rejected the Pathet Lao 'solution'; by the 22nd the talks had reached an impasse.[7] Souvanna Phouma then left Paris to attend the non-aligned summit conference in Cairo (5–10 October 1964). An attempt was made to revive the talks when he returned in mid-October; but without any basis for genuine compromise it was unlikely that they would make further progress.

The possibility of a new Gulf of Tonkin incident reappeared in

September. Washington had suspended the DE SOTO patrols after 7 August; two destroyers (the *Morton* and the *Edwards*) were now authorised to begin another surveillance mission along the North Vietnamese coast from 14 September. Four days later (on the night of the 18th, Vietnamese time) they reported another incident. Once again, Hanoi and Peking insisted that the 'attack' was an American 'fabrication'. But by the time their respective statements were issued (19 September), President Johnson had again suspended the patrols; and no further DE SOTO missions were authorised until late January 1965.[8] As on the previous occasion, it is impossible to obtain a clear picture of what exactly happened.

II

The month from mid-August to mid-September 1964 was also a critical period for Indonesia's 'confrontation' against Malaysia. Tension in that area had been mounting during July. The British and Malaysian governments were worried by the communal rioting which broke out in Singapore on 21 July and which resulted in at least 20 deaths over the next few days. The possibility could not be ruled out that the Indonesians, or their local Communist allies, might try to exploit the internal 'contradictions' of Peninsular Malaysia in pursuit of their campaign against East Malaysia. The riots coincided with a visit by Tengku Abdul Rahman to Washington, at the end of which (23 July) he and President Johnson issued a communiqué on United States military aid to Malaysia. Sukarno did not immediately respond to that unwelcome news. But Ambassador Jones was well aware that the announcement limited still further his own opportunity to keep American influence alive in Jakarta. Worse still, from his point of view, an amendment tabled in the US Senate by Senator Tower about this time sought to cut off aid to Indonesia altogether.[9]

In the wake of the Gulf of Tonkin Crisis, Sukarno made up his mind how to respond to the Johnson–Rahman talks. On 17 August – Indonesia's independence day – he denounced the United States in his famous *Tavip* speech, on the theme of 'living dangerously'.[10] The same day a small group of Indonesian irregulars landed at Pontian on the coast of Peninsular Malaysia. On 1–2 September a more substantial Indonesian air-drop took place at Labis, in Johor. Neither move was of major military significance, although Labis was a former stronghold of the Malayan Communist Party. The aim may have been to contribute to the internal destabilisation of Malaysia. That interpretation found some confirmation in an attempt to spark off new rioting in Singapore from 2 to 7 September.[11] It would appear that more was involved, however, for the landings and riots of the first week of September coincided with what may have been a serious crisis in Indonesian–British relations. Possibly fearing that additional Indonesian military moves were planned, the British ordered an aircraft carrier and two destroyers (then en route to Australia) to return to the area. If they attempted to pass through the Sunda Strait, the Indonesians might resist. The ships eventually passed through the Lombok Strait; but if the British aim was to deter further Indonesian action it succeeded. We can only speculate what might have been the outcome if this crisis had coincided directly with that in the Gulf of Tonkin one month before. In the event, tension eased in mid-September, when the United Nations Security Council discussed Malaysia's protest against violations of its territory by Indonesia. The debate lasted from 9 until 17 September; but then the Soviet Union used its veto to defeat a resolution which treated both sides equally and urged them to settle their conflict through fresh negotiations.[12]

Within Indonesia, Sukarno's position depended on balancing the power of the armed forces against that of the PKI and its mass organisations. A crisis at this moment had positive value in allowing him to strengthen the role of the former in relation to both 'confrontation' and internal security. The one substantive outcome of the heightened tension was a decree of 14 September, accelerating the implementation of the *Dwikora* command of May 1964 but also creating new 'regional authorities' under the ultimate control of General Yani.[13] Following that move, Sukarno felt sufficiently secure to embark on yet another foreign tour from late September to mid-November.

III

It would be going too far to suggest that the intensification of the struggle in South Vietnam during this period, and the apparent escalation of the 'crush Malaysia' campaign, were parts of a co-ordinated anti-American strategy. Nevertheless there was an increasing tendency for political speeches in Hanoi and Jakarta to emphasise the similarity between their respective struggles against a common enemy, American imperialism. Nor was mere rhetoric involved. Immediately following the Gulf of Tonkin crisis, Sukarno had accorded full recognition to the DRVN (which led Saigon to break off relations forthwith). On 14 August Truong Chinh and Prince Sihanouk both flew to Jakarta, where they were present when Sukarno made his *Tavip* speech three days later. In a speech on the 18th, Truong Chinh stressed Vietnamese support for the struggle in 'North Kalimantan' and for Indonesia's campaign against Malaysia. Whilst the coincidence of the two visits may not have amounted to a formal summit meeting, Sukarno and Sihanouk had talks in Bali on 19–20 August; whilst, on the same two days, Truong Chinh and Aidit were together in Bandung. The atmosphere was remarkably different from that of the 'Maphilindo' diplomacy a mere six or seven months before.[14]

Another common theme now beginning to emerge was the denial by all three countries (North Vietnam, Cambodia and Indonesia) of any suggestion that the United Nations might have a role to play in resolving conflicts in the region. On 17 August the Agence Khmer Presse reported Sihanouk's rejection, a week earlier, of the proposals of a UN commission which had recently enquired into the various Cambodian–South Vietnamese border incidents. On 19 August the DRVN foreign minister, in a message to the chairman of the UN Security Council, insisted that the United Nations had no right to investigate either the recent American 'acts of war' against North Vietnam or the 'US war of aggression' in the South. Those were questions for the co-chairman of the 1954 Geneva Conference.[15] Sukarno was not yet ready to go so far: Indonesia participated in the Malaysia-sponsored Security Council debate of 9–17 September, although later on (in January 1965) he would announce Indonesia's complete withdrawal from the United Nations.

Truong Chinh's visit to Indonesia had the same dual character as that of Liu Shaoqi in spring 1963. Ostensibly he was head of a national assembly delegation, which allowed him to present the views of the DRVN to non-Communist Indonesian leaders, and any contact he may have had with Sihanouk was also in this 'state' capacity. But his talks with Aidit were presumably Party-to-Party, and as such would contribute to the evolving pattern of inter-national Communist relations in East and South-East Asia. Truong Chinh was followed to Jakarta during the first week of September by the Japanese Communist leader Miyamoto, who immediately afterwards visited Peking for talks with Liu Shaoqi and Peng Zhen.[16]

It is possible therefore to discern two distinct anti-imperialist networks in Asia by this time: one involving the governments of China, North Vietnam, Cambodia and Indonesia; the other linking the Communist Parties of China, North Vietnam, Japan and Indonesia. In both, North Korea also began to play an important role by the end of the year. Within this essentially Asian context, it was possible to identify American imperialism as the principal enemy; and to regard the ongoing struggles in Vietnam, Laos and 'North Kalimantan' – and perhaps eventually also struggles in Thailand and elsewhere – as parts of one single anti-American movement. In the words of the Indonesian Communist Njoto, speaking at the PKI Bachtaruddin Academy in Jakarta on 25 September, South-East Asia had become 'the focal point of world contradictions'.[17]

There seems little doubt that Hanoi's relations with Peking were now closer than at any time since 1954. Two further indications of that trend were noted by Hanoi-watchers: on 15 September it was announced that the NLFSVN was to open a permanent office in Peking; and after 20 September, it would appear that Soviet newspapers ceased to be obtainable in North Vietnam.[18] Sino-Vietnamese relations cannot, however, be analysed solely in terms of a (hypothetical) connection between Peking and a solid 'pro-Chinese faction' in Hanoi. They depended on a more complex pattern of political-personal attachments, in which Hoang Van Hoan (the one Vietnamese leader to defect to China in 1979) may at this period have played as important a role as Truong Chinh. After visiting Cuba in late July, Hoan returned home only briefly before accompanying Li Xiannian to attend celebrations in Bucharest for the anniversary of Romania's liberation. He was again with Li Xiannian in Kunming at the beginning of September.[19] Thus he and Truong Chinh returned home at about the same time, and September was probably a month for 'taking stock' in Hanoi.

TABLE 17.1   *China and South-East Asia, August–September 1964*

China, North Vietnam, Cambodia	South Vietnam	Indonesia–Malaysia
13 Aug.: Seaborn again visited Hanoi.		14 Aug.: Arrival of Sihanouk and of Truong Chinh in Jakarta.
14 Aug.: Truong Chinh, Sihanouk both flew to Jakarta.	16 Aug.: Nguyen Khanh proclaimed himself president under new government 'charter'.	17 Aug.: Sihanouk's *Tavip* speech. Indonesian landing at Pontian.
18 Aug.: Sihanouk again proposed border talks with NLFSVN.		18 Aug.: Foundation of North Kalimantan Liberation League.
19 Aug.: DRVN rejected idea of a UN role in Indochina.		19–20 Aug.: Sihanouk was with Sukarno in Bali; Truong Chinh met Aidit in Bandung.
	21–2 Aug.: Start of new Buddhist demonstrations in Saigon, continuing for next week.	
22 Aug.: End of Sino–Soviet border talks.		
23–4 Aug.: Romanian anniversary celebration attended by Mikoyan, Li Xiannian, Hoang Van Hoan.	25 Aug.: Nguyen Khanh was forced to abandon his 'charter' of 16 August.	26 Aug.: Njoto became one of Sukarno's official advisers.
	27–9 Aug.: Mounting disorder in Saigon; Nguyen Khanh withdrew to Dalat.	
28 Aug.: Meeting of Souvanna Phouma and Souphanouvong in Paris.	29 Aug.: *Renmin Ribao*: 'US cannot save itself from fiasco in South Vietnam.'	30 Aug.: Truong Chinh left Jakarta for home.

1–2 Sept.: Li Xiannian and Hoang Van Hoan attended banquet in Kurming. Liu Shaoqi and Deng Xiaoping attended DRVN reception, Peking.

9–10 Sept.: Miyamoto in Peking; talks with Liu Shaoqi, Deng Xiaoping.

15 Sept.: *Renmin Ribao* warning to US not to take any action agains Cambodia.
15 Sept.: Report that NLFSVN was to set up its own office in Peking.

3–4 Sept.: Nguyen Khanh returned to Saigon; forced Nguyen Ton Hoan into exile.
9 Sept.: Washington decisions on next courses of action in Vietnam: NSAM-314.
13 Sept.: Abortive coup by *Dai-Viet* generals in Saigon. Khanh firmly in power.
14 Sept.: NLFSVN appeal for new offensive in South Vietnam; under way by 20th.

31 Aug.: Indonesian air force delegation began month-long visit to China.
1–7 Sept.: Miyamoto (Japanese CP leader visited Indonesia.
9 Sept.: Start of UN debate on Indonesia–Malaysia dispute.
13 Sept.: *Nhan-Dan* reaffirmed DRVN's support for anti-Malaysia struggle.
14 Sept.: Sukarno's decree creating regional commands, strengthening military power in Indonesia.

The current state of China's relations with the rest of the world were reflected in the list of distinguished foreign visitors to Peking at the end of September for the national day celebrations.[20] The USSR was represented only by trade union chairman V. V. Grishin, whereas Romania sent premier G. Maurer and Albania its minister of defence. From South-East Asia the two most important visitors were Pham Van Dong and Sihanouk: almost certainly a reflection of China's need to persuade Hanoi and Phnom Penh to agree, at least in principle, on the broader issues which had previously bedevilled relations between Sihanouk and the United States. Cambodia had reiterated its interest in border talks with the NLFSVN on 18 August; by November such talks were being arranged.[21]

Indonesia was not prominently represented in Peking on 1 October 1964, although the Chinese had given a warm reception during September to a military delegation led by the air force commander Suryadarma. On 28–30 September Sukarno himself (accompanied by Nasution) was visiting Moscow. But he is reported to have all but quarrelled with Khrushchev on that occasion, owing to his refusal to accept the Soviet line on the future of the non-aligned movement.[22] It would also appear that, although a new arms deal was made, the Russians were still reluctant to provide all the weapons Indonesia would have needed to mount a serious military campaign against Malaysia. It was then that Sukarno finally decided to 'choose Peking', and by early November he was holding talks with Zhou Enlai in Shanghai.

We do not, of course, know the full background to these events on the Communist side. It is conceivable, despite appearances to the contrary, that some kind of tacit understanding had emerged between Moscow and Peking which would allow the Russians to pursue *détente* in the West at the same time as the Chinese promoted revolution in Asia – without a final collapse of international Communist unity. In Europe, such an understanding would have enabled Khrushchev to fulfil his ambition of improving relations with West Germany, and, to that end, his son-in-law Adzhubei visited Bonn from 18 July to 2 August. As far as South-East Asia was concerned, such a strategy would have left Peking free to support the anti-imperialism of both North Vietnam and Indonesia. It would also have obliged the Vietnamese to depend on Chinese aid and support to a much greater degree than they may have liked. But any hint of an arrangement of that kind would be likely to generate acute conflict within the Soviet leadership itself. The subsequent change of leadership in Moscow, which brought to power Brezhnev and Kosygin closely supported by Suslov and Shelepin, would have spelled the end of any such understanding between the rival Communist powers.

In the aftermath of Khrushchev's fall, Hanoi quickly re-established its old relationship with Moscow – which, as we have seen, did not preclude continuing friendship with Peking. At that stage, too, the North Vietnamese leaders were finally able to address themselves to the problem which had been on their minds for some time: whether to implement the secret 9th Plenum Resolution by sending whole PAVN regiments to the South, in order to intensify the armed struggle there. Before we discuss the many questions surrounding that decision, however, we must look again at what the Americans were doing – and thinking – in the autumn of 1964.

Part V
1964-5

18 Washington Hesitates: the Autumn Debate

The Joint Chiefs of Staff . . . consider that such an accelerated program of actions with respect to the DRV is essential to prevent a complete collapse of the US position in Southeast Asia. They do not agree that we should be slow to get deeply involved until we have a better feel for the quality of our ally. The United States is already deeply involved. The Joint Chiefs of Staff consider that only significantly stronger military pressures on the DRV are likely to provide the relief and psychological boost necessary for attainment of the requisite governmental stability and viability.

> JCS Memorandum for the Secretary of Defense,
> 26 August 1964

During my first year in the White House no formal proposal for an air campaign against North Vietnam ever came to me as the agreed suggestion of my principal advisers. Whenever the subject came up, one or other of them usually mentioned the risk of giving Communist China an excuse for massive intervention in Vietnam. Rusk was concerned that putting direct pressure on North Vietnam might encourage the Soviets to raise the level of tension around Berlin, in the Middle East or elsewhere. I fully concurred. Our goals in Vietnam were limited, and so were our actions. I wanted to keep it that way.

> Lyndon B. Johnson, in *The Vantage Point* (1971)

I

The compilers of the *Pentagon Papers* paid special attention to the four months from mid-August to mid-December 1964, which they saw as the bureaucratic gestation period for the Vietnam strategy finally adopted by the president in the early part of 1965. The impression which emerges from their account is that of an administration preoccupied with one fundamental question: whether United States action beyond the borders of South Vietnam was necessary in order to deal even with the existing level of conflict. Apart from occasional references to increased infiltration along the Ho Chi Minh trail, hardly any account seems to have been taken of the possibility that Hanoi might already be thinking in terms of an *expansion* of its own role in the South. Thus American commentators regarded the eventual escalation, when it finally came, as entirely the product of decision-making in Washington. In attempting to analyse the American debate during the latter part of 1964 the present chapter will observe the same limitation; but Chapter 19 will then need to examine closely what was happening in Hanoi. In the final analysis, we must put the two sides together.

As early as 11 August 1964 a draft memorandum by William Bundy and his staff, taking up an idea which had originated with Ambassador Taylor, pinpointed 1 January the following year as the appropriate 'contingency date' for embarking upon 'systematic military action' against North Vietnam.[1] Quite why that date was chosen is not clear; it certainly represented a longer-term 'scenario' than the 30-day sequence Bundy had proposed in May 1964. It was now generally recognised that the conflicts in Vietnam and Laos could not be resolved by the same type of 'crisis management' that had proved successful in other areas. The use of force, and the threat of more force, was nevertheless still fundamental to the thinking of both William Bundy at the State Department and John McNaughton, his successor in the Pentagon's Office of International Security Affairs. Throughout the autumn of 1964 it was they who were chiefly responsible for drafting proposals, analysing the views of the various agencies, and making recommendations to the NSC 'principals': Rusk, McNamara and McCone.

For the actual decisions, however, it is necessary to look at the three occasions when the President, in consultation with his top advisers, gave approval to specific actions or contingency planning: namely 9 September, 2 November and 1 December 1964. The autumn debate thus involved three principal phases, of which the first (starting from the 11 August draft memorandum) ended with a White House meeting on 9 September and a NSAM (no. 314) the following day. A second phase occupied the interval from mid-September to the beginning of November, when Johnson was re-elected with a landslide majority. The third phase, again one of intense paperwork dominated by a new inter-agency 'working group', culminated in a series of high level meetings in late November and early December.

Already during the first of these phases it is possible, studying *Pentagon Papers* documents, to identify the main themes which would figure in the eventual strategy. Five main types of military action were being considered, each implying a greater degree of United States commitment and involvement than the one preceding it on the list. It is possible also to identify a spectrum of opinion regarding the range and intensity of the proposed moves under each heading; and regarding the speed at which they should be implemented.

(1) *Coastal and Maritime Actions*

Essentially this meant a continuation, perhaps intensification, of measures already approved in principle earlier in the year: destroyer patrols (code-named DE SOTO) in the Gulf of Tonkin; covert operations, by South Vietnamese units, authorised under OPLAN 34A. One suggestion was that the latter might now be acknowledged by Saigon, and therefore count as 'overt' action against the North; but that move was opposed by senior military officers.[2] Another proposal in early September, never acted upon, was to develop both forms of activity in ways that might deliberately provoke a fresh 'Gulf of Tonkin Incident' in order to justify further air strikes against the North. This suggestion, indeed, is the one piece of hard evidence which raises doubts about the original incidents of 2–4 August, although it does not (in itself) prove any provocative intent by the American side on that earlier occasion. On 10 September NSAM-314 did in fact approve the resumption of both the patrols and the covert operations, but on the understanding that they would be carefully separated from one another. In the event, as soon as a new DE SOTO patrol entered

TABLE 18.1   *Analysis of William Bundy's 'scenario' of 11 August 1964*

Phase I	Phase II	Phase III
1964 Until end of August 'Short holding phase', involving no new actions; continued support for 'Operation Triangle' in Laos; but suspension of OPLAN 34A operations and of destroyer patrols in Gulf.	*1964 September – December* (a) Resumption of 34A Operations and of destroyer patrols, but carefully separated from one another. (b) Leaks about joint US–GVN planning for action against North Vietnam. (c) Training of Vietnamese to fly jet aircraft. (d) Cross-border air operations in Southern Laos, reaching borders of North Vietnam by end of December. (e) If appropriate, 'tit-for-tat' air strikes against North Vietnam in reprisal for any major Communist actions.	*1965 January onwards* (a) Action against infiltration facilities and routes inside North Vietnam. (b) 'Next upward move' would be action against POL and communications targets; mining of Haiphong Harbour.

SOURCE   See note 1 (to this chapter).

the Gulf on 18 September, a new 'incident' *was* reported by the Americans – and as quickly denied by Hanoi and Peking. The patrol was immediately withdrawn and subsequent documents do not refer again to the idea of deliberate provocation.[3] Precisely what happened remains a mystery.

(2)   *Cross-border action inside Laos*

On one level this amounted merely to encouragement of the Vientiane government to use its American-supplied T-28 planes to bomb targets on the Ho Chi Minh trail in Southern Laos (called by Americans the 'Panhandle'). Such action was postponed in early August to avoid interfering with possible new tripartite negotiations, and talks between the Laotian leaders actually got under way near Paris on 28 August. As we have seen, they made no significant progress, and virtually broke down after 21 September. On 6 October Ambassador Unger was authorised to discuss air strikes with the Vientiane government; and the first raids on the 'trail' by T-28s took place on the 14th.[4] The use of American planes for the same purpose, however, was not approved until mid-December. Meanwhile the August documents also discussed the possibility of cross-border ground operations by South Vietnamese forces. By October it was clear that ARVN capability was quite inadequate for any significant moves of that kind, and the idea was abandoned. (Large-scale intervention in Laos by South Vietnamese ground forces had to wait until early 1971.) It was also evident by now that Prince Sihanouk would not give approval for cross-border actions (or 'hot pursuit') inside Cambodia.

Thus the opportunity for actual operations in this sphere fell far short of what Bundy had envisaged in his 11 August memorandum.

(3)   *'Tit-for-tat' reprisals against North Vietnam*

Here too, what William Bundy was recommending for the period down to the end of 1964 amounted to a continuation of the principle already established by the 'Pierce Arrow' strikes of 5 August. NSAM-314 authorised preparations for further reprisal attacks in the event of any major new Communist action against United States or South Vietnamese targets. But in practice the President was reluctant to authorise such action: for example in response to the attack on the Bien-Hoa airfield on 1 November. Eventually this principle was overtaken by more ambitious proposals for sustained air action north of the 17th parallel.

(4)   *Sustained air operations against North Vietnam*

A sequence of 'graduated pressures' might start with air strikes against infiltration routes and related targets. It might then proceed to such clearly military targets as the Phuc-Yen airfield, and might finally embrace the DRVN's limited range of economic targets. (The mining of Haiphong Harbour was also included.) By late August, the JCS were in a position to forward to McNamara a list of 94 targets for a sustained bombing campaign, and urged implementation at an early date.[5] There was still some ambiguity, however, in both military and civilian thinking, about the purpose of such a campaign: whether it should be designed mainly to destroy Communist military capabilities, or should seek to coerce Hanoi into abandoning its material and political 'support' for the NLFSVN. There was also room for disagreement about whether any level of bombing at all would achieve either objective. Some kind of action along these lines was what William Bundy proposed: if it began only after 1 January 1965, there was plenty of time to work out the details.

(5)   *Security Measures in South Vietnam*

Any decision to take direct action against North Vietnam was likely to provoke a response by Communist forces, probably in the form of more destructive terrorist attacks on American facilities and personnel in the South. Moreover, a sustained bombing campaign would depend at least to some extent on southern air bases. Measures to strengthen security in the South were therefore regarded as an integral part of any programme approved under the fourth heading. Already by mid-August both Ambassador Taylor and CINCPAC were thinking in terms of a range of possible actions extending from the deployment of 'hawk' missiles (at Saigon and Danang) to the creation of a full-scale United States base in Danang.[6] More immediately, it was evident that American dependents would need to be evacuated; but the timing of that move was an especially delicate matter in view of its likely effect on South Vietnamese morale.

The basic lines of disagreement between different branches of the American government and military machine were already evident in the documents generated by the first phase of the autumn debate. On the whole Ambassador Taylor, who commented on the Bundy draft in a cable of 18 August, was in favour of a strategy embracing all five areas of action. His reason for waiting until early 1965 before embarking on a 'carefully orchestrated' attack on the DRVN was to give the Khanh regime time to establish itself more firmly in power. (That was already a consideration even before the Saigon political crisis in late August.) But if the Saigon government collapsed, Taylor recommended an 'accelerated' programme of action against the North. CINCPAC and the JCS, in comments dated 17 and 26 August respectively, were in favour of accelerated action in any case. They opposed even Bundy's suggestion for a 'short holding phase' during the second half of August, fearing that any loss of momentum following the 5 August raids would be interpreted in Hanoi as a sign of American weakness or lack of resolve. (In that, they were probably correct.) If nothing else, they believed, the President should authorise continued deployment of United States strike forces to the area as a means of indicating his determination to go further if necessary.[7]

Another document, however, indicates that the JCS were themselves divided on certain issues. The most 'hawkish' line was that advocated by the air force and the marines, which would have required deliberate provocation of new incidents to justify an immediate air campaign. The chiefs of other services, and also the new Chairman of the JCS (General Wheeler) were one degree more cautious than that. It seems probable that underlying the debate within the JCS was a disagreement about the extent to which the United States could effectively respond to any direct Chinese intervention in South-East Asia by substituting air power for combat divisions on the ground.[8] Very probably some military leaders were already beginning to recognise the need for eventual deployment of American infantry, not merely for security duties but to participate actively in the war. But no proposals of that kind are mentioned in the *Pentagon Papers* at this stage.

Perhaps the most crucial question of all was that of political stability in Saigon. By early September American decision-makers were caught in a vicious circle. It could be argued that bombing the North was the one way to restore South Vietnamese confidence in Washington's determination to see its commitment through to the end. On the other hand direct military action against the DRVN would become pointless, if the South Vietnamese government it was designed to support fell apart under the first impact of a Communist response to American bombing. Ambassador Taylor was especially conscious of that danger and urged the need for effective 'pacification' of the provinces round Saigon before any moves were made against the North.

President Johnson himself would appear to have been especially conscious of this political factor during the White House meeting of 9 September. He seems to have used Ambassador Taylor's first-hand report on the situation in Saigon to convince the more 'hawkish' of his advisers that the type of action they were recommending could not be sustained. The NSAM (no. 314) which he approved the following day continued to place the main emphasis on actions within South Vietnam.[9] The President's reasons for adopting this cautious policy may also have had much to do with the election campaign, now approaching its most crucial stage; perhaps, too, there was an element of procrastination in his whole attitude to Vietnam. What seems fairly clear, given the documentary record so far available, is that there is little to justify the commonly held view that the President and his senior advisers had by this time already reached a consensus on 'escalation' and were merely awaiting the outcome of the election before implementing an agreed strategy in Vietnam. The President's dilemma may have been precisely the opposite: that there was *no* consensus at this stage; and Johnson, far more than Kennedy, needed such a consensus before finally committing himself to action.

II

During October, as the 1964 election campaign reached its climax, Vietnam policy was left on the back-burner in Washington. Nevertheless two decisions during that month were preliminary steps towards eventual escalation. In Laos, as we have seen, the government of Souvanna Phouma agreed to the use of its American T-28 planes to attack targets along the Ho Chi Minh trail, starting on 14 October. Secondly, moves were made towards greater co-ordination of United States diplomatic and military activities in the Indochinese region as a whole. A 'Co-ordinating Committee for Southeast Asia', comprising representatives of the American embassies in Saigon, Bangkok and Vientiane, together with a standing military committee drawn from MACV and MACTHAI, was designated to meet regularly in Saigon, presided over by Deputy Ambassador U. Alexis Johnson. In practice this meant the final reversal of the Kennedy strategy of treating South Vietnam (on the one hand) and Laos and Thailand (on the other) as separate problems. United States policy in Indochina as a whole would now be centred firmly in Saigon.[10]

On the eve of the election a new crisis erupted. On 1 November 1964 the PLAFSVN staged its most spectacular operation so far in the Saigon area: a mortar attack on the airfield at Bien-Hoa in which five American B-57 bombers were destroyed on the ground (and a number of others damaged) and four Americans were killed. This was precisely the kind of incident for which NSAM-314 had prescribed new reprisal raids against the DRVN. In addition to recommending punitive air strikes, the JCS urged immediate withdrawal of dependents from South Vietnam and the deployment of a United States combat unit to provide security around Saigon and Danang.[11] In a cable from Saigon, Taylor also urged retaliatory measures against the North. But the President, even though he was about to be re-elected with a landslide majority, rejected their advice and decided against overt retaliation. He again justified this continuing caution in terms of the weakness of the 'political base' in Saigon and the danger of a Communist terror campaign against American women and children still in South Vietnam. The immediate political situation in Saigon was particularly delicate at that moment, with a new civilian cabinet (headed by Tran Van Huong) due to take office on 4 November. The JCS remained unconvinced, nonetheless; on 4 November they placed formally on record their recommendation for stronger action.

On 3 November the President gave the debate on 'next courses of action' a more precise framework by appointing yet another interagency 'working group' (again chaired by William Bundy) to prepare a comprehensive new assessment of the situation for the NSC 'principals' and to analyse the main options now open to the Americans in Vietnam.[12] Despite what had happened at Bien-Hoa, this was not intended as a crisis measure. The new group was not an 'ExCom' of the kind which had met during the Cuba missiles crisis, or more recently during the Laos crisis of May and June 1964. Its proceedings were to be conducted at a lower level of the various agencies involved, to be followed by meetings of the 'principals' in the last week of November. Vietnam was no longer seen as a crisis but rather as a continuing problem – for which an appropriate strategy could be devised at greater leisure.

The terms of reference of the NSC working group did not include the option of working towards an early American withdrawal from Vietnam. We now know that a highly confidential memorandum favouring that course, written by Under-secretary of State George Ball, was circulated to Rusk, McNamara and McGeorge Bundy on 5 October 1964.[13] We also know that about the same time John McNaughton gave secret instructions to Daniel Ellsberg (then on his staff) to prepare a contingency plan in case withdrawal should prove necessary.[14] But that option was not taken very seriously in the corridors of power. Apart from the likelihood of an extreme reaction by the JCS, it was becoming clear to the President that events elsewhere in the region were moving against the United States. Sukarno as we shall see in the next chapter, visited Pyongyang and Shanghai in early November; and by the end of the month 'confrontation' was being intensified, forcing a more vigorous response by Britain and Malaysia. In such circumstances an American decision to abandon South Vietnam forthwith would have had disastrous consequences from the Western point of view.

Nor, it would seem, was the working group asked to consider the possibility of any large-scale deployment of United States ground forces to participate directly in the war against the PLAFSVN. That option only began to surface early in 1965, although it seems likely that it already figured as a possible course of action in the army's contingency planning. Nevertheless, special mention should be made of the massive military exercise which took place in North and South Carolina from 14 October to 12 November 1964, under the title 'Air Assault II'. Involving as many as 35,000 troops and large numbers of helicopters and planes, it was the final test of the 'airmobility' concept which the army had been developing over the past two and a half years.[15] (The eventual outcome would be the actual deployment to South Vietnam of the 1st Air Cavalry Division in August 1965.) It is possible that the President himself was by now convinced that troop deployments were the only ultimate solution if the military situation became really critical.

But almost certainly he still hoped to avoid such an extreme course of action.

The November working group thus continued to operate within the framework set out in William Bundy's 11 August draft memorandum, except that as the 1 January 'contingency date' approached it was necessary to define the options and their implications more precisely.[16] Bundy now set out three broad options, which are easily summarised:

A. To continue along present lines.
B. To embark quickly on a 'systematic programme of military pressures', against the full range of DRVN targets, which might eventually produce negotiations but should continue until American objectives were achieved.
C. To pursue present policies, plus 'additional forceful measures and military moves'; but with further action held in abeyance during hoped-for negotiations.

By the time the group reported to the 'principals' on 24 November, these options had been somewhat refined; but the differences between them remained essentially the same (see Table 18.2).

Two things emerge from the *Pentagon Papers* account of the way the three options evolved. First, 'Option B' was the course favoured by the JCS – possibly with the air force and marines taking the lead and the army and navy chiefs marginally less enthusiastic. In this the JCS were wholly consistent, having urged tough action against North Vietnam in a long series of memoranda throughout the year. (What they were advocating, it should be noted, was considerably more than the President was willing to approve even during 1965. Later, they would argue that the main reason why the United States lost the war was President Johnson's refusal to act on their advice in good time.) Second, it is clear that by November the civilian officials of the Pentagon's Office of International Security Affairs (headed by John McNaughton) were opposed to the immediate implementation of 'Option B', and that William Bundy took essentially the same line.[17] Thus the advocates of an extension of the war, to include action against North Vietnam, were now divided; the civilians (apart from Walt Rostow, who did not participate in this exercise) being rather less 'hawkish' than the military chiefs.

'Option C' was essentially the product of that split. It was an attempt by Bundy and McNaughton to devise a strategy that would avoid the risks inherent in a rapid escalation of the war –

TABLE 18.2   *Analysis of United states, opinions in Indochina, Autumn 1964*

Actions under consideration	Moves in September–October	November: 'Option A'	November: 'Option C'
I. *Cross-border actions, Laos:*			
(a) Laotian T-28 airstrikes in Southern Laos (against Ho Chi Minh Trail targets).	NSAM-314 authorised discussions on this with Vientiane government. First strikes took place on 14 October 1964.	(Already in progress)	(Already in progress)
(b) US airstrikes against such targets.	Urged by Ambassador Unger, but not approved, 13 October; only US fighter escort provided, for T-28 strikes.	Not mentioned specifically, but possibly allowed for.	Specifically recommended; first strikes authorised, on restricted basis, 12 December 1964: 'Operation Barrel Roll'.
(c) South Vietnamese air and ground actions inside Laos.	NSAM-314 authorised discussions with Vientiane; on 9 October, Ambassador Taylor indicated lack of capability for such actions on part of South Vietnamese forces.	Allowed for on a limited scale.	Allowed for; not emphasised.

II. *Actions against North Vietnam:*

(a) Covert operations by South Vietnamese forces north of 17th parallel, including coastal attacks from sea (OPLAN 34A).	NSAM-314 authorised resumption in principle (following suspension in August); actual authorisation given on 4 October.	Allowed for; no emphasis.	Recommendation that these be intensified.
(b) DE SOTO patrols in Gulf of Tonkin by US destroyers.	NSAM-314 authorised resumption; incident on 18 September led to further suspension by President.	Not mentioned specifically.	Allowed for.
(c) Tit-for-tat reprisal raids by US and South Vietnamese planes.	Advocated by JCS in September, but NSAM-314 approved only contingency planning; *no* reprisals authorised for Bien-Hoa attack on 1 November.	'Specific individual reprisals' recommended, for recurrence of Bien-Hoa type of attack, or any direct attack on US forces.	Overtaken by other elements of this 'option'.
(d) 'Graduated pressure' in form of continuing air strikes.	First mentioned in March 1964 (NSAM-288) in terms of contingency planning. Not mentioned in NSAM-314.	Ruled out, in any form, under this 'option'.	Recommended, in form of strikes against infiltration targets in southern part of DRVN; perhaps after a new action similar to the Bien-Hoa attack.

TABLE 18.2   *Analysis of United States' options in Indochina, Autumn 1964*

Actions under consideration	Moves in September–October	November: 'Option A'	November: 'Option C'
III. *Related actions in South:*			
(a) Withdrawal of American dependents and security measures involving small number of US troops.	Not mentioned in NSAM-314, or in discussion preceding it; had been explicitly ruled out in March 1964.	Not mentioned.	Recommended as necessary prelude to air strikes against North.
(b) Deployment of substantial US or SEATO forces (perhaps a division) on the ground, in northern South Vietnam.	Not mentioned in available documentation of September–October; but suggested by JCS, CINCPAC in August 1964.	Specifically ruled out under this 'option'.	Recommended as a possible action; not an integral part of this 'option'.

NSAM-314 was issued on 10 September; 'Option A' and 'Option B' are defined in the terms specified in a draft paper of 27 November 1964: 'Courses of Action in Southeast Asia'.

SOURCE *The Pentagon Papers: the Defense Department History of United States Decision-making on Vietnam*, Senator Gravel edition (Boston, Mass: Beacon Press, 1971) vol. III, pp. 192–7; 565–6; 659–66.

which, in any case, they believed would not deter Hanoi – but at the same time might break the impasse inherent in present policies. Their aim was an optimum 'level of harassment' of North Vietnam which they hoped would achieve American objectives without involving unacceptable risks. In that sense, the inspiration of 'Option C' was largely negative.

All three options assumed, ultimately, some kind of negotiated settlement to end the conflict. They differed in regard to the anticipated timing of serious negotiations, and also in their respective degrees of optimism about the eventual outcome. 'Option A' was seen as leading, in all probability, to an early settlement on lines favourable to the Communist side; possibly a total capitulation to NLFSVN demands on the part of a neutralist government in Saigon. At the other extreme, 'Option B' assumed that the negotiating phase would come only when Hanoi was obliged to come to terms with United States demands and virtually to call off the war in the South. The pressure might even be continued beyond that point, to enforce compliance with an actual agreement acceptable to Washington and Saigon. In view of the commitment to continuing military action which that option might require, it was suggested that its implementation be accompanied by some kind of presentation of the American case to the United Nations. That did not necessarily mean that the negotiations themselves would take place within a UN framework, from which Peking would automatically be excluded.

Between the two extremes, 'Option C' was designed to lead to negotiations based on the principle of 'bargaining': starting, perhaps, with an agreement by Hanoi to negotiate at all in return for an end to the bombing campaign or some limitation of it. Negotiations on that basis might well lead to a compromise settlement in which the United States would not achieve all its objectives; that was almost certainly one reason for the JCS rejection of 'Option C'. On the other hand, it was hoped that the start of negotiations might permit a lower level (and a slower pace) of military pressure than would be required under 'Option B'.

Given a completely negative North Vietnamese response to the Seaborn messages delivered on 18 June and 13 August, that logic may have been somewhat unrealistic. Nor was it likely that any other channel of communication would attain better results without considerable pressure being exerted upon Hanoi. It is true that U Thant had received some kind of reply to his own initiative via Moscow in mid-August, which he had passed on to the US Ambassador to the United Nations on 23 September.[18] He was upset to find, in mid-October, that the contact had not been followed up; but his memoirs offer no grounds for believing that a more constructive American response would have led at that stage to negotiations on any terms other than complete surrender by the Republic of Vietnam. In any case, the U Thant initiative does not appear to have been a factor in Washington's own definition of options.

The only real hope for negotiations on Vietnam, both now and later, depended on United States relations with Moscow and Peking. So long as the Russians and Chinese remained willing to give minimal encouragement to Hanoi, rather than bringing pressure to bear to secure a compromise as they had in 1954, there was little chance of a diplomatic breakthrough. 'Option C' was assuming that relatively restrained military action against North Vietnam would be sufficient to change the policies of both major Communist powers on that score: an assessment which in retrospect seems remarkably optimistic. Even 'Option B' might not have produced a significant change in that direction. Since it was never tried, in the form proposed by the JCS, that must remain a matter of speculation.

The members of the working group, as they debated the relative merits of 'Option B' and 'Option C', were keenly aware of the limitations involved in either course. 'Option B' was seen as having the better chance of producing an actual change of policy in Hanoi, provided it did not lead to an unacceptable expansion of the conflict. It assumed that at some point along the way, mutual deterrence would begin to take effect and that *both* sides would think twice before allowing a wider conflict to get out of control. 'Option C' would avoid that element of risk. But it was recognised that, if 'Option C' led to a more protracted military conflict because the DRVN refused to yield to the early phases of 'graduated pressure', Washington might still find itself having to choose between 'Option A' and 'Option B' at some later stage of the conflict. At that point a decision not to escalate further, but instead to modify the American negotiating position, might produce an even more complete collapse of the South than would happen now under 'Option A'. It might then be necessary to embark on the 'Option B' programme after all; whilst in the meantime the slow pace of 'Option C' would leave Hanoi and its allies more time to prepare effective military defences.

The working group nevertheless tended to favour 'Option C'. Much depended on what criterion was applied. Should the 'options' be judged in terms of their contribution to the achievement of one specific goal? Or should they be assessed in relation to the wider perspective of United States global policy? If the latter, then it was important to avoid a course of action which would be unlikely to win support in Western Europe and which would probably evoke outright condemnation across the 'Third World'. In recommending 'Option C', the civilian officials certainly had in mind those wider issues: the importance of Vietnam must be weighed against the negative consequences of a full scale military campaign there. Their preference for 'Option C' suggests that Bundy and McNaughton by now accepted that a compromise settlement – rather than outright 'victory' – was the only realistic objective. That in turn raised, once again, the question how firmly the United States ought to pursue its commitment to South-East Asia in general and to South Vietnam in particular.

Whilst everyone paid lip-service to the idea that the security of South-East Asia as a whole depended on stronger action in Indochina, Bundy and McNaughton were willing at least to mention the possibility that the actions they were recommending might not work. One passage in their initial draft, circulated around 10 November, implied that the main purpose of stronger action in Vietnam was to gain time to strengthen other areas of Asia. It might be necessary, in the end, to explain an American failure in Vietnam in terms of 'special local factors that do not apply to other nations we are committed to defend'. Those factors would include the past record of French errors; the fact that most other countries 'wrote off' South Vietnam in 1954; and the inability of the South Vietnamese to govern or defend themselves. The comments on that passage by Admiral Mustin (representing the JCS in the working group) were scathing indeed. In his view the United States commitment was real and binding: it was *American* judgements in 1954, not other people's, that were now at stake; the commitment must be honoured if the Americans were to avoid the worldwide repercussions of an 'abject humiliation'.[19]

Underlying this disagreement about commitment lay a difference of perspective which was to become increasingly important as time went on. The civilians (especially, in this case, Bundy's own Far Eastern Affairs Bureau at the State Department) were probably thinking mainly in terms of the South-East Asian region, where it was reasonable to hope that limited action in Vietnam would gain sufficient time to allow political change elsewhere to work to the advantage of the West. But the military chiefs were thinking more about the global chain of countries committed to military collaboration with the United States and to the strategy of 'containment'. In that perspective the 'domino' effect of an outright defeat in Vietnam might affect not merely the Indochinese peninsula and Indonesia but also more distant parts of Asia, perhaps as far west as Pakistan and Iran.

III

The NSC 'principals' met to discuss the draft memorandum of the working group on 24 November 1964; which proved to be only the beginning of a week-long series of meetings before they were able to produce an agreed recommendation to the President. On 27 November they were briefed by Ambassador Taylor, who still favoured action against the DRVN but was more concerned than ever about the immediate situation in Saigon, where the Buddhists had begun yet another campaign. This time their target was Tran Van Huong whose government had been in office for less than three weeks. On 26 November, the day Taylor left for Washington, a 'state of siege' had been declared and Westmoreland had had to dissuade Nguyen Cao Ky from staging yet another coup.[20] The worst rioting of this period came on 29 November – almost as if it had been deliberately planned to coincide with the critical stage of the Washington debate; and it probably had a direct effect, both on the recommendations finally made to the President on 30 November and on the President's own decisions the following day.

The 'principals' decided in the end to set aside both 'Option A' and 'Option B' – the two extreme alternatives – and to build their own recommendations around 'Option C'. They proposed a two-phase sequence of actions: the first phase, lasting for 30 days, to be devoted mainly to improving the political situation in Saigon; the second, starting early in the new year, to involve a gradual implementation of 'Option C'. At the White House meeting on 1 December the President accepted this plan in principle. But his formal authorisation of specific actions was limited to the first phase, which included limited American air action in southern

Laos but did not involve new operations against North Vietnam.[21] Phase II was held over for further consideration at the highest level in the light of events in Saigon. Nevertheless some effort was to be made to secure the support of United States allies for a probable expansion of the war: William Bundy visited Australia and New Zealand soon afterwards, and President Johnson had talks with British prime minister Wilson in Washington on 7–9 December.[22]

Unfortunately we know very little about the President's own deliberations on Vietnam at this point: in his memoirs he made no mention at all of the White House meeting of 1 December. A number of other clues suggest that serious differences of opinion existed at the highest level, possibly involving a clash between Rusk and McNamara. Rumours that the secretary of state opposed an expansion of the war in late 1964 were reported in the press the following February.[23] Although he has not written any memoir on his own account, it is generally agreed among other participants that Rusk's influence on President Johnson was considerable. As a native of Georgia – albeit a brilliant student who secured a Rhodes Scholarship to Oxford in the 1930s – he may have seemed less alien to the Texan President than the New Englanders who had dominated the Kennedy White House. The possibility must be taken seriously therefore that the policy of restraint which Johnson pursued during 1964 was essentially that of Rusk rather than his own. From the historian's point of view, of course, the bond of trust which clearly existed between the two men makes it all the more difficult to penetrate the barrier of confidentiality surrounding their frequent conversations at this critical period. Rusk himself, at a news conference on 3 January, took the view that the United States could afford neither to expand the conflict nor to withdraw from Vietnam.

It would appear that Rusk's greatest preoccupation was with the danger of another war with China. The Pentagon war games, in so far as they had any influence on official thinking, had been predicated on a range of possible assumptions about Chinese and Soviet reactions to American moves at each stage of several imaginary 'scenarios', and throughout the autumn debate the American intelligence community had been trying to estimate the likely responses of the Communist powers to various possible levels of United States action against North Vietnam. The element of uncertainty present in all such assessments generated a strong sense of risk amongst the civilian decision-makers. The JCS failed to dispel that fear by arguing that, in the final analysis, the risks for China were greater than those for the United States. But in retrospect the question logically arises whether this concern about direct Chinese intervention in the Indochinese peninsula was not

TABLE 18.3   *Washington decision-making and events in South Vietnam, November − December 1964*

South Vietnam	Washington
1 Nov.: PLAFSVN mortar attack on Bien-Hoa airbase, destroying and damaging US planes.	
	2 Nov.: White House meeting: decision not to retaliate for Bien-Hoa attack.
	3 Nov.: NSC Working Group established to formulate recommendations for the 'principals': William Bundy's 'project outline'.
4 Nov.: Tran Van Huong took office as prime minister of civilian cabinet; Phan Khac Suu as head of state.	4 Nov.: JCS again urged 'prompt and strong' reprisals for Bien-Hoa attack.
	10 Nov.: William Bundy circulated draft of parts of Working Group Memorandum.
	14 Nov.: JCS again urged early implementation of programme of continuing air strikes against North Vietnam; opposed 'tit-for-tat' reprisals.
18 Nov.: Communist side alleged air raid by US planes (from Laos) against targets in Quang-Binh province (no US information). Start of 'Operation Brushfire' (by ARVN units) against Communist positions at Ben-Suc: no significant contact reported.	18 Nov.: JCS reiterated its call for early action against North; including resumption of DESOTO patrols.
	21−4 Nov.: NSC Working Group producing final draft of its recommendations.
22 Nov.: Start of new Buddhist campaign against government of Tran Van Huong.	
	24 Nov.: Meeting of NSC 'principals' to discuss working group's three options: agencies differed about which to adopt.
26 Nov.: State of siege in Saigon. Ambassador Taylor left for Washington.	
	27 Nov.: NSC 'principals' briefed by Ambassador Taylor.

29 Nov.: Disorder in Saigon reached new peak, before order was again restored.

28–30 Nov.: NSC 'principals' held further meetings; reached agreement on recommending a two-phase plan to the president, in which phase II would include negotiation attempt.

1 Dec.: White House meeting: President authorised only first phase of action at this stage; no NSAM was issued.

3 Dec.: President gave new instructions to Taylor on need for reforms in South Vietnam.

4–8 Dec.: Battles at An-Lao (Binh-Dinh) and Binh-Gia (Phuoc-Tuy), at start of new PLAFSVN offensive.

4–9 Dec.: US consultations with Australia, New Zealand and Britain. (Wilson in Washington, 7–9 Dec.)

7–16 Dec.: US-Cambodian talks, New Delhi: failed to make any progress.

8–11 Dec.: Ambassador Taylor, back in Saigon, held talks with Nguyen Khanh and Tran Van Huong, to secure new government policies.

12 Dec.: NSC approved start of 'Operation Barrel Roll': US air strikes inside Laos.

---

perhaps exaggerated, throughout the critical period from late 1963 to early 1965.

Most Chinese military thinking about South-East Asia since 1949 had been geared to the concept of 'people's war' and the notion of revolutionary 'self-reliance'. The two big exceptions to that principle had occurred in Korea in 1950 and on the Sino-Indian frontier (a very limited action) in 1962: both cases where China's own borders had appeared to be threatened. An actual American invasion of North Vietnam in 1964 would undoubtedly have produced a similar response. Action short of that – coupled with the threat of action against China *only* if the PLA itself moved in – might not have had such dramatic results. At every stage when the Chinese might have intervened in strength during the next two years they chose not to do so; they provided only very limited support to Hanoi even at the height of the war. Ought the Americans perhaps to have been able to predict such restraint?

Without access to all the intelligence data at their disposal, it is not possible to attempt an answer to that question. But one day it must be asked.

There were, it is true, a few American officials who believed that the best policy towards China was one of moderation, which might open the way to an easing of tension. A memorandum by James Thomson (of the NSC staff) had argued in late October that 'there is a danger of pushing too far the thesis of Peking's responsibility for the South Vietnam crisis', and had suggested a gradual modification of Washington's attitude to Peking's admission to the United Nations. A week later the US Consul in Hong Kong had suggested a number of small initiatives which might bridge the 'enormous spiritual gulf' between China and the United States.[24] But thinking in the State Department remained utterly unsympathetic to such ideas, and the 125th ambassadorial meeting in Warsaw which took place on 25 November 1964 seems to have been devoted mainly to charges and counter-charges on the subject of banning nuclear tests.[25] A State Department 'intelligence note' two days later emphasised China's own extreme position on the United Nations issue – a demand for the complete expulsion of Taiwan – and suggested that a recent top-level meeting in Peking from 15 to 23 November had merely reinforced China's anti-American line. Without more information from both sides it is impossible to tell whether American intransigence evoked a 'hardline' Chinese response, or vice versa.

On 3 December President Johnson had a long session with Ambassador Taylor, at which they discussed the related problems of securing political and administrative reforms in South Vietnam and bringing about great stability there. Calm had returned by the time Taylor got back to Saigon, and on 8–9 December he discussed the latest American proposals with both Tran Van Huong and Nguyen Khanh. But the situation remained tense, and the Buddhists appeared to be deliberately seeking to prevent the political stability which the Americans so badly needed. Worse still, from their point of view, it would appear that Khanh had made some kind of deal with them; and that he was also by now in direct contact with the NLFSVN. Another round of demonstrations began about the middle of the month, provoking yet another coup on 19 December. The government itself was not overthrown, but Nguyen Cao Ky and Nguyen Chanh Thi (supported by Khanh) dissolved the High National Council from which the Huong cabinet had initially derived its authority. The following morning Ambassador Taylor confronted the generals and openly disagreed with Khanh; on the 22nd Khanh in turn spoke publicly of his differences with Taylor.[26] The political deadlock which followed lasted until late January and the crisis was not finally resolved until the second half of February, when Nguyen Khanh was at last forced into exile.

Meanwhile the situation on the battlefield continued to deteriorate, with ARVN suffering serious defeats at the hands of the PLAFSVN in Binh-Dinh and Phuoc-Tuy provinces during December; whilst the much vaunted *Hop-Tac* campaign, which was supposed to 'pacify' the provinces immediately surrounding Saigon, had made hardly any progress. The disastrous state of security in the capital area was demonstrated on Christmas Eve, when the Communists staged another terrorist attack in Saigon itself: a large explosion at the Brinks Hotel officers' billet, which killed two Americans and wounded over a hundred others. Once again Johnson was forced to the conclusion that the South Vietnamese 'base' was too fragile to permit immediate retaliation against the DRVN, and he continued to withhold authorisation for Phase II of the NSC's 'Option C'. But by 6 January 1965 William Bundy was observing, in a memorandum to Rusk, that 'the situation in Vietnam is now likely to come apart more rapidly than we had anticipated in November'.[27] The time for hard decisions was at hand.

19 Hanoi Decides

Some regular North Vietnamese Army units are known to have begun preparing for infiltration as early as April 1964. Several prisoners from the 95th Regiment of the 325th division have reported that their unit was recalled in that month from duty in Laos. . . . In October 1964 the first complete tactical unit of the North Vietnamese Army, the 95th Regiment, left the North. . . . It reached South Vietnam in December. The 32nd Regiment left the North in September or October 1964, arriving between January and March; and a second regiment of the 325th Division (the 101st) had left North Vietnam by December 1964. All of these dates of departure were prior to the beginning of US bombing of North Vietnam in February 1965. In short the evidence does not support the claim, sometimes made, that the sending of regular North Vietnamese units was only in response to the US bombing.

State Department paper,
May 1968

By mid-1964 guerrilla warfare had been expanded on the Tay-Nguyen (Central Highlands) battlefield. There was a requirement that we gradually develop regular warfare, maintain an offensive posture, annihilate large enemy forces and liberate territory. In view of these urgent requirements, on 1 May 1964 the Political Bureau of the Party Central Committee decided to set up the Western subregion of Military Region V, which was changed to the Central Highlands Front (B-3) in September 1964. . . . The armed forces of this Front were formed and developed from two sources: local armed forces which came of age in the local struggle movement, and mainforce troops sent South from the great rear area by the Ministry of National Defence.

The Anti-US Resistance War for National Salvation 1954–1975
(Hanoi 1980)

I

The decision by Hanoi to send whole regiments and divisions of the PAVN to South Vietnam, to fight as independent units rather than merely as external recruits for the PLAFSVN, has inevitably been a subject of great controversy. Critics of President Johnson's policies, inclined to attribute the escalation of the war entirely to American decision-making, have argued that North Vietnamese regular troops were sent South only as a response to American bombing north of the 17th parallel, which finally got under way in February 1965. The 'hawks', rejecting that conclusion, have insisted that Hanoi's decision was taken in principle at the VNWP 9th Plenum in December 1963. Neither of these interpretations can be accepted now, although it is evident that the secret resolution of the 9th Plenum was an important step along the road to the decision. Having said that, however, the historian is faced with the difficult task of attempting to establish the actual sequence of events more precisely; and also of analysing the Communist strategy on which the decision was based.

On the American side, hard evidence concerning the movement of substantial numbers of North Vietnamese troops down the Ho Chi Minh trail is available in two forms. First, while such movement was actually in progress, United States intelligence resources were brought to bear in an effort to measure the numbers involved; and although the resulting data are not yet available for research in their original form, they were the basis for regular estimates of the fluctuating level of infiltration which appear in more accessible intelligence assessments. In a cable from Saigon on 14 October 1964, Ambassador Taylor reported signs of 'a definite step-up in infiltration' and observed that if it were sustained at the current level for the remainder of the year the total number of North Vietnamese personnel reaching the South during the calendar year 1964 would be as high as 10,000.[1] Secondly, as the war progressed it became possible for the Americans to interrogate prisoners of war and so piece together information about the movement of specific units during 1964–5. From that source it emerged that the 95th regiment of the (PAVN) 325th Division, having begun training for the move in April, left the North in October 1964 and reached South Vietnam by the end of the year. Another regiment (the 32nd, formed specially for combat in the South) made the trek between October and early 1965; and a third (again from the 325th Division) began its southward move during December.[2] None of these units became engaged in actual combat before February or March 1965; possibly later. But the length of time required for the journey along the Ho Chi Minh trail meant that a substantive decision to deploy them in the South had to be taken at least three to four months before they could be used on the battlefield.

No reference to the presence of PAVN units in the South was allowed to appear in the Hanoi media so long as the war was going on: the Communist side persisted to the end in its claim that the DRVN had adhered strictly to the terms of the Geneva Agreement of 1954, and that the South Vietnamese struggle was a purely southern affair. Only after 1975 do we find a number of clues in Vietnamese sources which make it possible to reconstruct, in broad outline, the sequence of actual decision-making. The 1980 Hanoi history of the war tells us that as early as May 1964 the Politburo ordered the creation of a special military subregion for the Central Highlands (Tay-Nguyen), which in September the same year was redesignated the 'B-3 Front'.[3] That was the area where the use of mainforce PAVN units would later become a decisive factor – particularly in 1965 and again in 1975.

Another small but important clue comes from Van Tien Dung's memoir of the final campaigns leading to the conquest of South Vietnam. He mentions in passing that in September 1964 Nguyen Chi Thanh, after a secret mission to the South, made a speech to the Nguyen Ai Quoc Party School in Hanoi on the implementation of the 'internal section' of the 9th Plenum resolution. He also tells us that Thanh presented a draft strategic plan to the Politburo, which led to the promulgation (in the name of the Central Committee) of a formal resolution at the end of 1964.[4] This would imply that the Party leadership was debating the issue at least from September to December: the decision to send PAVN units to the South presumably emerged from that debate. Some troops began to move in October; but the final endorsement of Nguyen Chi Thanh's plan to use them on the battlefield may not have been given until the end of the year.

That the Hanoi debate was closely related to the secret resolution of the 9th Plenum seems evident; but that document was ambiguous at certain critical points. Even in its final form (the copy dated 1 January 1965) it did not explicitly record a decision about PAVN forces; it merely noted that 'the North must bring into fuller play its role as the revolutionary base for the whole nation'.[5] The main importance of the resolution was that it defined a new military strategy in the South, which could probably only be implemented immediately by using substantial numbers of North Vietnamese troops. Whereas during 1960–3 the emphasis of Party documents had been on working towards a 'general uprising', the long-term objective of the struggle was now defined as a 'general offensive and uprising'; that implied greater reliance on the military struggle. In calling for the 'development of the armed forces' in the South, the resolution indicated that they would include mainforce units as well as local forces and village militia groups. Whilst some mainforce regiments and battalions had begun to emerge from the developing revolutionary struggle inside the South, it would take time to expand their capabilities relying solely on Southern recruitment.

The first division-size unit of the PLAFSVN proper – the 9th Division, which incorporated two regiments already in existence – was created towards the end of 1964 and went into battle for the first time in Phuoc-Tuy province in December. At the turn of the year (28 December–3 January) it achieved a major success fighting the largest battle of the war so far, in which two ARVN battalions were annihilated trying to dislodge it from the Catholic village (and 'strategic hamlet') of Binh-Gia. The PLAFSVN was also making significant progress in the province of Binh-Dinh, which by this time was largely under Communist control. ARVN and the Americans suffered another serious defeat in a battle for the An-Lao subsector of that province on 7–8 December 1964.[6] Even so, a rapid expansion of the military struggle would require the introduction of trained personnel from the North to operate as mainforce units, at least in the Central Highlands area – where firepower would ultimately prove more important than either guerrilla warfare or political struggle amongst the local population. Delay in introducing PAVN units into that area might mean loss of the initiative which the PLAFSVN had gained during the 12 months since autumn 1963.

II

It is inconceivable that the Vietnamese Politburo made up its mind to send PAVN units to fight in the South without paying attention to the international situation, and particularly to the views of Peking and Moscow. The increasingly close relationship between North Vietnam and China, evident during the summer and autumn of 1964, might appear at first to indicate that the decision was encouraged (if not initiated) by Peking rather than by Moscow. But in the light of what has been said in earlier chapters about North Vietnamese decision-making in the early 1960s, it seems highly improbable that Ho Chi Minh would approve such a major expansion of the armed struggle unless he felt he could rely on Soviet as well as Chinese support. In their polemical publications of 1979, moreover, the Vietnamese were sharply critical of Peking's attitude to the war in 1964. One pamphlet of that later period refers to a secret visit to Hanoi by Deng Xiaoping towards the end of the year, during which he offered a major expansion of Chinese aid – on condition that the VNWP broke off all ties with the Soviet Union. The offer was promptly rejected.[7]

The Moscow 'coup' of 12–14 October 1964, in which Brezhnev, Kosygin and Suslov combined to force Khrushchev's 'retirement', had a significant impact on the Communist Parties of Asia. One result was that Zhou Enlai, accompanied by Kang Sheng and He Long, went to Moscow for the October Revolution anniversary. But although they stayed on until 13 November, for talks with the new CPSU leaders, no significant break-through was achieved. A week after their return home an article in *Hong Qi*, on the reasons for Khrushchev's fall, marked the resumption of ideological hostilities between the two Parties.[8] The Vietnamese Party leaders, on the other hand, may have had more reason to welcome the change and to improve their own relations with the CPSU at this point. On 3 November 1964 Pham Van Dong and Le Duc Tho left Hanoi to attend the October Revolution celebrations in Moscow; and it would seem that from Peking they flew in the same plane as Zhou Enlai. But after completing their respective talks with CPSU leaders it was noticeable that the two delegations left Moscow separately on 13–14 November.[9] Whilst it is unlikely that Pham Van Dong was able to resolve all Soviet–Vietnamese problems at one go, the door was kept open for further discussions.

Possibly the most important factor in North Vietnam's attitude to Peking at this juncture was the relatively backward state of Chinese military technology, compared with both the Soviet Union and the United States. *Nhan-Dan* had praised China's first successful test-explosion of an atomic bomb on 16 October 1964. But that event was more important as a symbol of China's

independent achievement than for its immediate military consequences. Chinese strategy in Vietnam still depended on the hope
of deterring hostilities north of the 17th parallel. If deterrence
failed and if Hanoi eventually did become involved in a direct
military confrontation with the United States, only Soviet
weapons would enable it to resist the type of military pressure the
Americans had in mind.

Hanoi's determination to secure support from *all* fraternal
Parties was reflected in the successful organisation of an International Conference for Solidarity with the People of Vietnam,
which met in Hanoi from 25 to 29 November 1964.[10] The Chinese
delegation led by Liu Ningyi was of noticeably higher status than
the Russian (led by Safronov). Nevertheless TASS made a point of
publishing a statement of Soviet support for Vietnam on 26
November, and the meeting was attended by delegations from all
the countries of Eastern Europe. If nothing else, the Hanoi
gathering demonstrated that the struggle in South Vietnam was
the one issue in world affairs on which the whole of the socialist
camp remained ostensibly united. In assessing the political realities
of 1964 we must be careful not to dismiss this appearance of
international unity in Communist support for Hanoi as merely
superficial. What mattered to all Marxist–Leninists in the immediate situation was the defeat of United States objectives in
South Vietnam. It was thus possible for the Vietnamese to draw
genuine support from many different quarters, and to create what
amounted to their own *ad hoc* united front against imperialism.

Meanwhile the Russians were gradually reaffirming their
support for the struggle in South Vietnam. Premier Kosygin sent a
message of support directly to the leaders of the NLFSVN on 17
November; and at the end of 1964 it was reported that the Front
would open its own office in Moscow – to match that already
functioning in Peking.[11] The improvement in relations between
Hanoi and Moscow may also have been reflected in the return to
prominence of Le Duan, who had not been very active in public
during the months since April 1964. On 20 December he was again
to the fore at the commemoration of the resistance anniversary in
Hanoi.

Towards the end of the year there were indications that North
Vietnam was receiving especially strong support from Pyongyang.
Whereas in previous years Vietnamese army day celebrations had
been attended by military delegations from China (1961) and the

Soviet Union (1962), it was reported on 18 December 1964 that the North Korean defence minister had arrived in Hanoi.[12] There is no evidence that Korean military personnel played any direct role in the fighting on the Communist side in Vietnam – whereas the Saigon government did secure a contingent of South Korean troops early in 1965. But the Koreans were in a position to offer other military assistance to Hanoi, which was probably welcome at a time when the Vietnamese wished to keep their distance from the Chinese.

III

The failure of Zhou Enlai's talks in Moscow, and perhaps also the failure of Deng Xiaoping's mission to Hanoi, may have been partly responsible for yet another shift in the balance of forces within the Chinese leadership towards the end of 1964. Another important factor in that change was almost certainly the virtual collapse of Sino-Japanese relations which occurred at about the same time. Since 1961 prime minister Ikeda had pursued an increasingly friendly policy towards Peking; but in late October he was forced to resign for health reasons. His successor was Sato Eisaku: a brother (despite their different surnames) of Kishi Nobusuke, who had been prime minister from 1957 to 1961. Like his brother, Sato was committed not only to close relations with the United States but also to friendship with Taiwan. Thus Chiang Kaishek once again found an opportunity, as in 1957–8, to put pressure on Tokyo to abandon its policy of expanding trade with the People's Republic. Although Sato continued to insist that Japan's attitude towards China had not changed, it became evident soon after he took office on 9 November 1964 that the momentum towards economic *rapprochement* with Peking had been lost.

Tokyo's refusal of a visa to allow Peng Zhen to attend the 9th Congress of the Japanese Communist Party from 25 to 30 November was interpreted as a serious rebuff to Peking. On 25 November *Renmin Ribao* responded with a sharp attack on the Sato government for its attitude towards China in general and towards the Taiwan issue in particular.[13] The full effects of the change would emerge early in 1965. But already by December it must have been apparent to Mao that any hopes of relying on further expansion of Sino-Japanese trade as an aid to China's economic recovery from the hardships of the early 1960s were doomed to disappointment. The effects on Chinese internal politics were not long delayed.

From July or August until late November 1964 it would appear that Liu Shaoqi was particularly influential, especially in shaping the new course of the socialist education movement in the countryside. But in December he ran into difficulties when one of his 'work teams' reported unfavourably on the model commune of Dazhai, situated in a remote and previously barren area of Shanxi province. The leading cadre in charge of Dazhai appealed to Zhou Enlai, and eventually to Mao himself. Not only did he secure a reversal of the work team's adverse judgement: on 30 December *Renmin Ribao* published Mao's latest instruction: 'Learn from Dazhai!' Whereas Liu had been bent on improving the quality of rural economic management, by conducting the 'big four clean-ups' campaign against local corruption, Mao was more interested in the principle of self-reliance – of which Dazhai was an outstanding symbol.[14] He was determined not to respond to Japan's latest rebuff by reverting to dependence on the Soviet Union. Greater self-reliance was the only alternative. Finally on 14 January a work conference of the CCP Politburo, probably under Mao's personal direction, approved a new '23-point' circular to govern the next phase of rural socialist education. That spelt the end of Liu Shaoqi's direction of the campaign. Meanwhile another sign of change was the promotion of Lin Biao, whose name appeared at the head of the long list of vice-premiers appointed by the National People's Congress at its closing session on 3 January.[15]

The change may also have had a direct bearing on Chinese policy towards the conflict in Vietnam. At the end of the year, as we have seen, the North Vietnamese finally reached a decision on sending at least some PAVN units into battle in the South – and on stepping up the formation of PLAFSVN mainforce divisions. So far from Mao Zedong being directly responsible for that move, he may well have seen it as a dangerous step from China's point of view. The likely result would be an American escalation of the war, which the Chinese were still anxious to deter. Mao's next move must be to avoid a direct confrontation with the United States.

Given the circumstances of late 1964, particularly the deterioration of Sino-Japanese relations and the apparent recovery of influence by Lin Biao, it was impossible to achieve a significant easing of tension through direct Sino-American contacts. The 125th ambassadorial meeting in Warsaw, on 25 November, appears to have concentrated mainly on the issue of nuclear weapons following the successful Chinese atomic test in mid-October; its results seem to have been wholly negative. By the end of the year – notably in an article in *Renmin Ribao* on 31 December – the Chinese were denouncing what they termed 'nuclear black-mail' in the form of the presence near the Asian mainland of the American submarine *Daniel Boone*, armed with nuclear weapons.[16] Yet they could not ignore the dangers implicit in a situation which might at some stage lead to another Sino-American war.

At this point the Chinese made two moves. On 8 January 1965 the National Defence Council authorised a number of changes calculated to improve the military capability of the Chinese armed forces, including an extension of the normal period of military service to allow more thorough technical training.[17] The following day (9 January) Mao himself gave an interview to the American journalist Edgar Snow – long regarded as a friend of China – which subsequently became the basis of an article published in European and Asian (but not the American) journals under a dateline of 17 February.[18] Much of what Mao said was in keeping with the previous strategy of trying to deter the United States from any escalation of the war, whether by air attacks against North Vietnam or an invasion of the South. Such action would result in a large war extending across South-East Asia, and would certainly involve Chinese intervention. But the most important passage of the interview was one which indicated that in present circumstances China would not move its own ground forces into Indochina.

Recalling Korea, Mao pointed out that in 1950 the Chinese had only intervened in force after the Americans had penetrated far beyond the 38th parallel, and had begun to threaten China's own territory. In the case of Vietnam, the Chinese would in similar circumstances respond to a call for help from Ho Chi Minh. But Mao believed that Vietnamese forces alone – if necessary, including those of North Vietnam – were sufficient to defeat those of the Saigon government within a fairly short period. In principle China would not engage in a direct conflict with the United States unless its own territory was attacked first. In practice the Chinese would prefer to see a negotiated settlement in Vietnam, based on a

return to the Geneva framework of 1954. Fifteen years later, in
their anti-Peking diatribe of 1979, the Vietnamese Communists
interpreted Mao's statement to Snow as a virtual invitation to
Washington to escalate the war.[19] At the time, it may have been
intended as one last bid to *avert* escalation – made in the knowledge
that Hanoi had already begun to move PAVN units into the
South.

IV

By late 1964 two different perceptions of the South-East Asian
revolution were beginning to crystallise: one Soviet, the other
Chinese. The Soviet perception – identified with Suslov and
Brezhnev rather than with Khrushchev – placed Vietnam on a
different level from other countries of the region. The DRVN was
already a full member of the 'world socialist system', having
reached the stage of building socialism, and was seen as a potential
Soviet ally in the long-term global power struggle. Hanoi's
aspiration to reunify Vietnam under its own rule was therefore
worthy of international support, even though it might involve a
larger conflict with the United States. The Russians had no wish to
allow this to become a direct confrontation between themselves
and the Americans; but they were again willing to give indirect
support in both the military and the diplomatic spheres. In this
view the Indochina conflict was not merely a case of 'anti-
imperialism'. It was above all a product of the world contradiction
between the capitalist and socialist systems, in a sense which did
not yet apply to any other part of South-East Asia.

By contrast the Chinese perception emphasised precisely that
wider anti-American significance of the struggle in South Vietnam, identifying it as one element in a pattern which also
embraced the anti-imperialism of Cambodia and Indonesia, and
which would gradually be extended to include armed struggles
against the governments of Thailand, Malaysia and the Philippines. That broader struggle would force the imperialists to
disperse their efforts to defend the 'free world' – until eventually
the Americans would have to choose between a major regional war
or a complete withdrawal from mainland South-East Asia and
Indonesia. Ironically the Chinese perception did not require
immediate expansion of the war in Vietnam itself, and there is no

reason to suppose that they encouraged the early use of PAVN units South of the 17th parallel.

Hanoi's refusal to rely exclusively on Chinese aid did not lead to a Sino-Vietnamese split at this stage: publicly the Chinese media were as committed as ever to the struggle in South Vietnam. But it made Peking even more anxious than before to develop its own influence elsewhere in South-East Asia. In the first place that meant continuing efforts to draw Cambodia into the anti-American struggle; and promoting a framework of Indochinese co-operation that would allow China to maintain direct relations with Cambodia – as well as with the Pathet Lao and the NLFSVN – rather than having to channel support through Hanoi. On 9 November Chen Yi was in Phnom Penh for an independence day rally at which Sihanouk called for an Indochinese People's Conference, to express the growing solidarity between Cambodia, North Vietnam, the NLFSVN and the Pathet Lao.[20] That conference finally took place, with Vietnamese support, in March 1965. In the meantime, Hanoi probably set greater store by the fraternal solidarity demonstrated at its own international conference in late November.

In keeping with the 'Maoist' perception of the South-East Asian revolution the Chinese were also keen to support nascent revolutionary movements in Thailand, and even in the Philippines. On 8 December the 'Voice of the People of Thailand' put out a manifesto issued by the Thailand Independence Movement (dated 1 November 1964); followed by the publication on 23 January of a statement by the Thailand Patriotic Front (dated 1 January 1965)[21] Although the relationship between those two organisations is somewhat obscure – they eventually merged later in 1965 – there seems little doubt that both were encouraged, if not initially sponsored, by Peking; and that the still secret Thai Communist Party was ideologically and politically much closer to the CCP than to the CPSU. In the Philippines a small anti-American demonstration in early October was followed by the establishment on 30 November 1964 of the *Kabataang Makabayun*, which organised larger meetings and demonstrations in late December and again in January. There too, it would seem that the inspiration was mainly Chinese.[22]

The main focus of China's interest in South-East Asia by now was Indonesia. Following his unsatisfactory visit to Moscow (mentioned in Chapter 17) Sukarno had had a friendly meeting

TABLE 19.1 *The international perspective, November – December 1964*

International Communist relations	Chinese relations	Vietnam and the war	Indonesia
21 Nov.: *Hong Qi* article on the fall of Khrushchev: resumption of polemical debate.			21 Nov.: PKI proposal to arm peasants and workers to form a 'fifth force' or militia.
		22–9 Nov.: Riots in Saigon. 24–30 Nov.: Series of high-level meetings in Washington to define new Vietnam strategy.	
24 Nov.: CPSU circular inviting other Parties to attend Moscow meeting in March 1965.		24 Nov.: Sihanouk denounced US–South Vietnamese violation of Cambodian frontier.	Late Nov.: Growing tension between the PKI and the 'Body for Promoting Sukarnoism'.
24 Nov.: to early Dec.: Li Xiannian visited Albania.	25 Nov.: Sino–American 125th ambassadorial meeting, Warsaw. 25 Nov.: *Renmin Ribao* attacked new Japanese government of Sato.	25–9 Nov.: Hanoi International Solidarity Conference; attended by Liu Ningyi, Safronov.	
25–30 Nov.: Japanese CP held its 9th Congress: Miyamoto criticised CPSU line.			

26 Nov.: Chen Yi left to visit Indonesia and Burma.	26 Nov.: US agreed to meeting with Cambodian representative in New Delhi (7–16 December).	26 Nov.: Sukarno's decree on confiscation of British firms in Indonesia.
		27 Nov.–3 Dec.: Chen Yi visited Indonesia. (Subandrio in Tokyo part of that time.)
29–9 Nov.: Mao's denunciation of US policy in the Congo, after fall of Stanleyville (24 Nov.); Tiananmen demonstrations on issue.		
		30 Nov.: Philippines: anti-American organisation formed. (3–8 Dec.: Chen Yi in Burma.)
	4–8 Dec.: Battles at An-Lao, Binh-Gia: PLAFSVN offensive.	4–7 Dec.: USIS libraries at Jakarta and Surabaya sacked.
3 Dec.: *Renmin Ribao* praised Japanese CP Congress.	8 Dec.: Thailand Independence Movement broadcast manifesto over 'Voice of People of Thailand'.	
6 Dec.: *Pravda* on the 'state of the whole people'.		
8 Dec.: Chen Yi, Li Xiannian both returned to Peking.		

SOURCES Monitored broadcasts, in *Summary of World Broadcasts: Far East*: for Indonesia, A. C. A. Dake, *In the Spirit of the Red Banteng: Indonesian Communists between Moscow and Peking 1959–1965* (The Hague, 1973) with the Chinese ambassador in Paris on 22 October. Two weeks later, immediately after visiting North Korea, he made a short stopover in Shanghai and had direct talks with Zhou Enlai on 4 November.[23] From that meeting it is possible to date the growth of a 'Peking–Jakarta axis', which continued until the stormy events of autumn 1965. Towards the end of November, Chen Yi visited Jakarta again to work out the details of what promised to become a lasting Sino-Indonesian alliance. As Sukarno veered towards Peking, the Russians again invited Subandrio to Moscow in mid-December, but to no avail. By this time only the Japanese were in a position to counter the further growth of Chinese influence and Sukarno himself was anxious to maintain that connection. He went to Tokyo in late October and again from 5 to 13 November, and Subandrio was there at the end of November.

Meanwhile the PKI seemed more inclined than ever to support the CCP line. One of the principal issues still dividing the Soviet and Chinese Parties was that of an international Communist conference: an idea which Brezhnev and Suslov were able to keep alive, even though the preparatory session had to be postponed from mid-December to March 1965. Invitations to that meeting were circulated on 24 November 1964, and its importance was emphasised publicly in a *Pravda* article of 12 December. The Soviet invitation was rejected not only by the CCP – predictably – but also by the Japanese and Indonesian Parties. (The Japanese CP was now sufficiently sure of its anti-Soviet position to hold its 9th Congress, from 25 to 30 November.) It was noticeable, too, that on the day the PKI announced its decision not to attend the Moscow meeting (14 December) one of its senior figures was holding talks with Miyamoto in Tokyo.[24]

In Indonesian domestic politics the PKI was now anxious to prevent the growth of any other organisation which might serve as a vehicle for Soviet policy: in particular the left-wing Murba Party and the 'Body for Promoting Sukarnoism' which it had sponsored earlier in the year. In Sukarno's absence (during October and early November) rumours had spread that he was in poor health and might soon die: tension between the PKI and its rivals consequently increased. During the month or so following Sukarno's return on 13 November the conflict came to a head; but the president himself eventually stepped in to protect the Communists – so long as they refrained from any attempt to mobilise the peasantry for a rural armed struggle. On 17 December he dissolved the 'Body for Promoting Sukarnoism', and a month later the Murba Party itself was banned. Within Indonesia this left only the armed forces as a counter to the PKI, and it was noticeable that from mid-January they attempted to bury their own differences in order to resist the proposal of the PKI that Sukarno should create an independent militia – outside the military chain of command – by arming the peasants and workers.[25]

American influence in Indonesia was now extremely weak; whilst the British economic presence (but not the Dutch) had suffered a final blow when Sukarno decreed the confiscation of British enterprises on 26 November. The anti-American mood was intensified in early December with attacks on the USIS libraries in Jakarta and Surabaya.

From mid-November the struggle to 'crush Malaysia' had also been intensified, and a marked build-up of Indonesian forces in Kalimantan followed by the end of the year. Fears of a change to more conventional military tactics led the British to respond in kind by reinforcing their units on the Malaysian side of the frontier. In the event, the only significant new development occurred in the diplomatic field. On 1 January 1965, when Malaysia was due to take its seat among the elected members of the UN Security Council, Sukarno announced that Indonesia would withdraw altogether from the United Nations: a move which Peking alone applauded, having been itself excluded from that organisation since 1949. Despite messages from the Soviet Union and Yugoslavia urging him to change his mind, Sukarno confirmed his decision on 7 January. Sukarno was now fully committed to closer relations with Peking, and on 24–7 January 1965 Subandrio held further talks with Zhou Enlai in the Chinese capital.[26]

The Americans were by now alarmed at what appeared to be China's growing revolutionary ambitions in South-East Asia as a whole. None of the documents so far available to outsiders provides direct evidence that President Johnson himself allowed events in maritime South-East Asia to influence his decisions on Indochina. But if the 'domino theory' meant anything at all, it focused attention on Vietnam as the one point in the region where it was possible – and seemed to be necessary – for the United States to act. What was at stake was not merely the future of South Vietnam but that of Indonesia and the whole region.

This was the context in which Hanoi finally took its decision to implement the 9th plenum resolution, and in which the Johnson

TABLE 19.2 *Asian relations, December 1964–January 1965*

China, North Vietnam	US Policy and the war	Indonesia, Philippines
18 Dec.: China: Supreme State Conference. 18 Dec.: PLA Navy shot down Taiwan reconnaissance plane over East China. 18 Dec.: North Korean military delegation arrived in Hanoi.		18 Dec.: Sukarno met Chinese ambassador in Jakarta.
	19–20 Dec.: Nguyen Cao Ky and Nguyen Chanh Thi dissolved High National Council in Saigon; confrontation between Nguyen Khanh and Ambassador Taylor: start of new political crisis.	
20 Dec.: Hanoi rally for anniversary of the Resistance; Le Duan again prominent. 21–2 Dec.: Opening sessions of Chinese National People's Congress: report by Zhou.		
	24 Dec.: Terrorist attack on Brinks Hotel (US billet in Saigon); Johnson again decided against retaliation. 26 Dec.: US nuclear submarine reported off Asian mainland.	25 Dec.: Anti-American demonstration in Manila.

	28 Dec.–3 Jan.: Main battle of Binh-Gia (Phuoc-Tuy province): first divisionsised operation by PLAFSVN; ARVN defeat.	
30 Dec.: Mao's slogan: 'Learn from Dazhai!'		1 Jan.: Indonesia announced intention of withdrawing from United Nations.
30 Dec.: Soviet letter to North Vietnam, promising support. Report that NLF-SVN will open its own office in Moscow.	1 Jan.: Date of final version of 9th Plenum Resolution on South Vietnam.	
31 Dec.: *Renmin Ribao* denounced American 'nuclear blackmail': reference to submarines off Asian mainland.	3 Jan.: Rusk's news conference: he still favours 'middle path' on Vietnam.	
		5 Jan.: Subandrio speech referring to a new and critical phase of the revolution.
3 Jan.: End of Chinese NPC session: new government included Lin Biao as first deputy premier.		
6 Jan.: *Renmin Ribao* article on Binh-Gia.	6 Jan.: US senior officials concerned at rapid deterioration of situation in Saigon.	
		7 Jan.: Sukarno confirmed decision to withdraw from United Nations.
	8 Jan.: South Korea announced decision to send 2000 troops to South Vietnam.	
9 Jan.: Mao's talk with Edgar Snow in Peking.		

SOURCES as for Table 19.1.

Administration had to interpret the resulting increase in 'infiltration' through Laos. The Vietnamese themselves were later to insist that their own objectives were *not* merely part of a larger Chinese strategy; and whilst the Chinese did not actively criticise the sending of PAVN units into South Vietnam, it is by no means clear that the move was actively supported by Peking. Even so, there is nothing to suggest that the Americans missed a significant diplomatic opportunity at this juncture, arising from either Sino-Soviet or Sino-Vietnamese differences. The fact that Soviet and Chinese support derived from conflicting ideas about the world revolution did not prevent the Vietnamese from exploiting circumstances which at last favoured an expansion of their own armed struggle.

20　February 1965: Escalation

The underlying difficulties in Saigon arise from the spreading conviction that the future is without hope for anti-Communist policy. Our best friends have been somewhat discouraged by our own inactivity in the face of major attacks on our own installations. The Vietnamese know just as well as we do that the Viet Cong are gaining in the countryside. Meanwhile they see the enormous power of the United States withheld and they get little sense of firm and active US policy. They feel that we are unwilling to take serious risks. ... Bob and I believe that the worst course of action is to continue this essentially passive role, which can only lead to eventual defeat and an invitation to get out in humiliating circumstances ... the time has come for harder choices.

> Memorandum to President Johnson from McGeorge Bundy,
> 27 January 1965

We believe that the best available way of increasing our chance of success in Vietnam is the development and execution of a policy of sustained reprisals against North Vietnam – a policy in which air and naval action against the North is justified by and related to the whole Viet Cong campaign of violence and terror in the South. . . . This reprisal policy should begin at a low level. Its level of force and pressure should be increased only gradually. . . . The object would not be to 'win' an air war against Hanoi, but rather to influence the course of the struggle in the South. . . .

> Memorandum from McGeorge Bundy, in Saigon,
> 7 February 1965

While it may be politically desirable to speak publicly in terms of a 'graduated reprisal' program, I would hope that we are thinking and will act in terms of a 'graduated pressures' philosophy, which has more of a connotation of steady, relentless movement toward our objective of convincing Hanoi and Peiping of the prohibitive cost to them of their program of subversion, insurgency and aggression in South-east Asia. We must be certain we are dealing from a posture of strength before we sit down at the bargaining table. . . . We should continue our military pressures, making general objectives publicly known while awaiting some sign that the DRV is ready to negotiate towards achievement of those objectives. . . .

> CINCPAC message (from Admiral Sharp) to JCS,
> 17 February 1965

I

The debate in Washington entered a new phase on 27 January 1965. That morning President Johnson, accompanied by McGeorge Bundy, conferred yet again with NcNamara on the question of taking stronger action against North Vietnam. In a memorandum prepared for that meeting McGeorge Bundy insisted that the time had now come to make a firm choice between two clear alternatives: either to negotiate a way out of Vietnam, accepting whatever sacrifices that might entail; or to 'use our military power in the Far East and force a change of Communist policy'.[1] McNamara, as well as Bundy himself, favoured the second course; in any event the issue should be argued out and the President should reach a decision. In taking this fresh initiative – despite the fact that Rusk did not concur – McNamara and Bundy were almost certainly influenced by the growing body of intelligence data indicating a build-up of PAVN forces in southern Laos. Movement of North Vietnamese troops into the Plaine des Jarres area had been noted in October; by late December the CIA reported that substantial numbers of them were moving further south. On 26 January a consolidated memorandum from the US Intelligence Board reached McGeorge Bundy's desk, noting both the build-up in Laos and also a further strengthening of Chinese defences in areas bordering on Vietnam.[2]

By the time the White House meeting took place the following day (11.30 a.m. in Washington, but already after midnight in Vietnam) the President and his advisers must also have been aware of the latest turn of events in Saigon. Following two more weeks of Buddhist rioting, Nguyen Khanh again seized control of the government on 27 January and dissolved the Tran Van Huong cabinet. The Americans had every reason to fear that his next move might be to make his own accommodation with the Communists: an anxiety borne out by the subsequent revelation that on 28 January Khanh received a direct communication from a leading member of the NLFSVN (Huynh Tan Phat), offering him 'friendly co-operation' if he continued to oppose any further United States intervention in Vietnam.[3] Although the new crisis in Saigon was not the main subject of the White House meeting, it can only have reinforced the President's fear that sooner or later he would need to take more drastic steps if he was to avoid an American humiliation in Vietnam. He was aware that Rusk still opposed deeper involvement, and he still needed a consensus. He nevertheless agreed that McGeorge Bundy should go to Saigon early in February, for consultations with Ambassador Taylor leading to the formulation of precise recommendations for presidential action.

It is now evident that the range of possibilities being considered by Johnson and Bundy at the beginning of 1965 was rather wider than that suggested by the *Pentagon Papers* account of the November debate, and that two quite different strategies for escalation of the war were under discussion by then. 'Option C' and 'Option B' of the earlier debate were in fact variations on a single theme, which had found its most coherent expression in the thinking of Ambassador Taylor himself. Both in November and in January, his strategy was based on three main principles: the restoration of political stability in Saigon; the revival of pacification and counterinsurgency; and the use of air power to compel Hanoi to abandon its support for armed struggle in the South.[4] The alternative strategy, virtually ignored by the *Pentagon Papers* in their analysis of this period, emerges from an exchange of cables between the President and his ambassador at the end of December and the beginning of January – whose existence was not publicly revealed until 1979. In a cable of late December 1964, Johnson indicated his own reservations about the effectiveness of bombing the North as a means of winning the war in the South. He went on to suggest that what was really needed was a greater American effort on the ground inside the South: 'We have been building our strength to fight this kind of war ever since 1961, and I myself am ready to substantially increase the number of Americans in Vietnam if it is necessary to provide this kind of fighting force against the Viet Cong.'[5] Replying to that cable on 6 January 1965, Taylor reiterated his belief that any substantial increase in the number of United States ground troops for use in security and combat roles was 'not now desirable'. For the time being the President accepted that conclusion and fell back on the two-phase strategy recommended by the NSC 'principals' at the end of November. Ultimately, however, his own strategy rather than Taylor's would prevail.

II

As McGeorge Bundy was preparing to go to Saigon – he left on 2 February – it was reported from Moscow that the new Soviet premier A. N. Kosygin would shortly visit North Vietnam during an Asian tour which would also take in Peking and Pyongyang.[6] This would be the first high-level Soviet delegation to go to Hanoi for just over two years, the first visit ever by a Soviet premier. It would also be the highest level Soviet mission to China since Zhou Enlai walked out of the CPSU 22nd Congress in October 1961, although Y. V. Andropov (who accompanied Kosygin on this occasion) had been there in January 1963. Even apart from the current crisis in Vietnam, therefore the Kosygin tour represented an important new initiative in the Communist world. To speak of a Sino-Soviet *rapprochement* would be going too far; but Soviet policy appears to have returned to the mood of early 1962, when Moscow's aim had been to avert a permanent schism in the international Communist movement. As on that previous occasion, the VNWP occupied a pivotal position.

As always in Soviet–Vietnamese relations, an important dimension of the visit was economic. Talks on matters of detail (which had begun earlier) produced a comprehensive new aid agreement signed by the two premiers on 10 February. In his speeches, Kosygin emphasised the value of fraternal assistance in the task of building socialism: a theme which some Americans saw as a hint that North Vietnam's economy was vulnerable to the threat of bombing, but which was more probably a reminder that the Soviet contribution to Vietnamese economic development was potentially far greater than that of China.

In the broader ideological and political context, Kosygin and Andropov may have been seeking to reassure the three ruling Parties in Asia about the nature of the international preparatory meeting of Communist Parties which was now due to take place in Moscow at the beginning of March. It was unlikely that the Chinese, the Koreans, or even the Vietnamese, would agree to participate. But it was possible to reassure them that Moscow no longer intended to use the meeting as a first step towards 'expelling' the CCP from the international movement. The main object of the preparatory session, when it finally met, seems to have been merely to strengthen Soviet leadership over the ruling Parties of Eastern Europe. Interestingly, the one Asian Communist country which belonged to the Soviet 'inner circle', Mongolia, was not included in Kosygin's itinerary but received a separate visit from Shelepin in early February.[7]

Perhaps Kosygin's most important task, in his capacity as head of the Soviet government rather than as a Party leader, was to ensure that ideological differences between the CPSU and other Parties were not allowed to develop into antagonism on the level of relations between states. In an international crisis of the magnitude of that now developing in Vietnam, it might still be possible to achieve a measure of unity on that vital issue. By the time he reached Pyongyang, Kosygin was able to proclaim that the Soviet Union, China and North Korea were indeed united in opposition to United States actions in Vietnam. Two days later (14 February), *Renmin Ribao* commemorated the fifteenth anniversary of China's treaty with Moscow with an editorial emphasising the value of Sino-Soviet unity.[8] It remained to be seen whether unity in principle would extend to agreement on the correct tactics for handling the actual crisis in Indochina.

It is not easy to assess the Soviet premier's attitude towards a possible escalation of the war in the months ahead. Later in the year (in an article of 11 November 1965) Peking accused Kosygin of having tried to persuade both China and North Vietnam of the need for a negotiated solution in Indochina.[9] If so, it is curious that Peking made no comment on that possibility at the time: perhaps, in February, even Zhou Enlai was willing to consider helping the Americans 'find a way out'. Certainly there were signs of Soviet diplomatic activity at that time. A TASS statement of 6 February renewed the call for another international conference on Laos; and on 17 February the British ambassador in Washington told Rusk that the Russians might be interested in reviving the Soviet–British role as Co-chairmen of the Geneva Conference.[10] It is less than certain that these moves were based on a real consensus in favour of serious negotiations; and highly unlikely that Hanoi had been persuaded of their value at this stage in the conflict. One cannot dismiss the possibility that the principal motive behind Soviet diplomatic activity at this point was to gain extra time for Hanoi; and in the process to confirm the Western image of Moscow as a 'moderating' influence in Indochina. Even though the Russians may have been willing to support the North Vietnamese war effort to a greater extent than formerly, they were still anxious to avoid a direct confrontation with the United States.

Whatever its initial purpose, Kosygin's stay in Hanoi from 6 to 10 February 1965 coincided with a sharp escalation of the military conflict. Starting in the early hours of 7 February and continuing until after Kosygin's departure, the PLAFSVN launched a major offensive in the area which had once been 'Interzone V' (southern Central Vietnam) and on the B-3 front (the Central Highlands). In four days, attacks at over twenty places produced substantial numbers of casualties – including, for the first time, a large number of Americans.[11] The most spectacular incidents, at Pleiku on 7 February and at Qui-Nhon on the 10th, made a major impact both in Saigon and in Washington. The Americans responded by making two series of bombing raids against targets north of the 17th parallel (Flaming Dart I and II) on 7–8 and 11 February. Shortly afterwards the Americans finally took a decision to embark on more sustained bombing of North Vietnam. For their part the North Vietnamese responded defiantly, with encouragement from both Moscow and Peking.

The motives behind the Communist offensive of 7–10 February must again be a matter for speculation. But in this instance – by contrast with the Gulf of Tonkin incident six months before – there is no room for doubt that the initiative was taken by the Communist side: it was they who provoked the Americans, not the other way round. One hypothesis which deserves to be taken seriously is that the offensive was a move by Southern Communist forces – perhaps with the encouragement of *some* leaders in the North – to thwart a suspected attempt by Kosygin to impose some new diplomatic settlement on Hanoi. If so it was a success, in that the American response left the Russians with no choice but to increase military support for North Vietnam. However, the presence of Marshal K. A. Vershinin in the Kosygin delegation suggests that the installation of defensive missiles in North Vietnam was already on the agenda even before the heightening of tension that occurred after Kosygin's arrival in Hanoi. Soviet determination to improve Hanoi's defence capabilities was confirmed by an official Moscow statement on 8 February.[12]

The impression that Moscow had in fact already made up its mind to give more assistance even before the offensive began suggests an alternative hypothesis which cannot be dismissed out of hand. The Russians themselves may have secretly wanted to provoke the Americans into attacking the North for either (or both) of two reasons. On the one hand, it would make it easier for them to represent an expansion of their own military presence in North Vietnam – for example, the manning of missile sites – as merely a response to aggression by the United States. On the other hand, they may have regarded the American attacks as a useful

TABLE 20.1 *The beginning of escalation, February 1965*

Hanoi, Peking, Moscow	South Vietnam, Washington
	3–8 Feb.: McGeorge Bundy's trip to South Vietnam; talks with Ambassador Taylor.
5 Feb.: Kosygin delegation in Peking, on way to Hanoi.	
6 Feb.: Kosygin arrived in Hanoi. TASS called for new international conference on Laos.	
7 Feb.: Hanoi Rally: Kosygin speech demanding US withdrawal from South Vietnam.	7 Feb.: Start of PLAFSVN offensive, including attack on US billet at Pleiku. McGeorge Bundy's memorandum from Saigon, urging 'sustained reprisal' policy.
8 Feb.: Soviet statement on strengthening defences of North Vietnam.	8 Feb.: 'Flaming Dart I': air strikes in Vinh-Linh and Quang-Binh provinces. McNamara requested JCS plan for 8-week bombing programme, between 17th and 19th parallels.
	9–10 Feb.: PLAFSVN attacks continued, in Binh-Gia area and provinces of Bien-Hoa and Binh-Dinh (including attack on US billet at Qui-Nhon).
10 Feb.: Kosygin and Pham Van Dong signed new Soviet–Vietnamese economic agreement. Kosygin left the same day. Peking: Mao and Liu attended rally in support of North Vietnam.	
11 Feb.: Peking: Kosygin met Mao and Liu. Later he left for North Korea.	11 Feb.: 'Flaming Dart II': more air strikes north of 17th parallel. Taylor urged more vigorous air action against North Vietnam.
	11–13 Feb.: Deployment of B-52s to Guam and Okinawa; they were not used at this stage of the war.
12 Feb.: Pyongyang: Kosygin speech emphasising unity of USSR and China in support for North Vietnam.	12 Feb.: State Department began work on final text of White Paper on Vietnam; it was published on 27 February.
13 Feb.: Chinese statement on Vietnam, repeating the threat of 'another Korea'.	13 Feb.: Johnson authorised a new pacification effort in South Vietnam; also a programme of 'measured and limited air action' against the North. (A plan to take the issue to the United Nations Security Council was abandoned.)
13 Feb.: DRVN asked International Commission to withdraw its teams from North Vietnam; they withdrew by 22 February.	

means to remind Peking of its ultimate dependence on Moscow in any major global confrontation.

In this latter respect the situation may yet again have been comparable with the Taiwan Straits crisis of 1958, when the Chinese had had to admit they could not afford to take on the armed might of the United States unless they strengthened their military ties with the Soviet Union: a course which Mao Zedong refused to take.[13] In 1965, as in 1958, there may have been some Chinese generals who would have welcomed an excuse for greater military preparedness, and would have gladly accepted a closer military relationship with Moscow if it led to modernisation of the PLA; Mao himself was probably again anxious to avoid such an alignment. For the time being he could only hope that his own tactics would be sufficient to deter the United States from expanding the war.

It was somewhat ironical that the Vietnamese, 15 years later, blamed Mao rather than Kosygin for being too ready to compromise with the United States. They interpreted Mao's interview with Edgar Snow on 9 January as a signal to Washington that China had no intention of becoming involved in a war on the ground in Indochina, and would only fight the Americans if China itself was attacked.[14] In the long run that was certainly Mao's position; but he also said a number of things calculated to deter the Johnson Administration from a course of action which might lead to a long and bitter land war across the whole of mainland South-East Asia. Deterrence was probably also the underlying purpose of a strongly worded Chinese government statement on 13 February, which threatened the United States with another Korea if it persisted in its present policy in Vietnam. A few days later, on 17 February, Liu Shaoqi went so far as to say that aggression against the DRVN was the same as aggression against China; but again the primary objective was probably to deter Washington rather than to enter into a new and more precise commitment to Hanoi.

The Americans themselves paid careful attention to the Snow interview. Their response would appear to have been made (in private) at the 126th ambassadorial meeting in Warsaw on 24 February, when they tried to reassure Peking that any action they might take against North Vietnam was designed to affect the situation in the South and not to destroy the Democratic Republic as a Communist state. By then President Johnson had made up his mind to embark on stronger actions against Hanoi; but his fear of

confrontation with China was an ever-present restraint throughout the next three years.

III

.

The initial American response to the Pleiku and Qui-Nhon attacks
was in many respects comparable with their response to the Gulf of
Tonkin incidents six months before. 'Flaming Dart I', on 7–8
February 1965, included air strikes in the Vinh-Linh area, just
north of the 17th parallel, and at Dong-Hoi in Quang-Binh
province. 'Flaming Dart II', on 11 February, consisted of a series of
additional strikes just north of the Demilitarised Zone. The
question which Johnson had to face next was whether he should
stop at that – as he had in August 1964 – or go on to implement
'Option C' in the form of a 'graduated' series of air strikes, not
linked to any specific incident in the South. Already on 7 February,
before he left Saigon for home, McGeorge Bundy was recommending action of that kind – under the label of 'sustained reprisals'. On
11 February, Taylor reiterated his belief that the bombing should
be sufficiently heavy to force Hanoi to change its whole policy, not
merely a response to the current level of guerrilla activity in the
South.[15] In the expectation that a policy of this kind would now be
adopted, the JCS authorised the deployment of B-52 bombers to
Okinawa and Guam for possible use against North Vietnam. The
deployment took place (11–13 February), although in the event
B-52s were not used for that purpose until very much later in the
war: the President was still too cautious for action on that scale.
Nevertheless on 13 February he approved an eight-week bombing
programme, prepared by the JCS in which all the targets lay south
of the 19th parallel.[16] It took another two weeks before even that
decision was implemented. The second half of February was taken
up by a number of initiatives in the diplomatic and political
sphere, some of which may have slowed the momentum towards a
larger war whilst others served to increase American determination to pursue the Vietnam commitment to its logical conclusion.
    The struggle for South-East Asia was now entering its most
critical phase. Although the Washington debate had come to focus
increasingly on Vietnam in the global context of 'containment',
the regional perspective remained important; and the situation in

Indonesia was now moving rapidly to the disadvantage of the United States. Sukarno's withdrawal from the United Nations had probably worried the Russians more than the Americans; the reverse was true of his economic moves in the second half of February. On the 15th, a day of anti-American demonstrations in Jakarta, the PKI-led workers on eight American rubber plantations in Sumatra took control by direct action. Ten days later the government submitted to Communist pressure to the extent of taking into its own hands the management (as opposed to formal ownership) of all American-owned estates. It was feared that the oil companies would be next. By 5 March, the United States had closed down both its military and economic aid missions and also the USIS libraries in Indonesia.[17]

It was no longer possible for the Americans to use even a limited aid programme to influence Sukarno's policies at this critical juncture. The logic of the 'domino theory' required some more dramatic demonstration of the continuing American commitment to South-East Asia; and that logic now prevailed. Whether the decision to bomb North Vietnam made an actual impact on events within Indonesia at this stage is impossible to say; perhaps not. The survival of any American presence at all in Indonesia would depend ultimately on the outcome of the conflict now taking shape between the PKI and the Indonesian armed forces: a conflict which could only be resolved inside Indonesia. But concern about what was happening there may have been among the factors which finally tipped the balance in favour of action in Vietnam at the end of February. One aim of 'Option C', after all, was to demonstrate American determination to the rest of South-East Asia, without producing consequences wholly unacceptable to Peking.

In Saigon the political crisis continued into February, with Nguyen Khanh still unable to dominate the situation completely despite his recent coup. Possibly the 'Flaming Dart' raids on the North made some contribution towards the recovery of political coherence in the South. After seemingly endless consultations between the various parties and groups, a new civilian government finally emerged on 16 February. The 'northern' Dai-Viet politician Phan Huy Quat became premier, with Nguyen Van Thieu as minister of the armed forces. At that point Colonel Pham Ngoc Thao made one last attempt to prolong the instability by staging another abortive coup on 19 February. He was quickly outmanoeuvred by the Armed Forces Council, which appointed

General Nguyen Chanh Thi to restore order in Saigon as the coup collapsed. At the same time the council insisted on the resignation of Nguyen Khanh as commander of the armed forces. On 25 February 1965, just 13 months after his first successful coup, Khanh was finally obliged to leave the country as 'ambassador at large'.[18] The Americans were at last satisfied that South Vietnam had a government which, although it lacked the administrative effectiveness of the Diem regime, seemed capable of restoring a semblance of political order – as well as being willing to support whatever action they might decide to take against the North.

Another significant development at this point was the withdrawal of the International Commission's remaining control teams from North Vietnam. Their removal was requested by Hanoi on 13 February, in the aftermath of the 'Flaming Dart' raids, on the grounds that the physical security of their personnel could no longer be guaranteed. The Commission protested; but when the request was reiterated a week later they had no choice but to give way: the last teams left the North on 22 February. The complete ineffectiveness of the International Commission by this time was reflected in its last two *Special Reports* to the Co-chairmen, on 13 and 27 February respectively.[19] The former, signed by the Indian and Polish members and accompanied by a dissenting Canadian statement, criticised the United States for the bombing raids of 8 and 11 February. That of 27 February, by contrast, dealt with the Commission's withdrawal from North Vietnam – but the Polish delegate refused to sign. Thus ended the 'experiment' which, in May 1955, General Ely had hoped would 'constitute a remarkable precedent on the international plane'.

Although the International Commission continued to maintain an office in Saigon, the Geneva framework which had given meaning to its original task no longer had any relevance to the conflict now taking shape. In his cable of 11 February, Taylor still tried to define the American objective as restoration of 'strict observance' of the Geneva Ceasefire Agreement of 1954. But the United States had by this time violated the conditions of the ceasefire even more obviously than the Communist side. It had also, in the eyes of many nations in the world, lost the propaganda battle over Hanoi's claim that it was the Americans and Diem who had sabotaged the political implementation of the Geneva final declaration. It was hardly possible, therefore, to justify action against Hanoi solely within the Geneva framework.

The State Department attempted to resolve this dilemma by preparing a 'White Paper' under the title *Aggression from the North*, which was finally published on 27 February 1965. It sought to demonstrate, by setting forth concrete evidence of infiltration of men and weapons into the South, the extent to which the DRVN controlled the struggle ostensibly waged by the NLFSVN.[20] Inevitably it was a controversial document, with critics protesting that the evidence for Hanoi's involvement was too insubstantial to legitimise the bombing. Many years later, it was even alleged that the most dramatic evidence offered – the capture on 16 February 1965 of a North Vietnamese ship full of Chinese-made weapons, at Vung-Ro in Phu-Yen province – had actually been faked by the CIA.[21] In retrospect the White Paper appears as a remarkably thin presentation given what is now known from Hanoi's own publications about the nature of Vietnamese Communist decision-making, and in view of Peking's statements about the supply of Chinese weapons. The historian is left wondering whether the reason for its inadequacy was an actual deficiency of intelligence on the American side, or a deliberate decision to avoid publishing information that might prejudice Western methods of intelligence-gathering. As the war progressed, this failure to demonstrate Hanoi's responsibility beyond all challenge or doubt was to have a disastrous effect on public attitudes towards United States policy both at home and abroad.

'Rolling Thunder' – the code-name given to the planned series of air strikes – had initially been scheduled to begin on 20 February but was then delayed, probably for diplomatic reasons. On 17 February the British ambassador in Washington reported his government's impression that Moscow might, after all, be willing to resume its role as Geneva Co-chairman in the hope of averting a military escalation. Rusk agreed to explore the idea further and a formal British approach to the Soviet Union was made on 20 February.[22] It elicited no immediate response. Instead, on the 23rd, the Russians made another proposal to General De Gaulle – whose initiatives were known to be regularly rebuffed by Washington. Nor did the meeting of United States and Chinese ambassadors in Warsaw on 24 February (mentioned above) produce any significant diplomatic opening, although it provided an opportunity for the Americans to explain that the operations they planned against North Vietnam were not intended to destroy the DRVN as a political entity. Later the same day President Johnson confirmed his decision on 'Rolling Thunder'; but bad weather caused further delay. On 25 February the President also approved the first deployment of combat units to South Vietnam: two Marine battalions which – despite opposition from Ambassador Taylor – had been formally requested by General Westmoreland on 21 February.[23] Already by then South Korean forces had begun to arrive, to reinforce ARVN's capabilities in southern Central Vietnam.

At this point Undersecretary of State George Ball made one last attempt to dissuade the President from allowing the war to escalate. On 24 February he forwarded to the White House the memorandum he had written for Rusk, McNamara and McGeorge Bundy in early October 1964; two days later (the 26th) it was the subject of a full dress debate at the highest level – and Johnson appeared to be taking Ball's arguments very seriously.[24] He did not change his decision on 'Rolling Thunder'; but the discussion that day may have strengthened his determination to pursue his own strategy in Vietnam, rather than give way to those who still argued for a rapid escalation of the bombing campaign once it began.

Any illusion that North Vietnam really intended to respond to a new Soviet diplomatic initiative, given sufficient time, was dispelled by the treatment given to J. Blair Seaborn when he again visited Hanoi from 1 to 4 March 1965. This time he was refused an audience with Pham Van Dong or any other top leader, and was obliged to deliver the latest American message to a lower-level official who had no authority to make any reply. Hanoi's own attitude left no room for effective diplomacy on the part of its allies. Perhaps in anticipation of more severe bombing than the Americans actually intended, an order for the partial evacuation of Hanoi and other cities was signed on 28 February and published four days later.[25]

President Johnson's decisions of February 1965 did not amount to a full presidential endorsement of the strategy advocated earlier by the JCS. 'Sustained reprisal' fell short of the 'systematic military pressures' recommended in November 1964. A comparison between McGeorge Bundy's memorandum of 7 February and the advice given by Admiral Sharp in a message from CINCPAC to

TABLE 20.2   *Final steps towards 'rolling thunder', February–March 1965*

Hanoi – Peking – Moscow	United States and Vietnam	United States and Indonesia
		15 Feb.: Anti-American demonstrations in Jakarta. Workers took over eight US-owned rubber estates in Sumatra.
16 Feb.: Soviet proposal for conference on Indochina; rejected by Hanoi.	16 Feb.: Phan Huy Quat formed government in Saigon.	
17 Feb.: Britain indicated to US signs of possible Soviet interest in a new peace effort in Indochina. Liu Shaoqi again said that 'aggression against North Vietnam is aggression against China'.	17 Feb.: CINCPAC message to JCS urging vigorous programme of 'graduated pressure' against North Vietnam.	
	18 Feb.: Decision to commence 'Rolling Thunder' air strikes on 20th; then postponed. First US-commanded bombing missions over South Vietnam (acknowledged, 24 Feb.).	18 Feb.: USIS library taken over by demonstrating youths in Jakarta.
19 Feb.: *Renmin Ribao* article rejected any negotiations on Vietnam before complete US withdrawal.	19–20 Feb.: Abortive coup in Saigon, led by Pham Ngoc Thao and Lam Van Phat; order restored by Nguyen Chanh Thi.	
20 Feb.: British approach to Moscow, to reactivate Geneva Co-chairmanship; no response.	20–1 Feb.: South Vietnamese Armed Forces Council met; decision to remove Nguyen Khanh as commander of armed forces.	

22 Feb.: International Commission withdrew its last teams from North Vietnam, after DRVN repeated its request on 20 February.

24 Feb.: 126th Sino–American meeting of ambassadors in Warsaw.

25 Feb.: Original date for meeting of Indochinese People's Conference, Phnom Penh; postponed until 1 March.

27 Feb.: International Commission made a *Special Report* on its withdrawal from the North; Polish member dissented.

28 Feb.: DRVN order for evacuation of Hanoi and other cities; published, 4 March.

1–9 March: Indochinese People's Conference convened by Sihanouk in Phnom Penh.

22 Feb.: Taylor opposed deployment of more than one battalion of US Marines to Vietnam; Westmoreland wanted two. (Two battalions approved, 25 February; they landed at Danang on 8 March.)

25 Feb.: 600 South Korean troops arrived in South Vietnam. Nguyen Khanh left Saigon.

26 Feb.: White House discussion of the Ball Memorandum.

27 Feb.: State Department 'White Paper' published: *Aggression from the North.*

2 March: First actual air strikes of 'Rolling Thunder' programme.

24 Feb.: Chinese atomic energy delegation arrived in Indonesia. Subandrio took control over Indonesian foreign trade.

26 Feb.: Government decision to take over management of all American-owned rubber estates in Sumatra.

1–3 March: Sukarno visited Cambodia. Early March: US decision to close offices of USIS, AID and MILTAG in Jakarta.

the Pentagon ten days later suggests sharply contrasting perceptions of the significance and value of air strikes. Bundy emphasised
both the gradualness of any series of attacks on the North and also
the need to relate it closely to the course of struggle in the South:
'the object would *not* be to "win" an air war against Hanoi. . . .'
Sharp, on the contrary, urged a programme of 'steady relentless'
pressure, to be continued until Hanoi showed itself ready to
negotiate on American terms.²⁶ Taylor also believed that the main
emphasis should be on forcing Hanoi to change its policy rather
than merely retaliating according to the current level of guerrilla
activity in the South. Underlying this difference of attitude was the
more fundamental one, already noted, between Taylor's view of
the conflict and that which Johnson himself was now coming to
accept.

Yet the President does not appear to have encouraged a
genuine, hardhitting debate within the Administration in order to
arrive at a clear decision between the two conflicting strategies. As
a master of the art of political compromise – which he had
practised with inordinate skill during two decades in the Senate –
he was more adept at commanding the illusion of consensus behind
each decision, day by day, than assessing the actual and potential
consequences of his own moves in the international power-game.
By choosing to expand American military involvement step by
step, without any declaration of war or the drama of a global crisis,
Johnson succeeded in avoiding a clear definition of his own 'war
aims'. The result was that in late February 1965 he authorised a
bombing programme which was too big for the Communist powers
to ignore, yet too small to achieve a major impact on Hanoi.

The first actual bombing raids in the 'Rolling Thunder' series
took place on 2 March 1965, when the Quang-Khe naval base and
an ammunition depot at Xom-Bang were struck by United States
and South Vietnamese planes. They were not immediately
followed up: a truly sustained programme of air strikes did not get
under way until the middle of the month. Meanwhile on 8 March
the two battalions of marines landed at Danang. By then, too, the
chief-of-staff of the US Army (General Harold Johnson) had
arrived in Saigon to discuss the possible deployment of one or more
infantry divisions to South Vietnam, although no immediate
decision was taken on that proposal. Ambassador Taylor remained
firmly opposed to a 'white man's war'; and even Westmoreland
was not yet convinced of the need for it. Nevertheless at the

beginning of March 1965 the United States became committed to a larger war in Vietnam. Its precise form and intensity were unpredictable; nor is it certain that Johnson had yet decided on all the military actions he was to take before the end of the year. But direct American participation in a 'limited war' against North Vietnam was now an established fact.

Notes

1. For details of these various sources, see the Bibliography, Part I below. The most important of the 'captured documents', the secret resolution of the VNWP Central Committee's 9th Plenum in December 1963, will be discussed at length in Chapter 13.
2. The most useful studies of the Sino-Soviet dispute in this period are those of Griffith (1964 and 1967). For Soviet politics in the later Khrushchev and early Brezhnev–Kosygin periods, see especially Linden (1966), Tatu (1969) and Slusser (1967 and 1973). Chinese politics during the years from 1962 to 1965 have received considerably less detailed attention than those of the 'great leap forward' and the 'cultural revolution' periods, immediately before and after. Among works that are especially useful, see Gittings (1967), Baum (1975), and Schram (1974).
3. As quoted in *Renmin Ribao*, 24 March 1966: *SWB/FE/2121/A1/1–2*.
4. See, for example, the works by Warner (1964), Halberstam (1965), Browne (1965), Shaplen (1966), Lacouture (1966); full details will be found in the Bibliography.
5. Notably Pike (1966), Thompson (1966), Duncanson (1968); also Mecklin (1965). For similar works on Laos, see Toye (1968) and Dommen (1971).
6. Hilsman (1967). Among general accounts of the Kennedy period, see Schlesinger (1965), which can now be filled out by referring to the same author's biography of Robert Kennedy: Schlesinger (1978). Note also Rostow (1972).
7. See especially Abel (1969), which was based partly on interviews with Robert Kennedy; the latter subsequently published his own memoir of this one crisis. Schlesinger (1978) is also especially useful in this connection.
8. Mention should be made, however, of the series of 'oral history' accounts collected by the Kennedy Library and the Johnson Library – some of which are already open to researchers, whilst others no doubt contain valuable information which will one day become available.
9. See Goulden (1969), Galloway (1970), Austin (1971), and Windchy (1971). The incidents will be discussed in some detail in Chapter 16 below.
10. For details see the Bibliography, Part I, below.
11. Gelb and Betts (1979); an essentially similar perspective is provided by the more readable study of Halberstam (1972).
12. For details of the presidential libraries see the Bibliography, Part I, below. A new period of serious research on this material may be said to have begun in

the early 1980s; one of its most valuable products thus far being Berman (1982).

13. See, among works listed in the Bibliography: Tolson (1973), Kelly (1973), Eckhardt (1974), and Collins (1975), all in the 'Vietnam Studies' series of the Department of the Army; also Whitlow (1977), Momyer (1978), and Buckingham (1982).

14. See Westmoreland (1976), Taylor (1972), Sharp (1978); also, among works by less senior officers, Palmer (1978); and for an analysis of counterinsurgency by one who participated in its early years, Blaufarb (1977).

15. For a study of this important aspect of United States intelligence-gathering, see J. Bamford, *The Puzzle Palace: America's National Security Agency and its Special Relationship with Britain's GCHQ* (London, 1982). But it has only a little to say about Vietnam, and hardly anything on the period before 1965.

16. See Herring (1983): Bibliography, Part I.

17. See Jones (1971); and for declassified cables, *DDRC* and *DDQC* provide a valuable guide. On Indonesia–Malaysia relations, see Mackie (1974), James and Sheil-Small (1971), Mayall (1977), and for a Japanese perspective, Nishihara (1976).

18. See especially the British publication, *Documents Relating to British Involvement in the Indochina Conflict 1945–1965*, Cmnd 2834 (London: HMSO, 1965).

19. The one attempt to study those exchanges in detail, using publicly available sources, is that of Young (1968); see also MacFarquhar (1971).

20. Two exceptions are worthy of special mention: Tran Van Don (1978), and Norodom Sihanouk and Burchett (1973); but neither is as informative as historians could have wished. Amongst Vietnamese-language materials, use has been made of some of the literature published by Buddhist organisations in South Vietnam, in dealing with the Buddhist Crisis of 1963 in Chapter 9. There is room for more research on South Vietnamese politics in the period after 1963.

21. See Gelb and Betts (1979).

22. The first memorandum in the series, not declassified until 1975, was that of 1 March 1964: it is reprinted in Porter (1979) vol. II, pp. 240–6; the others, dated 23 May (extract only), 11 August, and 24 November 1964, will be found in *PP* (Gravel), vol. III, pp. 167–8, 524–9; 610–28 and 656–66.

23. See, for example, Hilsman (1967) ch. xxxiv.

NOTES TO CHAPTER 2: DECEMBER 1961: COUNTERINSURGENCY

1. Schlesinger (1978) ch. xxi, section iii. On internal Cuban politics at this period, see Suarez (1967).

2. There is so far no detailed documentation for this meeting, nor for similar ones which followed during the early months of 1962; it is mentioned briefly in *PP*(Gravel), vol. I, p. 143. For the text of Kennedy's letter of 14 December 1961, see ibid., pp. 805–6.

3. Precise numbers of US troops assigned to duties in South Vietnam were kept secret at this period; but a detailed summary in a JCS paper of 9 January 1962 gives the number as 2646 at that time; the projected total for 30 June 1962 was already 5576: *PP* (Gravel), vol. II, p. 657. For NSAM-111 and the Taylor

Mission papers, in so far as they have been released, see ibid., pp. 73–120; and Rostow (1972) pp. 269–79.

4. US, Department of State, *A Threat to the Peace: North Vietnam's Effort to Conquer South Vietnam* (Washington, D.C., 1961). Much of the evidence consists of facsimiles and translations of documents showing that some at least of the guerrillas fighting in the South in 1961 (albeit natives of the southern zone) had been among the forces regrouped to the northern zone in 1954 and had recently reinfiltrated across the 17th parallel or through southern Laos. Such reinfiltration was in clear breach of the Geneva Ceasefire Agreement.

5. International Commission for Supervision and Control in Vietnam, *Special Report to the Co-chairmen of the Geneva Conference on Indochina* (London: HMSO, June 1962) p. 5.

6. These operations were authorised by NSAM no. 28, of 9 March 1961, reprinted in Porter (1979) vol. II, p. 94; there are also passing references to covert operations inside North Vietnam in *PP* (Gravel), vol. II, pp. 641, 653. But no full account has been made public and it is impossible to assess their overall scale or impact.

7. For the diplomacy of the Geneva Conference and meetings of the three princes (Souvanna Phouma, Souphanouvong and Boun Oum), see *Documents*, Cmnd 2834 (1965) pp. 176–8; *SWB/FE/831/C*; and Toye (1968) p. 175.

8. See Young (1968) pp. 249–50. He mentions no actual meetings at this period; but we know that as many as 14 ambassadorial meetings must have taken place in Warsaw between the 103rd on 7 March 1962 and the 118th on 7 August 1963. It is thus impossible, without access to more evidence, to relate Vietnam decision-making to Sino-American relations in late 1961.

NOTES TO CHAPTER 3: HANOI AND ITS ALLIES

1. The various stages of Ho's journey to Peking, Moscow and then back to Peking, between 12 October and 19 November 1961, were reported by VNA and NCNA: see *SWB/FE/768–801*; for his visit to the Baltic states, *SWB/FE/780/C2/2* and *SWB/FE/781/C/3*. Le Duan returned directly to Hanoi, passing briefly through Peking, in early November.

2. For a summary and interpretation of Pham Van Dong's tour, see P. J. Honey's account in *China Quarterly*, no. 8 (London, 1961).

3. 'Brief Introduction to the History of the Thai Communist Party', dated December 1977 and translated in Turton *et al.* (1978) p. 164; and a broadcast by the Voice of the Malayan Revolution, 5 July 1977, monitored in *SWB/FE/5560/B/6*. For Pham Van Dong's presence in Kunming, see *SWB/FE/720* and 722.

4. 'Resolution of an enlarged conference of COSVN, Month 10/1961', translated in Porter (1979) vol. II, pp. 119–23. For the increased guerrilla activity in October, see Warner (1964) p. 166.

5. For the composition and activities of the Ye Jianying mission, see *Peking Review*, 22 December 1961, and NCNA reports monitored in *SWB/FE/822*, 827 and 832. On Ye's early contacts with Ho Chi Minh, and the general background of Sino-Vietnamese relations, see K. C. Chen, *Vietnam and China 1938–1954* (Princeton, 1969). For background on relations of Chinese generals, see Whitson (1973).

6. The Politburo members who attended the VNWP reception on 30 December 1961 were Ho Chi Minh, Truong Chinh, Pham Hung, Vo Nguyen Giap and Hoang Van Hoan; see *SWB/FE/832/A3/2* and 833/A3/1.

7. The brief analysis of the Soviet crisis in this and the following paragraphs is based on a reading of Soviet broadcasts monitored in *SWB/SU/818–930*; see also the relevant chapters in Tatu (1969) and Linden (1966).

8. An attack on McNamara's speech appeared in *Krasnaya Zvezda* on 21 February 1962; the importance of developing Soviet military strength was also a theme in articles for Soviet Army Day, 23 February: *SWB/SU/877* and 879.

9. For Mao's speech, see Schram (1974) Text 8; on Liu Shaoqi's endorsement of Chen Yun's ideas in February, for which he was later condemned during the Cultural Revolution, see his 'self-criticism' of 23 October 1966, translated in *Collected Works of Liu Shao-ch'i 1958–1967* (Union Research Institute: Hong Kong, 1968) pp. 357ff.

10. *Peking Review*, 6 September 1963; Griffith (1964) pp. 36ff.

11. *SWB/FE/859/A2/1*; and for 20 January 1962, *SWB/FE/851*.

12. The 7th Plenum Resolution was reported by VNA on 19 June 1962: *SWB/FE/976/C1/1–7*; the fact that the plenum was held in April 1962 was revealed in *Nhan-Dan*, January 1970: see *VN Docs*, n. 76, Saigon, March 1970. See also *The Road to Happiness and Prosperity* (Hanoi, 1963).

13. *SWB/FE/878*, 880, 881, 884, 887. It was noticeable that Le Duc Tho was especially prominent in receiving the Soviet delegation, whilst Le Duan failed to appear throughout. For developments of 10 March 1962, see *SWB/FE/893–894*.

14. On Soviet relations with Cuba and the purge of Escalante, see Suarez (1967) ch. vi; also *SWB/SU/919*. The status of North Vietnam as a country 'building socialism' had been recognised by the CPSU as early as 1958 or 1959; certainly well before the VNWP Third Congress in September 1960.

15. *Peking Review*, 20 April and 4 May 1962; see also Maxwell (1972).

16. Dake (1973) pp. 153–5 and *SWB/FE/919*; for Soviet–Indonesian relations in February, see *SWB/SU/867*, 874 and 879, and also Dake (1973) pp. 139ff.

17. *Cuoc Khang-chien* (1980) p. 49. It should be noted that VNWP Politburo meetings and resolutions, as opposed to those of the Central Committee, were rarely reported publicly in the Hanoi media.

18. *SWB/FE/921* and 923; see also *Cuoc Khang-chien* (1980) pp. 50–1.

19. *Cuoc Khang-chien* (1980) p. 52. For the April COSVN document, usually known as the 'Chinh-Nam document', see Duiker (1981) p. 207; he cites it as Doc. no. 855 in the Pike Collection.

20. *Peking Review*, 19 January 1962, p. 22; for other Chinese material on Laos (including a strongly worded editorial in *Renmin Ribao* on 3 January) see ibid. 12 January and 2 February 1962. The contrast between North Vietnamese and Chinese views on the Indochinese revolutions is discussed more fully in Volume I.

NOTES TO CHAPTER 4: THE KENNEDY STRATEGY TAKES SHAPE

1. No detailed documentation is yet available on these meetings. The first two conferences in Honolulu are mentioned in passing by the *Pentagon Papers* (*PP* (Gravel), vol. II, pp. 143–4 and 451); no reference is made at all to the third, fourth or fifth such meetings, but that which opened on 23 July 1962 (ibid., p. 165) was the sixth. Nor do the *Pentagon Papers* make any mention of the Baguio meeting, whose importance was first publicised by the Chinese: see *Peking Review*, 23 March 1962, pp. 9–10, which incidentally also provided evidence of the care with which Peking was studying United States policy-making and objectives at that time. See also article by General T. R. Milton in *Air Force Magazine*, May 1978, p. 33.

2. For a discussion of the creation of MACV and the status of MAAG, see Eckhardt (1974) pp. 25–31, and Momyer (1978) pp. 67–9. The latter indicates that the Army and Air Force (within the JCS) favoured a unified theatre of command in Indochina; but the Navy supported CINCPAC in his opposition to the idea.

3. The text of NSAM-124 is printed in *PP* (Gravel), vol. II, pp. 660–1. The Special Group (CI) in fact grew out of an earlier Special Group (Augmented) responsible for clandestine operations against Cuba from late November 1961: see Schlesinger (1978) p. 513.

4. The evolution of the doctrine is examined in detail by Blaufarb (1977): see pp. 57ff.

5. Blaufarb (1977) p. 74; *PP* (Gravel), vol. II, p. 689. The text of the report was declassified in January 1980 and may be consulted at the US National Archives in Washington; some of its principal themes appeared in an article by U. Alexis Johnson in *Foreign Service Journal*, July 1962: cf. Blaufarb (1977) pp. 62ff. The 14 NSAMs on the subject can be identified from a list in the J. F. Kennedy Library, Boston.

6. For the expansion of the US advisory role, see *PP* (Gravel), vol. II, pp. 449–57, and Collins (1975). For the role of helicopter units at this stage of the war, see Tolson (1973) and Whitlow (1977).

7. *PP* (Gravel), vol. II, pp. 684–9; cf. also ibid., pp. 673–81 and 134–50.

8. For an official account of 'Operation Ranch Hand', the name given to the herbicide programme, see Buckingham (1982): for 1961–2, pp. 9–86. NSAM-115, apparently declassified in 1971, is available (photocopy) in the US National Archives, Washington.

9. See Kelly (1973) ch. ii; also Hickey (1982). Responsibility for the Civilian Irregular Defense Group Program, as it was called officially, was transferred from the US Mission to MACV during the first half of 1963.

10. Dommen (1971) p. 216; cf. also Schlesinger (1965) ch. xix, section 3. For the Rusk–Thanat statement, see *Department of State Bulletin*, 26 March 1962; and for documents relating to the Thanat visit, *DDQC 1976*, pp. 204–5.

11. NSAM-149 was declassified on 5 November 1979; a copy can be consulted in the US National Archives, Washington. For Nam Tha see Hilsman (1967); Toye (1968) pp. 180–2; *Cuoc Khang-chien* (1980) pp. 53–4; and for current broadcasts reporting the first phase of the final battle, *SWB/FE/*925, 927, 928.

12. NSAM-157, dated 29 May 1962, is reprinted in *PP* (Gravel), vol. II,

pp. 672–3; for the President's announcement of 15 May, on sending troops to Thailand, see ibid., p. 811.

13. The crisis is covered in some detail by Hilsman (1967) pp. 310–19, and is noted by Young (1968) p. 250; cf. also *Peking Review*, 29 June 1962.

14. For texts of these documents, see *Documents*, Cmnd 2834 (1965) pp. 178–86.

15. See US Air Force Memorandum of 17 February 1962: *DDQC 1976*, p. 35, item D (document in J. F. Kennedy Library, declassified in 1976).

16. For an account of Robert Kennedy's tour, see Schlesinger (1978) ch. xxiv. On the developing relationship between Japan and South-East Asia in the late 1950s and early 1960s, see Yanaga (1968) and Nishihara (1976).

17. Telegram from State Department to Jakarta, 12 February 1962, in *DDRC*, p. 558, item F; declassified, 1974.

18. For a detailed account of these negotiations and the American role, see Jones (1971) ch. xii.

19. The background to the claim is explored by L. G. Noble, *Philippine Policy towards Sabah* (Arizona, 1977); see also M. Liefer, *The Philippine Claim to Sabah* (Hull, 1968).

20. The Galbraith Memorandum was forwarded to McNamara for comment on 7 April, and the JCS commented on it (JCSM 282–62) on 13 April 1962: *PP* (Gravel), vol. II, pp. 669–72; for the JCS memorandum of 13 January 1962, forwarded to the President at their insistence two weeks later (JCSM 33–62), see ibid., pp. 662–66.

21. Originally published as Cmnd 1755 (London: HMSO, June 1962); reprinted in full in *Documents*, Cmnd 2834 (1965) pp. 195–203. See Appendix to Chapter 4, pp. 75–6.

22. Pike (1966) pp. 350–1 and 365.

23. G. Chaffard, *Les Deux Guerres du Vietnam* (Paris, 1969) pp. 267ff. Chaffard was in Geneva at the time and cites as source *Journal de Genève*, 29 August 1962.

24. *PP* (Gravel), vol. II, pp. 673–89.

25. *Ibid.*, pp. 175ff. Following the Honolulu Conference, the JCS formally directed CINCPAC to prepare the comprehensive plan on 26 July 1962; CINCPAC in turn forwarded the instruction to MACV on 14 August. MACV submitted draft plans to CINCPAC on 7 December 1962 and 19 January 1963, but it was not until 7 March 1963 that an agreed plan could be forwarded to McNamara by the JCS.

NOTES TO CHAPTER 5: CHINA'S ASIAN STRATEGY: A NEW PHASE

1. For the Chinese reply to Sihanouk's letter, see *SWB/FE*/1035/A3/1–2; for the British response, which suggested solving the problem through negotiations between Cambodia and her immediate neighbours, see *Documents*, Cmnd 2834 (1965), pp. 37 and 242. On relations between Thailand and Cambodia in this period, including the Preah Vihear dispute, see Nuechterlein (1965) pp. 249–57.

2. See *SWB/FE*/1054; for Mikoyan's visit to Indonesia, 20–31 July 1962, see Dake (1973) pp. 141–3.

3. Dake (1973) pp. 156–7.

4. Young (1968) p. 251, citing the *New York Times*, 21 September 1962. For the U-2 incident of 9 September, see *Peking Review*, 14 September 1962. Taylor's

tour of East and South-East Asia was mentioned in the press at the time, but little has been revealed about the content of his talks in various countries; see *SWB/FE/*1044ff.

5. *Peking Review*, 28 September 1962; cf. Maxwell (1972) part IV.

6. *Peking Review*, 28 September and 5 October 1962.

7. Jain (1977) pp. 67–8 and doc. 43; for more detail on the Matsumura visit, see *SWB/FE/*1048 and 1053–4.

8. Tatu (1969) p. 235; the exchange on this issue was first mentioned publicly in the first Chinese 'Comment on the Open Letter of the CPSU', *Renmin Ribao*, 6 September 1963.

9. *SWB/FE/*1047/B/1–2. A subsequent article in *Unen* (18 October 1962) was reprinted in *Pravda* on 1 November 1962 in circumstances which led some commentators to see it as a veiled attack on Khrushchev himself; cf. Tatu (1969) p. 276. These developments did not, of course, involve an open breach between Mongolia and China: in December Tsedenbal visited Peking to sign a Sino-Mongolian boundary agreement; see *Peking Review*, 28 December 1962.

10. The Communiqué issued immediately after the 10th Plenum appeared in *Peking Review*, 28 September 1962; for Mao's speech of 24 September, whose contents were revealed during the cultural revolution, see Schram (1974) Text 9. The importance of the reaffirmation of Mao's class line at this plenum was emphasised in the CCP Resolution on Party History, 27 June 1981: see *Beijing Review*, 6 July 1981, p. 19.

11. Mao referred to this question in his speech of 24 September 1962 (see note 10, above), although his main concern there was with China's internal class struggle. The contradiction between imperialism and anti-imperialism was emphasised strongly in the CCP 'Proposal' of 14 June 1963 (especially paras. 4 and 8); see Griffith (1964) pp. 261ff.

12. For Nguyen Duy Trinh's visit to Peking, see *Peking Review*, 28 September 1962; for the announcement of Peng Zhen's visit, *SWB/FE/*1051/i.

13. *Renmin Ribao*, 21 November 1979; translated in *Beijing Review*, 30 November 1979, p. 13. The same assistance was mentioned, specifying that the 'weapons' were in fact rifles and machine guns, by Hoang Van Hoan in an article about the same time: *Beijing Review*, 7 December 1979, p. 15.

14. *Cuoc Khang-chien* (1980) p. 32.

15. For the details of Peng Zhen's visit, see *SWB/FE/*1061, 1064–5 and 1070; also *Peking Review*, 5 and 19 October 1962. His biography is covered in some detail by Klein and Clark (1971).

NOTES TO CHAPTER 6: THE MISSILES CRISIS AND ITS AFTERMATH

1. The only source which, for what it is worth, appears to give an authoritative answer to the question when the decision was taken is Khrushchev (1971) ch. xx: he says that he first had the idea of installing missiles during a visit to Bulgaria, which from other sources can be dated to 14–20 May 1962. Tatu (1969) p. 235 suggests that the decision had emerged by the time of a visit to Cuba by Rashidov at the end of May. But conceivably some such strategy was already in Soviet minds at the time of the *Pravda* article of 11 April 1962, endorsing Castro's removal of Escalante.

2. The most useful accounts, on which the summary here is based, are those of Schlesinger (1978), Abel (1969), Allison (1971) and Pachter (1963); the last of which contains a useful selection of public documents. See also Watt (1970) pp. 66ff.; and *Documents on International Affairs 1962* (London, 1971).

3. For Western analyses of the Soviet view of the crisis, see Tatu (1969) and Linden (1966). Khrushchev (1971) ch. xx, offers a more 'authentic' Soviet view – but not necessarily a frank assessment of Soviet calculations before the Americans discovered the missiles; Khrushchev admits only to the 'defence of Cuba' interpretation.

4. Allison (1971) pp. 104–5, gives a comprehensive list of the weapons and sites installed in Cuba by the time the crisis ended. For the planned 'Philbriglex-62' exercise, see Abel (1969) p. 97.

5. As reported in the *New York Times*, 27 October 1962; article by M. Frankel, reprinted in Pachter (1963) pp. 188ff. For Mikoyan's remarks in New York, see Schlesinger (1978) ch. xxii, citing the testimony of a former Hungarian diplomat J. Radvanyi.

6. The point is emphasised, for example, by Maxwell D. Taylor in an article in *International Herald Tribune*, 13 October 1982; General Taylor was Chairman of the JCS at the time.

7. This analysis is based on the collection of statements included in Pachter (1963).

8. Rostow (1972) pp. 288–9. The contrast between the missiles crisis and the situation in Vietnam and Laos will be discussed more fully in Chapter 14 below.

9. These and other events in Moscow at this point are referred to by Tatu (1969) pp. 261–3, 274–5, 278. My interpretation, however, differs from his in suggesting that Khrushchev actually recovered some ground in late October and during November.

10. *Peking Review* (double issue), 30 November 1962; reprinted as a pamphlet (by Peking) in 1973. For an account of the events of the war, see Maxwell (1972).

11. See Hilsman (1967) pp. 327ff.

12. For details, see Tatu (1969) pp. 289–92.

13. On the East European Party Congresses, see Fejto (1974) pp. 183, and Slusser (1967) pp. 224–5; and on Tito's visit to the USSR, and its significance for Sino-Soviet relations, Griffith (1964) p. 85. These events are covered in greater detail in *SWB/SU* and *EE (Eastern Europe)/*1093–1132.

14. For details, see *SWB/FE/*1124–5, 1128, 1133 and 1136.

15. *Renmin Ribao*, 31 December 1962, reprinted in *Peking Review*, 4 January 1963; the passage is quoted in full at the head of the present chapter.

16. Research Memorandum RFE-59 (Hilsman to Secretary of State Rusk), 3 December 1962: *PP* (Gravel), vol. II, pp. 690–716.

17. *Cuoc Khang-chien* (1980) pp. 49–50.

18. The best American account of the Ap-Bac battle is in Palmer (1978) pp. 27–38; for the Communist version, see Le Hong Linh (1965) pp. 20–34. For Plei Mrong, see Hickey (1982) vol. II, p. 85.

19. The significance of the Soviet reaction to the Franco-German treaty is emphasised by D. C. Watt (1977) p. 7.

20. *SWB/FE/*1149–50, 1154–5. On the eve of Andropov's visit, *Nhan-Dan* published a new plea for Sino-Soviet unity; *SWB/FE/*1149/C2/1–4. For Novotny's visit and the joint statement at the end, see *SWB/FE/*1161, 1163.

21. The incident is reported in Tatu (1969) pp. 320–1. For the VNWP Politburo statement on 10 February, see *SWB/FE/*1173/C1/1–3; note also a remark by Vo Nguyen Giap on 5 February, to the effect that Sino-Soviet differences were merely temporary: *SWB/FE/*1169/C/1. For the PKI Central Committee meeting of 10 February 1963, see Dake (1973) pp. 204–5.

NOTES TO CHAPTER 7: LAOS: THE LIMITS OF 'DÉTENTE'

1. Sihanouk's speeches during the first half of March are summarised in *SWB/FE/*1194, 1200 and 1205; for his visit to China in February, see *Peking Review*, 22 February, 15 March 1963. Some Communists did eventually join the government as under-secretaries, notably Khieu Samphan and Hou Yuon: see *SWB/FE/*1279/B/1–2. The history of the Cambodian (Kampuchean) Communist Party at this period is still somewhat obscure. For Pol Pot's own version, in a speech of 4 October 1977, see *SWB/FE/*5634/A3/1–2; and for a Vietnamese version, including reference to the death of Tou Samouth, see *Nhan-Dan*, 26 May 1981.
2. For an account of events in Laos at this period, see Toye (1968) pp. 187ff.; for the Chinese version, *Peking Review*, 8 February 1963.
3. VNA, 7 January 1963: *SWB/FE/*1144/A3/6–7; for Souphanouvong's letter of 15 January, *Peking Review*, 8 February 1963, p. 7.
4. The tour was reported in the press; for the delegation's visits to China and North Vietnam, see *Peking Review*, 15 March 1963; *SWB/FE/*1197–9. Also at this period (20 February 1963) the first Laotian ambassador to Hanoi took up his post: *FE/*1182/A3/3.
5. *SWB/FE/*1217–18. The precise circumstances of the death were never cleared up, but the North Vietnamese were quick to blame the Americans, and *Nhan-Dan* had a long front-page article on the news. For Deuane's appeal of 12 March 1963, see *SWB/FE/*1204/A3/5; and for Pathet Lao accusations, contained in a statement by Singkapo on 10 April 1963, see *SWB/FE/*1224/A3/5–7.
6. The papers relating to the NSC meeting of 10 April 1963, together with those of 20–23 April 1963, can be found in the Kennedy Library: National Security Files, NSC Meetings 1963, Box 314.
7. For this and subsequent Sino-Soviet exchanges during 1963, see Griffith (1964) pp. 116ff.; also Tatu (1969) pp. 320–1.
8. The various stages of the Moscow 'power struggle' from March to May 1963 are discussed in detail by Tatu (1969) ch v–vi; for contemporary documentation, see monitored broadcasts in *SWB/SU/*1197–1421.
9. For these exchanges between London and Moscow, including several messages to Souvanna Phouma drafted by one side or the other but never sent, see *Documents*, Cmnd 2834 (1965) pp. 210ff.
10. For the record of these meetings, see note 6, above. The Meeting of 20 April also approved an order for preparation of contingency plans for action against North Vietnam, to be submitted to the President at a later stage; those plans were never implemented. Nor was there any NSAM on Laos at this stage.
11. French *aide-memoire* to Britain, 23 July 1963, printed in *Documents*, Cmnd 2834 (1965) p. 230.
12. Suarez (1967) pp. 181–2.

13. The speech by Le Duan was not immediately published, but appeared in *Hoc-Tap*, no. 4 (April 1963) and was later published in English under the title *Hold High the Revolutionary Banner of Creative Marxism, Lead our Revolutionary Cause to Complete Victory!* (Peking, 1964). The speech by Nguyen Chi Thanh appeared in *Nhan-Dan*, 14 March 1963, and was summarised in a VNA report: see *SWB/FE*/1201/C/1–3. (Some confusion was created by an error in the original monitoring which attributed Nguyen Chi Thanh's speech to Le Duan; it was corrected in *FE*/1207.)

14. Le Duan's speech of 18 May 1963 was later reprinted in his book, *On the Socialist Revolution in Vietnam* (Hanoi, 1965), vol. II, pp. 171ff. The Communiqué of the VNWP Central Committee's 8th Plenum was published on 29 April 1963; see *SWB/FE*/W211/B/13–21 for a long summary. For Nguyen Van Tran's visit to China, *SWB/FE*/1198/A3/8.

15. Liu's visit was given prominence in *Peking Review*, 17 and 24 May 1963, as had his earlier visits to Indonesia, Burma and Cambodia during the previous month. The latter will be discussed in Chapter 8 below. Note also V. Grishin's visit to Hanoi, as head of the Soviet trade union movement, 1–7 May 1963: see *SWB/FE*/1240/C1/1–2.

16. *Documents*, Cmnd 2834 (1965) pp. 221–2: Letter to Geneva Co-chairmen dated 20 June 1963; quoted in part at the head of the present chapter.

17. *Documents*, Cmnd 2834 (1965) pp. 219–20.

18. See reports of fighting in monitored broadcasts by both sides, 17–19 June 1963; *SWB/FE*/1278/A3/9–10; *FE*/1280/A3/5–6; for the Pathet Lao protest about the Indian and Canadian members of the International Commission visiting Attopeu on 19 June, without the Polish member, see *SWB/FE*/1285/A3/6.

19. *PP* (Gravel), vol. II, p. 726.

20. Again, see the account by D. C. Watt (1977) chs i and ii; also, for documents of the Sino-Soviet 'dispute', Griffith (1964) pp. 259–325.

NOTES TO CHAPTER 8: SOUTH-EAST ASIA: THE REGIONAL PERSPECTIVE

1. Liu Shaoqi's visits were covered in detail by *Peking Review*: 19 and 26 April (Indonesia); 26 April and 3 May (Burma); and 3, 10 May 1963 (Cambodia). His visit to North Vietnam was discussed in Chapter 7 above.

2. For an account of the Brunei revolt and its suppression, see James and Sheil-Small (1971) part I. For a survey of the diplomatic background in 1962–3, see Mayall (1977).

3. Dake (1973) ch. xiii provides a general account of the PKI view of 'confrontation' as it developed. For the Sarawak Liberation League founded in 1954 (which became the North Kalimantan Communist Party in 1965) see a short account given by Voice of the Malayan Revolution, 20 September 1980: *SWB/FE*/6536/B/1–4; and for Chaerul Saleh's organisation, as reported by Jakarta radio, *SWB/FE*/1130/A3/6.

4. The MCP statement of mid-December was reprinted by the PKI organ *Harian Rakyat* on 6 February 1963, but not broadcast by the Chinese until 27 March 1963: see Dake (1973) p. 186, n. 42; and for Subandrio's visit to China, ibid., pp. 174–5. Information about Chinese support for the 'North Kalimantan' guerrillas is based on Dake's interview with A. Malik in 1972.

5. *SWB/FE*1220/A3/4–6. For the first actual guerrilla attacks in Sarawak, see James and Sheil-Small (1971) pp. 57, 61–2.
6. Report to Senate Foreign Relations Committee by a four-man panel (headed by Senator Mansfield), 24 February 1963: in *American Foreign Policy, Current Documents 1963*, pp. 837–44.
7. The papers from this meeting were later published: Henderson (1963); the quotation at the head of this chapter is from Henderson's own paper, pp. 252–3.
8. For a full account of these events by the US Ambassador to Indonesia at the time, see Jones (1971) part III; cf. also Hilsman (1965) pp. 389–90.
9. Pike (1966) pp. 159–61, quotes from two 'pessimistic' captured documents of March–April 1963. The 'Crimp Document', a cadre's notebook believed to have been written about the same period, should also be mentioned in this context: see summary in Duiker (1981) pp. 208–11, based on Joint Publications, Research Service, *Translations on North Vietnam*, no. 2185. For Minh Tranh's article, *SWB/FE*/1215/C.
10. Thompson (1966) pp. 133–7; and National Intelligence Estimate, 17 April 1963 ('Conclusions'), printed in *PP* (Gravel), vol. II pp. 725–6. For the Honolulu conference of 6 May 1963, see ibid., p.p. 180–1.
11. *Documents*, Cmnd 2834 (1965) pp. 203–6. There was a further Soviet Note on the subject on 23 April; to which the British replied giving their reasons for rejecting extraordinary action by the Co-chairmen, on 18 May 1963; ibid., pp. 206–9.
12. *Nhan-Dan*, 8 April 1963, which gave a big front-page spread to the meeting and the speech by Hoang Quoc Viet. The questions in the House of Commons, on 25 March, were publicised by VNA: *SWB/FE*/1212/A1/1.
13. Buckingham (1982) pp. 81–6.

NOTES TO CHAPTER 9: VIETNAM: THE 'BUDDHIST CRISIS'

1. The only full accounts of the Buddhist movement of 1963 are in Vietnamese. One of the most detailed, which has been used here, is Quoc Tue, *The Struggle of Vietnamese Buddhism* (Saigon, May 1964, in Vietnamese); more detail on the movement in the provinces (notably Quang-Tri, Quang-Ngai, Khanh-Hoa, binh-Thuan and Dalat) will be found in Tue Giac, *History of the Vietnamese Buddhist Struggle* (Saigon, October 1964: in Vietnamese). For Western accounts of the Hue incident and its aftermath see *PP* (Gravel), vol. II, pp. 226ff.; Warner (1964) pp. 226ff.; Duncanson (1968) pp. 328ff., and Smith (1977) pp. 171ff.
2. Mai Tho Truyen, *Le Bouddhisme au Vietnam* (Saigon, 1962): a short but useful account (in French, English and Vietnamese) by a leading lay Buddhist figure of South Vietnam. It includes an important series of photographs covering such events as the 1951 Congress, the 1960 Buddha's birthday procession through the centre of Saigon, and several visits by leading Buddhists from other Asian countreis; but it gives no hint of 'persecution' of the religion at that stage.
3. Li Weihan, 'The Struggle for Proletarian Leadership in the Period of the New Democratic Revolution in China', originally published in *Hong Qi*, nos 3–4, 1962; translated in three instalments in *Peking Review*, 23 February – 16 March 1962. The passage referred to here will be found in *Peking Review*, 16

March, pp. 16–17. Li Weihan, head of the United Front Work Department of the CCP, appears to have been an associate of Chen Yun as well as of Liu Shaoqi.

4. The speech was published in *Hoc-Tap*, no. ix (1963), and summarised in *Renmin Ribao*, 29 October 1963; it is mentioned briefly in *SWB/FE/1393*. For a translation of the passage noted here, see Porter (1979) vol. II, p. 194.

5. *SWB/FE/1225/A3/10*. The head of the northern Buddhist Association was Thich Tri-Do, and it has been suggested that the syllable 'Tri' in his religious name meant that he belonged originally to the same Buddhist 'family' as the militant Hue Buddhist Thich Tri-Quang. ('Thich' merely means 'Venerable' or 'Reverend'.)

6. Nguyen Thai, *Is South Vietnam, Viable?* (Manila, November 1962).

7. *PP* (Gravel), vol. II, pp. 727ff. On the appointment of Lodge, see Schlesinger (1965) ch. xxxvii, section 3; apparently Kennedy himself, or at least some of his closest advisers, would have preferred to appoint Edmund Gullion to the post – but the State Department insisted on Lodge.

8. The early days of the American press corps in Vietnam are summarised briefly in P. Braestrup, *Big Story* (New Haven: Yale University Press, 1978), which deals mainly with 1967–8. Among those he mentions as already there by the summer of 1963 are: Malcolm Browne and Peter Arnett (Associated Press); Neil Sheehan (United Press International); David Halberstam (*New York Times*); Charles Mohr (*Times*) and Beverley Deepe (*Newsweek*). Mention must also be made of Nicholas Turner (Reuters) and Denis Warner (freelance, but formerly of the *Daily Telegraph*). Several of these reporters later produced books on Vietnam: see Browne (1965), Halberstam (1965), Warner (1964). An interesting discussion of the press problem from the official side appears in Mecklin (1965): the author, formerly himself a pressman, was in mid-1963 on the staff of the US embassy in Saigon.

9. See Browne (1965) pp. 175–82; as the pressman who took the photographs, he is able to give detailed eyewitness account of the event.

10. The Vietnamese Buddhists appealed to the UN Secretary-General as early as 18 May 1963; by early October, fearing that the subject might be formally debated by the General Assembly, Diem was willing to invite a UN team to visit South Vietnam; it arrived on 24 October, but left after the coup of 1 November. See Smith (1977) p. 177.

11. On the significance of the Draper Report, see vol. I, pp. 182–4.

12. For short but informative accounts of the coup-plotting of July–August 1963, see Tran Van Don (1978) pp. 87–95; *PP* (Gravel) vol. II, pp. 237–8; Shaplen (1966) pp. 197–201.

13. See Smith (1977) p. 175, citing the Saigon daily *Tu-Do*, 13 July 1963 and the *New York Times*, 8, 9 July 1963; cf. also *SWB/FE/1296* and 1297/B.

14. For the 'pagoda raids' and their aftermath, seen from various points of view, see *PP* (Gravel), |vol II,| pp. 232ff.; Mecklin (1965) pp. 180ff.; Halberstam (1965) pp. 228ff. For Reuters' 'solid tip', as reported by the US Consul in Singapore, see *DDRC*, p. 822, item A.

15. Cables reprinted in *PP* (Gravel), vol. II, pp. 736–40; for the notorious cable of 24 August, authorising support for a coup but not directly approved by the most senior officials, see ibid., pp. 734–5.

16. Memorandum of the meeting, made by SACSA chief Victor Krulak, in *PP* (Gravel), vol II, pp. 741–3.

17. Mecklin (1965) pp. 202–3.
18. Mao's statement was in response to a new appeal by Ho Chi Minh on 28 August; for it, and the reception of the NLFSVN delegation led by Madame Nguyen Thi Binh, see *Peking Review*, 6 September 1963; also *SWB/FE/* 1350–41.
19. See Sullivan (1978) pp. 68–9.

NOTES TO CHAPTER 10: INTENSIFICATION OF THE STRUGGLE

1. *PP* (Gravel), vol. II, p. 243.
2. Halberstam (1965) *passim*; for his account of the criticisms levelled by Porter and Vann, see pp. 172–6. One of his most important articles at the time, on the theme of the war, appeared in the *New York Times*, 15 August 1963: see pp. 190ff. Halberstam's own experience of the war in the Delta belongs to the period from October 1962 to November 1963.
3. See note 10, below.
4. Thompson (1966), especially pp. 137–9. His theory is well summarised in his earlier reports to Diem in September 1962 and March 1963: quoted at length, ibid., pp. 130–7.
5. See *SWB/FE/*1358.
6. The conference is mentioned, without any indication of source, in Pike (1966) pp. 102 and 162. Tran Van Tra's return to the South is noted in his own account of the events of 1973–5; see Tran Van Tra (1982) p. 219. He has not yet published a detailed account of the events of this earlier period.
7. *SWB/FE/*1348, 1349, 1353. The Vientiane incident may have been intended to prevent Souvanna Phouma's departure for New York to represent the Vientiane government at the United Nations. The three guerrilla actions in the Mekong Delta are mentioned (as Communist victories) by Moc Vien, *Vietnamese Studies*, vol. I (Hanoi 1964) pp. 84–5.
8. All these Chinese statements were immediately translated in *Peking Review*; see issues for 16 August, 6 September, 13 September and 27 September 1963. For a general account of Sino-Soviet relations in this period, including the Naushki station incident, Griffith (1964) chs xvii–xix.
9. *Peking Review*, 16, 23 August 1963.
10. 'Who will Win in South Vietnam?', translated in *Vietnamese Studies*, no. 1 (Hanoi, 1964); from which a key passage is quoted at the head of this chapter.
11. Aidit's visit to China, together with long extracts from his two 'reports' of 2 and 4 September, are covered in *Peking Review*, 6 and 13 September 1963. Cf. also Dake (1973) ch. xvi.
12. See Jones (1971) ch. iv; and Mayall (1977) pp. 16off.
13. 'Facts about Vietnam–China relations over the past 30 years', (known as the 'White Book'), published by Hanoi on 4 October 1979: *SWB/FE/*6238/A3/5. The relevant passage is quoted at the head of Chapter 8.
14. Aidit's departure from Peking on 21 September was reported in *Peking Review*, 27 September 1963; for Lukman's visit to Hanoi, see *SWB/FE/*1358/A3/4.
15. 'A Brief Introduction to the History of the Communist Party of Thailand', put out by the Party itself in 1977; text in A. Turton, J. Fast and M. Caldwell, *Thailand, Roots of Conflict* (Nottingham), (1978) p. 164.
16. Young (1968) p. 258; the same account indicates that the 118th meeting took place on 7 August 1963 and the 120th on 14 November 1963, but it

concentrates mainly on the arms control aspect of the 118th and 119th meetings. For a Special National Intelligence Estimate on greater Chinese militancy in South-East Asia, prepared for the meeting on 31 July 1963, see *DDQC 1975*, p. 235, item D.

17. *PP* (Gravel), vol. II, pp. 769–70; for the McNamara–Taylor Memorandum, on which the NSAM was based, see ibid., pp. 751–66. For the Krulak–Mendenhall visit, ibid., pp. 242–5.

18. The importance attached to this announcement, and the opposition of a number of key advisers, is discussed by Schlesinger (1978) ch. xxxi, section vii.

NOTES TO CHAPTER 11: THE OVERTHROW OF NGO DINH DIEM

1. See especially *PP* (Gravel), vol. II, ch. iv, section iv; Shaplen (1966) ch. vi; Halberstam (1965), ch. xvii; also Tran Van Don (1978).

2. *PP* (Gravel), vol. II, p. 764.

3. *The Times*, 7 October 1963.

4. For Harkins' cables to Maxwell Taylor on 30 October 1963, as well as those exchanged by Lodge and McGeorge Bundy on the same day, see *PP* (Gravel), vol. II, pp. 782–93; for the State Department assessment of 22 October 1963 (RFE-90), ibid., pp. 770–80. No text of Lodge's 23 October cable (Saigon 768) has been published; at the time it was held so tightly by the ambassador that even Harkins was not allowed to see it until late on the 30th.

5. McCone's attitude, together with extracts from a number of CIA cables, appeared during Congressional hearings in 1975: see US Senate, Select Committee to study Governmental Operations with respect to Intelligence Activities: *Alleged Assassination Plots involving Foreign Leaders* (New York: W. W. Norton, 1976) pp. 220–1.

6. This element of the coup is described in detail by Halberstam (1965) pp. 285ff. The officer involved was Col Nguyen Huu Co, who later took over command of IV corps from General Cao.

7. *PP* (Gravel), vol. II, pp. 782–3. The NSC meeting, alluded to only in passing by the *Pentagon Papers* author, is described by Schlesinger (1978) p. 778, on the basis of a paper in the Robert Kennedy collection.

8. McNamara Memorandum of 16 March 1964: *PP* (Gravel), vol. III, pp. 501–2; concern about the effectiveness of the new administration was already expressed in McNamara's earlier report of 21 December 1963: ibid., p. 494.

9. Pike (1966) p. 162, attempted to argue that the removal of Diem was actually a setback for the NLFSVN, since he had been a useful propaganda target; that interpretation placed too much emphasis on propaganda, as opposed to other dimensions of the Communist struggle. Pike does, however, notice the sharp increase in guerrilla activity and other incidents during November; ibid., p. 164.

10. See Moc-Vien in *Vietnamese Studies*, vol. I (1964) p. 86; Le Hong Linh (1965) pp. 35–55, has more detail on the attacks of 23–4 November. For the Hanoi meeting of the World Federation of Trade Unions, see *SWB/FE/*1384 and 1387.

11. The Honolulu meeting is described in different sections of the *Pentagon Papers*,

none of which gives a thorough and detailed account of it; see *PP* (Gravel), vol. II, pp. 274–6; vol. III, pp. 27 and 150–1.

12. See particularly Scott (1972), who argues that the compilers of the *Pentagon Papers* deliberately omitted the full text of NSAM-273 because it would have revealed an actual *lack* of continuity between the Kennedy and Johnson periods. Scott attempted his own reconstruction of the document from scattered quotations and allusions; when the NSAM was eventually declassified, it turned out that he had got most of it right. However, one passage is too cryptic to provide a full picture and the more detailed memoranda on which it was obviously based have not been declassified. For the full text of NSAM-273, see Porter (1979) vol. II, pp. 221–3.

13. For full text, see *PP* (Gravel), vol. III, pp. 494–6.

14. The documents of this committee have not been declassified, but its deliberations are noted in *PP* (Gravel), vol. III, pp. 150–1.

15. The changes of 6 January 1964 have received very little attention in secondary writings, but would have been important in the long run had they not been overtaken by the Khanh coup. For details, see *SWB/FE*/1447/A3/ 1–2.

16. For accounts of the coup of 30 January 1964, see *PP* (Gravel), vol. III, pp. 37–8; Shaplen (1966) pp. 230ff; Lacouture (1966) pp. 132–3.

17. For the government of 8 February 1964, see *SWB/FE*/1475/B/1.

NOTES TO CHAPTER 12: DIPLOMATIC IMPASSE

1. Schlesinger (1978) ch. 31, sections ix and x.

2. Undated memorandum, 'Observations on Vietnam and Cuba', Kennedy Library: Office File, Box 128; cited by Herring (1979) pp. 101–2. He does not attempt to relate the document to what is known of actual US–Cuban contacts, but assumes that the advice was completely ignored. Another anonymous and undated memorandum found in the Robert Kennedy papers (entitled 'South Vietnam, an Action Plan') also raised the possibility of sounding out the Soviet Union on 'the possibility of a neutralisation of all Vietnam on the basis of a change of leadership in South Vietnam'. See Schlesinger (1978) ch. xxxi, section ix.

3. The memorandum is quoted extensively by Schlesinger (1978) ch. xxiii, section viii; he also discusses the background to it, as well as the question of the assassination plot against Castro and the speech of 18 November: ibid., section ix.

4. Ibid. The Hilsman memorandum, addressed to Secretary of State Rusk, is apparently from the Kennedy Library: National Security File, Box 199: but I am informed by the Kennedy Library that it has not been declassified.

5. Mentioned in cable from US Embassy in Paris to State Department, 8 January 1964: *DDQC 1975*, p. 96, item E.

6. M. Maneli, *War of the Vanquished* (New York, 1971), quoted by Schlesinger (1978); cf. Sullivan (1978) p. 69.

7. For Faure's visit, see *Peking Review* , 8 November 1963.

8. See Young (1968) pp. 258–60.

9. The Chinese made a point of commenting on this aspect of the Barghoorn

affair, in terms which emphasised American unfriendliness towards Moscow: *Peking Review*, 22 November 1963, p. 24.

10. Borisov and Koloskov (1975) p. 241. By the 1970s, the Soviet version was critical of the Chinese attitude even at this point; but at the time they may have welcomed Peking's response. The border talks actually opened on 24 February and lasted until August 1964.

11. For Souvanna Phouma's optimism about Soviet intentions, evident during his visit to Bangkok on the way home, see *Bangkok Post*, 6 November 1963; and for the ceasefire and its breakdown, ibid., 18, 19 and 29 November 1963. For more detail on the Singkapo–Kong Lae meetings, see *SWB/FE/*1406–9 and 1412.

12. Sihanouk's speeches are reported in *Bangkok Post*, 13, 15, 20, 21 November 1963; for more detail, see *Principaux Discours, etc. de Son Altesse Royale le Prince Norodom Sihanouk: Année 1963* (Phnom Penh, 1963). For his formal message to the Geneva Co-chairmen, 24 November 1963, see *SWB/FE/*1421.

13. *Bangkok Post*, 16, 18 November 1963. For the background to the talks, see Gurtov (1971) pp. 98–100.

14. *Bangkok Post*, 7, 14 November 1963.

15. Jones (1971) ch. v. Some of the documents relating to US–Indonesian relations at this point have been declassified: see *DDRC*, p. 515, items A and C. Pressure regarding US aid to Indonesia came not only from Britain but also from Congress: the Broomfield Amendment in the House of Representatives, in July; and the Proxmire move, approved by the Senate on 8 November 1963, banning aid to Indonesia unless the President explicitly authorised it 'in the national interest'. On the army's attitude to 'confrontation', and Nasution's links with Azahari, see Crouch (1978) pp. 60–1.

16. *Bangkok Post*, 13–19 November 1963.

17. A series of State Department cables relating to Forrestal's mission has been declassified (albeit in sanitised form) and can be consulted in the Johnson Library: National Security Files, Country File Cambodia, Box 236. The information given here is drawn from that source.

18. *SWB/FE/*1423/A2/5; *FE/*1426/A3/1. The Cambodians, for their part, rejoiced at the death of Sarit: *SWB/FE/*1426/A3/3.

19. The incident is noted in Norodom Sihanouk and Burchett (1973) pp. 118ff.; for more detail see *Principaux Discours, etc.* (as in note 12, above) pp. 618ff., and also *Far Eastern Economic Review*, 9 January 1964, p. 49. For Son Sann's presence in Peking on 1 October: *Peking Review*, 4 October 1963.

20. For Sihanouk's speech on French aid, 6 January 1964, see *SWB/FE/*1452/A3/10–13; cf. also *Far Eastern Economic Review*, 16 January 1964.

21. Reprinted in *Peking Review*, 28 February 1964, pp. 9–12; for the Hilsman speech, see Hilsman (1967) and MacFarquhar (1971) pp. 201–5.

22. For his letter of 31 January 1964, see *SWB/FE/*1470; and for the Sam Neua meeting, *SWB/FE/*1460. The question of North Vietnamese involvement in the offensive of late January 1964 will be discussed further in Chapter 13.

23. The engagement is described in detail in James and Sheil-Small (1971) pp. 93–101.

24. For reports of Sukarno's meeting with Robert Kennedy, see *SWB/FE/*1457–8; and for Kennedy's subsequent visit to Jakarta, *SWB/FE/*1462. Cf. also Jones (1971) pp. 330–2; Mackie (1974) pp. 225ff.; and Dake (1973)

pp. 250–1. A speech by Aidit on 18 January 1964, demanding continuation of the 'confrontation' against Malaysia, was ignored.

25. Sihanouk's diplomacy, as reported at the time, is covered in *SWB/FE/* 1457–8; and 1461, 1463, 1468.

26. For Thanat's visit to Jakarta, 31 January–1 February 1964, see *SWB/FE/* 1468–9; and for the Bangkok meeting, *SWB/FE/*1473, 1475 and 1478. Sihanouk's talks with the Tengku and Macapagal in Cambodia, and their meeting with one another are covered in *SWB/FE/*1475, 1478, 1479 and 1480. No secondary work appears to have analysed these purely Asian exchanges in any detail.

27. For developments during Macapagal's visit to Indonesia and disagreements over the second Bangkok meeting, see *SWB/FE/*1491–3.

NOTES TO CHAPTER 13: HANOI AND MOSCOW: THE 9TH PLENUM

1. The communiqué was published in *Nhan-Dan*, 20 January 1964: *SWB/FE/* 1459/C/1–4; a translation was also put out, in pamphlet form, by Hanoi. Nothing was published in the Hanoi media about the discussion of the revolution in the South, which was kept strictly secret.

2. The text of a copy of the secret resolution (captured by American forces in the South) was eventually translated in *Vietnam Documents and Research Notes*, no. 96 (US Embassy, Saigon, July 1971). This copy is dated 1 January 1965, which probably indicates when it was circulated. Internal evidence suggests that it was actually written in February 1964, presumably on the basis of a draft approved at the 9th Plenum. See also *Cuoc Khang-chien* (1980) pp. 55–6, from which a passage is quoted at the head of this chapter.

3. See article of Nguyen Van Vinh, cited in note 11 below; 20 December 1963 was the third anniversary of the foundation of the NLFSVN.

4. *VN Docs*, no. 96 (Saigon) 1971, pp. 22–39.

5. *SWB/*1453/A3/2–3; *FE/*1456/A3/3–5; *FE/*1461/A3/3–4.

6. This upsurge in the fighting in various localities is brought out especially clearly in *Coup after Coup in Saigon* (Hanoi, 1964), a pamphlet which appears to have been originally completed early in February, with a postface dated 19 February 1964, and to have been published (in English) to draw the world's attention to the growing capabilities of the PLAFSVN.

7. McNamara Memorandum, 16 March 1964: *PP* (Gravel), vol. III, p. 501.

8. This was remarked upon in the State Department's 'White Paper' of February 1965: *Aggression from the North*. The northerners were at this stage used to reinforce PLAFSVN units; they did not yet operate as separate units of the PAVN.

9. *Cuoc Khang-chien* (1980) p. 59.

10. Ibid., p. 57.

11. VNA, 11 February 1964: *SWB/FE/*1478/C/3–11. The article came the day after Le Duan and Le Duc Tho ended a visit to Moscow. That issue of *Hoc-Tap* also included Le Duan's speech to the 9th Plenum; cf. note 13 below.

12. See, for example, an article in *Time* magazine, 8 May 1964, pp. 23–4, which goes so far as to categorise Le Duan as 'pro-Peking' at this stage. Such reporting is likely to have been based ultimately on US intelligence sources; but the historian has, as yet, no access to any records of the analysis on this

kind of question which must have been going on continuously within the intelligence community in Washington and Saigon.

13. *Hoc-Tap*, November 1963, put out by VNA on 16 November: *SWB/FE*/1410/ A2/1–5. Le Duan's speech to the 9th Plenum, *Hoc-Tap*, February 1964, was subsequently translated in his *On Some Present International Problems* (Hanoi, 1964) pp. 125–83.

14. The letter of 29 November 1963 was subsequently published, with other documents, in *Peking Review*, 8 May 1963.

15. For an analysis of Liu's report, which bears the date 30 November 1964 but may have been delivered earlier, see Yahuda (1978) pp. 178–81; no English translation appears to have been published. The Academy of Sciences conference was reported by NCNA on 24 November 1963, but with only a brief mention of speeches by Liu Shaoqi, Zhou Yang and Bo Yibo: see *SWB/ FE*/1414/A2/1–4. For Zhou Yang's actual report, put out by NCNA on 26 December 1963, see *SWB/FE*/1449/C; and *Peking Review*, 3 January 1964.

16. The 'instruction' of 12 December 1963 was mentioned in a talk by Deng Xiaoping in 1980, subsequently published in his collected works; see *Beijing Review*, 25 July 1983, pp. 17, 23.

17. The socialist education movement is analysed in detail in Baum (1975); for reports of the 'recent' PLA political work conference, appearing on 17–21 January 1964, see *SWB/FE*/1461 and 1467. It will be necessary for us to return to these aspects of internal Chinese politics in Chapter 16, below.

18. On the significance of the Vosnesensky articles, see W. G. Hahn, *Postwar Soviet Politics* (Ithaca: Cornell University Press, 1982) pp. 132–3; he discusses the events of 1949–50 and Suslov's subsequent role in criticising those who sought to defend Vosnesensky. For Suslov's disappearance in 1963, see Tatu (1969) p. 360; cf. also Linden (1966) p. 183.

19. The visit is discussed by Suarez (1967) pp. 191ff. For Mao's statement on Panama, and other Chinese material on Latin America, see *Peking Review*, 10 and 17 January 1964.

20. The apparent incongruity of Le Duan's position, as 'pro-Chinese' in 1963–4 and 'pro-Soviet' in 1979–80, is noted by Smyser (1980) pp. 79–80.

21. *Peking Review*, 28 February 1964, pp. 9–12; the same issue carried an article criticising operations of the US Seventh Fleet. Cf. Chapter 12, note 21, above.

22. The report was eventually published in *Pravda* on 3 April 1964; for complete translation, see Griffith (1967) pp. 204–69. For the circular of 12 February, which has never been published, see ibid., pp. 19ff.

23. For a discussion of the economic decisions of this plenum, see Linden (1966) pp. 193–6.

24. *SWB/FE*/1465/A2/1; *FE*/1468/A3/1–2; *FE*/1478/A2/1. Hoang Van Hoan was with the delegation in Peking (where Mao received them on 30 January 1964); it is not clear whether he also went to Moscow. For the impression that this mission was a failure from Hanoi's point of view, see the draft memorandum of William Bundy dated 1 March 1964: Porter (1979) vol. II, p. 242.

25. *SWB/FE*/1482/A2/1.

26. For the documents of 20 February–31 March 1964, see Griffith (1967) pp. 173–204. The period of relaxation in the Chinese attitude lasted until 7 May 1964, when the CCP rejected the CPSU proposal of 7 March: ibid., pp. 297ff.

27. See Baum (1975). Liu 're-emerged' in March, when he joined Zhou Enlai to receive a Japanese Communist delegation in Peking: see *Peking Review*, 27 March 1964.
28. *Peking Review*, 6 March 1964.
29. Ibid., 3 April 1964.
30. *SWB/FE/*1482/A3/9; *FE/*1486/B11. In March, Liu Shaoqi (who had not been prominent since November 1963) joined Zhou Enlai in greeting a JCP delegation in Peking led by Hakamada: see *Peking Review*, 27 March 1964.
31. The speech was reprinted in *Peking Review*, 20 March 1964.
32. For the Special Political Conference (27–28 March) and the meeting of the National Assembly which immediately followed (30 March–4 April), see VNA and Hanoi Radio reports in *SWB/FE/*1517–8 and 1521–3. Cf. also *Cuoc Khang-chien* (1980) pp. 57–8.
33. *PP* (Gravel) vol. III, p. 511.

NOTES TO CHAPTER 14: COERCIVE DIPLOMACY

1. NSAM-288 itself was very short: its main clause was to approve the Memorandum submitted by McNamara to the President on 16 March 1964; it then designated the new Assistant Secretary of State for Far Eastern Affairs (William Bundy) to co-ordinate its implementation. A copy of the NSAM itself is deposited in the US National Archives, Washington; for the full text of the McNamara Memorandum of 16 March, see *PP* (Gravel), vol. III, pp. 499–510.
2. For the full text of JCSM 46–64 (22 January 1964), see *PP* (Gravel), vol. III, pp. 496–9; an extract from JCSM 136–64 (18 February 1964) is given ibid., pp. 44–5.
3. See *PP* (Gravel), vol. III, 118–19, 142, 154ff. At one point this is described as an NSC meeting.
4. The text of William Bundy's draft memorandum, declassified in 1975, is reprinted in Porter (1979) vol. II, pp. 240–6; parts of it (but *not* the section on North Vietnam) were later incorporated into the McNamara Memorandum of 16 March 1964. It is clear from a passage in the *Pentagon Papers* (*PP* (Gravel), vol. III, pp. 155–6) that the section of the Bundy Memorandum dealing with action against the North was based directly on the interim report of a separate interagency group which had studied this question in the latter part of February; that report was also dated 1 March 1964, but we do not have the full text.
5. McNaughton's somewhat enigmatic role during 1964–5 is discussed in detail in Halberstam (1972) ch. xviii.
6. *PP* (Gravel), vol. III, pp. 161–2. The scenarios were probably related to a series of war games, played by the most senior officers and civilians; but no documentation relating to them has been released, and the impression of them given by secondary works is somewhat vague: e.g. Halberstam (1972) ch. xxi.
7. This difference does not emerge from the *Pentagon Papers* (compiled without access to internal JCS records), but is discussed briefly in Momyer (1978) pp. 13–14.
8. Rostow (1972) pp. 505–6; and *PP* (Gravel), vol. II, pp. 310–11. In another memorandum at this time, Rostow also urged the use of a Congressional

Resolution as a means of demonstrating the United States determination. For telegram from CINCPAC to JCS, 29 February 1964, see *DDRC*, p. 70, item B.

9. The memorandum on South Vietnam is quoted at length in *PP* (Gravel), vol. III, pp. 43–4; that on the wider situation in South-East Asia was declassified later: see *DDRC*, p. 839, item A.

10. Declassified in 1978; reprinted in Porter (1979) vol. II, pp. 247–9.

11. JCSM 159–64: *PP* (Gravel), vol. III, pp. 119, 158–9.

12. The idea was suggested by Britain in late February: see *Documents*, Cmnd 2834 (1965) pp. 246–7. For US cables relating to Cambodia in early March 1964, see *DDQC 1981*, pp. 93–5.

13. For telegrams relating to the Chantrea Incident, see *DDQC 1976*, pp. 53–4; the Vietnamese subsequently admitted responsibility for the incident, which occurred during a 'sweep' against Communist forces near the border.

14. The cross-checking operation was proposed by McCone on 7 January 1964 and approved by McNamara on 16 January: see *PP* (Gravel), vol. III, pp. 32–5.

15. NSAM-280, dated 14 February 1964: copy available in National Archives, Washington.

16. For details see Eckhardt (1974) pp. 38–42.

17. The *Pentagon Papers* contain two separate accounts of this conference (but without extensive documentation): *PP* (Gravel), vol. III, pp. 65 and 162–3. The Ottawa visit led eventually to the Seaborn mission to Hanoi in June, to be discussed below.

18. Schelling's book *The Strategy of Conflict*, originally published in 1960, was reprinted in 1963; it was the product of a year's work for the RAND Corporation at Santa Monica (California), on leave from Harvard University. He was subsequently invited to give the Stimson Lectures at Yale, in spring 1965, which were published as *Arms and Influence* (Yale University Press, 1966). Herman Kahn, also with RAND in the 1950s, had founded the Hudson Institute in 1961. His book *On Thermonuclear War* (1960) was followed by Thinking about the Unthinkable (New York, 1962); and by an essay *On Escalation*, originally prepared under a contract from the aircraft company Martin Marietta, and published as a book in 1965. For a general discussion of the origins of the 'military–political game', and the role of RAND, see Wilson (1970) pp. 68–71; and for an application of the theory to the Vietnam War in the years 1964–8, Thies (1980).

19. For the text of this cable, see *PP* (Gravel), vol. III, p. 511.

20. Rostow (1972) pp. 506–7; cf. *PP* (Gravel), vol. III, p. 123.

NOTES TO CHAPTER 15: THE THIRD LAOS CRISIS

1. Reported in *SWB/FE/*1527; for Souvanna Phouma's visit to Peking and his talks with Zhou Enlai, *Peking Review*, 10 April 1964.

2. For an account of the coup, see Dommen (1971) pp. 261ff.; it is also discussed briefly by Toye (1968) p. 192. For monitored broadcasts at the time of the coup, and the attempt to establish a new Revolutionary Committee, see *SWB/FE/*1533–4. The ostensible leaders of the coup were Generals Kouprasith Abhay (military commander in Vientiane) and Siho Lamphouthacoul (head of the paramilitary police force).

3. Souvanna Phouma informed the Geneva Co-chairmen of this decision in a message of 4 May 1964: his reply to their letter of 1 May 1964 expressing concern about the coup. See *Laos* (1970) p. 141.

4. For Phoumi Nosavan's loss of power following the failure of the coup, and particularly the implications of the affair for his financial position and control over the opium trade, see McCoy (1972) pp. 261–2. The effect of the coup was to produce a major power-shift within the rightist 'faction'; but it is not at all certain that that was its original intent.

5. For accounts of the offensive on the ground, see particularly the 'Message' of the International Commission for Laos to the Geneva Co-chairmen, dated 20 June 1964: partly reproduced in *Laos* (1970) pp. 144–7; also Dommen (1971) pp. 269ff. A brief record from the North Vietnamese side, which no longer attempts to conceal the fact that it was a joint North Vietnamese - Pathet Lao offensive – not just a 'mutiny' by left-wing neutralists, as was claimed at the time – will be found in *Cuoc Khang-chien* (1980) p. 59.

6. For the Sino-Soviet background at this period, including the text of the CCP letter of 7 May, see Griffith (1967).

7. Reported by VNA: *SWB/FE*/1557/A2/2. For the VNWP letter to fraternal Parties, dated 21 April and put out by VNA on 29 April 1964, see *SWB/FE/* 1542/C2/1; and for the visit of the French CP delegation to Hanoi, *SWB/FE/* 1541/A1/1.

8. US State Department, *Working Paper on the Role of North Vietnam in the War in the South* (May 1968), reprinted in *VN Docs*, nos. 36–7 (Saigon, June 1968). For an account of the sinking of the *Card*, see Le Hong Linh (1965), pp. 72ff.

9. Documentation on the meetings of this group is somewhat sparse, but its importance emerges from *PP* (Gravel) vol. III, pp. 167–71.

10. The *Pentagon Papers* discuss different aspects of these proposals in different contexts; but when the various proposals and memoranda of 21–7 May are studied in conjunction with one another, they can be seen to have constituted a significant 'debate' on US programmes in South Vietnam; see *PP* (Gravel), vol. II, pp. 318–20, 42 0–1 and 463–7; also Porter (1979) vol. II, pp. 268–70.

11. Summarised in *PP* (Gravel), vol. III, pp. 167–8; for the meeting of 25 May at which it was discussed, ibid., pp. 169–70.

12. For the diplomatic moves of 19–26 May, see *Documents*, Cmnd 2834 (1965), *Laos* (1970), and Dommen (1971) pp. 272ff.

13. The Polish proposal does not emerge very clearly from the published documentation, but the US reaction to it is indicated in a cable from Ball (in Washington) to Rusk (then in Bangkok) on 29 May 1964: Porter (1979) vol. II, pp. 272–4; cf. also *PP* (Gravel), vol. III, p. 171.

14. *PP* (Gravel), vol. III, 171–6; cf. also Momyer (1978) pp. 14–15.

15. *PP* (Gravel), vol. III, pp. 177–181 and 77–9. For the text of Bundy's draft resolution, and accompanying memoranda of 10–15 June, see Porter (1979) vol. II, pp. 281–8.

16. The Seaborn mission is covered by a section of the *Pentagon Papers* not released in 1971, but declassified in 1975: *USVNR*, VI.C.1; now available in Herring (1983) pp. 7–12.

17. These operations produced an immediate protest from Hanoi to the International Commission, but were not admitted by the American side until information about them emerged during the enquiry into the Gulf of Tonkin Incident: see Porter (1979) vol. II, p. 488.

18. This move was not publicised at the time but is mentioned, together with a similar proposal by Sihanouk to Nguyen Huu Tho on 18 August 1964, in a chronology of Vietnamese–Cambodian relations given in *Dossier Kampuchea*, vol. I (Hanoi, 1978) p. 56.

19. For details on these events, see Jones (1971) pp. 306ff.; Mackie (1974) pp. 230 ff.; James and Sheil-Small (1971) p. 119.

20. See Dake (1973) pp. 269–74.

21. For details see Tolson (1973) ch.iii; and Klare (1972) pp. 145–6.

22. On Taylor's first month in Saigon, see *PP* (Gravel), vol. II, pp. 326–9, and vol. III, pp. 79–83; on the planned increase in personnel, ibid., vol. II, pp. 468–71.

23. The 1 July ambush is one of the operations described by Le Hong Linh (1965) pp. 84–9; the attacks on special forces camps are recounted in Kelly (1973) pp. 54–6. For Saigon's allegation of the presence of PAVN regulars at Nam-Dong, in a broadcast of 9 July 1964, see *SWB/FE/*1602/A3/6.

24. Since this 'debate' related entirely to Laos and had nothing to do with Vietnam, it was not mentioned at all in the *Pentagon Papers*. However, some of the details can be gleaned from a series of (heavily 'sanitised') telegrams between the State Department and Ambassador Unger, covering the period 22 June to 6 August 1964, which are now available for study at the Johnson Presidential Library in Texas: National Security Files, Country File Laos, Box 274.

NOTES TO CHAPTER 16: THE GULF OF TONKIN CRISIS

1. The literature on this subject is considerable. The most useful secondary accounts are those by Goulden (1969), Austin (1971) and Windchy (1971). The principal 'primary' document is a staff study prepared for the Senate Foreign Relations Committee, and read into the Congressional Record on 29 February 1968 by Senator Wayne Morse; for text, see Galloway (1970) appendix 9; also Porter (1979) vol. II, pp. 486–94. For the President's own version of events, see Johnson (1971) ch. vi.

2. For a summary of these deployments, authorised by the Secretary of Defense on 4 and 7 August, see Goulden (1969) p. 236.

3. The text of Bundy's original draft, dated 11 June 1964, is reproduced in Porter (1979) vol. II, pp. 283–4; as is the text of the actual resolution of 7 August 1964, *ibid.*, p. 307. A comparison shows them to be quite different. Bundy's absence on holiday in August may explain why a new resolution was drafted by Chayes on 5 August: see Austin (1971) p. 289. Austin also disposes of the myth that Johnson had been carrying the resolution in his pocket for several weeks, waiting to use it.

4. In statements on 5 and 6 August, respectively: *SWB/FE/*1623/A3/1–2; *Peking Review*, 7 August 1964. An even more explicit admission that the PT boats actually fired on the *Maddox* is contained in *Cuoc Khang-chien* (1980) p. 60.

5. Moorer's message is reproduced in the Congressional staff report of early 1968: see Porter (1979) vol. II, p. 491; cf. also Austin (1971) p. 267.

6. Two State Department assessments are included in an NSC 'history' of the Gulf of Tonkin Attacks: Johnson Presidential Library, National Security Files, NSC Histories, Boxes 38, 39: Memorandum from W. W. Rostow to

Secretary of State, 5 August 1964; and Research Memorandum (RFE-56) by the State Department Bureau of Intelligence and Research, 6 August 1964. The second of these is reproduced in Porter (1979) vol. II, pp. 304–6. It is, of course, possible that the State Department was not privy to all that was known by CINCPAC and the Pentagon about the nature of the incidents.

7. Document probably emanating from CIA: Supplement to 'Vietnam Weekly', 16 July 1964: Johnson Library: National Security Files, Country File Vietnam: Southeast Asia Special Intelligence Material, vol. I, Box 48. The same source refers to completion of the airfield at Phuc-Yen. For the Chen Yi letter of 6 July and the *Renmin Ribao* editorial of 9 July, see *Peking Review*, 10 July 1964. We know that Zhou Enlai and Chen Yi visited Rangoon from 10 to 12 July, and a secret flight from Kunming to Hanoi immediately before that is perfectly credible: see *Peking Review*, 17 July 1964. The visit appears to be confirmed by the 'diary' of the Albanian leader Enver Hoxha: *Reflections on China* (Tirana, 1979) vol. I, p. 67.

8. *Peking Review*, 10 July 1964. For 'Operation Triangle', see Chapter 15 above.

9. See *Peking Review*, 3 and 10 July 1964.

10. *Washington Post*, 10 July 1964. The significance of this article as a deliberate 'signal' to Hanoi and Peking was commented upon by H. Kahn in his book *On Escalation* (New York, 1965) pp. 59–61.

11. Vietnam Press, Saigon, 9 July 1964: *SWB/FE/*A3/6. the report claimed that the engagement, occurring during the Lam-Son 122 campaign, had involved four battalions of PAVN troops belonging to the 9th regiment of the 304th division; but this was never confirmed and has generally been discounted as untrue. See, however, Hickey (1982) p. 97: he was at Nam-Dong camp when the attack occurred and says it was made by a 'reinforced battalion of Viet Cong, newly arrived from North Vietnam'.

12. For the Chinese statements of 14 and 19 July, see *Peking Review*, 17 and 24 July 1964; for the Hanoi rally, *SWB/FE/*1611/C1/1 and 6–7. What must now be recognised as unduly alarmist reports appeared in the Western press at this time; e.g. an article by V. Zorza in the *Guardian* (London and Manchester) on 21 July 1964, which said 'analysis of Peking statements indicates that Chinese troops are now poised for action in North Vietnam'. For a general discussion of Chinese deterrent 'signals' at this period, see Whiting (1975) ch. vi.

13. Both points figured in the summary put out by VNA, 27 July 1964: *SWB/FE/* 1621/A3/2–4; for the full text, see Vo Nguyen Giap, *The South Vietnam People will Win* (Hanoi, 1965).

14. Nguyen Chi Thanh's role will be discussed in Chapter 19, below. He and Giap both appeared at a Hanoi ceremony on 7 August 1964 to honour the PAVN personnel involved in the Gulf of Tonkin Incidents and in shooting down a US plane on 5 August; Le Duan was again absent. See *SWB/FE/* 1626/A3/1.

15. See Baum (1975). Remarkably little reference was made to the socialist education movement in *Peking Review*, possibly because it was not yet based on a full consensus within the CCP leadership. On the movement to 'Learn from the PLA', see Gittings (1967) pp. 254ff.

16. For the Peking Opera festival, and the text of Peng Zhen's speech to it, see *Peking Review*, 7 August 1964; for Jiang Qing's criticism of Peng Zhen in that connection, and her own role in the festival, see R. Witke, *Comrade Chiang Ch'ing* (Boston, 1977) pp. 309ff.

17. *Peking Review*, 17 July 1964. For Mao's remarks of 10 July, and other aspects of Sino-Soviet relations in this period, see Griffith (1967) pp. 365ff.

18. *SWB/FE/*1624/C2/1–3. This article did not appear in *Peking Review*, although that journal carried a news report of Luo's activities to commemorate Army Day on 31 July–1 August: see issue of 7 August 1964, pp. 11–12. On that occasion the PLA chief of staff warned the Americans that if they ignored China 'your claws stretching into South-East Asia will be chopped off'.

19. For Butler's visit to Moscow, see *Documents*, Cmnd 2834 (1965) pp. 239–41; for the Chinese reply to the Soviet Note, *Peking Review*, 7 August 1964; and for the views of Hanoi and Khang Khay, *SWB/FE/*1618, 1619 and 1624.

20. The Vientiane Cabinet meeting, presided over by Souvanna Phouma early on 4 August, was reported the same day: *SWB/FE/*1624/A2/1. For the meeting with Unger and U. Alexis Johnson on the 3rd, see Telegram from Vientiane to State Department, 3 August 1964: included in the NSC History of the Gulf of Tonkin Attacks, cited in note 6 above (Box 39, Tab. 40).

21. The article was eventually noticed by the US Embassy in Vienna and reported in a telegram to the State Department on 3 August 1964, which is also included in the NSC History cited in note 6 (Box 38, Tab. 18).

22. See the map, summarising the North Vietnamese version as circulated in 1964, in Goulden (1969) p. 228.

23. This earlier patrol is mentioned in a Memorandum for the Record, prepared by 'Colonel Steakley's people' and dated 1 August 1964: included in the NSC History mentioned in note 6.

24. *SWB/FE/*1623/A3/1. For the official statement and the editorial about the Nam-Can incident on the Laos–North Vietnam border, see *SWB/FE/*1621/A3/1–2 and *FE/*1623/A3/2.

25. Telegram from US Consul, Hong Kong, to State Department, 6 August 1964: included in the NSC History mentioned in note 6 above (Box 38).

26. Statement on Vientiane Radio, 2.30 p.m. on 5 August: *SWB/FE/*1624/A3/6.

27. For broadcasts of North Vietnamese and Chinese statements on 5–6 August 1964, see *SWB/FE/*1624 and 1625; for the Chinese statement and the *Renmin Ribao* article of 6 August see *Peking Review*, 7 August 1964, Supplement.

28. The two Taylor cables of 3 August 1964 were included in the NSC History cited in note 6 above (Box 38, Tabs 18, 20).

29. Seaborn again met Pham Van Dong in Hanoi on 13 August 1963: *USVNR*, VI. C. For documents relating to the message to be sent via Seaborn, see *PP* (Gravel), vol. III, pp. 519–22. For U Thant's initiative, see his memoir, *View from the UN* (1978) pp. 62ff.

30. These moves are noted in CIA Memoranda on the 'North Vietnam Crisis', 11–12 August 1964, to be found in Johnson Library: National Security Files, Country File Vietnam, Box, 48.

31. Mentioned in *Renmin Ribao*, 21 November 1979, as translated in *Beijing Review*, 30 November 1979, p. 14.

32. This exchange of letters, also from the Johnson Library, is reprinted in Porter (1979) vol. II, pp. 302–4.

33. *PP* (Gravel), vol. III, p. 130. The failure to link the air strikes of 5 August to North Vietnamese action in Laos and South Vietnam was noted with some concern by Ambassador Taylor, in a cable of 9 August 1964: *ibid.* pp. 522–4.

NOTES TO CHAPTER 17: 'THE FOCAL POINT OF WORLD CONTRADICTIONS'

1. The best published account of this crisis is to be found in Shaplen (1966) ch. ix. See also *PP* (Gravel), vol. III, pp. 85–7; and daily coverage in the Western press, e.g. *New York Times*.
2. CIA reports of 3–10 June 1964, declassified in 1976: *DDQC 1976*, p. 21, items D and E. Cf. also Shaplen (1966) p. 246.
3. In January 1975, Khanh himself distributed copies of a letter of support he had received from Huynh Tan Phat in January 1965: Porter (1979) vol. II, pp. 345–6.
4. *PP* (Gravel), vol. II, pp. 522–3.
5. For text, see *SWB/FE/1659/A3/6–7*.
6. The best account of the FULRO revolt is that by Hickey (1982) ch. iii. Not only was he an eyewitness; in 1970 he was able to visit Phnom Penh and to discuss the incident with the Cambodian figure thought to have masterminded the revolt. For Hanoi's decision in September to improve its command structure in the Central Highlands, which now became the 'B-3' front, see Chapter 19 below.
7. For NCNA and VNA reports of these meetings, broadcast on 16, 18 and 23 September 1964, see *SWB/FE/1653*, 1661, 1662 and 1666; cf. also Dommen (1971) p. 278, and *Laos* (1970) p. 150.
8. For the Gulf of Tonkin incident of 18 September 1964, see *PP* (Gravel), vol. III, pp. 194–5; but unfortunately a key passage is sanitised. There is also a report on the incident, declassified in 1976, in the Johnson Library: National Security Files, Country File Vietnam, Box 77. The DRVN foreign ministry statement of 19 September, together with a statement by Luo Ruiqing the same day, can be found in *SWB/FE/1662/A3/1–3*; see also *Peking Review*, 25 September 1964. The decision to send out a new patrol was based on NSAM-314 (10 September 1964) which will be discussed in Chapter 18 below.
9. Jones (1971) pp. 342–3.
10. Jones (1971) 345ff.; the full text of the speech appears in *SWB/FE/1635–6/C*.
11. For accounts of the Singapore riots in July and September, and of the Pontian and Labis landings, see Mackie (1974) pp. 255–7 and 259–62.
12. Whereas the Gulf of Tonkin incidents have received detailed scrutiny, it is still impossible to piece together from British and Australian reports the various moves that were made in this early September affair; but see Mackie (1974) pp. 261–2. He also summarises the UN debate, pp. 264–7.
13. *SWB/FE/1659/A3/1*; cf. Crouch (1978) p. 76. *Dwikora* was the name given to the command to 'crush Malaysia'.
14. For reports of the visits of Truong Chinh and Sihanouk to Indonesia, see *SWB/FE//1632*, 1633, 1637, 1648. The North Vietnamese reiterated their support for Indonesia in an editorial in *Nhan-Dan*, 13 September 1964: *SWB/FE/1657/A3/6–7*.
15. *SWB/FE/1635/A3/1* and *FE/1637/A3/3–6*.
16. Reports of Miyamoto's visits were monitored in *SWB/FE/1650*, 1653, 1655, 1656, 1658; he was in Peking on 10 September and left Canton for home on 14 September 1964.

17. He attributed that phrase to Sukarno. The same speech is quoted at the head of the present chapter; see NCNA report of 4 October 1964: *SWB/FE/*1675/A3/3–4.

18. Smyser (1980) p. 76 citing *China News Analysis* (Hong Kong) no. 544, 11 December 1964.

19. For his and Li Xiannian's travels, see *SWB/FE/*1632, 1647, 1650 and 1653; Hoan returned to Hanoi on 3 September 1964.

20. *Peking Review*, 2 October 1964.

21. For Sihanouk's presence in Peking from 27 September to 7 October 1964, see *SWB/FE/*1669, 1670 and 1676; and for his meeting with Pham Van Dong on 28 September *SWB/FE/*1674/A3/4. Pham Van Dong returned home, via Nanning, on 9 October: *SWB/FE/*1680/A3/7. The decision to hold border talks between Cambodia, North Vietnam and the NLFSVN was announced on 15 November 1964: *SWB/FE/*1711/A3/4–5. But a news report early in January 1965 indicated that the talks themselves, held in Peking sometime in December, had failed to produce agreement: *New York Times*, 6 January 1965.

22. Dake (1973) pp. 289–90.

NOTES TO CHAPTER 18: WASHINGTON HESITATES: THE AUTUMN DEBATE

1. 'Next Courses of Action in Southeast Asia': a paper drafted on 11 August 1964, partly on the basis of a cable from Taylor the previous day. The main part of the text was submitted to Saigon, Vientiane and CINCPAC, for their comments, on 14 August: *PP* (Gravel), vol. III, pp. 524–37.

2. For the list of OPLAN 34A operations proposed by MACV for the month of September, see *PP* (Gravel), vol. II, pp. 553–4. For differences of opinion within the JCS on whether to make these operations 'overt', see General Wheeler's memorandum of 9 September 1964: ibid., pp. 563–4.

3. The text of NSAM-314, dated 10 September 1964, is printed in *PP* (Gravel), vol. III, pp. 565–6; for the suggestion that DE SOTO patrols and OPLAN 34A operations might be combined in a deliberately provocative way, being discussed on 8–9 September, see ibid., pp. 562 and 564. The incident of 18 September was reported in the press, and again denounced as an American 'fabrication' by the Chinese media. See Chapter 16, note 8.

4. State–Defense message to Unger, 6 October 1964: *PP* (Gravel), vol. III, pp. 576–7; see also pp. 133–4. The rightist general Phoumi Nosavan was in Washington at that time; but his ideas for a major expansion of covert ground operations in northern Laos appear to have been rebuffed: ibid. p. 580.

5. The JCS 'Target Study for North Vietnam' was said (26 August) to have been 'recently forwarded' to the Secretary of Defense, who acknowledged it at the end of the month: *PP* (Gravel), vol. III, pp. 551 and 555–6; cf. Momyer (1978) p. 15.

6. CINCPAC comments on Bundy's draft memorandum, in cable to JCS, 17 August 1964; and Taylor's comments on same, in cable of 18 August: *PP* (Gravel), vol. III, pp. 542–8.

7. The documents are reprinted in *PP* (Gravel), vol. III, pp. 542–8 and 550–2; cf. note 6 above.

8. A hint of such a debate is contained in a memorandum from the Assistant Secretary of Defense (Comptroller) to McNamara, dated 24 August 1964: *PP* (Gravel), vol. III, pp. 549–50; but other relevant documentation remains classified. For Wheeler's memorandum of 9 September 1964, indicating differences among the Joint Chiefs, see note 2 above.

9. Johnson (1971) pp. 119–20.

10. The details of this decision were beyond the terms of reference of the *Pentagon Papers*; but one cable reprinted there (Saigon to State Department, 10 October 1964) indicates the formal establishment, of the committee, its membership, and its responsibilities: *PP* (Gravel), vol. III, pp. 579–80. In the absence of any access to the record of its proceedings, the precise role of SEACOORD in subsequent events is impossible to assess.

11. A brief glimpse of the potential importance of this crisis, had the President chosen to handle it differently, is given in a cable from JCS to CINCPAC, 1 November 1964: *PP* (Gravel), vol. III, pp. 209–10, 587. For the President's own view of the event and his reasons for inaction, see Johnson (1971) p. 121.

12. The proceedings of the NSC Working Group are covered in great detail by the *Pentagon Papers*: see *PP* (Gravel), vol. III, pp. 206–48 and (for documents) pp. 588–683. The members of the group included William Bundy, Michael Forrestal, Marshall Green and Robert Johnson (all of the State Department), John McNaughton (Defense Department), Harold Ford (CIA) and Admiral Lloyd Mustin (representing the JCS).

13. It would appear that there were only five copies of the original 74-page memorandum, entitled 'Validity of Assumptions Underlying Vietnam Policies'; and that a copy did not reach the President himself until early in 1965. At least one copy is in the Johnson Library, but (as of September 1983) has not yet been declassified. Ball himself, however, has written about the memorandum and the gist of its contents in his article 'Top Secret: the Prophecy the President Rejected,' *The Atlantic*, CCXXX (July 1972).

14. This was later revealed by Ellsberg himself in a BBC interview: see Charlton and Moncrieff (1978) pp. 173–5.

15. Tolson (1973) pp. 54–5.

16. The analysis which follows is based mainly on *PP* (Gravel), vol. III, pp. 215–31.

17. One document which indicates the strength of ISA feeling against 'Option B' is a memorandum sent to William Bundy on 23 November 1964, signed by McNaughton's deputy (Harry Rowen) but representing their joint view: *PP* (Gravel), vol. III, 642–4.

18. U Thant, *View from the UN* (London, 1978) p. 64.

19. 'Comment on draft for Part II of Project Outline on Courses of Action in Southeast Asia': Memorandum from Admiral Mustin to William Bundy, 10 November 1964: *PP* (Gravel), vol. II, pp. 621–8.

20. *PP* (Gravel), vol. II, p. 342; for the demonstrations of this period see Western press reports of late November.

21. For the meetings of 24 November to 1 December, see *PP* (Gravel), vol. III, pp. 236–51. Operation 'Barrel Roll', involving a limited number of air strikes in southern Laos by US planes, was authorised on 12 December 1964 and began two days later: ibid., p. 254. For MACV's dissatisfaction with the restricted level of action authorised, see Westmoreland (1976) p. 110.

22. *PP* (Gravel), vol. III, pp. 257–8. The main purpose of the Wilson visit was to negotiate on NATO defence issues; the British delegation also briefed the Americans on Malaysia. The *Pentagon Papers* indicate that Johnson gave Wilson a full briefing on Vietnam; in his memoirs Wilson barely mentions the subject, beyond noting that, as one of the Geneva Co-chairmen, Britain could not offer even token assistance to the United States in Vietnam: see H. Wilson, *The Labour Government 1964–1970* (London, 1971): Penguin Books edition (1974) p. 79.

23. *The Times* (London), 16 February 1965. A more explicit reference to differences between Rusk (on the one hand) and McNamara and McGeorge Bundy (on the other) occurs in a memorandum from McGeorge Bundy to the President on 27 January 1964; to be discussed in Chapter 20 below.

24. These two documents are to be found in the Johnson Library: National Security Files, Country File China, Box 238; together with the State Department intelligence note of 27 November 1964, referred to later in this paragraph.

25. Young (1968) pp. 261–2. This meeting followed exchanges between the two governments arising from the Chinese atomic test on 16 October. There is no indication, in any of the public references, to suggest that Vietnam was also discussed.

26. The quarrel between Taylor and Nguyen Khanh is documented in Porter (1979) vol. II, pp. 336–9; the crisis in Vietnamese–American relations was sufficiently serious to receive front-page attention in the *New York Times* on 23 and 24 December 1964. One report noted that this was 'the most direct clash with Vietnamese leaders since the veiled threats levelled against the regime of Ngo Dinh Diem before it was overthrown'. See also Shaplen (1966) pp. 294ff.

27. *PP* (Gravel), vol. III, pp. 684–6.

NOTES TO CHAPTER 19: HANOI DECIDES

1. Saigon to State Department, 14 October 1964; reprinted in *PP* (Gravel), vol. III, pp. 583–4. Taylor was inclined to attribute the increased infiltration to the Communists' need to make good casualties suffered in the fighting in the South; he did not detect any significant change of strategy on the Communist side.

2. U.S. State Department: *Working Paper* (May 1968) in *VN Docs*, nos 36–7.

3. *Cuoc Khang-chien* (1980) p. 62.

4. The relevant passage appears in full in the Vietnamese text, printed in *Nhan-Dan*, 13 May 1976; it is translated somewhat loosely, omitting key details, in Van Tien Dung, *Our Great Spring Victory* (New York, 1977) p. 207. Other indications of Nguyen Chi Thanh's influence in Hanoi in the latter part of 1964 are noted by Smyser (1980) pp. 78 and 85; he mentions a public speech on 21 December 1964 and a secret report for the Politburo dated 20 November 1964. The latter, captured by US forces inside Cambodia in May 1970, is clearly an important document; Smyser says he has a copy in his possession but he uses it only sparingly, and it has never been published in a full translation.

5. See text of the secret resolution, translated in *VN Docs*, no. 96 (Saigon, 1971); the form of the document captured by US forces was dated 1 January 1965

and was stated to have been made in only ten copies. The resolution as a whole is discussed more fully in Chapter 13 above.

6. For the battles of Binh-Gia and An-Lao, see Le Hong Linh (1965) pp. 110–38; also *Cuoc Khang-chien* (1980) pp. 63–6. They were part of a new PLAFSVN offensive, which in the Binh-Gia area lasted until early March 1965. For the formation of the 9th Division, which soon became known to American intelligence, see Palmer (1978) p. 52. The importance of Communist military activity in Binh-Dinh province generally was noted by Westmoreland, in Sharp and Westmoreland (1968) p. 95.

7. *Chinese Aggression against Vietnam: the Root of the Problem* (Hanoi, 1979) p. 17; an English-language statement, probably compiled and circulated while the war of February–March 1979 was still in progress, since it describes events only down to the end of February. The precise date of Deng's visit is not indicated but it certainly came after the Gulf of Tonkin Incident.

8. *Hong Qi*, 21 November 1964; translated in *Peking Review*, 27 November 1964; see also Griffith (1967) pp. 61–5. It should be noted that this article was *not* presented as a continuation of the earlier *Renmin Ribao-Hong Qi* 'comments' on the CPSU statement of July 1963; the 'ninth comment' of 14 July 1964 proved to be the last in that series.

9. *SWB/FE*/1700, 1702, 1710 and 1711. Pham Van Dong did, however, stop in Nanning on the way home, where he met Chen Yi on 14 November: *SWB/FE*/1710/A2/1–2.

10. The proceedings were published as a pamphlet by the conference itself, in English: *International Conference for Solidarity with the People of Vietnam against U.S. Imperialist Aggression and for the Defence of Peace* (Hanoi, 25–29 November 1964).

11. Reported in *The Times* (London), 4 January 1965; for Kosygin's message of 17 November, see Pike (1966) p. 342, who identified this as the first Soviet message directly to the NLFSVN. An additional indication of increased Soviet attention to Vietnam, and positive willingness to support Hanoi, will be found in Janos Radvanyi, *Delusion and Reality* (South Bend, Indiana, 1978) pp. 37–8. A former Hungarian diplomat, he notes that the Gulf of Tonkin incident made no impact in Budapest; and that the first sign of a change in the Soviet attitude to Vietnam came during a visit to the Hungarian capital by Brezhnev and Podgorny in January 1965, when they blamed Khrushchev for his neglect of both Vietnam and Korea.

12. *SWB/FE*/1739–41. The delegation stayed until 26 December 1964, then visited Peking for two days on the way home: *Peking Review*, 1 January 1965. Note also that the North Korean president, Choe Yong-kim, paid a visit to Cambodia in mid-December, on his way home from Africa: *SWB/FE*/1738 and 1741. For the Hanoi rally of 20 December, attended by Ton Duc Thang, Le Duan and Vo Nguyen Giap, see *SWB/FE*/1741/A3/7.

13. *Peking Review*, 4 December 1964. A useful summary of Japansese political developments during the year will be fund in *Annual Register 1964* (London, 1965) pp. 360–3.

14. On this movement, and the significant changes of December 1964–January 1965, see again Baum (1973).

15. *Peking Review*, 8 January 1965. It will be recalled that Lin Biao's career advanced considerably, in similar circumstances, in April–May 1958: see Volume I, pp. 109–10.

16. *Peking Review*, 1 January 1965. The Pentagon confirmed that the nuclear submarine had left Guam for waters off the Asian mainland on 26 December 1964. For the 125th ambassadorial meeting (the first to be publicly reported since the 120th just over a year before), see Young (1968) p. 261.

17. *Peking Review*, 15 January 1965, and press reports of 20 January 1965. The meeting was convened by Liu Shaoqi rather than by Mao himself.

18. The full text of the Mao–Snow interview became available to Averell Harriman on 12 February 1965; a copy (of the published version) was circulated to top officials in Washington a month later. See Johnson Library: National Security Files, Country File, China, Box 238. The fact that the interview had taken place was reported briefly in *Peking Review*, 15 January 1965.

19. See Hanoi's 'White Book', October 1978: *SWB/FE/*6238/A3/14; citing a passage in Edgar Snow, *The Long Revolution* (London, 1973).

20. A Soviet delegate, N. G. Ignatov, also attended the rally; see report by D. Bloodworth from Phnom Penh, *Observer* (London), 15 November 1964; also *SWB/FE/*1706/A3/4.

21. Weatherbee (1970) pp. 30–44; he gives the translated text of both documents.

22. See A. Guerrero: *Philippine Society and Revolution* (3rd edn 1979) p. 50. At the time when the book was written (1970), its author was chairman of the (Maoist) Communist Party of the Philippines. One should not overestimate the significance of these events for the mainstream of Philippine politics, but they reflect a new additional strand in Chinese strategy.

23. *SWB/FE/*1701/A3/1–2; Dake (1973) p. 326. Zhou and He Long flew specially to Shanghai for the meeting, which took place on the eve of their visit to Moscow. On 6 November, a Sino-Indonesian air communications agreement was signed in Peking: *SBW/FE/*1705/A3/2. Dake also discusses the visit of Chen Yi to Indonesia, from 27 November to 3 December 1964; ibid., pp. 328–9.

24. Dake (1973) pp. 314–5; *Peking Review*, 25 December 1964; and for Lukman in Tokyo, *SWB/FE/*1738/A3/2. For the Sino-Soviet background at this period, see Griffith (1967) pp. 64–5; and for the Japanese CP 9th Congress, *FE/*1719/C and *Peking Review*, 11 December 1964.

25. For details of the internal political conflict in Indonesia, which came to a head at a Bandung conference of political parties on 12 December 1964, see Dake (1973) pp. 300–6; and Mackie (1974) pp. 279–83.

26. Dake (1973) pp. 329ff.; and for the departure from the UN, ibid., pp. 315–17. On the build-up of forces on both sides of the border, see James and Sheil-Small (1971) pp. 152–3; no major change in Indonesia tactics actually occurred.

NOTES TO CHAPTER 20: FEBRUARY 1965: ESCALATION

1. Extract printed in Berman (1982) pp. 38–9, from NSC History: Deployment of Major US Forces to Vietnam. For the original, see Johnson Library: National Security Files, Aides File, McGeorge Bundy: Memos to the President, vol. 8, Box 2; declassified November 1977.

2. Johnson Library: National Security Files, Country File Vietnam: Southeast Asia, Special Intelligence Material, vol. 3, Box 48; heavily sanitised.

3. Reprinted, from a translation distributed by Nguyen Khanh in January 1975, in Porter (1979) vol. II, pp. 345-6. This letter indicates that Phat had written to Khanh in similar vein on an earlier occasion; but no date is given. For a CIA cable indicating suspicion about Khanh's relations with Hanoi, where one of his half-brothers was living, see ibid., p. 339. Khanh's contact with the NLFSVN in late 1964 is also discussed by Tran Van Don (1978).

4. Outlined in his 'briefing' for the NSC Principals on 27 November 1964: *PP* (Gravel), vol. III, pp. 666-73.

5. Johnson's cable to Taylor, sometime in late December 1964, as quoted in Berman (1982) pp. 34-5. Taylor's reply (6 January 1965) and Johnson's further cable (7 January) are also summarised and quoted by him: ibid., pp. 35-7. The whole sequence is drawn from the NSC History on Deployment of Major US Forces, cited in note 1 above.

6. Kosygin's plan to visit Vietnam was announced in Hanoi on 31 January 1965: *SWB/FE*/1774; the various stages of his tour are covered by *SWB/FE*/ 1778-90. Besides Kosygin, the delegation included Party secretary Y. V. Andropov, deputy foreign minister V. V. Kuznetsov, deputy minister of defence K. A. Vershinin, minister of civil aviation E. F. Loginov, and a deputy chairman of the State Committee for Economic Relations, G. S. Siderovich; see *SWB/FE*/1779/A2/1. For a US intelligence assessment of the purpose of the visit, dated 1 February 1965, see Porter (1979) vol. II, pp. 346-8.

7. *SWB/FE*/1779/A2/4. For a discussion of the Moscow Meeting of 1-5 March 1965, see Griffith (1967) pp. 83-91. He notes that already by 22 February the status of the meeting had been toned down by the Soviet press; and that in effect it was no more than an inconsequential 'consultative' session

8. *Peking Review*, 19 February 1965.

9. *Peking review*, 12 November 1965; for the relevant passage, see also Griffith (1967) pp. 460-1.

10. *PP* (Gravel), vol. III, pp. 276 and 325ff; for the TASS statement of 6 February, *Soviet News*, 8 February 1965.

11. The Pleiku and Qui-Nhon incidents were front-page news in the Western press, but other attacks received less attention. The larger picture emerges from monitored Communist reports: e.g. VNA, 17 February 1965, which noted 'fourteen big battles' between 7 and 10 February: *SWB/FE*/A3/7-8. The offensive must have been planned much earlier; it may have been intended originally to coincide with Tet (the lunar new year) which in 1965 fell on 2 February. For an account of the Pleiku incident and its consequences, by an American journalist in South Vietnam at the time, see Browne (1965). Cf. also Berman (1982) pp. 42ff.

12. Soviet statement of 8 February, following US bombing of North Vietnam: for text, see *Soviet News* (USSR Embassy, London), 9 February 1965.

13. The comparison with 1958 was made explicitly by an article in *Izvestiya*, noted by the commentator V. Zorza in the *Guardian* (Manchester), 15 February 1965.

14. The text of the Snow interview, originally published in Europe and Asia under the dateline 17 February 1965, was being studied by Averell Harriman in Washington as early as 12 February. See copy at Johnson Library: National Security Files, Country File China, vol. II, Box 238. For Hanoi's interpretation in 1979, see *SWB/FE*/6238/A3/14.

15. For McGeorge Bundy's memorandum of 7 February 1965, and extracts from Taylor's cable of 11 February, see *PP* (Gravel), vol. III, pp. 309–17.

16. The decision was reported in detail in a cable from the President to Taylor on 13 February 1965: *PP* (Gravel), vol. III, pp. 321–2.

17. Several cables from Jakarta relating to these developments (dated 26 February and 2, 3 and 5 March 1965) have been declassified: see *DDRC*, p. 27, item C; p. 595, items C, D, G; and p. 596, item A. Another ominous development from the US point of view, was the arrival in Jakarta on 24 February of a Chinese atomic energy delegation; see Dake (1973) pp. 334–5.

18. For an account of this crisis, see Shaplen (1966) pp. 310–12; relevant broadcasts from Saigon will be found in *SWB/FE/*1789, 1791 and 1792.

19. Published by HMSO London, in March and April 1965: Cmnd 2609 and 2634.

20. US State Department, *Aggression from the North: the Record of North Vietnam's Campaign to conquer South Vietnam* (Washington, D.C., 1965); the main passages are reprinted (together with a critical comment in *I.F. Stone's Weekly*, XIII, 8 March 1965) in Gettleman (1966) pp. 300–41. For a brief discussion of the decision to publish the paper, see *PP* (Gravel), vol. III, p. 330.

21. The allegation, by a former CIA officer, was made in 1982 in the context of a growing debate about 'external involvement' in the guerrilla war then in progress in El Salvador: see *International Herald Tribune*, 24 March 1982. The incident at Vung-Ro is briefly referred to, without comment, in *Cuoc Khang-chien* (1980) p. 32. For a contemporary report by Vietnam Press (Saigon), 21 February 1965, see *SWB/FE/*1792/B/2; it would seem that an incident of some kind certainly occurred.

22. This initiative is described in detail (but with a 'sanitised' omission) in *PP* (Gravel), vol. III, pp. 325–9.

23. *PP* (Gravel), vol. III, pp. 400–3; 417–23.

24. Ball's interventions in the Vietnam debate in February 1965 are discussed in detail in Berman (1982) pp. 46–52.

25. *Nhan-Dan*, 4 March 1965: see J. M. Van Dyke, *North Vietnam's Strategy for Survival* (Palo Alto, 1972) p. 126. For the third Seaborn mission, see *PP* (Gravel), vol. III, p. 330; and more fully, *USVNR* (portion declassified in 1975) VI.C.1.

26. The relevant passage of the CINCPAC message is reproduced in *PP* (Gravel), vol. III, p. 318; cf. also Sharp (1978) chs V and vi.

Bibliography

I DOCUMENTARY SOURCES

(1) Official Government Publications (non-Communist)

The following items in this category deserve special mention:

(i) *Documents relating to British Involvement in the Indochina Conflict 1945–1965* (London: HMSO, 1965). Cmnd 2834 (referred to in notes as *Documents*, Cmnd 2834, 1965).

(ii) *Select Documents on International Affairs*: no. 16, *Laos* (Canberra: Department of External Affairs, April 1970) (referred to in notes as *Laos*, 1970).

(iii) US State Department: *A Threat to the Peace: North Viet-Nam's Effort to Conquer South Vietnam* (Washington, D.C., December 1961).

(iv) US State Department: *Aggression from the North: the Record of North Vietnam's Campaign to Conquer South Vietnam* (Washington, D.C., 1965).

(v) Official United States pronouncements on foreign relations are regularly published in the *Department of State Bulletin*. A selection of statements relating to Vietnam is to be found appended to the four volumes of *The Pentagon Papers* (Senator Gravel Edition): see below.

(vi) A number of volumes relating to the official history of various aspects of the Vietnam War have been published by the Government Printing Office, Washington, D.C., on behalf of different branches of the United States armed forces. Those which have been used in the present study will be found listed under author in the second part of the Bibliography.

(2) United States Archives

No archives of this period have been deposited by US Government Departments in the National Archives. A small number of photocopies of National Security Action Memoranda have been deposited there by the NSC, and are referred to in footnotes as necessary.

For the limited number of individual documents which have so far been declassified, it is necessary to consult the following:

(i) *Pentagon Papers:* the name usually given to the official, and originally classified, history of United States decision-making on Vietnam compiled within the Office of the Secretary of Defense between June 1967 and January 1969. In addition to

412

the 'short' version published by the *New York Times* in 1971, two longer versions are available (excluding the last four 'books', relating to negotiations):

(a)   *PP* (Gravel) refers to: *The Pentagon Papers: the Defense Department History of United States Decision-making on Vietnam: Senator Gravel Edition.* (Boston, Mass.: Beacon Press, 1971) 4 vols.

(b)   *USVNR* refers to: *United States–Vietnam Relations 1945–1967.* US Congress, House of Representatives, Armed Services Committee (October 1971) 12 books.

The additional four 'books' were eventually declassified in 1975 (see *DDQC 1975*, p. 60, item B); they have since been published (but in a 'sanitised' version):

(c)   G. C. Herring (ed.) *The Secret Diplomacy of the Vietnam War: the Negotiating Volumes of the Pentagon Papers* (Austin: University of Texas Press, 1983).

(ii) *Presidential Libraries:* The White House archives of each Administration are normally deposited in a presidential library, administered by the US National Archives but situated away from Washington in the individual president's home state. Two such libraries contain archives relating to the period 1961–65, some of which are already open to scholars:

(a)   John F. Kennedy Library, Boston (Massachusetts).
(b)   Lyndon B. Johnson Library, Austin (Texas).

In both cases, the materials relating to foreign affairs are to be found in the National Security Files, kept by the Special Assistant for National Security Affairs and his staff.

A growing number of such documents has been (and continues to be) declassified under presidential Executive Orders, either on the initiative of the Presidential Library itself or through use by individual scholars of the Freedom of Information Act. In some cases, such declassification is subject to a document being 'sanitised', which means that only a photocopy is available from which certain passages have been excised.

Among the series of documents kept at the Johnson Library, special mention should be made of two 'National Security Council Histories' which are relevant to this period. Each consists of selected (classified) documents relating to a particular topic; they have been substantially reproduced on microfilm by University Publications of America, Inc., Frederick, Maryland:

(a)   *Presidential Decisions: Gulf of Tonkin Attacks of August 1964.*
(b)   *Deployment of Major US Forces to Vietnam, July 1965.*

In addition to declassified documents, both these presidential libraries also have a number of 'oral histories', recorded and transcribed, by officials of the two administrations. Those so far released for research vary considerably in their coverage of events, but some are very useful.

(iii) *Declassified Documents Reference System:* Inaugurated in 1975 by the Carrollton Press, Inc., Washington, D.C., this series attempts to make more easily available many of the documents recently declassified: it comprises a series of catalogues, listing and briefly summarising each document, together with microfiche copies of the documents themselves. The documents are drawn from all the major government departments dealing with defence and foreign relations; some of the originals are from the two presidential libraries indicated above.

(a) *DDRC* refers to *Declassified Documents Retrospective Collection*, published in two volumes in 1975.
(b) *DDQC* refers to *Declassified Documents Quarterly Catalogue*, published quarterly from 1975 and still in progress.

Individual documents are referred to by indicating the year (of the Catalogue), page number, and item letter.

(3) Communist Documentation

(i) *Monitored Broadcasts:* Considerable use has been made of *Summary of World Broadcasts*, published several times a week (at this period) by the BBC (Caversham, England). For researchers working in the United States, it may be more convenient to use the publications of the Foreign Broadcasting Information Service (FBIS). In fact, since the Anglo-American agreement of 1947, actual monitoring of Far East broadcasts has been carried out by FBIS on the basis of a division of labour with the BBC. In the present volume, two series have been used:

SWB/FE refers to the Far East series;
SWB/SU refers to the Soviet Union series.

The *Summary* contains translations (in full or in summary) of broadcasts from a variety of radio stations; many of which, particularly in Communist countries, broadcast in whole or part the text of articles from the principal newspapers and periodicals. The following are the most important Communist publications which have been used in this indirect form; in certain cases it has been necessary also to consult *Nhan-Dan* in the original.

(a) Hanoi: *Nhan-Dan* ('People'), daily.
              Hoc-Tap ('Studies'), theoretical organ of the VNWP.
(b) Peking: *Renmin Ribao* ('People's Daily'), daily.
              Hong Qi ('Red Flag'), theoretical organ of the CCP.
(c) Moscow: *Pravda* ('Truth'), daily organ of the CPSU.
              Izvestiya ('News'), daily organ of the Soviet government.
              Krasnaya Zvezda ('Red Star'), daily organ of the Soviet armed forces.

(ii) *Communist Publications in English:* The following two periodicals have been especially useful:

(a) Peking: *Peking Review*, published weekly; after January 1979, it became *Beijing Review*.
(b) Hanoi: *Vietnamese Studies*, published monthly; it began to appear in the autumn of 1964, and the first issue was devoted largely to the struggle in South Vietnam.

In addition, both Peking and Hanoi published a growing number of pamphlets and short books in English or French during this period; for reference to individual titles, see the second part of this Bibliography.

(iii) *'Historical' Materials published in Hanoi:* A small number of individual works deserve special mention under this heading:

(a) *Facts about Vietnam–China Relations over the Past Thirty Years* (known as the 'White Book'), published by the Foreign Ministry in Hanoi on 4 October 1979 and made available to the diplomatic community (in English). The text used in the present volume is that monitored from VNA (in English) and printed in full in *SWB/FE*/6238, and 6242 (6, 11 October 1979). For replies by the Chinese government and by Hoang Van Hoan, then in exile in Peking, see *Beijing Review*, 23 November, 30 November and 7 December 1979.

(b) *The Anti-US Resistance War for National Salvation* (in Vietnamese: *Cuoc Khang-chien chong My Cuu-nuoc*) *1954–1975*, published by the People's Army of Vietnam, Hanoi, 1980. The text used in the present volume is the FBIS translation published by the US Joint Publications Research Service, Washington, D.C., June 1982. (Referred to as *Cuoc Khang-chien*, 1980.)

(c) *Concluding the Thirty Year War* (in Vietnamese: *Ket-thuc cuoc Chien-tranh 30 nam*), by Tran Van Tra, published in Ho Chi Minh City (Saigon), 1982. It is the last of five volumes of memoirs which he plans to write, but the only one published so far, dealing mainly with the years 1973–5. Translated by Joint Publications Research Service, and published in FBIS, *Southeast Asia Report*, series, Washington, D.C., February 1983.

(iv) *Captured Communist Documents:* The only Communist source materials not officially published or broadcast at one time or another, and the only materials on the Communist side that are comparable with Western archives, are those captured in the field by units of the American or South Vietnamese armed forces or security services. Much more research is needed on these materials, some of which are to be found in the collections made by Douglas Pike and Jeffrey Race. Others are not yet accessible for research. In the present volume, only limited use has been made of materials of this kind. Some are translated in Pike (1966) and in Porter (1979). For one particularly important example, see: 'Resolution of the Ninth Plenum of the Vietnam Workers' Party Central Committee, 1963', translated in *Vietnam Documents and Research Notes*, no. 96 (Saigon: US Embassy, July 1971) (referred to as *VN Docs*).

(4) Published Collections of Documents

In addition to official collections indicated above, the following are useful:

M. E. Gettleman (ed.): *Vietnam: History, Documents and Opinions on a Major World Crisis* (New York: Fawcett Publications, 1965); also published in Penguin Books (Harmondsworth, 1966). Includes much of text of the US 'White Paper' of February 1965.

G. Porter (ed.): *Vietnam: the Definitive Documentation of Human Decisions* London and Philadelphia: Heyden, 1979. Volume II contains documents from the period

1955–75, including a number of United States documents declassified after 1971 and printed here for the first time.
J. Galloway: *The Gulf of Tonkin Resolution* (Rutherford: Farleigh Dickinson University Press, 1970). Appendices include texts of the documents surrounding the Resolution itself and of the Congressional Hearings of 1964 and 1968.

II SECONDARY WORKS

This section does not include peripheral works, cited occasionally in individual footnotes.

Abel, E. (1969) *The Missiles of October: Twelve Days to World War III* (London). (Original US edition entitled *The Missile Crisis*, appeared in 1966.)

Allison, G. T. (1971) *Essence of Decision: Explaining the Cuban Missile Crisis* (Boston).

Austin, A. (1971) *The President's War* (Philadelphia).

Baum, R. (1975) *Prelude to Revolution: Mao, the Party and the Peasant Question 1962–1966* (New York:).

Berman, L. (1982) *Planning a Tragedy: the Americanization of the War in Vietnam* (New York).

Blaufarb, D. S. (1977) *The Counterinsurgency Era: US Doctrine and Performance, 1950 to the Present* (New York).

Borisov, O. B. and Koloskov, B. T. (1975) *Soviet–Chinese Relations 1945–1970* (Bloomington, Indiana). (Translated from the Russian originally published in Moscow, 1971.)

Browne, M. W. (1965) *The New Face of War* (London).

Buckingham, W. A. (1982) *Operation Ranch Hand: the Air Force and Herbicides in Southeast Asia 1961–1971* (Washington, D.C.).

Charlton, M. and Moncrieff, A. (1978) *Many Reasons Why: The American Involvement in Vietnam* (London).

Collins, J. Lawton (1975) *The Development and Training of the South Vietnamese Army, 1950–1972* (Washington, D.C.).

Crouch, H. A. (1978) *The Army and Politics in Indonesia* (Ithaca, NY).

Cuoc Khang-chien (1980) see Part I of Bibliography, above.

Dake, A. C. A. (1973) *In the Spirit of the Red Banteng: Indonesian Communists between Moscow and Peking 1959–1965* (The Hague).

Documents, Cmnd 2834 (1965) see Part I of Bibliography, above.

Dommen, A. J. (1971) *Conflict in Laos: the Politics of Neutrality*, 2nd edn (London).

Duiker, W. J. (1981) *The Communist Road to Power in Vietnam* (Boulder, Colorado).

Duncanson, D. J. (1968) *Government and Revolution in Vietnam* (London).

Eckhardt, G. S. (1974) *Command and Control 1950–1969* (Washington, D.C.).

Fejtö, F. (1974) *A History of the People's Democracies: Eastern Europe since Stalin* (Harmondsworth, Middx.) (Translated from French edition, originally published in 1969.)

Galloway, J. (1970) see Part I, of Bibliography, above.

Gelb, L. H. and Betts, R. K. (1979) *The Irony of Vietnam: The System Worked* (Washington, D.C.).

Gittings, J. (1967) *The Role of the Chinese Army* (London).

Gott, R. (1970) 'The Conflict in South-East Asia', in D. C. Watt, *Survey of International Affairs 1962* (London).

Goulden, J. C. (1969) *Truth is the First Casualty: The Gulf of Tonkin Affair, Illusion and Reality* (Chicago).

Griffith, W. E. (1964) *The Sino-Soviet Rift* (Cambridge, Mass.).

Griffith, W. E. (1967) *Sino-Soviet Relations 1964–1965* (Cambridge, Mass.).

Gurtov, M. (1971) *China and Southeast Asia: The Politics of Survival* (Lexington, Mass.).

Halberstam, D. (1965) *The Making of a Quagmire* (New York).

Halberstam, D. (1972) *The Best and the Brightest* (New York).

Henderson, W. (1963) *Southeast Asia: Problems of United States Policy* (Cambridge, Mass.).

Herring, G. C. (1979) *America's Longest War: The United States and Vietnam 1950–1975* (New York).

Hickey, G. C. (1982) *Free in the Forest: Ethnohistory of the Vietnamese Central Highlands 1954–1976* (New Haven, Conn.).

Hilsman, R. (1967) *To Move a Nation: the Politics of Foreign Policy in the Administration of John F. Kennedy* (New York).

Hoxha, Enver (1979) *Reflections on China: Extracts from the Political Diary*, 2 vols. (Tirana).

Jain, R. K. (1977) *China and Japan 1949–76* (London).

James, H. and Sheil-Small, D. (1971) *The Undeclared War: the Story of the Indonesian Confrontation 1962–1966* (London).

Johnson, L. B. (1971) *The Vantage Point: Perspectives of the Presidency 1963–1969* (New York).

Jones, H. P. (1971) *Indonesia, the Possible Dream* (Stanford, Calif.).

Kahin, G. McT. (1975) 'The Pentagon Papers, a Critical Evaluation', *American Political Science Review*, vol. LXIX, no. 2, June.

Kelly, F. J. (1973) *US Army Special Forces 1961–1971* (Washington, D.C.).

Khrushchev, N. S. (1971) *Khrushchev Remembers*, trans. by S. Talbott, vol. I (London).

Klare, M. T. (1972) *War Without End: American Planning for the Next Vietnams* (New York).

Klein, D. W. and Clark, A. B. (1971) *Biographic Dictionary of Chinese Communism 1921–1965*, 2 vols. (Cambridge, Mass.).

Lacouture, J. (1966) *Vietnam, Between Two Truces* (London). (Translated from French edition, published in 1965.)

Laos (1970) see Part I of Bibliography, above.

Le Hong Linh (1965) *Ap-Bac: Major Victories of the South Vietnamese Patriotic Forces in 1963 and 1964* (Hanoi).

Leifer, M. (1983) *Indonesia's Foreign Policy* (London).

Linden, C. A. (1966) *Khrushchev and the Soviet Leadership 1957–1964* (Baltimore).

McCoy, A. W. (1972) *The Politics of Heroin in Southeast Asia* (New York).

MacFarquhar, R. (1971) *Sino-American Relations 1949–1971* (Newton Abbot).

Mackie, J. A. C. (1974) *Konfrontasi: The Indonesia–Malaysia Dispute 1963–1966* (Kuala Lumpur).

Maxwell, N. (1972) *India's China War* (Harmondsworth, Middx.). (Original edition appeared in 1970.)

Mayall, J. B. (1977) 'Malaysia, Indonesia and the Philippines: Prelude to Confrontation', in D. C. Watt, *Survey of International Affairs 1963* (London).

Mecklin, J. (1965) *Mission in Torment: An Intimate Account of the US Role in Vietnam* (New York).

Momyer, W. W. (1978) *Air Power in Three Wars* (Washington, D.C.).

Nishihara, Masashi (1976) *The Japanese and Sukarno's Indonesia: Tokyo-Jakarta Relations 1951-1966* (Kyoto and Honolulu).

Norodom Sihanouk and Burchett, W. (1973) *My War with the CIA: Cambodia's Fight for Survival* (London).

Nuechterlein, D. E. (1965) *Thailand and the Struggle for Southeast Asia* (Cornell, Ithaca).

Pachter, H. M. (1963) *Collision Course: The Cuba Missiles Crisis and Coexistence* (New York).

Palmer, D. R. (1978) *Summons of the Trumpet: US-Vietnam in Perspective* (San Rafael, Calif.).

Palmerlee, A. E. (1968) 'The Central Office of South Vietnam', in *Vietnam Documents and Research Notes*, no. 40 (Saigon).

Pike, D. (1966) *Viet Cong: The Organisation and Techniques of the National Liberation Front of South Vietnam* (Cambridge, Mass.).

Porter, G. (1979) see Part I of Bibliography, above.

Prouty, L. F. (1973) *The Secret Team* (Englewood Cliffs, NJ).

Rostow, W. W. (1972) *The Diffusion of Power: An Essay in Recent History* (New York).

Schlesinger, A. M. (1965) *A Thousand Days: John F. Kennedy in the White House* (Boston, Mass.).

Schlesinger, A. M. (1978) *Robert Kennedy and His Times* (New York).

Schram, S. (1974) *Mao Tse-tung Unrehearsed: Talks and Letters 1956-71* (Harmondsworth, Middx.).

Scott, P. D. (1972) 'Vietnamisation and the Drama of the Pentagon Papers', in *The Pentagon Papers*, vol. V (Boston). (This volume, although published as a supplement to the Gravel edition of the *Pentagon Papers* by Beacon Press, has nothing to do with the text of the *Papers* themselves; it consists of a series of essays by critics of the war, including this one.)

Shaplen, R. (1966) *The Lost Revolution in Vietnam 1945-1965* (London).

Sharp, U. S. Grant (1978) *Strategy for Defeat: Vietnam in Retrospect* (San Rafael, Calif.).

Sharp, U. S. Grant and Westmoreland, W. C. (1968) *Report on the War in Vietnam, as of 30 June 1968* (Washington, D.C.).

Simmonds, E. H. S. (1968) 'The Evolution of Foreign Policy in Laos since Independence', in *Modern Asian Studies*, vol. II.

Slusser, R. M. (1967) 'America, China and the Hydra-headed Opposition: the Dynamics of Soviet Foreign Policy', in P. H. Juviler and H. W. Morton (ed.), *Soviet Policy-Making* (New York).

Slusser, R. M. (1973) *The Berlin Crisis of 1961: Soviet-American Relations and the Struggle for Power in the Kremlin* (Baltimore).

Smith, R. B. (1977) 'Vietnam', in D. C. Watt, *Survey of International Affairs 1963* (London).

Smyser, W. R. (1980) *The Independent Vietnamese: Vietnamese Communism between Russia and China 1956-1969* (Athens, Ohio).

Suarez, A. (1967) *Cuba: Castroism and Communism 1959-1966* (Cambridge, Mass.).

Sullivan, M. P. (1978) *France's Vietnam Policy: A Study in Franco-American Relations* (Westport, Conn.).

Tatu, M. (1969) *Power in the Kremlin: from Khrushchev's Decline to Collective Leadership* (London). (Translation from French edition, published in 1967 under the title *Le Pouvoir en URSS*.)

Taylor, J. (1976) *China and Southeast Asia: Peking's Relations with Revolutionary Movements*, 2nd edn (New York).

Taylor, M. D. (1972) *Swords and Plowshares* (New York).

Thies, W. J. (1980) *When Governments Collide: Coercion and Diplomacy in the Vietnam Conflict 1964–1968* (Berkeley).

Thompson, R. G. K. (1966) *Defeating Communist Insurgency* (London).

Tolson, J. J. (1973) *Airmobility 1961–1971* (Washington, D.C.).

Toye, H. (1968) *Laos, Buffer State or Battleground* (London).

Tran Van Don (1978) *Our Endless War: Inside Vietnam* (San Rafael, Calif.).

Tran Van Tra (1982) see Part I of Bibliography, above.

Warner, D. (1964) *The Last Confucian: Vietnam, South-East Asia and the West* (Harmondsworth, Middx.) (revised edn for Penguin Books).

Watt, D. C. (1970) *Survey of International Affairs 1962* (London).

Watt, D. C. (1977) *Survey of International Affairs 1963* (London). (This was the last in this valuable series of annual surveys.)

Weatherbee, D. E. (1970) *The United Front in Thailand: A Documentary Analysis* (Columbia, South Carolina).

Westmoreland, W. C. (1976) *A Soldier Reports* (New York).

Whiting, A. S. (1975) *The Chinese Calculus of Deterrence: India and Indochina* (Ann Arbor, Michigan).

Whitlow, R. H. (1977) *US Marines in Vietnam: The Advisory and Combat Assistance Era 1954–1964* (Washington, D.C.).

Whitson, W. W. (1973) *The Chinese High Command: A History of Communist Military Politics* (New York and London).

Wilson, A. (1970) *War Gaming* (Harmondsworth, Middx.).

Windchy, E. G. (1971) *Tonkin Gulf* (New York).

Yahuda, M. B. (1972) 'Kremlinology and the Chinese Strategic Debate', in *China Quarterly*, vol. XLIX.

Yahuda, M. B. (1978) *China's Role in World Affairs* (London).

Yanaga, Chitoshi (1968) *Big Business in Japanese Politics* (New Haven, Conn.).

Young, K. T. (1968) *Negotiating with Chinese Communists: The United States Experience 1953–1967* (New York).

Index

For the subject-matter of the tables, see the List of Tables on pp. vii–viii.